# Advance Praise for *Nothing Personal*

"[A] warm, witty, and rigorously honest memoir, a '*Confessions of an English Opium-Eater*–type exposé on dating apps'...Against all odds, this unsparing, must-read portrait of modern dating and sex is also a love story."
                                        — ***Kirkus Reviews*, starred review**

"[A] candid and provocative memoir...Sales's funny, fresh approach will resonate with many single readers, as well as anyone concerned about the ways technology enables capitalism to invade personal lives."
                                                        — ***Publishers Weekly***

"Nancy Jo Sales has been a leading chronicler of our digital culture, its joys and pathologies. Sales is a gift—her journey is powerful and raw, and her humor amidst it all makes it difficult to put the book down. Brava, this is a masterpiece."
                        **—Danielle Citron, author of *Hate Crimes in Cyberspace***

"For those of us questioning what courtship even means in the age of dating apps, Nancy Jo Sales is a guide and a much-needed voice of reason who has swiped, sexted, and survived. *Nothing Personal* will be remembered for translating the world of twenty-first-century sex and romance."
                                **—Marisa Meltzer, author of *This Is Big***

"Groundbreaking...I love Nancy Jo's honesty and her connection with her own brain, heart, and soul. It's so unbelievably refreshing to read the words of a woman that are so based in truth, her truth. I love this book so much. I didn't want to put it down."
                                                              **—Peri Gilpin**

"Nancy Jo Sales has written an unflinching confession and thoroughly researched exposé of how big tech has affected the way we relate now. Amid so much hot sex, I found myself chilled to the bone."

**—Iris Smyles, author of *Dating Tips for the Unemployed***

"An adrenaline-fueled romp through the world of online dating. At once hilarious and disturbing, Sales recounts not only how this technology shapes our experiences of love and dating, but also how it transformed her."

**—Breanne Fahs, author of *Burn It Down!***

"Through a personal narration that opens your mind to the world of relationships biased by a culture manipulated by technology, *Nothing Personal* explores an unimagined reality for some and the lived dating experience for many. Throughout the narrative, this book will keep you going down the rabbit hole."

**—Dr. Ayanna Howard, dean of Ohio State University's College of Engineering**

"Nancy Jo Sales is officially the world expert of dating apps. For years, she's been a rare voice exposing the underbelly of hookup tech. The retaliation by Tinder to her earlier work didn't stop her from penetrating the industry harder. Now, she's reincarnated as a user taking us on the harrowing journey of her own hookups while telling us the ugly truth about the misogyny these companies perpetuate."

**—Carrie Goldberg, author of *Nobody's Victim***

"A wonderful, wonderful book. Nancy Jo Sales has always been a brilliant chronicler of the sexual mores of our time. But *Nothing Personal* manages the enjoyable feat of reading like a touching memoir, a well-researched and balanced feminist treatise, and a frequently funny journey through funny/sad love stories like *Sex in the City* for the smartphone era. Like most smartphone excesses, dating app romances can be awful, but Sales is a great literary Virgil."

**—Dimitry Elias Léger, author of *God Loves Haiti***

# Nothing
# Personal

ALSO BY NANCY JO SALES

*American Girls*

*The Bling Ring*

# Nothing Personal

## My Secret Life in the Dating App Inferno

# Nancy Jo Sales

hachette
BOOKS

New York

Copyright © 2021 by Nancy Jo Sales

Cover design by Amanda Kain
Cover photograph © plainpicture/Ute Mans
Cover copyright © 2021 by Hachette Book Group, Inc.

Hachette Book Group supports the right to free expression and the value of copyright. The purpose of copyright is to encourage writers and artists to produce the creative works that enrich our culture.

The scanning, uploading, and distribution of this book without permission is a theft of the author's intellectual property. If you would like permission to use material from the book (other than for review purposes), please contact permissions@hbgusa.com. Thank you for your support of the author's rights.

Hachette Books
Hachette Book Group
1290 Avenue of the Americas
New York, NY 10104
HachetteBooks.com
Twitter.com/HachetteBooks
Instagram.com/HachetteBooks

First Edition: May 2021

Published by Hachette Books, an imprint of Perseus Books, LLC, a subsidiary of Hachette Book Group, Inc. The Hachette Books name and logo is a trademark of the Hachette Book Group.

The Hachette Speakers Bureau provides a wide range of authors for speaking events. To find out more, go to www.hachettespeakersbureau.com or call (866) 376-6591.

The publisher is not responsible for websites (or their content) that are not owned by the publisher.

Print book interior design by Abby Reilly.

Library of Congress Cataloging-in-Publication Data
Names: Sales, Nancy Jo, author.
Title: Nothing personal: my secret life in the dating app inferno / Nancy Jo Sales.
Description: First edition. | New York: Hachette Books, 2021. |
Identifiers: LCCN 2020029602 | ISBN 9780316492744 (hardcover) | ISBN 9780316492799 (ebook)
Subjects: LCSH: Online dating. | Man-woman relationships.
Classification: LCC HQ801.82 .S25 2021 | DDC 306.730285—dc23
LC record available at https://lccn.loc.gov/2020029602

ISBNs: 978-0-316-49274-4 (hardcover), 978-0-316-49279-9 (ebook)

Printed in the United States of America

LSC-C

Printing 1, 2021

*For Donald Suggs Jr.*

The act of sex may be nothing, but when you reach my age you learn that at any time it may prove to be everything.

—Graham Greene, *The End of the Affair*

# Contents

# One

Look. I bedazzled my mask."

I'm FaceTiming with Constance at the beginning of the pandemic. She's told me she wants this to be a "ladies night in the time of corona." I didn't know we were supposed to get dressed up for the occasion, so I'm wearing my usual jeans and an oversized sweatshirt with the logo for the band Kiss on it. Constance is in a blue evening gown, which she says she put on because she "might not ever get another chance." She's done her dark hair in carefully sculpted layers that make her look like a character on *Dynasty*. I'm drinking an IPA; she has champagne. I'm not sure how to get an angle that doesn't make me look like a melting candle. She looks fabulous.

She holds up a gold lamé surgical mask she's affixed with fake crystals that spell out "New York." It's the city where we live. She stretches the mask across her face with smiling eyes. She seems happier than I've seen her in years.

"Dick thinks it's so cute the way I have to make everything a fashion statement," she tells me.

Dick is the guy Constance met on Tinder a few weeks ago, when the spread of the coronavirus started to get bad. His name is Richard, she says, but she calls him Dick, like all his close friends do.

"He's my quarantine bae. Do you know what that is, a 'bae'?" she asks.

I tell her yes, I know.

Constance is in her mid-fifties, like I am. We met in Carl Schurz Park when our daughters were small. "I had my sixteenth birthday at Studio 54," she told me with a wistful smile that day, the first time I ever remember reminiscing about how things used to be when I was young.

Years later, I would see the picture Constance posted on Facebook of a red-lipped beauty in a Madonna-style bustier, a glamorous shot of her taken at the now-shuttered Lucky Strike, from back in the days when we were running around New York, meeting men.

"Do you remember how much fun it was?" she said dreamily, that day in the park.

"Yes," I said. I did.

I didn't want to tell her about the times I remembered that weren't so great, about the bad dates that went seriously wrong. She seemed to be the type who wanted to look back with rose-colored shades.

"We were so *gorgeous* then," she said.

In her thirties, Constance married a hedge fund guy, and for years she lived the life of a Scarsdale wife and mom. Then her husband lost everything in the Great Recession and began to drink. Constance started selling real estate after leaving him, which she did after he pushed her down in an argument and broke her rib. Now, she's on her own, living in a studio uptown.

About six months before the virus hit, she discovered Tinder.

And now this guy, Dick, age sixty, is living with her.

"He's my corona husband," she tells me with a giggle.

I've seen that the New York City Department of Health has just issued "Sex and Coronavirus Disease" guidelines saying it's not safe to hook up with people you meet online, but I don't mention it. I don't want to sound like a scold.

"Sounds great," I manage to say.

"We've literally been together all the time since our first date, so how is it any different if we were married?" Constance says defensively, although

I've said nothing to dissuade her from having this relative stranger move in with her.

"Sounds like you *are* married, from how I remember it," I tell her.

Dick is still going out to work every day, she says, but when he comes back, she's Lysoling the bottom of his shoes and washing his clothes, "so everything's clean."

"You're doing his laundry?" I ask.

"But he's doing so much for *me*," she insists.

"Omg, Omg, no. This poor woman. He's just using her," texts my friend Abigail when I tell her about Constance, later.

Abigail is twenty-seven and an inveterate online dater. She's told me lots of stories over the years about dating app culture and its chilling effect on relationships.

"He's gonna be out the door as soon as isolation ends," she texts.

"That's what I'd be worried about too," I text her back.

But then, who knows how any of this is going to end?

Covid-19 isn't like anything we've seen before, so there's no way of knowing what its long-term effects on dating and relationships will be. There have been reports, ever since shelter-in-place orders went into effect, that online dating has surged. Which comes as no surprise, since millions of people are now trapped at home, feeling lonely, horny, and bored, not to mention desperate and scared. Tinder reported that on March 28, 2020, its users swiped more than three billion swipes, more than any single day in the company's eight-year history.

The online dating industry has been rushing to capitalize on its newly captive audience, adding video-chat capabilities to its apps and launching new, social-distancing-friendly sites. Video dating has already been deemed "the new normal" by sectors of the media which always seem ready to champion the latest technological innovations in dating. The news has grown effusive in describing how online dating companies are doing their best to help isolated singles "stay connected" and "keep a dialogue going." I've seen pieces which read like synopses of rom-coms about people falling in love through their laptops.

Then in April of 2020, CivicScience, a polling company, published a study saying that 71 percent of unmarried couples who didn't usually live together but were quarantining together were reporting a spike in their sex lives.

"It's just sex, sex, sex, all the time!" Constance tells me with a throaty laugh.

For no good reason, I feel a little twinge of jealousy.

I've been watching all this with interest because, for the past few years, I've been writing about sex, love, and dating in the digital age. I wrote a book about teenagers and social media and made a documentary film about dating apps—none of which has given me confidence that online dating is the path to love or lasting relationships.

But then, what is? I've wondered.

"We were walking in the park with our masks on," Constance says, still talking about Dick. "And I asked him, 'We're not a thing just because of quarantine, right?' And he was like, 'Absolutely not!' So I know it's been a whirlwind with him, but he says such nice things to me, and I'm not used to anyone saying nice things. He thinks I'm *amazing*."

I don't want to tell her what I've been hearing from the women who've been sending me texts and emails since "love in the time of corona" began (I see the phrase is already getting more than four billion results on Google). Surprisingly, they say nothing much has changed in the dystopian world of online dating, despite the onset of a global pandemic. They've sent me screenshots of guys wanting to "quarantine and chill," "looking to smash with masks." It's the usual kind of stuff, but now that there's the threat of contagion, the numbers game online dating is so often described to be has a different calculation: How many will wind up sick? Or dead?

"At first I was really excited," said a young woman named Ariel I interviewed for the *Guardian*, "because I thought, Okay, now the guys are going to have to do the work to actually get to know us because they can't come over. But then I start swiping and there's all these profiles saying things like, 'Covid-free and have a bunch of toilet paper, who wants to hang out?'"

A young man DM'd me after that piece came out, claiming that "women are doing the same things." "Okay, send me screenshots," I told him. When he didn't, I asked him, "You're not getting any matches, are you?" "No," he said, and asked me if I had any advice on how he could "get busy on lockdown."

I've wondered what I would be doing if I were dating now. Would I be convincing myself I couldn't get sick, justifying my recklessness, running out to meet some man? Would the idea of not being able to kiss anyone make me thirst for a certain someone's lips?

But then, I think, it's impossible to imagine myself doing the things I used to do, with everything I've been through that got me to this point.

"It's not like he's going to do anything to endanger me," Constance goes on. "I mean, we're being really safe."

"Uh-huh," I say.

"He's the only thing I have to look forward to," she says plaintively, like a teenager arguing with her mother. "I don't see any other human beings. Ashley"—her daughter—"won't come over now because she says he might be contaminating my apartment. She's like, 'Mom, you just started dating, you don't even know him.'"

"Well, she's kind of right," I say.

"I know," says Constance, her voice going low. "But he said he loves me. I just can't believe anybody would say that to me. It's been so long."

● ● ●

It's strange to think how much the world has changed in the few months since I last saw Constance. It was a cold winter night. I was snuggled down in my bed, at home in the East Village, where I've lived now for about twenty years. My apartment is small but cozy and colorful, full of

5

paintings and photographs, knickknacks and books. Once, when I was in my twenties, I got a reading from a psychic at a party named Kermit who told me, "You're surrounded by books." I remember I was so excited when he went on to say, "You will make it as a writer," although I was a bit miffed to hear it would be by writing about kids. As a younger and less experienced person, I think I considered children a less important subject. But how wrong I was about that, and how right Kermit the psychic was about everything.

I didn't really want to see Constance that evening, but she kept texting and calling me on the phone. "I'm at Pardon My French"—a little French bistro near my apartment building—she said, sounding distraught. So I climbed out of bed and went and found her there. She was sitting alone in a back booth of the crowded bar. I could see the flicker of disappointment on her face when I showed up in my jeans and sneakers. She was in her usual designer wear, which was looking almost vintage since she hadn't had the funds to shop in a while. Chanel circa 2005.

"Sorry," I said rather crankily, sitting down. "I didn't have time to get dressed up on such short notice."

"It's fine," she said, regarding me with mild pity. I could see she'd already had a few martinis.

Then she put a hand on my wrist and gave me a level look. I thought she was going to tell me she was ill or something, God forbid.

"I had sex," she said.

"Hello, waiter?" I called. I could see I was going to need a drink.

Constance had started using dating apps, she told me. Like most online daters, she was using more than one. She was on Tinder, Bumble, Hinge, and Match, she said. And now, after almost thirty years of being faithful to the same man, she had hooked up with a guy she met on Tinder. But she didn't want it to be just a hookup.

"And then I sent him another text, and another, and another, and he didn't answer!" she cried. "And I had even told him he was the first person

I'd had sex with since Don"—her ex-husband—"and after that, he doesn't return my *texts*?"

I listened, not saying a word. I knew just what she was going through; I'd been through the same things. But it was a secret I felt I couldn't share with her. I'd always been afraid that Constance would judge me if she knew about my past on dating apps.

"Do you think he found out my real age?" she asked anxiously. "My profile says fifty-one—well, okay, I'm not fifty-*one*. But he saw me in daylight, so it's not like he didn't have a chance to see the lines on my face."

"You don't have lines on your face," I said. At least, I couldn't see any in the dim light. But then, my eyesight isn't what it used to be.

"I'm so upset!" Constance said, checking her phone again. "This guy still hasn't texted me back!" He was a guy, she said, who lived in New Jersey. I was surprised by the idea of Constance going all the way to Jersey to have sex, but then, I had been to Queens.

"I checked this morning," she went on, "and I could see that he'd been online already. So why hasn't he texted me back?"

Constance was starting to annoy me now—she was sounding too much like me.

"Online dating is a sham," I growled at her. "I'm supposed to be an expert on this stuff, remember?"

"I know!" she said. "That's why I wanted to talk to you—because I need your advice!"

"My advice is to get off dating apps," I said.

"Then how will I ever meet a man?" she demanded.

"Why do you even need a man?" I asked. "Aren't men sort of the problem?"

She looked chagrined then, staring into her glass, and instantly I felt bad.

"I'm sorry, Constance," I told her. "I just think you deserve better."

It was then I realized the real reason I was mad at Constance was for making me think about the young man I had sent away. I had met him on a dating app four years before, and now I didn't know if I was ever going to see him again.

But then, I never knew when I was going to see him even when we were seeing each other regularly. He came and went—no labels, everything up in the air—which is so often how things are these days. Which I'd told myself was fine with me because, you know, I'm *busy*, I don't *want* a relationship.

I thought of his pretty face on the pillow…

"Maybe we've been chasing the wrong things," I said to Constance. "Maybe we should be happy with what we have."

We were women in our fifties, and nothing and everything about dating had changed. We had careers, we had children. But we were alone.

"And maybe that's okay," I told her.

"But don't men want love? Is love just…over?" she asked.

Before I could answer, I felt my phone buzz inside my purse.

My heart leapt.

It was him.

I threw down money. I made excuses. I ran out of the bar.

"Are you coming back?" Constance called after me.

● ● ●

Then I was running through the streets to meet him, running like a madwoman, as if in a dream. I was running past stores and restaurants and bars I'd passed by hundreds of times before, but now they seemed alive with technicolor beauty, like in a 1950s musical, because he had texted me. I'm surprised I didn't burst out singing.

Even the arrangement of the letters of his name in the green bubble on my phone screen thrilled me: A-b-e-l. Abel.

"Hola there lovely how goes it?" he'd texted.

And even though I knew he wasn't really inquiring as to my well-being, but looking to see if he could come around again and have sex—even after

I had told him that I never wanted to see him again because he had done something which, finally, I could no longer explain away as the result of his youth, or this challenging time for relationships—I texted back, "Hey!"

Then I slowed down to a walk along Second Avenue, wondering why my legs had carried me along so quickly, without my even thinking, as if that little text ding had been the ring of the bell that had summoned Pavlov's puppy. I thought of Jaron Lanier, the Internet philosopher with the wild dreads, talking about how we are all being made into dogs by the behavior-modification algorithms of social media.

"Please don't be insulted," Lanier wrote. "Yes, I am suggesting that you might be turning, just a little, into a well-trained dog, or something less pleasant, like a lab rat or a robot."

I stopped in my tracks and saw myself looking wild-eyed in a store window.

Was this me, the so-called expert, demonstrating the very thing I worried the tech invasion of dating was doing to women: robbing us of our free will, making us obedient to whistles?

Or was this all part of a personal pattern that I had been repeating forever?

Or did I really just love this young man? Was he, after all, my last grand passion, which I would be a fool to deny myself?

I thought about it all on the walk back home. If I had been committed to anything, all these years, it had been to avoiding examining any of this too closely, because it had worried and frightened me, and perhaps because such examination would have made it impossible to have love in my life, or what I had called love.

And suddenly I felt as if I didn't know myself anymore. And what would be worse than winding up alone would be not knowing the person I had wound up with. All I knew for sure was that I never wanted to be looking for love in the dating app inferno again—I couldn't go back there, back into the whirlwind.

● ● ●

I met Abel one night in the summer of 2015, when I had been on dating apps for about a year. It might be hard to remember, now that these platforms have so overwhelmed dating for people of all ages, but in those days, being on a dating app was seen by middle-aged people like me as kind of creepy, so I had been using them in secret.

It was a year in which I had spiraled out of control, like a cartoon cannonball gleefully whizzing into the sky, in full denial that at any moment it's going to explode. But I didn't have to admit that what I was doing was kind of crazy—not even to myself—because dating app dating was becoming normalized and even celebrated in a cultural nanosecond.

I was keeping it together in one part of my life while unraveling in another. The work was still being done, the bills were being paid, my daughter was being fed and clothed and loved. The laundry was folded, her homework checked. Meanwhile, this other, secret me was using dating apps like an addict uses drugs.

It didn't help that this drug was free and constantly available and always waiting for me on my phone—waiting to help me feel good, to feel comforted and reassured, to feel something and nothing at all, to have some skin-to-skin contact, to get off, to feel high, to feel wanted and loved by a prowling procession of young men in their twenties who had no intention of loving me; or maybe they didn't know what they wanted. I never got to know most of them well enough to say. I did get to know some things about them, though, which I'm going to tell you about here.

They had nose rings and man buns, beards and beanies, porkpie hats and tattoos. They were musicians and writers, baristas and bartenders. One of them was a self-described "artisan barber," another a Wall Street bro, and another a marketing executive for a start-up. Some of them were atheists, and some called themselves "ethically non-monogamous." Some of them wore skinny jeans. One of them rode a skateboard over the Williamsburg Bridge to come see me. It had a horny devil emoji painted on it.

• • •

I drove like a maniac back to New York that summer night I met Abel. I was coming home from dropping off my daughter at a Spanish language immersion camp being housed in a redbrick liberal arts college in a tiny town in Vermont. She was fourteen at the time, but we were very close (a wry friend called us Big and Little Edie), and we had never been separated for more than a few days, so I'd stayed for about a week in the town, making sure she was liking her program okay and dealing with my own anxiety over being away from her.

I was taking daily trips to the local five-and-dime to buy her things: a shower caddy and some colored pens and pencils and a screen for her window and a cover for the lumpy old mattress at the school and a sunscreen with a higher SPF number and some boxes of those Nutella cookie sticks she's fond of. I'm a single mom by choice, although my choice to have a baby came about after I accidentally got pregnant by a man I was barely dating in 1999. And yet having Zazie turned out to be the best choice of my life.

At night, I was sending texts to her secret cell phone—her first cell phone, a device verboten by the school—to check in and see how she was doing. "How's it going?" I'd ask, and she'd send me a GIF of Carlton on *The Fresh Prince of Bel-Air* doing his happy dance, and I'd send her back a GIF of Pee-wee Herman doing his "Tequila" dance; and so it would go on, both of us trying to make each other laugh, by the light of our phones, in our respective rooms.

I was staying at an empty, fussy, Victorian bed-and-breakfast run by a pinched-faced woman who clearly hated me, for reasons I couldn't quite understand. Breakfast was always already over, and no, she said, she didn't know of any good hikes in the area. It made me wonder if maybe she had been awake the night I entertained a visit from a local college student I met on Tinder. He wore a baseball cap, was nondescript, polite; the sex was bland, and not overly loud. He left in the morning without a word.

But maybe, I thought, she had heard the squeak of the screen door opening and closing.

It was in Vermont, one night, when I was having a beer at the grungy bar on Main Street, that I became aware that Tinder—still a relatively new thing back then, launched in December of 2012—had made its way to places like this little middle-of-nowhere town. Sitting down the bar from me were some rough-looking guys in coveralls, swiping away on the app, discussing their matches.

"I have over forty matches," one of them crowed.

I scooted closer.

Being a reporter, I was used to striking up conversations with strangers, and online dating was something I had actually been doing a story on for the magazine I work for, *Vanity Fair*. So I asked these guys how they were finding this new dating app dating.

They were shruggingly enthusiastic.

"Everybody in this town has already fucked each other," one of them explained. "You can get girls in Albany on this thing."

"You'd drive all the way to Albany to have sex?" I asked.

"Apparently you don't understand the male species too well," he said, grinning.

He was probably right about that, I thought, zooming down I-95 on my way home to meet up with the guy I'd been talking to on Tinder—Abel. But the real question was why I was continuing to date guys from dating apps when I knew the whole enterprise to be *fakakta*, as my Russian grandfather would have called it.

I had spent the last few months doing the aforementioned story—which I'd just emailed in to my editor; I'd been writing up there in Vermont as well as helicopter parenting—and what I had been hearing from the scores of young people and experts I had interviewed had only reinforced my sense that there were a lot of things about this new type of meeting and mating that were sort of sick, if not dangerous.

There was the commodification these apps were inspiring. "It's like ordering Seamless, but you're ordering a person," said a young man in my story.

There was the dating FOMO they were spreading like a virus. "Apps like Tinder and OkCupid give people the impression that there are thousands or millions of potential mates out there," David Buss, an evolutionary psychologist, had told me.

There was the way in which this explosion of options was affecting straight male psychology, exacerbating the sexism that had always existed in dating. Young men were treating women as objects, young women had said: "They're just looking for hit-it-and-quit-it on Tinder."

Of course, not all straight men were as cavalier—or thought to be as "successful"—in their experience on dating apps as the Wall Street bros I wrote about in my piece; but these seemed to be the type of guys dating apps were designed for, so I led with them.

"Guys view everything as a competition," said the young man I called Alex the Tinder King, whom I spoke to one night in a bar filled with swiping singles. "Who's slept with the best, hottest girls? It's setting up two or three Tinder dates a week and, chances are, sleeping with all of them, so you could rack up a hundred girls in a year. Tinder has made everything so much easier."

With the help of dating apps, said Alex the Tinder King, he was sleeping with a different woman almost every night of the week. He couldn't remember all their names; his roommates had to help him fill in the blanks. "It's less personal for sure," he said. "You could talk to two or three girls at a bar and pick the best one, or you can swipe a couple hundred people a day and choose the best one on Tinder. The sample size is so much larger. I think it's great. Tinder is the bomb."

I suppose my face must have betrayed my feelings, as I listened to him, because he asked me: "So do you think this culture is misogynistic? I'm just curious. Because objectively I think our dialogue might sound absolutely misogynistic."

He said it, not I; and yet, for me, my latest story was about the ways that dating apps were weaponizing misogyny, something no piece on the dating app craze had yet explored. I'd reported on the dick pics and abusive, harassing messages young women were routinely receiving on these apps—57 percent of women ages eighteen to thirty-four, according to a survey by the Pew Research Center in 2019—as well as the bad sex and unwanted, rough sex young women told me they were encountering in hookups, which some of them attributed to the popularity of online porn among their straight male counterparts.

I had no idea that these revelations would cause so much agitation, especially among the heads of some of the dating app companies—that was to come. To me, it all seemed kind of obvious, when you looked at it closely, and I was puzzled by how other pieces on online dating could talk about it without ever mentioning its uglier aspects.

My last day in Vermont, I'd received a digital galley from my editor, who had headlined this story "Tinder and the Dawn of the 'Dating Apocalypse,'" using a joking quote from a young woman I'd interviewed. But I was already starting to think that the mass spread of dating apps was like a sign of the end of the world. And yes, I do mean end of the world in the same way that the melting of the polar ice caps is a sign, and the mass extinction of species is a sign—signs of an unprecedented moment in which we have to wonder whether life on this planet is going to continue as we know it, or if we're all just totally fucked.

"But just one more time," I told myself that night, speeding home so I could fix myself up before the arrival of the guy from Tinder.

●　●　●

It did occur to me, as I hurtled down the FDR, the highway that snakes along the east side of Manhattan, that I was acting kind of crazy, weaving in and out of traffic like Gene Hackman in the chase scene in *The French Connection*.

I'd made it back to the city in four hours flat, as if entrusted with delivering the antidote for a dying snake-bite victim. When the skyline of New York came into view, I'd said aloud, "Thank God," because I was home, where I could be myself for a little while—or this other, secret self that I was, sometimes, ever since I'd discovered dating apps, those shiny little portals to casual sex.

It wasn't like I was new to the concept of free love, once a great hobby of mine, slowed down considerably since I'd become a mom. The gossip website *Gawker* had once called me a "hard-partying good-time girl," which I took to be a sexist slam at my liking for men, as I was never much into alcohol or drugs, unless you count love as a drug. (Would they refer to, say, Nicholas Kristof as a "good-time boy," no matter how many people he'd slept with? Never.)

But then, dating apps had taken casual sex to a whole new level. Sex wasn't just casual anymore—it was mechanized, and it could be instant. "Like, after an exchange of, like, six messages," as one young man I interviewed said.

When Graydon Carter, then the editor in chief and my boss at *Vanity Fair*, first asked me to do a story on these newfangled mobile dating sites, I tried to get out of it. I didn't want to have to tell him that I was on these things—not that I thought he would have been shocked to hear it. I had never made much of a secret of my romantic misadventures before, mainly because making jokes was one of the only ways I knew to keep from wanting to jump out a window over them.

Graydon was a legendary editor and a cosmopolitan sort of guy. With his windswept gray hair and patrician features, he looked like a Founding Father who shopped at Brooks Brothers. He'd once called me a "screwball," which I'd decided to take as a term of endearment, since he was a big fan of classic films. I'd always hoped that he meant I was like Rosalind Russell in *His Girl Friday*, a quirky yet reliable newswoman, instead of just a screwball. But I thought not even Graydon would have felt completely comfortable hearing what I had been up to on dating apps over the last year, so I gave him a truncated version:

"There was a guy with a skateboard," I said, "a guy with a rottweiler, a French guy who smelled like cigarettes and followed me down the street shouting 'whore,' uh, ha ha…"

"Oh, that's great!" said Graydon. "So you know how dating apps work!"

Yes, I knew how they worked. I could have written a *Confessions of an English Opium-Eater*–type exposé on dating apps—but I guess I'm doing that now.

I knew about the endless swiping, messaging, talking to strangers, the tiresome, exhausting, never-ending threads, the repetitive dates (swipe, text, meet, drink, fuck) with an assembly line of weirdos—all of which was beginning to feel like *Groundhog Day* playing on Pornhub. I knew about the default sex, which was either very hot or very not, and then never talking to that person again, or having to block him because he won't stop trying to talk to you even when you wish he would disappear as easily as a profile pic on which you'd swiped left.

I knew about all this from my seat at the window, looking out on my Macy's Thanksgiving Day–sized parade of man-children with man buns, none of them over the age of twenty-eight, most of whom seemed to see me as a trophy fuck, a climb up MILF Mountain—that is, when they weren't trying to hit me up for networking opportunities or asking me to help them fix their websites and résumés: "You're a writer, right?"

I knew about all this, too, from the teenage girls I'd been interviewing for the book I was doing on social media and how it was affecting their lives.

Pause for a sidebar regarding timeline here:

In the roughly five years covered in the book you're reading now, I was researching and writing a book called *American Girls: Social Media and the Secret Lives of Teenagers* as well as shooting and editing a documentary film entitled *Swiped: Hooking Up in the Digital Age*, also working on a bunch of articles, all while trying to survive as a journalist and support my family after being turned into a salary-less freelancer along with most of the other writers at *Vanity Fair*. About a week before Christmas of 2008, I received a letter from Advance Publications, also known as Condé Nast, informing me that the regular monthly paychecks I had been receiving for the last eight years would stop in January of 2009—upon which I had a four-day panic attack, and decided I better reinvent myself.

It was the girls and young women I was interviewing for *American Girls*—hundreds of them, from California to Indiana to New Jersey—who had first clued me in to the rape culture underpinning the world of online dating. "Just looking for a rape victim to get freaky with," said one of the vile dating app messages they'd shown me. "Do you have any rape fantasies?"

I'd woken up that very day of my wild ride home from Vermont to a big, hairy dude on OkCupid messaging me: "Wanna fuck?" It was the first thing I saw when I opened my eyes, for the hand does heed the whispering call of dating apps when they seductively nudge at you, even through semiconsciousness: *Hey, hottie, come swipe…*

I knew about all this—I'd been studying this—and yet, cut to a close-up of me barreling down the highway with my face scrunched up like a fist from thinking about all this, and here I was, rushing home for my date with the guy from Tinder, with whom I'd been talking on text for about two weeks like an excited schoolgirl: "Hey, *you!*"

But had I paused for a moment to consider *why* I was doing this? Was I having a midlife crisis? Using sex with twenty-five-year-olds as a way to stave off my fear of *dying*? Or was I the bearer of such a bottomless pit of internalized misogyny that I was just blithely going along with whatever the patriarchy was currently telling me to do—offering up myself digitally and bodily to the next fuckboy who wanted to experience my night moves?

But there was no time to think about all that now, going seventy miles an hour in rush-hour traffic. Not now, when I was cutting off the outraged dad in the Beemer, who for a second looked like he wanted to come at me, bro. "Don't worry, bud, I see your kids in the back seat," I signaled to him with a nod.

I was jetting ahead of him so I could get home in time to shave my legs in case I'd be having sex that night with the guy from Tinder. Which I kind of hoped I would.

•  •  •

Abel, Abel of the beautiful lankiness which wrapped itself around me like a locket.

The night I met him, he was twenty-three. I know—that's young. But if you're worried now that I corrupted this innocent youth in some lurid scene reminiscent of Mrs. Robinson locking Benjamin Braddock in the upstairs bedroom, nude, hold on. These kids today know from casual sex, coming of age in peak hookup culture, about which some cranky mansplainer always seems to want to tell me: "It doesn't exist, things have always been this way." But they haven't. Hookup culture is, in fact, a thing—a thing with a vast body of research examining it, going back to its inception around two decades ago— and recognizing this is a necessary step, I think, toward any real understanding of the global warming of sexual relations in the digital revolution.

A 2012 study by research scientists at the Kinsey Institute for Research in Sex, Gender, and Reproduction reported that 80 percent of undergraduates across genders and sexual orientations said they had had hookup sex, here characterized as sex without any expectation of a relationship. By the time of this study, hooking up was already replacing "more traditional forms of courtship," such as going on dates. And this study was released shortly before Tinder took off, landing like a meteor in the midst of our already dinosaur-like rituals of courtship. Ever since then, it's hard not to see how dating apps—of which there are now thousands of versions being used by hundreds of millions of people across the globe—have sent hookup culture into overdrive, like when the starship in a sci-fi flick blasts into light speed on its way to an unknown galaxy. "We are in uncharted territory," Justin Garcia, the executive director of Kinsey, told me.

"So chances are this Abel isn't some choirboy," I was thinking, getting closer to home, my foot seemingly unable to let up on the gas. I also knew that he was no callow youth from his many suggestive texts. He hadn't hit me up with any horny devil emojis yet, or asked for nudes (I don't send nudes, although like the majority of women who've used dating apps, I've received my share of unsolicited dick pics, one of which visually compared its subject to a can of Monster Mutant Super Soda in order to illustrate size and girth). However, he'd been flirting with me in a way that suggested some experience with the ladies, as well as an offbeat sense of humor.

He'd been texting me in the persona of a courtly southern gentleman (or so I thought, as yet unaware of the extent to which he was a bona fide country boy), which I'd taken as a sign that he had some idea of how overly determined all of this dating business is—and always was, even before Big Dating co-opted it for big profits.

"You sure are perdy," he texted. He told me he "liked a good snuggle and sech." And when his Gomer Pyle bit got too corny, instead of succeeding in being a commentary on corny, I'd just look at his profile picture again...

Oh, that picture of Abel. How many times had I looked at that picture in the last couple of weeks? I wondered, whipping along. And what about that particular picture had captured my attention, as opposed to the thousands of others I'd seen in the relentless stacks of profile pics on dating apps? Maybe it was because it looked like an album cover from the seventies, the era in which I'd formulated my idea of what constitutes an attractive man: longish hair, scruffy beard, and a rock 'n' roll vibe suggesting a loosey-goosey attitude toward sexual orientation; think Paul Rodgers of Free strutting across the stage belting out "All Right Now" at the Isle of Wight concert in 1970, a clip I've watched on YouTube more times than I would like to have to confess to.

He was sitting on the floor of some music studio, playing a bass guitar, wearing a beanie, boots, and jeans, looking like the dictionary definition of "hipster man," but thoughtful and gentle, bent down over his strings with an expression which seemed to say that, in this time of the great techno suck of our souls, he had somehow preserved his soul.

"Oh, but listen to you now!" I scoffed. "Sounding like somebody who doesn't know the score to this online dating horror show, projecting your own fantasies onto this virtual stranger!"

As if I hadn't been on enough dates with knit-cap-wearing hipster dudes to know that their pictures were as curated as an ad campaign by Don Draper. As mine were.

And what about that guy who'd looked just great in his pic, but then he took off his hat and he had vampire ears, which he had had surgically attached to his head? (He was a goth from Orlando.) That was one of those nights when I bid a hasty retreat, coming up with a fake-text excuse: "Oh no, the babysitter says I should come home now..."

● ● ●

Careening off the highway onto Houston Street, I was starting to get apprehensive. What did I really know about this guy? Nothing really, at least nothing that could be confirmed with the usual sleuthing searches on Facebook, LinkedIn, and Google. "Most women these days could immediately be hired by the FBI," one of my young women friends joked. Social media had turned us all into dating spies, which only seemed to make us better at hiding in plain sight.

But this Abel was strangely Internet absent, I'd noticed. I couldn't even find his last name, which he hadn't told me, and I hadn't wanted to spook him with my suspiciousness by asking him (in those days, Tinder was still all but anonymous). I only knew that he was from Tennessee, or so he said, and that he had a busy work schedule, or so he claimed. But working at what? I was dying to know. His answers to such questions had been jokingly vague: "I do a bit of this and that," he'd texted.

And, of course, I hadn't been able to experience any of those in-person indicators which evolutionary biologists say we've developed over tens of thousands of years in order to be able to determine whether someone can be trusted—which, on some level, means trusted with our very lives. I didn't know how he sounded; we hadn't spoken on the phone—it just wasn't done. And I didn't know how he moved or how being around him felt. And, oh, how I *wanted* to know how he sounded, moved and felt—and *smelled*—how I'd fantasized about it all on those lonely jogs along the piney roads up in Vermont...

"But hold on a minute now," I was thinking, steering my rental car into the treacherously narrow Avis garage on East 11th Street, "that's just blind lust! That's the tech lords tapping into the lonely waves in your brain and igniting them with a shot of ego, spiking your excitement that this nice-looking young man is coming over to your *house?*"

"Oh, what have I done?" I fretted, hurrying along the streets of the East Village, wrestling with my rolling bag, fully registering now how I was breaking all my own rules by inviting this young guy I had never seen before to come to my home. In the past, I had always insisted on meeting my matches in public, despite the usual attempts to "just come over with a bottle of wine," "Netflix and chill." But then, when none of them ever killed me, I guess I got used to the idea—"Well, he's not going to *kill* me"—normalization being the name of this roulette game. What's more, after a couple of weeks of flirty-dirty texting with Abel, I felt like I did know Abel—which, of course, I did not. But, as another young woman friend said, "Your guard is further down because it's like, oh, I know you, I've looked at your Instagram."

"And what if he does kill you?" I asked myself as I stood in front of my bathroom mirror, blow-drying my wavy red locks, from which I had plucked a few white hairs—Ow!—nearly burning my scalp. Oh, that would look just great: "Journalist investigating the world of online dating is murdered by Tinder date." Like what happened to Warriena Wright, the poor New Zealand woman who fell fourteen floors to her death on a Tinder date in

2014. She was twenty-six. Her iPhone captured sounds "consistent with him choking or strangling her....She pleaded to be allowed to go home before repeatedly screaming 'no.'" She seemed like the canary in the coal mine we hadn't stopped swiping long enough to really think about.

Oh…

So should I tell someone this guy is coming over? I wondered, pulling on my cutest jeans, which I noticed had somehow shrunk—"Hey," I thought, cramming myself into them, "did I leave them in the dryer too long?"—and the Fleetwood Mac T-shirt I had had since I was a teenager, now as thin and full of holes as my attempt to appear young and fresh.

But then I realized I couldn't text any of my young women friends, my babysitters and bar buddies and former sources on stories, who seemed to look at me as a kind of New York mom, a sort of OG of dating who was old enough to know what all of this had been like before social media, and who could reassure them in their feeling that, yes, this was all truly fucked up—and always was. Because even though we'd discussed how we were all on dating apps, those problematic little cattle prods of desire, I wouldn't want them thinking that I sanctioned this sort of thing—allowing some random dude to just come over to my house without checking him out in a public place first. Not that it would necessarily keep us from getting raped or killed, which we didn't talk about as much as we should.

And then I realized I couldn't text any of my older women friends either, my friends from high school and college and former jobs, almost all of whom were married and at home cozily reading the *New Yorker* and scrolling on Facebook and sipping pinot grigio or pinot noir (sometimes all at the same time). On top of which, I was pretty sure that most of them already thought I was more than a little bit strange for *choosing* to be a single mom, and at this point I didn't think any of them had even heard of Tinder.

"Hey, so I know we haven't talked in a while, but I just wanted to let you know that this twenty-three-year-old guy I've never seen before is coming over to my apartment to probably have sex with me, so if you don't hear back from me in like an hour, call the police, okay?"

Oh no...

So I realized I was going to have to go through this alone.

Alone, alone.

"How did I wind up alone?" I wondered, brushing on mascara, admiring my big green eyes. How they sparkled! "And look at those gorgeous lips," I thought, applying lip gloss. "So kissable..."

I was thinking all this, you see, as a way of gearing myself up for having a twenty-three-year-old survey me and decide whether I was worth that right swipe. "I hate that moment when they walk in," said one of my young women friends. "You always feel like you'll never measure up to their expectations, no matter how hot you look..."

But that wasn't really what was bothering me now, was it? I asked myself.

I looked at myself in the mirror, putting down the tube of lip gloss.

And I knew that, deep down, what was really bothering me was that no matter how much I told myself "all I wanna do is fuck," what I really wanted was love, true love, a love where there is equality and respect and tenderness and orgasms for all; it was what I had always wanted.

*BUZZ.*

And there he was.

"I don't want to die! My child needs a mother!" I was thinking, reeling toward the front door, my heart now beating like a bouncy ball. Was this the moment when my familial history of heart disease was going to kick in? I was already on Lipitor!

Still, I buzzed him in, and, as he was coming up the stairs, I glanced around my kitchen for something to protect myself from what I was now certain was going to be an immediate, murderous assault. And I spied on my kitchen counter the gold metal candleholder filled with pens and pencils and a pair of scissors, and—I know this sounds crazy, but isn't everything about meeting up with a stranger off a dating app to have sex with kind of crazy?—

I took the scissors and slipped them in the back pocket of my jeans. What I would do with these shears, if necessary, I wasn't sure, but I had seen *Dial M for Murder*, and I knew they might come in handy.

I opened the door.

And there was Abel, a young man from Tennessee, recently arrived in New York.

Dark hair, cut shorter than in his picture; tan skin (I'd find out later, his father was an Argentinian guitar player who'd rolled through town, capturing his mother's heart). Full lips; soft, wide-set, caramel-colored eyes; high cheekbones ("My mama's granddaddy was a Shawnee," he'd tell me, when we got to talking). Medium height. Skinny. Wary. He seemed shy. Oh my goodness, I was thinking, he *is* shy. He reminded me of a glossy two-year-old rescue puppy who wasn't quite sure what was going to happen to him, and I was the face on the other side of the cage, deciding whether I was going to take him in.

We stared at each other a moment.

"Hey," he said.

"Hey."

And we smiled.

And I let him in.

• • •

That was four years before the night I so unceremoniously left Constance sitting in a French bistro to go running to meet up with this same young man. Four years before I slowed down to a walk along Second Avenue, wondering why I was rushing to see him all over again.

It was four years in which a lot had happened to make women angry, to make us want and demand change: the election of an avowed pussy grabber to the US presidency; the ascension of an alleged sexual assaulter to the Supreme Court; attacks on reproductive rights and civil rights, for starters.

The Women's March of 2017 was the biggest single-day protest in US history. The #MeToo movement, which kicked off that same year, had grown to international size, with women all over the world speaking out about sexual harassment, assault, and rape.

It was four years in which a lot had happened for me professionally: I wrote a book, made a film. And yet, here I was, running back to this young man as if he had never hurt or disappointed me—as if he were my savior.

"But why?" I asked myself, even as I continued on my way to meet him.

Why do the women who want men *still* want them, I wondered, even when we know we don't really need them, and, in fact, they've continually let us down?

What are the lies we tell ourselves to keep opening the door?

Something the feminist academic Elizabeth Armstrong said to me began to ring in my ears: "We need to puzzle out why women have made more strides in the public arena than in the private one."

As I passed by the dive bar with the neon sign where Abel used to have a few beers with his work buddies before coming to see me, I glanced in the window, as I had so many times before, hoping to see him. There, I spied the guys in flannel shirts like he wore, and the bartender who looked like one of the dudes I would have hooked up with before Abel came along and became the only one.

Then he texted that he was waiting for me, standing outside my building.

"Well, let him wait," I thought, putting my phone away. I had some things to think over—I had a decision to make. Was I really going to just run right back to him after all I'd learned in my more than forty years of dating?

And how far back did this go, I wondered, this conundrum of how much a woman should be willing to put up with from a man? To my mother? My grandmother? Were there cavewomen who got divorces? How many women were going through the same thing that I was that evening, asking, "Should I stay or should I go?"

I thought of the Wordsworth poem: "The Child is father of the Man..."
And is the woman the daughter of the patriarchy? I asked.

• • •

My parents met on the beach in St. Petersburg, Florida, in 1955. My mother was a long-legged midwestern gal with a short Audrey Hepburn haircut and squinting green eyes. She'd been told "men don't make passes at girls who wear glasses," so she often left her pair at home, once resulting in her being hit by a car. She was twelve at the time, and came out unscathed, she said, although my grandfather scolded her for inconveniencing the newlyweds who had run into her.

My father was a short, blond, energetic Jewish boy from Miami, living in St. Petersburg while attending Stetson University College of Law. He wasn't what you'd call handsome, but he had what Kramer on *Seinfeld* called "the Kavorka," an inexplicable, irresistible appeal for women. He was given to histrionic displays of affection, my mother said; he once sold his blood to buy her a nightgown. She was so overcome by his attentions that she agreed to marry him. "I barely knew your father when we got married," she told me. "I think I felt sorry for him. I have that thing where you feel like you have to be the caregiver."

In their wedding photo, it's as if I can see the origins of two major strains of my personality and even my sexuality, right there in this odd family portrait, taken in the chapel at Stetson. Standing on one side of the frame are my Indiana grandparents, and on the other side my Russian grandparents. My Indiana grandparents look like humble, respectable folks. I remember them as being very calm and quiet—almost too quiet; you could always hear the grandfather clock ticking in their house. They were churchgoing Christians who reserved judgment of others, or at least any expression of judgment. Their response to almost anything you might tell them was, "Oh, that's nice."

My grandfather was a postman and World War I veteran who played the cornet in a local Navy band. My mother said she remembers women flirting with him wherever they went, which he pretended not to notice. My grandmother, a sweet-looking lady in a dainty hat, had a charming way of talking out of one side of her mouth; she'd had an early stroke. Nothing about her meek appearance suggested the wildness of her past.

She was a former farm girl, schoolteacher, stenographer, and suffragist who had marched for the women's vote in Chicago; in faded, sepia-tone pictures she can be seen posing on mountaintops with her girlfriends, with whom she had traveled the country, wearing trousers. "My mother was a flapper," my mother said. "Before she married my father, she was having the time of her life."

But then in the 1930s, when my grandmother was already in her thirties, her friends set her up with my grandfather, a widower with a young daughter (my aunt). He was looking for a wife. "And she became a housewife and took care of his kids," my mother said. "Because that was what you were supposed to do. Nothing else you did was really admired."

And then on the other side of this family pic, we see the Russians. I mean them no disrespect when I say they look completely insane. It's not just the expression on their faces—open-mouthed shock and brow-knitting rage, all baffling, given the occasion—but their clothes, which are ill-fitting, awful, and look as if they have been slept in. My grandfather's glasses are bizarrely fogged up and my grandmother's hat is askew. They're both grossly overweight, like big blocks of solid life force. They look kind of scary; but they also look interesting.

They were storytellers. When I see their faces I can hear their voices, with their thick Yiddish accents, telling their raucous tales of the old country and their various disreputable relatives here in America (one of my grandmother's brothers was a racetrack gambler known as Morris the Horse, allegedly an inspiration for Damon Runyon). My grandparents met in my grandmother's family's general store, which served the Jews of Louisville, Kentucky. My grandfather was delivering oranges from Florida when he saw my grandmother standing behind the counter. My grandfather would drive down to Florida with a load of apples, sell the apples to buy oranges, and then drive back up north and sell these. Family rumor has it that this was all really a front for his business distributing bootleg whiskey, which he stored underneath the fruit in his truck. He changed his name from Seltzer to Sales while on the run from the cops.

My grandfather was "tough," my father used to say, with that uncomfortable admiration some abused children never seem to be able to escape from feeling for their tormenters. "When I was a kid I thought my father's fist was coming out of my ear," he would tell us, with a nostalgic laugh that always made me shudder.

But before I could resent my grandfather for setting in motion this family cycle of pain, I would remember his place further back in the cycle: When he was sixteen he left his town in Russia after a pogrom in which he saw his father shot dead by Cossacks. He worked his way across Europe to Antwerp with his cousin Israel and caught a ship to America.

The brothers and sisters he left behind all died in the Holocaust and were never mentioned. In his latter days, he sat in his junkyard with his snarly dog, selling auto parts and yelling for my grandmother—whom he called Shmaltz (like "Fats")—to bring him his lunch. "She was the real brains of that family," my mother said. "Can you imagine what she might have done with her life if they'd let her go to college? But she got pregnant with your aunt and had to marry your grandfather."

And finally, in the middle of this family pic, are my mother and father. My father is looking at my mother as if she's the most beautiful thing he's ever seen. "I had to buy him that suit," she told me. She'd been working in the art department of the *St. Petersburg Times*. She wanted to be an artist, but once she got married she became a housewife, like her mother.

"Your father was such a lost soul, I wanted to help him," she told me. "Sometimes I gave him money. My mother kept saying, 'Are you sure you want to *marry* him?' And I'd say, 'I'm almost twenty-one, I can get married if I want.'"

My mother did look beautiful that day, in her lacy, white, tea-length wedding dress, like something Debbie Reynolds would wear; but in the picture, she's crying. People must have thought they were tears of joy. My grandmother is extending a hand to her, as if to console her.

•  •  •

The way people used to meet seemed like fate, like magic, I thought as I walked along, on my way home to meet Abel that night after leaving Constance. Is the secret ingredient of love really accident, to which scientists attribute the beginnings of life itself?

So just how would I ever meet anyone again, if I ended it with Abel now, once and for all? How long would it be before the organic sort of meetings in which my parents and grandparents had found each other vanished forever?

These chance types of encounters already seemed to be endangered— the young women and men I interviewed were always telling me, "No one approaches anyone in person anymore." They talked about sitting in classes and bars and cafés and just wishing they had the guts to talk to that person sitting next to them, but instead going on a dating app or social media to try and find someone. The tech industry's colonization of dating had changed human behavior so quickly, it seemed we were already losing the ability to connect on our own, to court and spark.

But I knew it was dangerous to romanticize the past, and courtship has always been fraught with inequality. My mind flashed to an interview I had done for my documentary with Moira Weigel, the dating historian and author.

It was 2016 and we were in the living room of the Brooklyn brownstone where Weigel had grown up. She was home, visiting from Cambridge, where she was a fellow at Harvard. I was there with my cameraman and soundman, Daniel Carter and Austin Plocher, two wonderful, bearded young guys. Weigel, a pretty, redheaded woman in her early thirties, was sitting in front of me on a dining room chair, talking about the ways in which people used to meet and mate.

"The whole idea of dating and meeting a partner through dating is relatively new historically," Weigel said. "For most of the history of the United States and elsewhere, people have usually met through family members or religious leaders or community leaders in supervised settings. Before there was dating, there was this ritual called 'calling.' You would sit with your mother or your aunt or whomever in the parlor, and a young man who might be interested in you could come visit you socially in your home."

And then, in the late 1800s and early 1900s, she said, "you have women starting to move to the cities to work and going out in public spaces, getting the freedom to meet and mix with men on their own, but also the responsibility of finding their own partner. There were more men and women in the streets, mingling in dance halls, and this becomes a matter of great concern to police and social workers."

I remembered then how, even as a little girl, when I would watch old movies on the TV in the kitchen as my mother made dinner, I had wondered on what authority the women in some of those early Hollywood films were always being sent away to "detention houses" and "reformatories," just for being deemed "loose" or having a baby out of wedlock, like Barbara Stanwyck in *Shopworn*.

"We haven't done anything those society debutantes don't do," gripes a character in the Jean Harlow vehicle *Hold Your Man*, "but do you ever hear about those society girls being sent up?" I remember actually worrying that if I had sex I could go to prison.

Years later, I read *The Trials of Nina McCall* by Scott W. Stern and learned about the "American Plan"—a shocking, rarely discussed government program in which women actually were incarcerated just for being deemed promiscuous or immoral, and therefore a risk for spreading STIs.

"For much of the twentieth century," Stern wrote, "tens, probably hundreds, of thousands of American women were detained and subjected to invasive examinations for sexually transmitted infections," sometimes sterilized, beaten, or sexually abused. Women in poverty and women of color were especially targeted. And how telling that this cruel exercise in misogyny, racism, and classism was implemented at the height of the women's suffrage movement, in the 1910s, when women were demanding political autonomy, as well as asserting more independence in their personal lives by doing this revolutionary new thing called dating.

"The authorities were really very worried," Weigel said. "There was a lot of anxiety about women having control over their own lives and not having family and social protections. I think, to a lot of early twentieth-century onlookers, dating looked like sex work. I think they really did think it was a form of prostitution."

"It basically is like getting a free prostitute, in a lot of men's eyes," I remembered Elizabeth Armstrong saying when I interviewed her for my piece about online dating. I can't count the number of times since that I've heard someone say something similar. "It's like getting a free prostitute," they say, or, "Why do women put themselves on there like prostitutes?" Usually it's a sexist man who's saying this, or sometimes a woman who seems to feel superior to other women because of their sexual choices. Dating has always been threatening to patriarchy, it seems, because it means a loss of control over women's bodies, and so, historically, it has whipped up sexist attitudes—and still does.

"For me," Weigel said, that day in Brooklyn, "the real turning point is when you start having mobile dating apps—then everyone has it on their phones and can sort of be dating all the time. You can Tinder in traffic. The effect of mobile dating apps is to feel like you should always be putting yourself out there, always be promoting your 'product.' It's this application of the logic of consumer capitalism to private life," she went on, "in this way that romantic and sexual desire are used almost like a lure to get you to keep consuming."

And in a society which shames women for being too sexually available—too "easy"—it's striking to see how current corporate ventures into the dating realm are designed to make women constantly available.

It was when courtship became a public rather than a private affair, according to dating historians like Weigel, that it became subject to market forces. And this is perhaps more evident now than at any other time in the history of dating, with the advent of digital technology.

"Maybe we don't think of it as part of the economy," Weigel said, "because a lot of apps are 'free,' but what you're doing when you swipe and swipe, swipe up and 'super-like,' is you're providing valuable data to companies like IAC."

IAC is InterActive Corp, the controlling shareholder of Match Group, Inc.—the biggest of Big Dating companies, with forty-five dating services used all over the world, including Tinder, Match, Plenty of Fish, OkCupid, and Hinge. For a long time, online dating businesses like Match Group avoided admitting that their services were selling users' data, encouraging the impression that they were turning profits through subscriptions and ads alone. But then in 2020, a study by the Norwegian Consumer Council (NCC), a government nonprofit organization, confirmed what many had long suspected—that just like other ad-tech companies, many of the biggest dating sites, including Tinder, OkCupid, and Grindr (which is owned by San Vicente Acquisition LLC), do share the vast amounts of personal data they collect from users with advertising companies and marketers, who then use it to target consumers.

With dating sites, this information can be extremely sensitive, involving users' sexual orientation and preferences, gender identity, drug and alcohol use, and religious beliefs. The NCC discovered, for example, that OkCupid was providing an analytics company with data regarding its users' political views, sexuality, and drug use. And this type of "sharing" is typically done without users' explicit knowledge or consent, potentially violating a 2020 California privacy law, as well as the European Union's General Data Protection Regulation, an administrative code concerning data privacy.

"The big shift with dating," Weigel said, "is that courtship now happens in spaces that are owned by other people"—people who want your money and your data, people who don't necessarily have your happiness in mind, but just want you coming back for more.

"A bartender doesn't care if you get married to the person you're having a drink with," Weigel said, "and in fact, it would be better for the bar if no one ever got married!" She smiled at the irony of it all.

● ● ●

By the time I was born, my mother had already realized she'd made a big mistake in marrying my father. The relationship wasn't shaping up the way she had thought it would, as suggested by his early courtship. He wasn't acting like a gobsmacked suitor from one of the Hollywood movies she'd seen at the double feature every Saturday growing up in Indianapolis. He wasn't morphing into one of the perfect dads in the magazine and television ads the men of Madison Avenue were churning out, trying to entice her to buy new furniture and household appliances.

She was trying her best to become the perfect little housewife as seen in these ads, serving up pound cakes and pot roasts and setting the table just right. But my father wasn't acting like a *Father Knows Best* kind of father—he wasn't even acting like the other fathers on our block (none of whom were consistently princes). He wasn't grilling hot dogs in the backyard or playing football with us kids in the street at dusk. He was doing whatever he wanted. Which was not that.

Our street was hot and bare and lined with small white houses. North Palm Beach was a newly minted suburb. There was hardly any vegetation except for the lawns, just a few skinny palm trees which gave off the air of embarrassed, naked adolescents. It was as if a giant bulldozer had pulled into whatever fecund Florida forest had been there before and vomited up a massive amount of asphalt and concrete, killing life, so that the suburbanites could move in and begin theirs.

The dads were all young professionals—doctors, lawyers, dentists, accountants—and the moms were mostly housewives who wore aprons throughout the day. Everybody was white and Christian, except for a smattering of Jews, like us, who weren't making a big deal out of it. Nobody ever said anything openly about race—not even when the family next door took their daughter out of our elementary school when our class was integrated. My mother pursed her lips and told us, "That wasn't nice," and my father said, "If I ever hear about you being rotten to any of the Black kids, you're gonna see the back of my hand."

On Sundays, my mother would take me and my two older brothers to the Presbyterian church, where she played the organ. Apparently, my father thought this would provide a good image for his budding law practice. My brother Danny, always the rebel, the future punk rocker, would lead me and my other brother in singing the wrong words to hymns ("Oh, North Palm Beach, how foul the smell!") and making farting noises, and my mother would get so embarrassed. I noticed she didn't tell my father about it, though. She was protecting Danny.

I have few memories of my father before about the age of eight. "Because you didn't see him," my mother told me. "He wasn't there." She left his dinner on a hot plate in the kitchen and sometimes he didn't make it home to eat it, so it would be sitting there in the morning.

Looking back, I think my father must have been bored by suburban family life. I think he might have been one of those people who would have been happier never getting married. But he was doing what was expected of him. He was doing what everybody else was doing, just like people now. His escape was his work. He was getting a reputation as the kind of divorce lawyer you called when you wanted a pit bull—which, as a formerly bullied Jewish boy, hazed by the guys at the University of Chicago (they once got him drunk, drove him to Wisconsin, and left him there without his coat, his sister told us), must have felt pretty good.

Being a man, he could come and go as he pleased. So he came and went. He drove a Mustang convertible he would purr away in every morning when it was still dark out. I sometimes heard some of the other mothers and fathers on our block call my father a "workaholic," which they said disapprovingly, as if they were saying "alcoholic." Which some of them were. Drinks on the patios at twilight were a regular thing, as all kids knew, because we would run from house to house stealing cheese and crackers and pigs in blankets, running barefoot across the pesticide-soaked lawns. Passing through these gatherings, I sometimes heard the adults murmuring things about my parents. I was already a little eavesdropper, a listener at keyholes, fascinated by secrets, secrets about my own family.

"Do you think he sees other women?" I heard one of the mothers say languidly one evening as my father roared off in his car.

"If he does, he's crazy," said a father who was standing there, swatting a bug off his thigh.

My mother was the pearl of Oyster Road: beautiful but "too thin," they said. They didn't talk about anorexia back then; they just said she "wasn't eating." Her long, black, Emmylou Harris hair started falling out, making clumps in the comb, which scared me when I would see them in the bathroom trash. Years later, my mother told me that her doctor had asked her, "Is anything making you unhappy?" Like a sad song I could hear in the background, I knew my mother was unhappy. She would play sad songs on the piano. She would get a look on her face when she drove us in her station wagon, as if she wanted to drive us all away from there.

I tried to be what the adults called a "good little girl." I baked cakes in my Easy-Bake Oven. I took care of my Baby Tender Love. I played with my big-bosomed Barbies and dressed them up in smart fashions. I watched *Bewitched* and *I Dream of Jeannie*, my favorite shows, both of them about women who hide their incredible powers to serve their husband and "master." I wanted to be magic. I felt a wildness inside me I didn't know what to do with. I ran around the house, pretending to fly on my toy broomstick. I would stay in my room, which my mother painted pink because she said girls liked pink, and read books from the adult shelves, which were always more interesting, revealing things I sensed were going on underneath the surface.

I would go into my father's study and write stories on the typewriter. Everybody seemed to think this was so funny of me to do, though I couldn't see why; to me it felt necessary. They were stories about woodland animals having marital disputes ("Mr. and Mrs. Chipmunk had a fite"), which ended grimly ("'What would you do without me?' she said. He said, 'Go on living'"). I wrote stories about love: "X was a dog. I saw him. I loved him. Oh, oh, X."

I fell in love with a little boy down the street and fantasized about taking my mother's dulcimer and strumming it on his lawn with my hair in my face, like a lady I'd seen on TV. But I didn't dare. I went to the library on my banana seat bike and read a book on how people have sex. I was interested in sex. Once, when I was sitting on the toilet, a bold-eyed little lizard appeared on the windowsill, on the other side of the screen, and his crimson throat started pulsing in and out, in and out, while he was staring right at me, and I knew that this had something to do with sex, and I was both freaked out by it and quite flattered.

But I never felt I could talk to my mother about these things, because I didn't want to upset her—she already seemed upset. My mother didn't talk to me about much of anything in those days: "Time for dinner." "Oh, that's nice." She made the food, she gave the hugs, but it felt like she wasn't there.

I knew that my father sensed my mother was unhappy, too, and I knew that he felt very guilty about that. He would get frustrated and yell and sometimes he would become violent. I saw him tip over his glass-topped desk. I saw him hit my mother. He hit my brother Danny too, when he said

Danny was "talking trash." "What are you, some kind of hippie?" my father would say whenever Danny's hair grew longer than a soldier's in the Vietnam War, which was always on the TV news, a disturbing green blur.

I often found it hard to breathe. I would get up from bed in the middle of the night and go running into my parents' room. Doctors didn't talk about anxiety back then; they just said it was "wheezing." They gave me yellow pills called Quibron and a vaporizer.

My father would bring my mother gifts as penance: perfume, clothes, a toaster oven, and, once, a diamond ring (which, almost fifty years later, my mother gave me to sell in the Diamond District, to help fund my documentary). But the presents didn't seem to make my mother any happier. Years later, she told me how it made her feel strange to know that there were women in the streets marching for her rights—marching against the very things she was experiencing on Oyster Road, things that she felt she couldn't talk about with anyone she knew.

And then, one day, my mother disappeared. She was gone for a few days, and then she came back. Soon after she came back, my father came home in the middle of the day and played Frisbee on the lawn with my brothers, still wearing his white button-down shirt and tie. I felt bad because he didn't know how to throw the Frisbee—it went up and down instead of sideways, and everybody felt awkward. I listened at the door when he went in his study and got on the phone. "She's giving me a week to get out of the house," I heard him say. I knew what it meant. I ran next door and told my best friend, Teedie. "Oh, you poor thing," she said with her southern twang. But I remember feeling an immense sense of relief, like when you can finally throw up after a long, painful stomachache.

● ● ●

As I walked back home that night after leaving Constance—wondering if I was going to let Abel back into my life, my body, my heart—I passed by

Sake Bar Satsko. I looked in the window to see if Satsko or any of my young women friends were there, but it was a busy night and the place was looking rowdy, with rounds of sake bombs being downed, so I walked on by.

It had been one of the great boons to my existence, fifteen years earlier, when Satsko opened her sake bar in my neighborhood. I had wandered in there one night, not long after it opened, after having a fight with my then husband. I had staggered out of our apartment in a weeping rage, still wearing my bathrobe, needing a moment away from him to calm down. When I came in and sat at the bar—and Sake Bar Satsko is mostly bar, a little hole-in-the-wall bathed in the light of red lanterns—Satsko made no reference to my strange attire and, after a few minutes, set before me a bowl of bright green edamame.

We started talking, sharing the snack and a couple of glasses of wine, and soon I was telling her everything about myself and wanting to know everything about her. It turned out that we had the same birthday, were both single moms to daughters, and had lived lives full of adventures with men, but had now grown skeptical about the benefits of associating with them.

"Oh, I'm done with them," Satsko said in her decisive way. "One day you'll be done with them too, and you'll be so happy!" She gave her infectious laugh, which always felt a bit like she was laughing at you, too, but in a way that made it easier to laugh at yourself.

After that, Satsko's became my *Cheers* bar. The owner's charming presence attracted a lively and eclectic young crowd. It was through becoming a regular there that I developed my circle of young women friends, with whom I found myself sharing stories of dating and dating apps.

How I wished I could run into some of them now, I thought as I walked along. I wanted to talk to them about Abel. Abigail, Emily, Samantha, Kira, Dolly, Molly—where were they tonight? I wondered. They were the first women in my life with whom I felt I could speak frankly about men, because they were talking about them in a way that was new to me. They weren't apologizing for how they felt or what they wanted; they weren't sugarcoating their experiences in an attempt to seem successful at relationships. They didn't slut-shame each other, or themselves, and they didn't seem to think it strange that an older woman like me actually had a sex life. They were the most feminist young women I had ever known—all the more striking because they were living in a time of great misogyny, when at any moment they might be bullied or harassed online, where they spent a fair number of hours daily.

"Thank God there wasn't Instagram when I was in college," said Abigail on a typical night at Satsko's, scrolling through the feed on her phone.

Abigail was twenty-five when we met. She was fashionable and fun, a rep for a music label who looked like Phoebe Cates's twenty-first-century little sister. I followed her on Instagram, where she could often be seen in her stories, vamping in some self-ironically alluring pose.

"Look at this," she said, scrolling through her feed. "We all look the *same*."

She wriggled her shoulders, satirically kittenish, doing an exaggerated duckface.

"I think objectification got worse with dating apps," Abigail said, "because you were already posting hot pictures of yourself online in case some guy would check you out. And then everybody was on dating apps, which were specifically *for* hot pictures—and then dating apps got linked to Instagram and Facebook and Snapchat.

"So now any time you post anything," she went on, "you have to be thinking some guy might be checking you out off of Tinder or Bumble or wherever. The male gaze is constant. But that's all of social media," she added. "I've had guys I don't even know slide into my DMs like, 'Hey, girl, I like that ass.' Like, I'm supposed to be flattered by this? Like that's the most important thing about me?

"But then"—she smiled—"I *did* kinda post all those pictures of my ass looking hot."

We laughed. We drank more sake.

After the pandemic hit, I called Abigail to see how she was doing. I'd seen her in her Instagram stories, dressing up to go on fake dates for the amusement of her followers. She lit candles and made herself elaborate dinners and pretended to be having conversations with some wonderful fellow. It was funny, but it also made me sad. I wanted her to have some wonderful guy. I felt like Jimmy Stewart watching his Miss Lonelyhearts neighbor in *Rear Window.*

"Oh, it's better than talking to real men right now," she told me on the phone. "I was under the illusion that maybe men were going to try and take the time to really get to know me now that we can't leave our apartments, but they just keep badgering me about coming over. And when I was like, 'No thank you,' one of them accused me of being a 'tease' because I don't want to get Covid! A bunch of them have asked for nudes, like, right away. Since they know there's not even a chance of meeting in person, the objectification has become total."

● ● ●

It was perplexing that dating apps, which were supposed to be fun to use, were making us miserable, and so we would talk about that when we met up at Satsko's. It was perplexing, too, that we were still on these things, and that there seemed to be no other choice now but to be. Wasn't the essence of feminism about having choice?

It was for all these reasons, Emily said, that she had stopped using them. "I gave up on dating apps because the respect is zero," she told us one night at the bar. Emily was twenty-six and studying for her PhD in psychology. She reminded me of Taylor Swift in her long-forgotten emo phase, with her dyed black hair.

"The bar is so low," she said. "You have some guy who has no perceptible job with this long list of demands in his profile, saying he won't settle for less than perfect. Check him out."

She held up a Tinder profile she had screenshotted for "Jonathan," a doughy young man in a panama hat. "Must be: blonde or brunette," his profile said. "Be fit and toned, go to the gym 4 times weekly. Be no more than 5'11" and no less than 5'4" in height. Be available at all times. Give good head. Be able to cook and clean. Devote as much of your time to me as possible. Have a steady income of at least $70,000. Have own apartment that I can crash at occasionally. If you fit these criteria, swipe right. I will not settle for anything less. Also not interested in BBWs"—meaning "big, beautiful women"—"and no single moms."

"Well!" I said, with mock outrage. I was a single mom who wasn't exactly small.

Everyone laughed.

The young women I met at Satsko's were accomplished and smart and thoroughly flummoxed by what dating had become. It was sitting at the bar, listening to them talk about the disrespect they were encountering from the men they met on dating apps, that I started to think about how online dating had become the site of a potent new wave of backlash—the same hostile reaction to the gains of the feminist movement identified by Susan Faludi in her 1991 bestseller named for this phenomenon.

It seemed to me that, as women had achieved more and more professional and political power, the destabilizing trend with which they now had to contend was the outrageous sense of entitlement and disrespect from the men they were dating and with whom they were having sex. And the new technology of dating, which encouraged men to think of women as less than human—as hot pictures, as objects—was enabling such disrespect to become normalized. It had made the once unacceptable mundane.

My young women friends talked about men who wouldn't commit to dates, much less relationships—and worse. "After that guy on Tinder just left me standing at the entrance to BAM [the Brooklyn Academy of Music] with two tickets to *Parasite*, I was like, *that's it*," Emily said. "And then there was the Bumble dude who straight up slapped me in the face while we were having sex."

41

She mentioned the incident with the brave and unsettling, no-big-deal off-the-cuffness with which I'd heard other young women tell tales of assault, or near assault, as if it was nothing surprising—which statistically, of course, it's not. According to the Centers for Disease Control and Prevention (CDC), nearly one in five women in the United States have been sexually assaulted. But even beyond this well-known figure, there was something else going on. I was hearing, not only from the women I spoke to at Satsko's, but many others I was talking to for my book and film, that it had now become a routine part of dating for some guy to start being violent in bed with you, and not as part of a mutual interest in BDSM.

A 2019 study at the Indiana University School of Public Health found that nearly a quarter of adult women in the United States have felt scared during sex due to a male partner becoming unexpectedly violent. And it seems this trend isn't just happening here, but other places around the world. In a 2019 study done by the UK's Centre for Women's Justice, nearly 40 percent of women under the age of forty said they had experienced "unwanted slapping, choking, gagging, or spitting during consensual sex." This study described a "growing pressure on young women to consent to violent, dangerous, and demeaning acts."

"When you told him to stop, did he accuse you of not being sex positive?" Abigail asked Emily with a frown.

"Oh, of course," Emily said. "He tried to act like I was a boring vanilla loser because I didn't want to be smacked around. So after that I decided I was just going to try and meet people in real life. And so I met this guy in the Nike store. He sold me shoes. He was cute. He asked for my number. And then we start texting and he won't make an actual plan—he was being flaky, like most guys these days.

"So I told him, look," she said, "I'm old-school, if you want to see me you have to make a real date with a time and place and you have to show up on time, like our dads used to do. And he texts me back"—she gave a wait-for-it look—"*Ooh, daddy issues.*"

"Oh my God," we said. "Oh, no."

"Daddy issues is a what really gross dude-bros like to say when they're talking about why women like to have sex," said Amy, who was bartending that night, handing Emily a beer. "Like it couldn't just be because we actually like to have sex—like, there must be something wrong with us, or we must be sluts because daddy didn't pay attention to us or paid too much attention."

We said, "Mm-hmm."

"But who doesn't have daddy issues in patriarchy?" Abigail asked. "It is literally a system based on the daddies being in charge so they can fuck women over. I don't have issues with men because I have daddy issues—I have issues with them because I watch the news. I have issues with men because one in five women are raped."

"What I want to know is, if I have daddy issues, then why are you the one asking me to stick this dildo in your butt?" Amy asked.

We laughed.

● ● ●

Amy was the one, among the enchanted group I discovered at Satsko's, to whom I felt the closest. She was Satsko's daughter, her mini-me, with a breast-plate of intricate, colorful tattoos. It was Amy who had come up with the phrase "pussy affluenza" to describe the sense of entitlement in heterosexual men brought about by the explosion of options provided by dating apps. She was the first one to talk to me about a "dating apocalypse."

She was a little bit older than the other women I'd usually find at the bar, a few years which made a big difference in terms of technology—kids who'd gotten their phones at fourteen versus twenty. People in their early thirties had been able to see firsthand the seismic shift in dating which had occurred with the introduction of these devices.

"Dating when I was in high school was still super sweet," Amy had told me. "You would call each other up and go to the movies. People would actually say, 'This is my boyfriend. This is my girlfriend.' It was like, we're gonna hold hands a little bit and then enter the world of sex together. It's crazy to me that kids will never have that again," she added. "Everything has changed. As soon as I got a PalmPilot, guys were asking me for nudes."

Which, she said, she did enjoy sending and receiving, sometimes, though never unsolicited. "A nude is like a vampire; it has to be invited in," she joked.

Amy said that she had initially embraced the changes brought about by technology, believing it would all lead to more sexual freedom and happy experimentation in relationships, but now she wasn't so sure. "Like the idea of being in love suddenly seems unattainable," she said. "I haven't had a serious relationship in six or seven years. Sometimes I'll have these weird moments where I'll get all weepy and wonder, when am I gonna have that again? Is it even possible anymore?"

It reminded me of a thread I had seen on Twitter around Valentine's Day. "I don't know who needs to hear this today," the Tweeter wrote, "but I'm 23 and I've never had a relationship. I've never been asked on a date. For so many years, this has made me feel absolutely horrible about myself. But I'm learning I'm not the only one."

A deluge of comments followed, in which young women and men commiserated about the difficulty of finding love in the digital age. And if not love, then just someone who would be respectful and kind. "I just want a guy who will be nice to me and text me back," said a tweet I saw from another young woman.

"Where's Abel?" Abigail asked me one night at the bar.

"Oh, he's off in the woods somewhere," I said offhandedly, as I did whenever I didn't know where he was, pretending like I didn't care.

● ● ●

How I wished I could go back to that night in 2015 when he stood in my kitchen for the first time. How I wished that I could wind back the clock to that first moment, when there was so much promise: the beginning of a love affair.

Where had it gone wrong? I wondered on my walk back home, the night he texted me when I was out with Constance. "Whatever happens tonight," I thought, "if this does have to end all over again, please just let me relive that moment I first saw him…"

"Hey," I had said, "come on in."

And so we began.

In my mind's eye, it always plays in close-ups of his face, his eyes, his lips. We stare at each other and smile as if we've known each other forever and are seeing each other again after a long time apart: "Oh, hello again. There you are."

Who can account for attraction? That immediate feeling of connection? Not the brogrammers whose algorithms had arranged our meeting. For even as I stood there grinning at him goofily, my heart hammering away from the excitement of finally meeting him, I knew the promise of dating app algorithms was a con. No study has ever found that they work any better than pure serendipity in predicting the future success of a match—in fact, studies have shown that these algorithms promote superficiality, pushing on us those who most resemble others we've already chosen, in the same way Zappos suggests shoes. And if you get swiped on a lot, then you get pushed to the top of the stack, getting more and "better"—meaning better-looking—matches, while others who get swiped on less are pushed down, down, made into actual bottom-feeders by the cold selection of lines of code.

However, this doesn't deter dating app companies from telling their users that algorithms will find them love. eHarmony, the first algorithm-based dating site, launched in 2000, still boasts a "scientifically proven" matching system despite offering no evidence of their "proof." In 2012, *Scientific American* reported that the company had not provided members of the scientific community with information about its matching algorithms that could be used to verify claims about them being scientifically based. In 2018, Britain's Advertising Standards Authority banned an eHarmony ad which included the line, "It's time science had a go at love," on the grounds that it was misleading. And yet, in 2020, the eHarmony website still read: "What happens when you apply scientific research to dating behavior? A whole lotta love!"

"I'm Abel," he said, stepping inside.

"I know," I said, exhaling. "Hiiii…"

I opened my arms to him, and he came to me without hesitation, and we stood there, holding each other, our faces buried in each other's necks— one of the many things that happened and was about to happen that had never happened to me before on any dating app date. We kept hugging and hugging until we were hugging each other hard and fast, like we both needed to hug someone, like we had reunited after a long, difficult journey. I'll never forget that moment of touching him for the first time, feeling his slender body with its sinewy muscles wrapped around me…

Then he pulled back his head and looked at me with a funny little smile.

"Goodness," he said. "I guess I came to the right place."

It was then I realized that his accent was no act, not the ironic humor I suspected him of attempting when we were texting—he was just country. I knew that rolling intonation from many childhood summers spent at the camp in the Blue Ridge Mountains my mother sent us to so she could finally have some time to herself. Suddenly I was there, hearing the way the ladies in the kitchen always sounded like they were singing when they'd ask us: "Y'all want some more biscuits?"

Oh, yes, please.

All in a rush, I heard the sound of the rushing brook that ran through the camp and the old swinging bell they would ring to wake us up in the morning after a night of perfect sleep in our cabins, and the kids singing "Edelweiss" in the lodge at twilight, when you could see fireflies dotting the darkness. That's how far back he went for me—to summers in the mountains, where I felt safe, away from everything that was wrong at home, and where everything smelled good, like pine trees and freshly cut grass.

He smelled like cologne.

"Aw," I thought, "he put on cologne for me, this Abel."

Then he muttered something I couldn't quite catch, because he was Heath-Ledger-in-*Brokeback-Mountain* hard to understand, and just as pretty. But before I would have to ask him "What'd you say?," I kissed him.

Now, there had been a number of kisses in the year since I'd started using dating apps—some things just shouldn't be counted—and many more in the years before they were ever invented, but somehow this kiss felt like the kiss I'd been waiting for all my life. Like the kiss in *Spellbound* when Gregory Peck and Ingrid Bergman kiss for the first time: she closes her eyes, and all you see is door after door opening slowly, one after the other, until finally it's a door opening to the sky . . .

Allow me to introduce myself: Nancy Jo, movie buff and incorrigible romantic.

Or maybe it was just that I was so starved for a kiss with some passion in it, after the past year of such rough, impersonal encounters. Or maybe it was that I knew that it might be the last time I had a chance like this—because I was swearing off dating apps, once and for all, I promised. Or maybe it was because I was getting older.

"Goodness *gracious*," he murmured.

Then his hands went down around my hips, and he let go of me and went walking back a step. And I saw that he was holding up the scissors I had put in my back pocket, in case I needed to kill him—in case he was going to try and kill *me*.

He held them aloft, looking at them quizzically. It was as if he was trying to say something, but he couldn't quite get it out, like he might have a stutter—oh, and I saw that he did have a stutter.

"What you doin' with these?" he said finally.

"Oh, I—" I cast about, trying to think of how to explain it. A giant pair of scissors in my pocket. "Um—"

"I ain't gonna hurt you," he told me.

It was the first thing that made me love him, I think—that he immediately understood, without my having to explain. That he didn't see me as paranoid or crazy, but as a woman who knew there was reason to be scared. Scared of a strange man in her house. Scared of men.

That he knew I had cause, and that he wasn't offended, and didn't try to make it about him. That his first thought was to allay my fears, and not to attack me for wanting to protect myself. All of this made me want to kiss him again.

"I'm not gonna hurt you either!" I said.

He handed me back the scissors. I put them on the counter.

"Can I have some water?" he asked. "I'm feeling a little light-headed. I think I gotta sit down..."

"Guileless and sweet," I thought, smiling, getting him his water as he wandered into my living room. Maybe I was gonna love this one a little bit.

● ● ●

I'd seen one great love. And I suppose that ever since it started, it had been my ideal. It was the love of my mother and my stepfather, the man she left my father for. They've been married now almost fifty years.

When my mother went away for a little while, it was with him. I happened to be there on the day they met. It was at the home of a neighbor lady, whose younger brother was visiting Oyster Road with a bearded college classmate. I remember peeking out from behind my mother's soft green skirt and hearing her voice become lilting in a way that I had never heard before. I remember her rocking back and forth on her flat sandals. And I knew she was flirting with the young man with the beard.

She was thirty-seven and he was twenty-seven at the time. They caused a bit of a scandal on Oyster Road. The day she drove us out of the suburbs in the station wagon with our suitcases and the dog, my brother Danny stared out the window and said, "You're doing the right thing, Mom. There's nothing for us here."

When I wonder what love is, I think one possible definition might be the feeling that my stepfather, a former French literature major who resembled Adam Sandler, exhibited in wanting my mother so badly that he was willing to take on her three strange, difficult children. Danny was sullen, obsessed with chess, and plagued with the worst case of acne I've ever seen, poor guy; my other brother was a nervous eater and into doing magic tricks; and then there was me, with my gold, octagon-shaped glasses, freckles, and braids, which I insisted on wearing after reading *Pippi Longstocking*, whose heroine I idolized for her bravery and physical power, although I myself was so sensitive I cried at least once a day. We were not cute, I realize now, and we were rather terrifying.

But love my mother my stepfather did—if there was no other proof, he took my brother to a magic convention—and she loved him. They were crazy in love, always "smooching," as my stepfather liked to say; they couldn't keep their hands off each other, which seemed to annoy my brothers to no end, but I thought it was lovely. "Love is all you need," I thought, just like the Beatles sang. And the effect of love was that my mother was happy now, always beaming and blushing. She still seemed far away from me, somehow, but in a different way that was preferable. She was eating again. And I had stopped wheezing, which everyone attributed to the "change of air."

We moved into a little yellow house with a Spanish tile roof and a front porch with a wooden swing, where I would read hundreds of books over the next few years—every novel I could get my hands on, from *Charlotte's Web* to *Middlemarch* to *Invisible Man*.

My stepfather owned a restaurant in Coral Gables, that lush and beautiful suburb of Miami, with its streets framed with canopies of oaks and banyans. The place was a little hippie watering hole nestled in a Publix shopping plaza.

It was called the Spiral, after the spiraling properties of yin and yang, the Chinese concept of dualism, which was somehow connected philosophically with the Zen Buddhism–influenced macrobiotic diet, of which my stepfather was a great advocate. The problem was he couldn't cook; but my mother could. She was such a good cook, it made me sad for the other kids sometimes, when you would go over to their houses for dinner and wonder how they could stand to eat whatever was being served (like in "Rapper's Delight" when Wonder Mike says, "The macaroni's soggy, the peas are mushed / And the chicken tastes like wood").

After my mother became the head chef at the Spiral, the restaurant came into its own. All that creative energy she had, which had never been remotely tapped, was now flowing into the restaurant's vegetarian lasagna and shrimp tempura and the creamy miso dressing on cornucopia-like salads. After she came on the scene, the place transformed into an unlikely Miami hot spot, attracting some counterculture celebrities such as Abbie Hoffman and Jerry Rubin, whenever they were in town. And then there were our homegrown stars, like the impossibly cool cats of KC and the Sunshine Band and the lionlike Bee Gee brothers, who moved to Miami in the mid-seventies.

"Your parents owned that hippie restaurant?" a former editor of *Sports Illustrated* asked me in the nineties, when I was a newbie reporter at *People* and working in the Time, Inc., building. "Whenever I was in Miami I used to go there to check out the hippie girls," he said. "None of them wore underwear."

The creepiness of his comment aside, it's true that the Spiral was a hothouse of sexual revolution sex, full of romantic intrigue, which I found out about in my usual way, by listening when no one thought I was. "What's an orgy?" I remember asking my brother Danny, who just laughed and called me a "perv." Talk of sex was happening openly and gleefully at the Spiral in a way that I had never heard on Oyster Road. "I love my lady to be on top!" I remember one of the customers announcing as I cleared the table (in those days, no one seemed fazed by having a ten-year-old working in a busy restaurant).

Our head waiter was a dashing young Cuban guy named Roberto, whose ongoing barrage of sexual innuendo was as much of a draw as his good looks. I remember him walking up and down the aisles to "Jive Talkin'" playing on the radio, the red hankie in his back pocket flapping jauntily against his tight jeans. Looking back, I can see that the Spiral was an oasis of tolerance for many of the people who gravitated there, and I think the credit for this really goes to my stepfather, who was that rare type of guy who never judged anyone for who they were.

● ● ●

But that didn't mean that the gender roles in our household were any less traditional, which I noticed even as a little girl. I was the one who cleared the table as my brothers and stepfather sat kibitzing over their desserts and my mother did the dishes. My mother was devoted to making elaborate dinners for her young husband. "I was just taking care of somebody again," she told me ruefully, years later, talking about going from one marriage right into the next. We ate so much, I became positively rotund, and I couldn't help but feel ashamed that my legs, coming out of my scooter skirts, weren't coltish and straight like I knew they were supposed to be—like Marcia's on *The Brady Bunch*—but chubby and curvy, with my freckled knees.

"What is happening to you?" my mother asked me one day, when I could no longer fit into any of my clothes. I saw her face flash with a disgust I associated with how she felt about my father. I knew that she saw my father in me—I looked like him, I didn't look like her. After she said this, I went to the garage to cry, as I did whenever my brothers hit me, which they often seemed to be doing. "Well, what did you do to them?" my mother would ask, if I complained. My brothers had learned that this was how boys treated girls, and I don't think she saw the connection to my father, or knew how to tell them differently.

I was ashamed of my weight, ashamed of my crying. I escaped into

51

books. I rode my banana seat bike to the Waldenbooks on Miracle Mile in downtown Coral Gables every Saturday to buy more books. I escaped into movies. I would go by myself to the art deco Miracle Theater, where I sat in the balcony alone, one afternoon, riveted, watching Tatum O'Neal in *Paper Moon*. My mother told me she didn't want me to see this film because the little girl in it smoked and swore—but that was exactly why I wanted to see it, because the little girl was breaking the rules, and I was already getting the sense that the rules were rigged against girls.

It thrilled me, seeing a little girl like me being smart and savvy enough to con the con men in her world, and survive by her wits. Watching it again, years later, I realized that another reason I might have been so affected by this film was the tangled relationship between the little girl and her father, played by Tatum O'Neal's own father, Ryan O'Neal. In some ways, their relationship mirrored mine with my father—both on- and off-screen, from what I've gathered from the celebrity gossip mill and Ryan and Tatum's later attempts at reconciliation in the painful-to-watch-it's-so-close-to-home 2011 reality show *Ryan and Tatum*. O'Neal was like a handsomer, Irish version of my dad—in short, a misogynist with a heart of gold—and Tatum was the child who called him on his bullshit.

But I hadn't started doing that yet. After my parents divorced, we saw my father on the weekends. He would drive down from West Palm Beach to see us—about a seventy-mile trip—or he would send one of his secretaries to come and get us. The secretaries, always strikingly pretty young women, were always preferable. My father was the worst driver I've ever been in a car with—it's actually amazing that we survived our childhoods with him at the wheel, particularly when he would drive us after dark, as he had night blindness and could barely see ten feet in front of him. On top of this, he had a permanent case of road rage—lots of swerving and honking of horns. And then, when we finally arrived at his apartment, he almost always found another reason to be mad at someone, usually Danny. He had stopped hitting Danny, thankfully, probably having been sufficiently put in check by the divorce.

My father's apartment was a standard seventies bachelor pad, decorated by his young women friends, who also picked out his albums (Paul McCartney singing "Jet," the lyrics to which caused me to look up the word "suffragette"). I could hear them whispering and giggling in the mornings when he was sneaking them out before we got up. There were *Playboy*s and *Hustler*s hidden under my father's bed, which I saw my brothers take into the bathroom with them when he went to work. I knew that my father was going through something, and that part of how he was dealing with it was with sex.

It had no doubt given him a jolt that his beautiful wife had left him for a man ten years younger than he. He referred to my stepfather as "the hippie on the motorcycle," although my stepfather didn't own a motorcycle. My father, who had a Don Rickles–like knack for coming up with a put-down, would often ask us whether we were "getting enough protein" now that we were being raised vegetarian and "living on gruel." He filled up our time together with activities we wouldn't have chosen, such as going to Monkey Jungle in Miami, where, back then, the spider monkeys roamed free and would crawl up your legs, begging for peanuts, which always scared me. My father seemed to realize that these outings were miserable for us, and to make up for it, he gave us stuff that my mother didn't like us to have, like Atomic Fireball candy and *Mad*. He let us to stay up late and watch the off-color Dean Martin celebrity roasts. I can still hear his rough laugh.

He knew I liked books, so he gave me books—classics like Dickens, Dickinson, and Austen. "Be the doctor, not the nurse," he told me, an attempt at being encouraging which managed to be both empowering and offensive to nurses. "If any boys come near you, tell them your father is capable of homicide," he told me, laughing. Of course, I knew he was only kidding, but it made me never want to tell him anything about what was happening between me and boys and men.

● ● ●

A lot was happening. My boobs were growing, and boys were noticing, and men were, too. By the sixth grade, I had a serious pair of knockers—a word I hate, but which I use now to convey how it sounded to me when I heard a grown man use it as I bounced by him one day on Miracle Mile: "Nice knockers, kid." I really needed a bra, but I was too embarrassed to ask for one, and my mother seemed too embarrassed, in her midwestern way, to bring it up. So I tried to hide my bouncing boobs under sweatshirts and oversized T-shirts that said things like "May the Force Be with You" and "Keep on Truckin'."

But the boys in my school were still very aware of what was going on under my clothes, and if they didn't see for themselves, there was the mass alert from our PE coach, who took to calling me Big Red. Thanks, Mr. Novak. I missed twenty days of school that year, claiming sore throats and stomachaches, but really I was avoiding the mockery of the boys.

And then there were the daily assaults of a particularly psycho boy named Roger.

Roger was the boy who followed me into the walk-in closet at the back of our homeroom nearly every day and grabbed my boobs. The closet was where my orange school patrol belt and plastic helmet were kept, and I was allowed to go and get them before leaving class five minutes early in order to attend to my patrolling duties. At that time of day, the other kids in the class were usually running around, talking loudly and packing up their things, and our teacher was preoccupied with end-of-the-day concerns. Roger was always lying in wait, with a shit-eating grin on his face, as he watched me grow more and more nervous about what was about to happen.

When Roger came upon me in the closet, I'd try and dodge him, doing shimmy-shimmy shoulder moves I'd copied from Mercury Morris, the halfback for the Miami Dolphins (my father took us to all the home games), but this only seemed to make Roger all the more determined. He always got in his squeeze.

I never told anyone about what he was doing to me. I was mortified by the fact that he had singled me out for this ugly ritual, and I didn't want anyone thinking about my boobs any more than I suspected they already were. I couldn't imagine having that conversation with our teacher, a perpetually disapproving-looking lady who wore a large gold cross, nor with my easily embarrassed mom. It wasn't something I had ever heard anyone talk about. I'd never heard the words "sexual assault" or "harassment" in a movie or on TV, where they did sometimes mention rape, but it was always presented as something very shameful for the woman. I was afraid that if I said anything, everyone would laugh at me—not Roger, but me—which very well might have happened. And so I resigned myself to being Roger's sexual object, which felt as horrible as it sounds.

He always snickered, during his flashes of groping, like he was enjoying getting away with something. Years later, I was reminded of him at one of our drinking sessions at Satsko's, when Abigail said, "They say humiliation is the emotion we feel most deeply—it's how women are silenced." I thought, yes, and there's something even worse to consider: the way humiliation conditions girls to be accepting of sexual violence.

● ● ●

Even as a little girl, I was aware of the basic principles of feminism, as well as the concept of right and wrong, which to my mind are almost the same thing. I knew that the things that were happening to me were caused by inequities in the treatment of my gender, a subject very much in the news, with the fight for Title IX and the ERA.

I'd been hearing about feminism since I was six, when I remember sitting on the couch with my groovy teenage babysitters—long-haired sisters in bell-bottoms and fringe—watching *The Dick Cavett Show*, and they clapped and cheered for the lady on TV who was yelling at the man with the pipe who was making women dress up like bunnies.

When I looked up the clip on YouTube, years later, there was feminist author and activist Susan Brownmiller telling Hugh Hefner, "You choose to see women as sex objects, not as full human beings." (When I interviewed Hef decades later, in 2001, he hadn't changed a bit; he had seven women living with him, all in their late teens and twenties. "I'm an *orgy* guy," he told me.)

I remember my brothers scowling when I did a little dance when Billie Jean King beat Bobby Riggs in the nationally televised "Battle of the Sexes" tennis tournament in 1973; and I remember the episode of *The Partridge Family* about the girl who starts a "women's rights" group called the Power of Women (POW). "All they wanna do is throw out that phony double standard and stop being treated like second-class citizens," said Laurie Partridge, my former TV queen.

But why wasn't I learning about the history of the women's movement in school? I wonder now. Why weren't we all learning about the Grimke sisters, Ida B. Wells, and countless others? It wouldn't be until college and beyond that I would learn about women's struggle for equality, but what a difference it would have made to me, and what a difference it would make to girls now. Decades later, schools are still not teaching the story of women as they should. Women are still "not well integrated into US state history standards," according to a 2018 study.

Instead, I found myself trying to protest without an abundance of language to do it with. I'd already gotten into arguments with neighborhood boys about whether girls could do everything they could do, or if they were as smart or strong. "Yeah, but you can't do *this*," said one of the boys, whipping out his floppy little penis—the first one I'd ever seen—and shooting a stream of urine at me. This got a big laugh from the other kids.

I knew there were women out there in the world who were fighting so that women and girls wouldn't be treated this way, and I wondered when they were going to deliver me from this. I don't remember anybody ever telling me what to do when bad things happened to me, if I were catcalled or groped or harassed. Back then, nobody I knew ever talked about such things, and nobody admitted that they happened to girls all the time. I think too few people do even now. I've interviewed girls who have told me their parents have no idea that they've been bullied or pressured into sharing a nude picture—or, sadly, even raped. They don't want to upset their parents, they say; they don't want to feel judged or ashamed.

● ● ●

Does misogyny affect girls' health? It was certainly affecting mine.

In the sixth grade, I developed symptoms of what I could later identify as OCD. Weird things had started happening in my brain. I had to throw the towel up in the air three times after showering or I was afraid something terrible would happen to me. I had to brush my teeth in time to the tune of "Turkey in the Straw" (Why this song? I have no idea) or someone would find out about the things Roger was doing to me at school. I had to have everything in my room pointing up and to the right, or I would fail a test or get in trouble somehow. I still do these things, sometimes, when I'm feeling particularly anxious. A shrink once told me, "You felt like you needed to be in control, because things were happening to you that were beyond your control."

And just when I was starting to wonder if maybe I should tell someone about all this, because it was all getting pretty strange, my body changed on me again. Sometime between the seventh and eighth grades, it emerged from its sweatshirt cocoon looking like a Vargas pinup.

The boys at school were always making lists, rating the "foxes" in our grade, and I was never on these lists, except when the boys were separating the girls into body parts and I landed in the category of "best tits." But now—oh, wow. "Look at me now," I marveled, surveying my naked body in the mirror. I went and snuck a pair of my mother's high heels and put them on and looked at myself naked again, thinking, "Hey, I look just like a stripper!" And what was I going to do with this amazing bod? I knew that what I was supposed to do was to show it off so others could ogle and desire it and rate it favorably. I knew I had to show it to the world.

Suddenly, I wanted to buy lots of things: tube tops and tank tops and Candie's high-heeled sandals and Love's Baby Soft lip gloss—"Because innocence is sexier than you think," said the ads, which had pucker-mouthed models who looked younger than I was. I wanted to buy things to help me look sexy, because now I was in possession of the holy grail: a teenage girl's beautiful body. I wanted to cause a sensation like Brooke Shields in the Calvin Klein ads. "You wanna know what comes between me and my Calvins? Nothing," said Brooke, who was fourteen, like me.

I wanted to be sexy like the whispery-voiced women on *Charlie's Angels* (my brothers had the famous Farrah poster up in their room, like every other boy), even though I hated how they acted dumb, like Suzanne Somers on *Three's Company*. I still wanted short-shorts like hers. I wanted to look sexy like Olivia Newton-John as Sandy when she comes out in her leather pants at the end of *Grease*, after she stops acting like an uptight little virgin people made fun of ("Look at me, I'm Sandra Dee"). I took pictures of myself naked in my room with a camera on a tripod, lolling around on my bed. It's amazing to think of how these photos came back from the lab without a hitch—it was a different time, as they say. If there had been an Internet back then, my boobs would have been all over it. I would have been doing all kinds of dances on TikTok.

Looking back, I can see that none of this actually had anything to do with sex—it was sexualization, a most powerful form of social conditioning which grooms girls to turn themselves into sex objects, and can make them anxious and depressed, among other things, studies say. For here I was, a proud little feminist, now furiously pedaling my bike to Walgreens to buy more lip gloss instead of to Waldenbooks to buy more books. I wanted to look sexy—but I knew I wasn't ready to have *sex*. I wanted men to want me, but I didn't want to have to do anything about it, and I was horrified whenever they expected me to.

"How about you come back to my hotel room with me?" a man of about forty whispered at me one day in a store, breathing down my neck.

"I'm fourteen!" I protested.

"That's okay," he said, leering.

I ran away.

The waiters at the Spiral—hippie boys of twenty-two, twenty-three, all of whom looked like extras from the set of *Almost Famous*—were always smirking now when they talked to me, touching my hips, my waist. When I was working as a bus girl, clearing tables, it wasn't unusual for some male customer to covertly grab my ass. My first kiss, if you can call it that, was from a thirty-year-old dishwasher who stuck his tongue in my mouth, slimy and sweaty as hell. "Ewww!" I exclaimed, turning on my heel. From then on, I zoomed in and out of the dish room so fast, banging down the bus trays so hard, that not a few plates were smashed.

There was a waiter named Pisces who was always figuring out ways to be the one to drive me home, car rides during which he would put his hand on my knee and hold forth about his devotion to the Indian guru Meher Baba. "We had to tell him to cut it out," my mother said, years later. "We thought it was so weird he wanted to drive you everywhere."

But then why didn't you talk to me about it? I wanted to ask her, though I didn't say anything. It was one thing to talk about what had been done to us, something else entirely to ask why we hadn't protected each other.

● ● ●

Living with misogyny requires a lot of compartmentalization. How else to accept the fact that a man has hurt you and treated you with disrespect, and yet you want to run back to him and take him inside you again and again?

I asked myself these things as I walked along that night after leaving Constance, wondering what my choice about Abel was going to be. Because once you get into choice—the things you choose, rather than what just happens to you—you get into an area where you might see a lot of contradictions in yourself, contradictions in what you want versus what you do, and in what you think is right versus what you want.

These puzzles went back, for me, to the beginnings of my choosing men at all. I remember, in ninth grade, wondering how to square the fact that men were harassing me on a fairly constant basis with the prevailing notion that, in order to achieve happiness and social success as a girl, I had to have a boyfriend.

But I did want a boyfriend, and I wanted a boyfriend for reasons other than just the promise of status. I wanted to be kissed and touched. I wanted to know about sex. I had already figured out that that little button down there between my legs felt very good when touched, and I was starting to wonder if there was a way to get a boy to touch it (not always so easy to arrange even now, as many women can attest). I knew that it was called a clitoris from my library reading of *The Joy of Sex*, although I had never heard a single person say this word out loud—and rarely do even now.

But I didn't want to be touched by just anyone. I wanted to be touched by someone who loved me. I wanted to be loved—adored. I wanted a boy to love me in the enthralled, devoted way Gomez Addams loves Morticia. "*Cara mia!*" he would exclaim. "You set my blood aflame!"

I wanted a boy to talk to me the way Jimmy Stewart talks to Katharine Hepburn in *The Philadelphia Story*. I had seen this film on Miami's Channel 6, which ran a double feature of classic movies every afternoon, and which I would often watch, alone in my room, while applying face masks and doing leg lifts and homework. When that scene came on where Jimmy Stewart and Katharine Hepburn are drunk and arguing after a party, tingles of excitement went up my sides all the way to my neck. When Stewart says, "There's a magnificence that comes out of your eyes and your voice and the way you stand there and the way you walk—you're lit from within!" and then grabs and kisses Hepburn... Well! I thought, I would do almost anything to get a boy to talk to me like that!

I might even let him do things to me if he would say such things—and mean them, of course. But how did you get a boy to say these things? And would he say them if you let him touch you? Or would that just make you kind of a slut? I already knew that this was a sexist word, applied freely to girls who let boys do things to them, but I wasn't sure how to find my way out of this particular catch-22, being fourteen and wanting to know what it was like to do things with boys. On my own terms.

●  ●  ●

In the ninth grade, I picked a boy named Sean to be my boyfriend. I think I chose him well. He was a nice boy, one of the nicest I've ever dated to this day. Back then, he was low-hanging fruit, a nerd boy in the group of smart nerds who wore *Star Wars* T-shirts and quoted lines from Steve Martin's comedy albums ("Let's get small!"). Despite my newly hot bod, I was still considered a geek, a freak, and therefore undatable by less nerdy candidates.

But Sean was cute, despite his hair, a huge blond afro which resembled a clown wig. He didn't seem to know that he was cute, nor did any of the other girls in our grade. But I saw it. And I liked it. And so I decided I was going to make him fall hopelessly in love with me, though I didn't really know him well. We had only one class together, chemistry, where he always sat in the back with the other nerd boys, drawing ballpoint pen pictures of the *Millennium Falcon*.

"How do you get a boy to like you?" I asked my mother, a subject I instinctively knew she would warm to.

"Make him cookies," she said, adding that her own mother had told her that "the way to a man's heart is through his stomach."

Unable to, or refusing to, do anything in a normal way, I made Sean one single, king-sized peanut butter cookie about the size of a medium pizza. Within an hour of me delivering it to him at the end of his wrestling practice, we were frantically making out under the bleachers on the PE field, our lips all crumbly with said cookie.

After that, we started making out everywhere and at every possible opportunity. We made out after school in my bedroom when my mother and stepfather were at work, and at night after we'd been talking on the phone till 1 or 2 a.m. We'd get so horny we couldn't stand it anymore, and he would ride his bike through the streets and sneak up to my bedroom and we would make out some more. Once, we almost got caught when my little brothers woke up (my mother had had twins at forty-two, a couple of cute, rough-and-tumble little guys), and so Sean and I started making out on the kitchen floor by the back door, so that he could get out quickly if needed.

But we weren't just making out—we were doing "everything but," as we used to say. I sat on his face this way and that. He fingered my clit. I sucked his dick. I found that I loved dicks—or at least, I loved his, which seemed to bode well for my future experience of penises. I discovered there was this whole narrative with dicks, where they would get hard and grow and explode and collapse in ecstasy. A dick told a story all its own, and I loved being in command of that narrative.

I loved all the feelings I was feeling in this wonderful new escape into someone's arms—the thrill of a mouth, a tongue—all the transportive sensations where you didn't have to think about anything except this body you were experiencing. I loved the way Sean seemed so concerned about me and whether whatever he was doing was making me feel good. "Does this feel good?...Does this?" he would ask. There was a feeling in the zeitgeist at the time that it was a point of pride for a man to show some consideration for a woman in bed (as seen in the great ballads of Barry White), and I feel such affection for him, thinking back on how he was trying to do that.

And then one night, we were lying there in the dark and he looked at me, splayed naked across the kitchen floor. "This body," he said, running his fingers along my side.

"Do you love me?" I asked.

I don't really know what made me ask him this; it just seemed like it was time for him to tell me. It was what always happened in movies and books, that a man and a woman would kiss and somebody would say, "I love you." I had been waiting for him to say it.

"Do I love you?" he said, sitting up. "I don't know if I *love* you, exactly. I *like* you," he said. I liked him too. We'd been spending a lot of time together, hanging out, walking home from school, talking about movies and music. I'd introduced him to Elvis Costello, whom I'd learned about from my cool big brother Danny. We made out to *My Aim Is True*.

"I'm not sure I know what love is," he said, looking worried. "Do you love me?"

When he put it like that, it made me wonder if I did. What was love, after all, and did I love him? It made me think of all the reasons I actually might *not* love him. I didn't like the way his breath smelled sometimes; I didn't like it that he didn't have fuller lips. I didn't like the way I had to pretend he was giving me an orgasm; I hadn't actually had one yet. I hadn't wanted to correct him in whatever he was doing, as I was afraid it would spoil things, undermine his confidence, make him think I wasn't sexy. And I knew from seeing women in movies have sex, that women were supposed to have orgasms immediately and constantly, and everybody thought that was very sexy.

"I don't know," I said.

I realized that maybe I'd made a mistake in thinking you could just pick someone out of the blue and make him fall in love with you; maybe that wasn't the way it worked. But then, how did it work? I wondered.

"Well, do you think we're going to have sex?" I asked him.

He lay back against my shoulder and said with a smile, "Oh, I think we will…"

There was no reason for him to doubt it. Things were certainly moving that way. We hadn't yet entered the Moral Majority era and its condemnation of teenage sex. But there was something about the way he said it—like it was a foregone conclusion, like he *knew* I would do it—that maybe tapped into all of the semi-threatening messages I'd ever received about being a "nice girl." Or maybe I just bristled at his sudden air of entitlement, I don't know, but the next day, I broke up with him. Standing by our lockers in school, I told him, "This just isn't working for me," repeating a line I'd heard some actress say in a movie.

Years later, in the wake of his divorce, he called me from a hotel room in Tallahassee where he was lying in bed with a pack of ice on his dick, recovering from a reverse vasectomy (he'd started dating a younger woman who wanted to have kids), and he told me angrily that my breaking up with him so abruptly and without any good explanation had been the worst thing that had ever happened to him. He made me feel so bad about it that I told him to come to New York and have sex with me, as if I owed him this. (Although, to paraphrase a popular slogan about men and women, I didn't owe him shit. Anyway he never did come.) I didn't tell him what I was really thinking: "Well, if that's the worst thing that ever happened to you, then you're doing okay…" I didn't tell him about what happened to me just a few weeks after our breakup.

● ● ●

It happened at the University of Miami, just a few blocks from where I lived. I was with my friend Janice, who was a year older than I and had already slept with the police officer she would eventually run away with. She was sexy and she taught me to be sexy—how to swing my hips when I walked and tie my shirts up above my belly button and nonchalantly lean over to reveal my cleavage. She said, "It drives men crazy."

"Let's go to the University of Miami and meet some guys," she said one day after school.

We sat in the grassy quad pretending to be students, and then we were in some boys' dorm room drinking beer and watching *Match Game* with Gene Rayburn. And then all of a sudden, Janice and her guy weren't there anymore, and I was lying on a bed making out with this college freshman.

I could hardly believe it, because he had a real mustache like Mark Spitz on the Wheaties box and his body felt so incredible, so much bigger and stronger and more muscular than Sean's. It was a real man's body, I thought; I put my hands all over it.

"You're so wet," I remember him saying, inserting his fingers in my vagina. He wriggled out of his shorts.

"No, no, I don't think I'm ready for this," I told him. "*Stop*." But it was too late; he was already inside me. I turned my face to the wall. It hurt so bad at first, but then I went somewhere else in my mind, thinking of my cat Puff and how he was so grumpy all the time and didn't like anyone but me to touch him...

I rode my bike home, trying not to sit on the seat because it stung. It was late. I stopped a block away and unhooked my bike chain. "Where have you been?" my mother screamed at me from the front porch. She was furious about me worrying her and missing dinner. I told her that the chain on my bike had broken and that I'd had to walk it home from somewhere far away. I never told her what really happened. It wasn't until years later, when I was reading accounts of women describing their sexual assaults, that I realized I had been raped.

● ● ●

I started using dating apps in 2014 to get over a guy named Axel Wang. I was despondent, heartbroken, and a young friend said to me, "Why don't you just go fuck somebody on Tinder?"

But before I can explain what made me fall for a guy like Axel, I have to back up a couple of years, to 2012. That was thirty years after I had been a teenager, thirty years in which I had gone to college and graduate school and worked for a while as an English teacher in Japan, and then moved to New York City and gotten married and divorced from a college classmate and become a reporter and a writer and had my daughter and settled in to life in the East Village, a single mom to my middle schooler and companion to an aging German shepherd named Boo.

We were happy. I was happy, being Zazie's mom, enjoying attending to every little thing she needed done: making her breakfast in the mornings and having talks with her about feminism, which I slipped into our conversations like I dripped vitamin drops into her juice. We watched *I Love Lucy* on the Hallmark Channel in the mornings as I brushed her hair, talking about how Lucy was subversive—and also not—and pondered why the ads for cleaning products always showed women fighting over who had a cleaner tub. It became kind of funny; we would giggle. What an absurd way to portray us women! We talked about which was a better book, *Jane Eyre* or *Wuthering Heights*, and how we wished David Bowie was our friend, or Michelle Obama.

We had so many conversations, I and my little girl, who loved to talk-talk-talk and draw and paint pictures and dance as old, white-whiskered Boo looked on with cloudy eyes. Things were good. Except for whenever a man came around, or I let one come, interestingly enough.

In 2012, my life changed with the death of Amanda Todd. She was the fifteen-year-old Canadian girl who was driven to suicide by a new kind of torture. Cyberbullying doesn't seem a strong enough word. If it had been the Middle Ages—and this might be a new Dark Age, however lit up it is with our LED screens—Amanda Todd would have been made a saint, the patron saint of girls on social media.

She was cyberbullied, cyberstalked, sextorted, beaten up, and left lying in a ditch by a mob of kids at her school. Her family kept moving, trying to escape her ruined reputation after an older man she met online screenshotted a picture of her breasts and circulated it around the Internet. She hanged herself after posting a haunting video of her turning over cards with her suicide note. "I have nobody. I need someone," she said.

I wanted to be that someone. Lying in bed, unable to sleep at night, I would think of her, and the girl I used to be.

When I asked my boss, Graydon, if I could do a story on girls and social media, he suggested that I look at not just one of these tragic cases that were coming up more often in the news—Steubenville, Audrie Pott, Rehtaeh Parsons, and many more—but spread my net wider to see if these were signs of a more pervasive cultural problem. No one was really talking about how social media was affecting the lives of girls. Few were talking about the pressure to get likes, or the related rise of sexualization online, where girls were rewarded for looking hot. There was still this idea, relentlessly pushed by the marketing teams of Silicon Valley—as well as certain academics, some of whom were discreetly funded by tech—that social media was always harmless and fun and socially progressive, and any criticism of it in regard to how kids used it amounted to a moral panic.

But when I talked to girls, I heard a different story.

"Social media is destroying our lives," said a sixteen-year-old girl in LA.

"So why don't you go off it?" I asked.

"Because then we would have no life," she said.

What was most troubling to me about these conversations I had started having with girls was what I was hearing about how social media was changing the power dynamic in dating, intensifying old sexist attitudes as well as generating new kinds of misogynistic behavior. Boys were casually asking girls for nudes, which they saw no problem with sharing nonconsensually. Boys were communicating with girls online in ways that amounted to sexual harassment, although nobody was calling it that yet. Boys were availing themselves of their exponentially increased access to girls through social media platforms, which seemed to be heightening their sense of power, as well as whetting their appetite for acting like players.

"It leads to major manwhoring," as one girl said.

I was sitting with a sixteen-year-old girl on a bench at the Grove, the mall in LA, in early 2013, when she took out her phone and showed me a new dating app called Tinder. She said that she'd been using it to try and find a random dude to lose her virginity to after she'd had her heart broken by another guy who'd said that he loved her, but then she found out he was "talking to" several other girls on social media simultaneously.

"I mean, I should have known," she said. "All men are basically whores."

She said she'd met up with a guy from Tinder at a mall, and he'd wanted her to get in his car, but she refused, so they wound up going to a Pottery Barn and making out on a couch. She said she found the whole experience depressing.

Tinder had only been out a few months, but kids were already on it— and, as I write this, still are. Though the app banned thirteen-to-seventeen-year-olds in 2016, kids still make fake profiles to join. There are no age checks on dating apps, despite many documented cases of sexual assaults and rapes of minors, some as young as eleven and twelve years old. Big Dating has remained silent in the face of evidence that children are being harmed through the use of their products. Which should really tell you all you need to know about Big Dating.

In 2020, the Subcommittee on Economic and Consumer Policy of the US House Committee on Oversight and Reform launched an investigation into the lack of age screening on dating apps owned by Match Group, Meet Group, New Grindr, and Bumble Trading, citing "dangerous and inappropriate situations" involving minors. Finally, the government is taking note of the dangers; hopefully it won't give up until dating apps are held accountable.

Remembering my own curiosity about sex and the sexualizing influences that had so affected me when I was a girl, I could understand very well why underage kids were going on these apps. To me, watching that girl swiping at the Grove that day, Tinder had the look of a thing that was going to change everything. I never dreamed what it would mean for my own life.

• • •

When my story on girls and social media, "Friends Without Benefits," came out in *Vanity Fair* in the fall of 2013, it went viral. Millions of people were reading it all over the world. I started to get emails from people in places as far-flung as Sweden and Indonesia saying things like, "It's just like that here": parents telling me about terrible things that had happened to their daughters online, girls talking about their experiences with cyberbullying and harassment. It felt like this was a subject I should keep reporting and writing about, so I sent a proposal out to some publishers and got the chance to do the book that would become *American Girls*.

And then one night in early 2014, after I had started reporting that book, I was walking home from the subway past a bar in my neighborhood called Manitoba's, and I glanced in the window and saw some guys I had a feeling I should talk to.

Manitoba's is an old punk bar on Avenue B, dark and grungy with a wall of booths which are optimal for making out in or—so I would soon learn—small enough to enforce a closeness, and with perfect lighting. Manitoba's was about to become my go-to bar for Tinder dates, because it was just around the corner from my house, making it easy to break away and get home quickly, if necessary, and no one knew me there.

But I wasn't on any dating apps yet. I was just passing by when I saw these boisterous young guys through the window. They had the sloppy smiles of men you could get to talk. So I went in and sat down next to them and asked if they had ever heard of Tinder.

"I swipe right on every girl," one of them said rowdily.

"All guys do," another said. "We swipe right on every girl. It's just a numbers game. The more you swipe right, the higher the chances you'll bang."

"Tinder's like the most efficient pussy-delivery system ever invented," said another.

The others laughed. "Good one!"

There were three of them. They were soldiers, part of an Army reserve unit near Albany, come into the city for a night of fun. They were all in their early twenties, with buzz cuts and loud-colored polo shirts, drinking Yuengling. In the coming months and years, as I continued to report on technology and dating, I would hear a lot of guys talk in this callous way about meeting women online, but hearing it for the first time, I felt kind of rattled. They sounded so delighted, so giddy with this new technology that was making it so much easier for them to "smash."

"What's it like?" I asked. "Do you go on dates?"

"Noooo," they said, laughing.

"Why not?"

"You don't have to," one of them said. "To be perfectly honest, you don't have to."

"Why spend the money?" another asked.

"Blow jobs for free? Hey, I'll take it!" said another.

As I tried to maintain the frozen smile on my face, I noticed a fourth member of their group, who was standing off to one side, not saying much. He looked a few years older than the others, in his leather bomber jacket.

"I don't really know these yahoos," he whispered hotly in my ear. "I'm their sergeant, but it's just the reserves."

His name was Axel, he said, steering me over to a booth to have a more private conversation. He was short and compactly built, with small dark eyes and big white teeth. He reminded me of Sluggo in the *Nancy* comic strip, with his stubbly head.

"Not all guys are like that," he reassured me unconvincingly, with his raspy gangster's voice. "They're just young and dumb and full of cum, know what I mean? When you get older you want to settle down. Like me. I have a wife. Or I did…"

He told me his wife had left him for another guy while he was away in Iraq; but I would find out later that his wife had actually left him for a guy she met while they were swingers in a polyamorous community. Axel told me a lot of lies that night, and most other nights. He never went to Iraq; he had a desk job stateside during the war. His name wasn't even Axel Wang—it was Anthony Romano. He was an Italian kid from Staten Island. He just liked the name Axel Wang—he thought it sounded cool—and so he had changed it, weirdly enough. For a long time, I assumed he was part Chinese, until he confessed that, no, he wasn't, "but a lot of people think that—it doesn't hurt with diversity hiring." I was astonished.

He told me he was thirty-two; he was twenty-eight. He told me he wanted to be a journalist and was doing a graduate degree in journalism at a good college—this much was true, and may have accounted for why he glommed on to me that evening: his roving ambition. He saw me as a connection. He told me he was a cameraman for a major TV network—actually he was a production assistant—and that his deepest desire was to make a documentary film about sex trafficking.

"How are you going to do that?" I asked him, interested.

He told me about his plans with such earnestness that I believed him. Or did I believe him because I wanted to, because I found him strangely hot? What in the world ever made me get involved with Axel Wang? I've wondered many times. It's true, he had a bad boy sexiness. But why do women fall for bad boys in general? It's a peculiar phenomenon. Psychologists say that our attraction to such men, with their grandiose sense of entitlement, sociopathic tendencies, and propensity for violence, is determined by natural selection— a desire to partner up with a man who could, say, kill saber-toothed tigers— but I don't buy it. I think it must be that living with misogyny trains women to become attracted to misogyny itself, scarily enough. Because what's a bad boy if not a misogynist?

And then there was the fact that Axel was in the Army—a man from the military, no less, the driver's seat of patriarchy—which irrationally made me trust him even more. Soldiers were good guys, I remember thinking, soldiers were guys who could handle stuff. And so this Axel was going to make a documentary film...I had to admit, I was a bit jealous.

"Where do you get the camera equipment?" I asked him.

We went outside to keep talking while he smoked a cigarette. If I'd had a movie camera back then, I would have panned to the other soldiers at the bar and recorded what I imagine were their knowing grins as they watched their very sexually active sarge exit with the curious MILF. I suspect, at least, that was the category they put me in, as a way to account for any interest they might have had in a woman in her forties. (I was forty-nine at the time, and still holding up pretty well.)

I think of my sexual history as divided into BZ and AZ—"Z" for my daughter, Zazie. I had strict rules about not bringing someone home with me; I didn't want her to have to experience the discomfort of knowing a strange man was in the house with her mom. So, AZ, you could count the number of guys on one hand, but BZ—now there was a time. I sometimes missed those days, when romantic adventures could commence when you least expected it.

It felt like BZ all over again, when I found myself sitting in Axel's car, making out with him not twenty minutes after we had left the bar. He was parked right in front of my building, so I agreed to get in his beat-up Toyota Corolla with him, because I wanted to hear more about how one goes about making a documentary. And suddenly he was all over me, climbing on top of me like an overexcited bulldog. But he was so funny and weird—moaning my name in his Staten Island accent—that it made me want to laugh rather than scream. I pushed him back onto his own seat when he tried to get his hands down my pants. He wanted to have sex right there in the front seat.

"I live on this block!" I told him, shoving him away. "I have to go upstairs and let the babysitter go home!"

"I'll wait for her to leave," he insisted. "I'll stay here until you let me in."

There were red flags flying with this guy like a parade for the anniversary of the Chinese Communist Party, but did I pay attention? I'm reminded of that line of Karen Hill's in *Goodfellas* after Henry asks her to hide his gun: "I gotta admit the truth. It turned me on."

But there was also something else going on, something that had nothing to do with sex; it was ambition, all right, but not Axel's this time—it was mine. After I went upstairs and got into bed, I started thinking about that guy out there in his car and his outsized confidence in his plans to make a film. And I wondered: Why can't I be like that? Why can't I do that? Why do men always seem to think they can do whatever they want? And why did I so often doubt myself, thinking that the things I wanted to do were impossible, or that no one would let me do them?

Then I sat up in bed and I realized that, hey, *I* wanted to make a documentary film. And not because Axel Wang had said he wanted to, but because I had wanted to ever since I had interviewed that girl at the Grove in LA. I remembered then how, as I'd sat there listening to her talk, I'd seen flashes of her telling her story on-screen. Because I knew that what she was talking about—the ways that technology was weaponizing misogyny and undermining the possibility of relationships and love—was so unprecedented, and so dark, that people needed to hear about it, and not just in a book, but in a film. And then it just seemed so *right* to me that I'd met Axel Wang that evening, because I was going to make a documentary about girls and social media, and he was going to be the cameraman and help me do it.

"Call me tomorrow," I texted him.

• • •

We came to each other gently, at first, Abel and I, the first time we made love. I say "made love" as I would never have described my encounters with any other guys I met on dating apps. It was the night we met.

It felt like such a relief, to be with someone, finally, who was sweet and sensuous, I almost started to cry. Thankfully, though, I kept my feelings at bay, because there was already so much going on with us, with me being older, I was afraid I might scare him, if I hadn't already.

I could see that he was trying to impress me with his confident strokes, his ability to last. I got a sense of just how young he was, and how much he wanted to show me he was a man who could please a woman. Prince playing on my playlist, his face euphoric in the candlelight.

We fell into a groove and got lost in each other.

"How does it feel?" I whispered to him.

"Feels warm," he said.

Early the next morning, I woke up and found him wrapped around me. I hadn't felt a man hugging me from behind in bed like that in so long. I had taken to stuffing a pillow behind me to create the feeling of someone next to me in the night. They had products for this now, "body pillows" for this lonely time in which we lived, in which almost half the adult population is single, and more than half of single people are women.

Often it's our choice, to be single—a complicated choice, one that I myself had made over and over again, chucking men right and left when they angered or displeased me, or when I realized that I had no other choice but to get away, because they were hurting me or bringing me down.

And yet, it felt so good, now, to be cuddling with someone. All mammals seem to like to cuddle, to nuzzle and spoon, even some reptiles do. Cuddling releases oxytocin, the so-called love hormone, which our brain spews ecstatically when we're touching, making us feel bonded. Studies have shown that touch is vital to our mental and physical well-being at all ages. (Though some people prefer not to touch, of course, often as the result of traumatic experiences.)

As soon as shelter-in-place orders went into effect due to the pandemic, I noticed how people were talking about their sorrow over the loss of touch. Mental health professionals started publishing articles about how this could be as hard on people as anything else about the crisis. Almost instantly, Facebook rolled out a new hugging emoji—a face hugging a heart. As if this could replace our need to give and receive affection through physical contact.

It made me think about how unfortunate it is that hookup culture has put so much emphasis on the stark act of sex while downplaying the need to cuddle and hug. Cuddling is usually avoided in hookups, confusing as it can become to bond with someone you might not ever see again, someone you don't want to lead on—or, at least, that's what you sometimes tell yourself, as you hold back to keep from getting hurt. But how deprived we feel without this, I remember thinking, feeling Abel wrapped around me, like a lion with its mate. I snuggled back into him.

And then, suddenly, we were fucking again—well, good morning, sir!

He held me tight, pulling my hips to him as he thrust into me and I pushed back, my hand balancing against the wall. His fingers were on my clit, moving around and around just the way I like. What man had ever done that without having to be shown? The sex was faster and harder than the night before. We didn't say anything after it was over. He fell back asleep almost immediately, snoring a little on my shoulder.

I extricated myself from his embrace and got up to go to the bathroom.

When I saw myself in the mirror, I laughed out loud. I looked horrible. I looked happy, with my blotchy skin and messy hair, as if I'd just emerged from an explosion. I sat down and peed, chuckling to myself about what I had been up to, to acquire this look of a woman who had been properly fucked, for a change.

And then it hit me: We hadn't used condoms.

I'd just fucked a stranger all night and hadn't used a condom?!

I thought of my friend, the late Donald Suggs, the journalist and gay-rights activist, my daughter's spiritual father. I imagined him shaking his head at me from on high (he'd passed away from a heart condition in 2012), asking, in his kindly baritone, "Why don't you want to protect yourself, sweetie?"

"How could you *do* this again?" I asked myself.

It wasn't the first time I'd messed up. Ever since I'd discovered dating apps, I'd been sliding. In dating app dating, condoms didn't seem to be a thing— which had unnerved me, at first, as someone who went to college during the AIDS epidemic, when condoms became a given; but then, I guess, I just got used to it, like most everybody else in hookup culture. I'd sworn to myself ever since my last round of negative tests, however, that I would never, never, never not use condoms again. But then here came this beautiful stranger on a night when I was feeling so lonely and as if this was my last chance to ever have sex again. And it just happened...

"Oh, but now you sound like a teenager," I scoffed, flushing the toilet, washing my hands. I didn't sound like someone who should know better—not like someone who'd been interviewing hundreds of young people about sex and dating over the past couple of years and arguing with them about the continued need for prophylactics. Arguing against their protestations that "this isn't the eighties" and "it doesn't matter, everybody's on PrEP"—the HIV-prevention drug, which, no, everybody was *not* on, and even if they were, it still didn't prevent a lot of other troublesome STIs.

"Condom fatigue," as it's known to safe-sex educators, is so significant a phenomenon that it has had an impact on the condom industry. In 2015, Trojan did a study to look into the reasons behind decreased condom use and found that nearly 40 percent of people who didn't use a condom during their last sexual encounter hadn't discussed safe sex first. Such lack of communication is one of the hallmarks of hookup culture, in which you're not likely to know the person you're having sex with all that well, something the introduction of dating apps only seems to have aggravated.

Abel and I hadn't said a thing about safe sex. We just fell into bed.

In 2019, the CDC reported that cases of syphilis, gonorrhea, and chlamydia had reached an all-time high the previous year, and public health officials have said they believe that dating apps are one of the reasons. The impact of dating apps on public health has been identified as so serious a problem that health officials have sought the cooperation of dating app companies to track and prevent outbreaks. Some of these companies have resisted, not wanting to be involved in STI prevention because of the stigma associated with admitting that their products could be contributing to the rise of infections. In 2015, Tinder responded with a cease-and-desist order when the AIDS Healthcare Foundation put up billboards and bus ads across LA warning that online encounters on dating apps like Tinder and Grindr could lead to unsafe sex. Under pressure, the following year, Tinder agreed to add a health and safety section to its app, as did other major sites such as OkCupid and Grindr.

"But who reads that?" asked a young man I spoke to. "And who really cares?"

As the Covid-19 pandemic began to spread, I wondered if dating apps were factoring into this new public health crisis. Not many people were asking this question in public, with the exception of an opinion piece I saw in the *New York Times* in March of 2020: "Can we really afford to rely on horny people forced to stay at home all day to 'make the best-informed decisions' about everyone else's health?" the playwright Philip Dawkins wrote. "History—and my Grindr inbox—tells us no," he said, reporting how men on the gay dating apps Grindr and Scruff were still hooking up, despite the danger of becoming infected with the coronavirus. "In my inbox—an invitation to a group-sex party," said Dawkins, going on to urge dating app users to be responsible, despite his own observation that not everyone could be relied on to do so. Later, news stories reported that the virus had been found not only in saliva, but in semen.

"My friend broke quarantine to have sex and got Covid," said a woman I follow on Twitter in a viral tweet of May of 2020.

"Thank goodness it wasn't something treatable, like syphilis," one commenter noted sarcastically. But other commenters were jocularly sympathetic with the Covid catcher. One man tweeted: "Worth it." A woman responded: "What about all the people that slutted it up and didn't get Covid. We rarely hear their heroic tales."

"A side chick is testing my willpower daily," commented a man. "Can't do it, but she's not making it easy. Apparently doesn't give [a fuck] about a pandemic, constantly sending nudes and telling me to stop being scared. And we're in NY."

"Oh your side chick huh? Hope your [girlfriend] finds out," replied a woman.

●  ●  ●

Standing in my kitchen that morning, after spending the night with Abel for the first time, I was starting to get really anxious.

Who was this guy I'd just fucked all night without a condom? I asked.

I got so anxious, I went looking through his backpack, which was sitting on my kitchen floor, where he'd left it. Yes, I was anxious about *my* mistake, and yet here I was, sitting on the floor, snooping through his things, as if something I would find in them would tell me whether I had contracted a sexually transmitted disease from him.

Or maybe it was just that I was a shameless snoop, and dying to know all his secrets because I already liked him so much and still knew so little about him.

After our instantaneous make-out session just after his arrival, we had gone up to my roof to drink some beers. As we looked out at the city, the knockout New York skyline glittering in the distance, he told me a little about himself. But not much. He was very good at avoiding my reporter's questions, turning them into self-effacing jokes.

"Where do you live?" I asked.

"In between the shadows," he said with a wink.

I did learn that he worked on the construction crew of a high-end fashion company, building stages and sets. I knew the brand by reputation; it was kind of a fancy place to work.

"What's it like being around all those models?" I asked.

"They're perdy," he said, "but they're too skinny." He put a hand on my bubble butt.

I blushed.

"Why'd you move to New York?" I asked.

It was in the flicker of hesitation I saw on his face, as if he was deciding whether he should tell me that story—perhaps wondering if telling me now, before we had sex, might change what I would think of him and then the sex would never happen—that I saw that other thing that was drawing us together: the insecurity he was carrying around about who he was, as deep as the insecurity that had led me to lie to him already, telling him, "You know, I've never done this before, met up with someone on a dating app..."

I wasn't telling him the whole truth about myself either, and yet I wanted to know everything about him: Did he want to be a musician like his father, the Argentinian guitar player? Did he go to college? Did he see other women? Did he have a girlfriend? How often did he use Tinder? And was he going to break my heart if I kept liking him as much as I did after talking to him for just ten minutes?

"I tell that story, we'd be here all night," was all he offered.

Now it was the next morning, and I was on the floor of my kitchen rummaging through his backpack. It was a big backpack—the kind students carry when they trek across Europe—and it held an inordinate amount of things: long underwear, socks, pants, T-shirts, briefs, a sweater and a wooly hat, a receipt for a slice of pizza, a toothbrush and toothpaste, roll-on deodorant, ACE bandages, half a carton of Marlboros, a little plastic container of a weed and a one-hitter pipe, several crumpled $1 bills, a frayed phone charger, a harmonica, a ukulele... So much stuff to be carrying around on your way to a Tinder date, I thought, looking through it, putting his clothes to my face and breathing in the spicy, young man smell of him.

And suddenly it dawned on me, as I sifted through it all: This is the sum of his possessions. This is his world he's carrying around. I remembered him talking about how he liked that his workplace had a couch in the basement and beer in the fridge, and I realized: Because that's his house. I could see that he'd been telling me without telling me that he slept there sometimes when he had nowhere else to go.

And was he doing that now? I wondered. Using this hookup with me as a place to crash?

I had heard about this—there were even terms for this: "Tinder surfing," for when somebody couch surfs at the homes of the matches they've met on dating apps. I'd interviewed a French girl, Ellie, whom I'd met at Satsko's, who told me she'd come to New York on an internship and never bothered to find a place to live—she just stayed with hookups. And then there was the term "hobosexual," for someone who did this consistently, who found shelter going from hookup to hookup.

"Oh my God," I thought. "Is Abel a hobosexual?"

It struck me as so sad, at first—"He's homeless!"—that I wanted to go into the bedroom where he was still sleeping and cradle him in my arms. I started thinking about how even basic living requirements had become so impossible for young people, and how hard it was for them just to pay rent and survive. I tried to think of ways I could help him: "Well, he could live here with me while Zazie's still away at camp; after all, Bob Dylan used to crash on people's couches before he was famous, and so did Kurt Cobain…"

"Wait, what?! What are you saying?"

My mind reeled at seeing where it automatically wanted to go—to helping this random dude and not to protecting myself from being played by this, this *hobosexual*!

And *was* I being played? I wondered. To think that I might just be an easy mark for this young man who needed a place to perch. *Oh no.* Had I become that desperate older lady who will forgive a man anything as long as he would show up and fuck her?

My stomach lurched, thinking of that infamous letter Benjamin Franklin wrote to a young friend in 1745, entitled "Advice to a Young Man on the Choice of a Mistress." Broad-minded Ben recommended that "in all your Amours you should *prefer old Women to young ones*" (italics his). He was very complimentary about us older ladies' greater experience and knack for conversation. He even allowed that fucking us felt the same as younger women—especially if you put a basket over our heads. "So that covering all above with a Basket," he wrote, "and regarding only what is below the Girdle, it is impossible of the two Women to know an old from a young one." Always practical, Franklin further pointed out that older women can't get pregnant—but above all, he said, "They are *so grateful*!!"

Oh dear.

Was Abel just using me, I wondered in horror, and did he just give me a sexually transmitted disease?

I marched into the bedroom to confront him.

"Mornin'," he said, grinning at me, one eye open. And then, "What's wrong?"

"We didn't use condoms," I blurted out, not quite knowing what to say.

"I'm clean," he said, pulling me onto the bed and maneuvering me around to spooning position, nuzzling the back of my neck.

"I just think we should talk about it," I said. "Mmmm..."

I could have asked him for more details; I could have demanded to see his test results. I could have asked if he had a place to live. But the most striking part of this moment was that I didn't want to ask him anything, when he was wrapped around me like that. I didn't care.

The warmth of his embrace made me feel safe, and I started telling him about myself, about my book and my film and how important they were to me, and how everything was kind of screwed up right now (I'd been experiencing some professional snags and worries), and how nervous I was that they wouldn't work out.

"I just want them to be really good!" I said.

"Aw, you'll figure it out," he said, squeezing me from behind. "Look at all them books you read." He meant the books on the bookshelves lining my walls.

Then he started fucking me again. And I have to say, it made me feel a whole lot better.

● ● ●

I have a friend, a woman my age, who tries to be helpful by pointing out all the things that are wrong with me. I think many women have had a friend like that. Elise, who is married with three kids and lives in Connecticut, says that my problem is I date men who are "beneath" me.

"You know what I mean," she says, insisting she's not being snobbish.

Elise's husband is a rich guy who likes to remind everyone he has "fuck you money." She posts lots of pictures on Facebook of her daughter riding their horse, Richter. Elise's life looks so perfect on social media, I sometimes wonder why she needs to go to a therapist, which she has done for so long that she seems to think it qualifies her to psychoanalyze everyone around her.

"You date men who are beneath you because you don't really want a man," she tells me. "It gives you the perfect excuse to finally get rid of them—that, and your self-esteem issues."

"But doesn't almost every woman living under patriarchy have some self-esteem issues?" I've asked her. "And is it any wonder, when we're so often told we don't measure up?"

Too fat, too thin, too pretty, not pretty enough, too loud, too opinionated, too whatever—we hear this from the time we're little girls. And so I think our inevitable self-esteem issues must always be affecting our choices in regard to men, if it's men we want.

But I've never believed that anyone is beneath me, or that anybody's above anybody else. I do seem to have a type, though, and I've dated a fair number of hot messes—but sometimes they come to *me*. Which opens up a whole other interesting conundrum: Just how does that guy swaggering toward you from across the room know that he's going to fit your pattern like an Escher woodcut?

Take Buckley, the last guy I dated seriously before I met Axel. I thought Buckley was a successful lawyer; it turned out he was a penniless wreck. He reached out to me on Facebook by sending me a picture of a margarita. This type of thing had been happening to me with guys I knew from high school and college, as well as countless other hapless men, ever since I went on Facebook. My romantic life, like everyone else's, had been drastically changed by social media long before dating apps ever came along. Women friends my age who were single started telling me this was happening to them in the mid-to-late-2000s. "It's the 'Hello beautiful, thank you for your friendship' message that turns into 'What are you wearing?' in about five exchanges," said a friend in her forties.

We were experiencing the same type of things as the teenage girls I was interviewing, except the guys hitting up us older ladies were often married. You'd go and check their Facebook pages and there they were with their wives, on biking trips through Ireland or idyllic-looking wine tours through Spain. "Love this guy!" their wives would post, patting the balding pates of these very same guys who had just sent you a Facebook-generated GIF of exploding hearts—or, worse, a picture of a dick.

When I talked to Justin Garcia, the executive director of Kinsey, he pointed out that the Internet has made it possible for people from all walks of life who might never have known each other before to meet, and that this has been a positive development for LGBTQ+ people and other marginalized communities. It's a really important point, and one that should be included in any discussion of the pros and cons of online dating. But it's also true that the Internet has made it infinitely easier for people who are married or in relationships to meet people they would have never met before, in order to cheat.

It was suddenly no longer necessary for a man to, say, sneak out to a pay phone to call his sweetie; he could talk to her on his computer while sitting in bed next to his wife. What's more, he could tell himself—not to mention the women he was involved with—that it wasn't really cheating: "I never touched her!"

That's actually what happened to Buckley: his wife left him for a guy she met on Facebook, which now figures in more than 30 percent of divorces, according to an oft-cited study. Buckley was still very bitter about it all when he sent me that virtual margarita. He wasn't used to getting the fuzzy end of the lollipop. He was a preppy boy from an old New York family. When we knew each other at boarding school—where I went for my last two years of high school, after my mother and stepfather moved to New Hampshire to open a cheese shop, burned out on running the Spiral, and where some of the male teachers liked to remind us girls how much better things allegedly were at the school before we were allowed to matriculate—he looked like the villain in a John Hughes movie. After college, he went to Wall Street to seek his fortune in the go-go eighties. He was nowhere near my romantic ideal, but I thought he was rich, and after my regular paycheck stopped, I was close to bankrupt; I was looking for someone to save me from my economic distress. It went against my feminist principles to pin my financial security on a man, but I was behind on my mortgage. And so I convinced myself that Buckley was fascinating.

The relationship was...irritating. Buckley's children were the first teenagers I had ever been around who were glued to their phones. Like zombies, those kids were, with their phones. But Buckley didn't see the need to moderate their behavior. He was constantly on his phone himself, usually texting back and forth with his ex-wife.

It's a curious thing, how people don't seem to get all the way divorced anymore. "When your father and I got divorced," my mother said, "we never talked to each other again, and that was fine with me. Wasn't that the whole point of getting a divorce?" I think the change came about because of cell phones, which give divorced couples the ability to keep trying to work out their issues—or perhaps just needle each other—under the guise of responsibly co-parenting.

This seemingly noble mode of separation feels like sheer hell for the people who date these consciously uncoupled couples. It turns you into the narrator of Daphne du Maurier's *Rebecca*, seeing ghosts of your putative rival everywhere. Because now, she is everywhere.

I found myself checking up on Buckley's ex on Facebook in a semi-obsessive fashion, checking to see if she was prettier, happier, or married to a handsomer guy than the one I was dating—the one she'd dumped. "Once I found his ex-girlfriend's account, oh my God, I was always on there," said Dylan, a young woman in New York I interviewed for my documentary. "Like, oh my God, I can't believe he was with this bitch, she doesn't even know how to dress. She's not even that cute!"

But maybe dealing with this type of thing was just what you had to put up with in order to date anyone in middle age—or so I'd started to think, in my more anxious moments, probably after I'd read another story about how women in their fifties are less likely to ever date again than to have a piece of fuselage from an airplane fall on their heads.

Fifty was looming—fifty! It was the first number that had ever scared me. Fifty sounded old. And fifty with no steady income sounded terrifying.

But although Buckley was supposed to relieve my financial woes, I was actually spending money on him. It was a long-distance relationship, since Buckley had relocated to Arizona to be near his children after his wife had moved them out there to be with the guy from Facebook, so I was spending money on travel. No, Buckley didn't buy my tickets; he was devoutly frugal. He didn't seem to feel like he had to do much of anything to keep this relationship going—and why should he, when I was doing everything?

I was setting up the Skype calls and putting on shows for him like a free webcam girl. When I visited him, I even cleaned his house. "Poor Buckley," I thought, "I will cheer him up by scrubbing his tub." But no, Buckley's house was a mess because Buckley had never been taught that he had to clean up after himself.

He was home most days, listlessly playing the stock market while he waited for his father to join the stock exchange in the sky. Except that Buckley's father wasn't going anywhere any time soon; he ate Kellogg's Corn Flakes with whiskey poured on them every morning and piloted vintage cigarette boats around Lake Placid. He was ninety.

It was Sofia Coppola who saved me financially, when she came along in 2010, interested in making a movie out of an article I'd written about a group of teenage burglars in LA known as "the Bling Ring." If not for this unlikely turn of events, I would have had to sell my apartment, or do something else entirely. Since the bottom had fallen out of the journalism market, friends who used to be big deals in my field were now selling real estate or freelance editing. It was scary, suddenly not knowing how I was going to make a living.

But this *Bling Ring* money wasn't life changing, nor was the money I got for doing a little movie tie-in book. I sent a copy of it to Buckley, who told me, with his mid-Atlantic accent, that "this really wasn't the sort of thing [he] would read." Poor Buckley, he'd wanted to become a writer, too. He sent me love poems I knew were partially plagiarized, though I never said anything.

●　●　●

As I walked along the night I went to meet Abel after leaving Constance, watching all the people rushing home—most of them, I suspected, following the same paths they always traveled—it seemed to me that we were all swirling around in our patterns, patterns of where we walk and whom we love. We repeat what's familiar, whatever leads us back to a place we know, even when that place isn't a happy home. And for me, this meant that all paths led back to Oyster Road, where the women's work had made the men's lives possible.

It had been the same for me in my earliest adult relationships; I supported the careers of my partners over my own—not that I liked doing so, but I felt a pressure to. It was that way with my first husband. We went to college together. I was captivated by him from afar because he gave impromptu concerts in the dining halls, in which he banged away passionately on the piano while wearing a cape. He looked like a young John Cusack acting in a vampire movie. It all seemed so romantic to me, at twenty.

After college, we ran into each other in New York at a dinner party thrown by some mutual friends, which was one of the ways people used to meet and have sex and get married, back in the days before dating apps and smartphones: wine-fueled dinner parties at our cramped Brooklyn apartments. He turned my head with his talk of "living the life of an artist." After a quickie courtship, we got engaged. I confess it was mostly my doing. I was ecstatic, thinking I would be the wife of this brilliant young man who was already making good money with what he called his "art." He wrote soap opera music.

But then, just a few weeks before our wedding, he quit his job so he could write an opera based on a graphic novel—bewilderingly so, as he hadn't made any attempts to obtain the rights to this book or even contacted the author. I was too young to know that there are these Ralph Kramden sort of men in the world who decide to do things that make absolutely no sense, and a woman has to put her foot down or proceed at her own peril. I just thought he was brilliant and had no doubts he could pull this off.

Most days, he sat at home in our Williamsburg apartment—Williamsburg, Brooklyn, circa 1990, when it was still just nuclear waste glowing along the waterfront and Polish pickle stores, not fixed-up and fancy like it is now—hammering away on his keyboards, stopping for breaks to watch Blockbuster videos, while I worked at a dead-end job at the Brooklyn Public Library. It gradually became clear to me that I was going to be the one in the marriage with a day job, even though our dream as a couple had been to pursue a life in the arts together, like Percy Bysshe and Mary Shelley or John and Yoko. I wanted to write novels.

"Why must I work and you don't have to?" I finally got up the nerve to ask. I wasn't always the outspoken gal I would become—or actually I was, but I had learned to mask my true nature behind imitations of Hollywood actresses being soft-voiced and ladylike, so as not to intimidate my male counterparts.

"Because I am a genius and you are not," my husband said.

And I almost immediately started cheating on him.

It pained me to see an article in the *Harvard Business Review* in 2017 entitled "If You Can't Find a Spouse Who Supports Your Career, Stay Single," which reported that—nearly thirty years after I learned that inequality can follow a woman even into a marriage with the man of her dreams—women are still grappling with this "ambition-marriage trade-off."

Unfortunately, the subject still seems rather unmentionable. A young woman I follow on Twitter tweeted in 2019: "Finding a cishet male partner who doesn't want to knock you down a few pegs or compete with you is trickier than a lot of talented women artists unapologetically pursuing their paths are willing to discuss."

And yet I don't blame anyone but me for the failure of my first marriage. I had persuaded myself that getting married was my burning desire. But looking back, I realize that I was trying to please just about everybody *but* myself. I wanted to please my mother, who seemed to be enjoying presiding over my wedding planning like a matriarch played by Irene Dunne. As a woman who had been taught that social success means marrying off your daughter to a nice young man, she seemed very happy to assume this role. I wanted to make her happy, and also for her to see that somebody wanted me forever. As a girl who had been taught that social success means having a man want you, I wanted everybody to see this.

"Why didn't you tell me he quit his job?" my mother asked me, years later, when the subject of my first ex-husband came up.

"Because I was afraid, I guess. Afraid to admit I was making the wrong choice," I told her.

I think I got married, too, because I was starting to feel like a loser, and marriage seemed like something that would validate me as a grown-up woman. I was twenty-five, it had been four years since I'd graduated from college, and I felt like I had nothing to show for it, unlike some of my high school and college friends, who were already zooming ahead in their careers, some of them even publishing books. I'd been floundering around, trying to find my own path forward, writing terrible short stories that kept getting rejected by smaller and smaller literary magazines. Looking back, I can see that what I was looking for in my first husband was something he could never give me, and perhaps no man ever could. I wanted someone to help me become the self I wanted to be: a writer.

● ● ●

Abel stayed for a week, after that first night we met, a week in which we made love twenty-four times. Of course I counted, sitting at my kitchen counter dreamily making hash marks on an old envelope after he went off to work.

I guess the number made me feel sure he wanted me. Zazie was still at camp, and I hadn't had a chance to indulge in a days-long affair like this since she was born. I was used to taking my dating app dates up to my roof to have sex, or downstairs to our building's little gym. I would never go to a man's apartment, partially out of safety concerns but also because I didn't want to spend any more time than I had to on the whole disheartening process.

"This is definitely the best Tinder date I've ever been on," I told Abel, rolling back on the pillow, my heart racing from another orgasm.

He smiled and took my hand.

We made love in my bed, which is the size of a cot, the only size that will fit in my room. When we moved in, Zazie got the bigger bedroom because she had more toys and stuff. So Abel and I slept close together, always touching, our feet curled around each other's.

We made love on the couch, in the shower, on the floor. We made love in the middle of the night, waking up at the same time, full of desire. We made love joyfully, laughing sometimes at the intensity of our passion.

"You sure got a lot of books," he said, staring up at my bookshelves after we'd made love on the living room rug one night. "You read all these books?" he asked.

"Not all of them," I said. "I want to read them all someday."

"I'm think I'm gonna learn a lot from you," he said, after a moment.

My heart leapt.

Guys on Tinder dates didn't usually refer to the future. Any mention of the future was to be avoided, in case it suggested future contact. Young women and men I'd been interviewing had described a "contest to see who could care less," in which you wouldn't want to ever suggest to someone that you actually liked them and wanted to see them again.

But everything about Abel was different. The culture of detachment didn't seem to have taken hold of him yet. I wanted to reward him for being so sweet. I rewarded him with kisses and blow jobs. I thought his dick was perfect. It hit all my spots just right. "Not too big, not too small," I gushed to my lady friends at Sake Bar Satsko.

"Goldilocks dick," said Amy, with a knowing look.

I rewarded him with food. He loved to eat. He ate like he didn't always get enough food. We ate tacos and pizza, his favorite things, and then I started to cook for him. I was waiting for him with meals like a devoted little wife when he came home from work.

I'm not really much of a cook—my mother the chef was strangely guarded with her deep knowledge—but I can make a few things really well, like turkey. I made him a fifteen-pound turkey. He ate almost all of it.

"Don't watch me when I eat, now," he said with a smile. "I eat like an animal."

He did. I loved it. His table manners reminded me of the charmingly un-couth creatures in *Fantastic Mr. Fox*, a film we watched together. We watched movies he liked and movies I liked, sharing our picks, getting to know each other. He picked *Inglourious Basterds*, and did bits from Lieutenant Aldo Raine, whose extreme southern accent as played by Brad Pitt was not far off from his own. "We're gon' be doing one thang, and one thang only—killing Nazis," he quoted, and I giggled like an idiot.

I picked *Princess Mononoke* because he said he liked animation and super-heroes, and so I thought he would like this story of a young prince who saves the world. He did. He lay watching it with his head in my lap as I stroked his thick, wavy, dark hair and his beautiful head, with its high forehead and cheekbones. "You look like a pirate," I whispered to him.

We stayed up late and picked songs off our iPhones to share with each other. He introduced me to a punk brass band called the Stumblebums. We danced around. But there was still something a little shy in it all, until we started making love again. That's when it seemed like we had known each other forever. That's when any anxiety I had ever felt over the twenty pounds

I had put on since I was his age and the C-section scar that hatched its way across my lower midriff disappeared, because he didn't seem to mind or even notice. "I'll tell you a little secret," said a Park Avenue plastic surgeon I went to see after I had Zazie, worried that I would never get another man without a tummy tuck. "Men don't really care about any of this," he said. "Not if they like you. Don't waste your money." Turned out he was right about that.

● ● ●

One night we were smoking cigarettes by the kitchen window—Oh, did I mention I was smoking again? And not using condoms?—when he asked, "What's Cha-noo-ka?"

He was staring up at the top of my refrigerator, looking at my box of Chanukah candles.

"You mean Chanukah?" I said. "The Jewish holiday? Right around Christmas?"

He looked puzzled. And then, as if he was catching on, he said: "You're Jewish?"

"Uh-oh," I was thinking.

*Oh, please don't say something anti-Semitic, please don't say something anti-Semitic, I know you're from down there where they ride around with Confederate flags flying on their trucks but please don't say something anti-Semitic...*

"Well, yeah, I mean, my dad was," I babbled. "My mom converted after she married my stepfather. But it was the seventies and I think the rabbi was an atheist. Then I converted when I was in my twenties. But looking back, I think I only did it because my first husband wanted to convert before we got married—which I never really understood because I wasn't observant or anything. He used to read the Torah on the toilet. Which I always found sort of disrespectful—"

He seemed to be trying to process.

"Um, have you ever slept with a Jewish person before?" I asked.

"I don't think I ever *met* a Jewish person before," he said.

He looked at me with a little glint in his eye.

"Oh, well, I mean, you must have," I told him. "How long have you been in New York? New York has like a million Jews, so chances are you've probably met one by now, especially if you work for a fashion company. Jews are big in the arts…"

"Hmm," he said, considering all this. And then, smiling, "I told you I was gonna learn a lot from you."

He winked. I wasn't sure then if he'd been putting me on. It was the first time I saw how he used the expectation of him being a rube to tease people. Fantastic Mr. Abel.

"Are you making fun of me?" I asked, slapping him on the shoulder.

And then we were "wrastling," as he liked to call it, playing a kind of sex Twister, trying to pin each other down. "Now I have proved my dominance over you," he would declare, grinning ear to ear, as he crushed me to the floor. And then we were kissing and fucking again until we both got rug burns.

I had a playmate. For the first time in…well, maybe ever. The men I'd dated had often been competitive and angry men who weren't much fun.

He wasn't like that. He was funny. He would do impressions of the high-strung fashionistas at his workplace, who he said clicked around in heels and yelled: "Abel! Abel! Where are you?" He put his hand on his hips. "Do you know how to hang drapes?"

He told me more about himself. He described the town he came from as so small, there was "just a caution light." His said his mother ran a day care in their house. His father the guitar player hadn't been around much when he was growing up. He and his mom lived "on the Black side of town," he said, and some of the kids at school would call him a "spic."

His Argentinian grandparents looked elegant. They were socialites who had immigrated to Miami in the 1950s after the rise of Perón. He showed me a picture of them he had on his phone, a black-and-white photo taken in a nightclub. There was his grandfather, who looked so much like him, in a tuxedo, with his slicked-back hair, sporting a Clark Gable mustache, and his grandmother, with her orchid corsage and pearl-encrusted dress. He said he never saw them much but hoped, one day, they were going to bring him into the family business.

I liked the way he played my guitar. He played Led Zeppelin's "Going to California" one morning not long after I met him; it was a song that reminded me of my childhood, not only in its vintage but its melancholy sound, which made me think of that moment when my mother pulled the station wagon out of our driveway and we left Oyster Road forever. It was a song about not giving up on love even after someone has treated you "unkind."

"Never let them tell you that they're all the same," say the lyrics.

Listening in the kitchen, making my coffee, I thought, "Yes."

It was a song that sounded like it should be on the soundtrack of our budding romance. In the retrieval system of love and desire, in which we look for love with those who remind us of others we've lost or left behind, I felt that I had found him—or that he had been delivered to me, against all odds, by a ridiculous dating app.

We went to Satsko's one night and he met some of my neighborhood friends and played his ukulele, sitting at the bar. My friend Nariman laughed and told me, aside, "Oh my God, Nancy Jo, this guy is so into you."

And I said, "He *is*?"

I just knew that I felt relaxed. Relaxed like I was on vacation from the self who gave me so much trouble with men, the one who was always worried and anxious and overthought everything, even now, when I knew that I should be gearing up for my wise-old-woman phase.

I just knew that I liked myself with him. As the relationship gurus say, I was my "best self" with him. I felt like the me I could be when I was with my daughter or my closest friends. Would it be going too far to say that I had never been this comfortable with a man before? Did it make any sense? I knew that it didn't, and that I must be romanticizing again. But I decided not to overthink this either. I decided that I was just going to let myself enjoy this little sexcation and not care about anything else but the now—which I had learned how to do with a man, finally, at the age of fifty, after a year spent in the dating inferno, where chaos reigned. Abel felt like my reward for that year in dating hell, a year in which I had learned to let things stay loose and not care about what came next. Which is hard, when you can't get enough of someone and feel like you don't ever want them to go away.

I knew that New York would change him, that dating apps would change him, as would other temptations that had never presented themselves to him back in the small town where he was from. It was an evolution I'd seen before. How long would it be before he became just another fuckboy I joked about with my friends, as a way not to feel the pain of his disappearance or disregard?

I found myself saying a little prayer: not yet, not yet.

# Two

I left my first husband for a tabloid reporter named Jason. He saw me in the office where he worked when I went there to interview for a job. I didn't get the job, but I did get Jason, who followed me out onto the street and started chatting me up. I thought he was devastatingly handsome. He wore a leather jacket and a skull ring. He looked like Paul Reiser trying to look "downtown." He was in his forties and I was in my late twenties. He lived with his girlfriend, a cantankerous artist, and so it felt like high drama when we both left our partners and moved in together, into a dusty little apartment on the West Side Highway. I thought we were madly in love. By the end of our first few months together, he was beating me up.

I'd started doing freelance copy editing and fact-checking at newspapers and magazines to make ends meet while I was still trying to write a novel—places like *Soap Opera Digest* and *High Times*, the weed magazine, where I once argued with some of the editors about the facticity of the line, "Man has long known that cannabis eases the pain of childbirth."

Jason was always digging up dirt on celebrities for the tabloid he worked for. He was a gossip reporter, a sleazy, Sidney Falco–esque character, which I didn't quite get for a while; I just thought he was edgy. The tip-off should have been when he had a "slipup" smoking crack, but I was still pretty naive and told myself he was some kind of genius.

Once, he had an assignment where he had to find out whether a certain TV star was dating a teenage girl, and he was having trouble with it. "Why don't you ask kids?" I suggested. "Kids always know everything about each other." It was just a hunch. I wanted to help him, so I ventured out on my first-ever reporting adventure, finding my way to some clusters of private school kids hanging out in Central Park. Within a few days, I knew everything anybody needed to know about thirty-nine-year-old Jerry Seinfeld and his seventeen-year-old, private school student girlfriend, Shoshanna Lonstein. I don't know how I knew how to do this, I just did. I'd seen a lot of movies about reporters, and my favorite comic-book character was Brenda Starr, with whom I identified as a fellow redhead. Jason took the information gratefully and told his bosses he had reported it.

When the story of Jerry Seinfeld's teenage girlfriend broke across several news outlets, I was surprised more wasn't made of the age difference. It seemed like a sign that we hadn't come so far from the days when I was in high school, and people just laughed when I told them grown men had come on to me.

I still found the whole reporting experience thrilling, however, and I started to wonder if I could make my living as a journalist. Impressed by my beginner's luck, Jason started asking me for help on things he was working on. He asked me what I would do to get the information he needed; he asked me to edit his copy. You would think he would have continued to be grateful for the assistance, but it only seemed to make him mad when I asked if he could get me a job as a reporter at the tabloid.

"Trying to take my job?" he said, looking at me funny.

"Of course not!" I said.

It became an argument. And he slapped me.

He started hitting me regularly after that. He punched me, shoved me, pushed me down. He once beat me up so bad I was taken to St. Vincent's Hospital. Someone in our building had heard me screaming and called the police. "You deserve better than this," the cop who put the handcuffs on Jason told me.

I refused to testify against him, so the case was dropped. I didn't want anyone to know that, once again, I had chosen wrong, that I had left my husband only to jump into a physically abusive relationship. I was ashamed of it. I thought it must be my fault, somehow, that I had brought on this treatment.

Of course, it's never a woman's fault, not one of the one in four American women who are victims of severe domestic violence—which I knew in my head, but I was still worried that I had done something wrong, or that there was something wrong with me.

Plus, I thought I loved this guy.

And I was afraid of him.

When shelter-in-place orders were issued for Covid-19, the news became filled with stories about a rise in domestic violence all over the world. I couldn't stop thinking about the women and children who were trapped inside with their abusers. What would it be like, if we were all stuck inside with my frustrated, angry father? I wondered. Or if I was still with Jason?

The United Nations secretary-general, António Guterres, urged for "all governments to put women's safety first as they respond to the pandemic." It was a welcome sentiment. But has this ever been the case, that governments "put women's safety first"? I wish it were.

The Covid disaster brought into focus a different public health crisis: the lack of protection for women and children suffering domestic violence. The Trump administration had been rolling back such assistance for years, with massive cuts to federal programs designed to help victims, such as counseling services, shelters, legal aid, and other programs which receive grants under the Violence Against Women Act. Trump's crackdown on immigration had also caused undocumented immigrant women to fear seeking help, lest they risk deportation.

I thought about all this when I saw a tweet from a teacher I follow: "Best sentence so far from a student final: 'The pandemic has not only made life worse for women and girls globally, it has reminded us that for a lot of us, it was never really okay to begin with.'"

• • •

When I finally left Jason after almost two years, he didn't want to let me go; or he didn't want to stop hurting me. And he had a new weapon to do it with: the Internet.

My first experience of this exciting new cyberworld everybody was talking about was online harassment. It was a journalist friend who clued me in to the dismaying fact that my old boyfriend Jason was "talking shit about [me] online."

"How can he even do that?" I asked. I was mortified. At that point, all I knew about the Internet was AOL. Jason was posting unflattering photos of me on various sites—one where I was asleep and drooling on a pillow, another where I was jokingly fondling a banana—as well as putting up false stories about me, links which would follow me around for decades.

"What can I do?" I asked a lawyer.

"Nothing," he said, shrugging. "The laws haven't caught up."

That was 1993, more than twenty-five years ago, and since then the problem has grown into a plague. People still have little recourse in the face of online harassment, which happens more often to women and girls, and to women and girls of color or who are LGBTQ+ most often. Even after the passage of laws against cyberbullying in nearly all fifty states, men continue to attack women online, and few are ever prosecuted. I think people who continue to insist the Internet is "neutral" and "benign" must be people who have never been cyber-bullied, unlike the 40 percent of American adults and nearly 60 percent of American teenagers who have, according to surveys by Pew in 2017 and 2018.

But Jason didn't stop with posting nasty things about me online. When I started making some headway in my career, he wrote letters to my employers, attacking my character and claiming that he, not I, had written my stories (which was false; I had a restraining order against him). He didn't leave me alone until another guy I'd started dating, a *Life* magazine photographer named Gary, threatened him with a baseball bat when he showed up one day outside Gary's building. Jason had followed us. He'd been stalking me—turning me into another statistic, one of the one in six women who get stalked, usually by boyfriends, husbands, or exes.

"Guy like that only understands one thing," Gary said, when he came back inside with the bat. "Guy who'd hit a woman isn't even a man." He had a strange little smile on his face, as if he had enjoyed the confrontation. And though I'm grateful to this day to him for scaring off my stalker, it still makes me queasy, remembering that little smile of his.

Years later, I would think of Jason whenever I would see a dating app profile where the guy said he was a feminist. Sounds like a good thing, right? But it always rang false to me, like advertising which co-opts feminism in order to sell women products. When I asked some young women about it, they told me they'd had the same reaction. "'I'm a feminist' on Tinder is another way of saying, 'Just tryin' to get my dick wet,'" said Kim, a student at the University of California, Santa Cruz.

Because Jason had said he was a feminist, too. He liked to take me to strip clubs like the Baby Doll Lounge and Billy's Topless—which, under his guidance, I thought was so daring and cool. "They *like* being strippers," he told me. "It turns them *on*." I'll never forget the look on the face of the stripper he'd convinced to come home with us as he paid her the two hundred dollars he'd promised her (my money). She just looked tired, like she wanted the night to be over so she could go home and get some rest.

● ● ●

What would have become of me, and where would I be now, if someone hadn't taken a chance on me? I wondered that night, walking along, on my way home to meet Abel after leaving Constance. I felt like I was going to cry.

"Not now, not now," I told myself. "Not now when you're on your way to see him."

Even knowing I had reason to not want to see him, I still didn't want him to see me crying. I worried how it would look, to him, to see me so upset—and also how I would *look*, with puffy eyes. Which made me want to cry all over again, to think that I still cared what anyone thought about how I looked. I wondered when I would be free from all that.

I felt I had to sit down to collect myself, to think a moment before I kept walking home. I sat down on the bench in front of my friend Ahmet's café on East 7th Street, across from Tompkins Square Park. I saw him through the window, making food in his kitchen. He waved.

I texted Abel, "On my way." I fished in my bag for a tissue. The tears were coming.

And suddenly, sitting there, I was seeing myself the day I moved out of the apartment I had shared with Jason, dashing out with my things while he was at work so he wouldn't come back and catch me leaving. With the help of my friend Lisa—a student at Parsons, an eccentric artist who wore turbans—I moved into a studio in the West Village, a hundred and fifty square feet on West 12th Street. I remember Lisa laughed and said, "This looks like a cabin on a boat." And she didn't mean a yacht. The bed was a loft just a few feet from the ceiling because there was no space for a bed on the floor. But it was mine, all mine, my first apartment of my own. I felt like I had made a giant step forward, escaping Jason and getting this place, though I could barely afford the first month's rent.

I knew I was privileged. I was white and expensively educated. I was also broke. My parents were of the World War II generation that said, "Good luck, kid! You'll figure it out!" when you graduated college. I got no financial help. I hadn't been in much contact with my family lately; we'd become estranged since my divorce and my tumultuous relationship with Jason. They seemed to feel uneasy with the person I was becoming, which made me want to stay away, not wanting to listen to their questions and judgments. *I* didn't even know who I was just then, so what could I say when they asked me what was going on? I needed someone to believe in me—in the me I wanted to become.

That person was Jeanie Pyun, then an editor at *Mademoiselle*, who started hiring me to write for her. She let me write about Jason (we changed his name). She assigned me lifestyle stories and movie reviews. Jeanie was one of those young women who seemed to effortlessly have it all together, and I looked up to her. *Mademoiselle*—which folded in 2001, one of the first casualties of the demise of print—was a lady mag, one of those sexist publications I had always resented for making women feel anxious about themselves through their relentless pushing of impossible beauty standards. But it also had a history of hiring fabulous women writers such as Sylvia Plath and Joyce Carol Oates, and so I was thankful for the chance to see my byline there. Whatever Jeanie gave me to do, I tried to make it great.

As I started on my path as a journalist, I noticed that most of the young women I knew who wanted to be writers and editors were finding more luck getting work at women's magazines than at hard news publications. For women of color, there seemed to be even less opportunity; most were finding work at the handful of Black women's magazines or the up-and-coming hip hop magazines—some of the best gigs in town, but limited in number. Today, this hiring bias has only gotten slightly better. According to a 2019 report from the Women's Media Center, "Despite some gains, men still dominate in every part of the news, entertainment, and digital media." The percentage of white and male employees in newsrooms in 2018 was still higher than in the overall US workforce, according to Pew.

This state of affairs started to become apparent to me when I would go into newsrooms, trying to find a job, and I would look around and see a sea of white guys. "Why should I hire you," an editor at a major newspaper asked me, with a condescending smile, "when there are ten young men applying for this job who have more clips with more hard-hitting stories?" Maybe because the only stories anybody had assigned me so far were on things like the best acne washes and the new pussy-waxing craze (which, I said in my piece, was connected to the boom in online porn, with its hairless performers; even when I did frivolous assignments, I tried to sneak in my feminism). It was a catch-22 he was unable or unwilling to see. And it pissed me off.

It's funny to think of how unthreatening and accommodating I tried to appear in those days, so as not to upset anybody with my ambition and drive. For who were the pop culture icons us professional gals were supposed to model ourselves after in the early nineties? Why, bubbly, smiley Meg Ryan and Julia Roberts, or adorably self-doubting Jennifer Aniston. (I don't blame the actresses for this, but rather the male-dominated system that cast them in sexist roles where they never complained about gender inequality.)

Meanwhile, I was practically boiling inside. I was pissed off that the young men I'd gone to high school and college with who'd gone into journalism were already doing so much better professionally, when most of them hadn't done as well academically as I. I was pissed off about how men had treated me in relationships. I was pissed off that some of my family members now seemed to see me as damaged goods because I had gotten divorced, which was ridiculous for all kinds of reasons, including the fact that my mother and father were divorced and my father was a divorce lawyer. It was like my friend Amy once said: "I feel like to be a young woman nowadays is to be in a mild, constant state of rage." That's just how I felt, back then, in my late twenties.

Around this time, I developed a health condition which seemed to produce a metaphor for my general mood. My bladder burned. I felt like I had to piss all the time! It was maddening—so maddening that a couple of times I sort of casually considered suicide: "What am I gonna do about this? Well, I guess I can just kill myself…" Suicidal ideation with interstitial cystitis, an inflammation of the lining of the bladder, is not uncommon, and I hope if anybody reading this is feeling this way, you'll seek and find the help you need.

Eventually, in my thirties, I would be properly diagnosed and successfully treated for my illness. But not before a male urologist gave me a "breast exam," which he told me was a necessary part of his examination (it was not), and a male psychiatrist asked me if I had "wet the bed as a child," and how was my sex life with my husband? And how many times a week did I masturbate, and what did I think about when I did? Whatever connection he thought all this had with my urgent need to pee, he never explained. And then there was the Zen Buddhist monk physician in orange robes who just laughed at me merrily and said, "Oh, you *are* pissed off!"

I didn't know how pissed off I had a right to be. I wish somebody had let me know.

And I wish somebody had told me what to do when a man dangled work while putting his hands on your bod—like the editor at *New York* magazine who invited me out for drinks after reading a piece I did for *Mademoiselle* on tantric sex and touched my boob in the cab on the way home. It wasn't the first time someone had touched my boob without asking, but it was the first time it had happened in a professional situation. At least, I *thought* it was a professional situation: we'd been discussing me working for him. It's amazing how during these murky occurrences, your mind starts automatically doing calculations, like a sexual harassment abacus: "Well, if I get mad about him grabbing my boob, then he might not give me an assignment, but if I don't, then I might have to sleep with him, and then he still might not give me an assignment, and I might not ever get anywhere in this business. So is this what you have to do to get ahead? Maybe I'll just go back to waitressing…"

So I kissed him back. And he gave me an assignment. And then another, and another one. I did five front-of-the-book stories and three feature stories before *New York* finally put me on staff, so I don't think having sex with my editor was actually the reason I was hired there. The man who hired me, Kurt Andersen, then the editor in chief, was a kind and brilliant guy we were all intimidated by. "Well, I think you've proven yourself," he said in his mild way, over breakfast at Forty Four, the restaurant in the Royalton Hotel. I remember he had yogurt, I had pancakes. I thought I would plotz, as my Russian grandmother would say. I was so excited to get a real job as a writer.

I just wish my editor had helped me get the shot without putting sex into the mix. Maybe he didn't see it that way. Many people in the office were having relationships; it wasn't frowned upon back then. Work was just another place where we used to meet people to date and have sex with. But then, my editor never actually told anybody he and I were having sex (and I was telling myself it was more than just sex), because, as he informed me several months into our affair, he had "met someone." Meaning someone he was also fucking. Not long after I joined the staff of *New York*, they got married. He took me aside at his wedding and kissed me, sticking his tongue in my mouth (he was drunk), and whispering in my ear, "This doesn't have to end." I was so relieved when he went to work in television.

● ● ●

The offices of *New York*, in those days, were at 50th Street and Madison Avenue, in the same art deco skyscraper where Jennifer Garner works as an editor in the 2004 time travel rom-com *Thirteen Going on Thirty*.

"That's where *New York* magazine was!" I yelped at Zazie when we watched this movie on cable together when she was about nine. I felt like I was seeing a childhood home, a place where I had grown up—and, in a way, it was. I was a little past thirty myself when I started working there, a late bloomer professionally, so psyched to have a spot at the hottest magazine in town. It had been a long road getting there, and I was determined to keep proving myself.

I remember a lot of mornings getting my coffee at Patisserie Claude, the bakery on West 4th Street, after I had pulled another all-nighter. Soon, the all-nighters started to pay off, and there was a little moment there where I was the It Girl, getting asked to talk about my stories on the radio and television—which I always hated doing, becoming instantly shy about the way I looked. Whenever I saw myself on TV, it seemed to me that I appeared imperfect and odd, not smooth and coiffed like ladies on TV were supposed to look. And fat! I was a size eight, back then, but Bridget Jones, our single girl avatar, was a size eight, and she was obsessed with being overweight. It all seems so crazy now.

But I loved my new job. I loved it so much. It was the thing I had loved most in my life up until then. I loved the way it was making me feel about myself—like I had a voice, like I was somebody. I wanted my stories to stand out, to have an edge, and a rocking kind of rhythm, like Joan Jett singing "Bad Reputation."

And yet, as much as I was enjoying my new job and all the adventures it was enabling me to have—chasing Leonardo DiCaprio around town, finding out about the secret lives of the "prep school gangsters," doing the first cover story on Gwyneth Paltrow—it didn't escape my notice that, for the most part, the male writers at *New York* got the more "serious" assignments, while girls like me got to write about fashion and style and celebrities and, in my case, teenagers, a subject nobody ever took very seriously. However, I decided that if they were going to make me the teen reporter, then I was going to be the best. "She is to the American adolescent what Jane Goodall is to the Tanzanian chimpanzee," Graydon wrote about me, years later, in his editor's letter, which may be the nicest compliment I've ever received (with apologies to the teens).

But despite the fact that the stories I was doing, on youth culture in particular, were getting a lot of buzz, I found out some years into my tenure at *New York* that I was still being paid significantly less than my male counterparts in equal jobs. This salary discrepancy was explained to me by the fact that these men "had families," which actually not all of them did. And then when I got pregnant and asked for a raise, I was told, "Nancy Jo, you can't get a raise just because you're pregnant." It was frustrating.

And when can women expect the gender pay gap to close? Apparently not for another 257 years, according to a 2019 study from the World Economic Forum. And do people really think this has no effect on how men see women in the workplace?

The atmosphere in the offices of *New York* made Sterling Cooper Draper Pryce (the ad agency in *Mad Men*) look woke. I'm not sure the three editors in chief I worked under ever fully knew what was going on, but maybe they should have. There was a male writer there, a young man who resembled a gnome, who kept a list of "girls in the office I want to fuck"—a list on which I did not appear, and which he bandied about loudly with some of the other guys in the office, who all took it very jocularly. There was a fairly constant stream of commentary about the attractiveness of the young female assistants and the sexiness of their clothes, the slip dresses and minidresses that were popular at the time.

Yes, it was 1996, not 1966, but it felt like middle school all over again, and the backlash to feminism was on. Lad mags like *Maxim* were making a splash on the newsstands, and Howard Stern was on the radio doing "butt bongo" on strippers and locker-room talk with Donald Trump. Katie Roiphe, the media's designated young feminist, was writing about how date rape was just an overblown whine. The Victoria's Secret fashion show was the new pop culture event we were all supposed to be just dying to watch. And if you didn't laugh along, or at least keep your mouth shut about what you really thought about all this, then you weren't considered a cool girl—you were a drag, a bitch, and didn't you know we had moved past the *tediousness* of political correctness and into the perpetually ironic?

Just five years after Anita Hill testified before the Senate Judiciary Committee, setting off a national conversation about sexual harassment in the workplace, nobody was talking about sexual harassment, at least not at the place I worked. Quite the opposite, in fact: to even mention it was to be seen as a problem.

I once did an interview in which a male celebrity whipped out his dick right in front of me. When I came back to the office and told everyone about it, wide-eyed and upset, some of the men just laughed, and some of the women laughed along with them. A young woman on the staff (who went on to do very well in journalism), gave me the nickname "Nancy Ho," which some people seemed to think was just sidesplitting.

"Oh, but it's just a *joke*," she said, when I let her know I didn't appreciate it. She ended up marrying the guy who kept the list, so I can't help but feel bad for her.

• • •

The slut-shaming nickname was no doubt a swipe at my busy sex life. I wasn't the only woman in the world exercising her right to cat around—I was just fool enough to talk about it in the office, usually as a way to regale my coworkers with funny stories from the weekend, or to deal with my own distress over the bad behavior of some of the men I was having sex with.

It seemed safe to talk about it, because this was the era of women writing titillating sex columns, like Candace Bushnell with "Sex and the City" over at the *New York Observer*. It even seemed kind of feminist to talk about it, to declare one's sexual freedom. But what no one ever mentioned was how a woman is always taking a risk when she starts talking about what she's really been doing behind closed doors—perhaps like I'm doing now.

What was happening was that I had a good job, and I was looking good—I was working out for the first time in my life, now able to afford a membership at a gym—and I was feeling myself, as they say. In my thirties I finally felt like I could handle men, and I wanted them to handle me. I met men everywhere—at parties and dinner parties and bars and out in nightlife, at places like Don Hill's and Club USA and Limelight and Palladium and Nell's and Lot 61 and Chaos and Shine and the downstairs inner sanctum of Life. Life was where, on a Thursday night, you might see Puffy and Jay-Z and Mariah and J.Lo and assorted other stars, all perched on their banquettes, rapping along to the genius hip hop of the era: Tupac and Nas and Biggie and Missy and Busta Rhymes, who would show up sometimes, looking amazing. Q-Tip and the then teenage Mark Ronson were the regular DJs.

"It's Cotton Club," said my friend Gary Harris, the late music executive and writer, one night as we sat looking around at the room, feeling dazzled.

I got into these places because I was a reporter covering nightlife, following my sources around, but that didn't keep me from ending the night with some cute guy who had pulled me out onto the dance floor. I loved to dance, and back then, we danced a lot. I danced with Mase to "Feel So Good" ("Bad,

bad, bad bad boy / You make me feel so good") at Puffy's twenty-ninth birthday party at Cipriani Downtown. I liked a bumping dive on Houston Street called Den of Thieves, where one night I ran into some members of the Wu-Tang Clan, which turned into a very long, smoky weekend.

But I don't actually remember if the sex I was having in those days was good or bad. I remember the moments, like the night I sat holding hands with a guy as we watched our dogs play on my terrace on East 22nd Street, where I had moved; or when I held a guy in my lap, as he told me about how his father had died of AIDS; or when a guy and I lay in bed and laughed together, watching *Austin Powers: International Man of Mystery* on video after we had sex; or the night a guy and I sat at a bar and talked for two hours about *The Miseducation of Lauryn Hill,* which we'd both just listened to for the first time, blown away. I wanted more of these types of moments with one person, long-term. I felt it in my bones when Liz Phair sang, "I want a boyfriend." But boyfriends suddenly didn't seem to be as available as they once were.

"Whatever happened to a boyfriend?" Phair asked.

It used to be that if you slept with someone a few times and hung out a bit, then he was your boyfriend, at least for a while. It didn't mean you were going to get married, necessarily, but you were going to be exclusive, more or less; cheating was still seen as an actual transgression. But as the nineties progressed, more men were expecting to have casual sex outside of the boundaries of a relationship, and so were many women. It was the dawning of hookup culture, although nobody was calling it that yet.

Researchers at Kinsey date the inception of hookup culture to around 2000—the same year Tom Wolfe wrote about a new, emerging definition of "hooking up," which used to mean just meeting up but now meant "a sexual experience." But I think the change in sexual culture was actually already well underway in the mid-to-late nineties due to a convergence of many factors—most significantly, the spread of the Internet and the availability of online porn. The Internet meant that everybody in the world was at your fingertips—or so it seemed—in AOL chat rooms, via instant messenger, and on countless other new social-networking services. So why settle on just one person? People were getting freaky with anonymous strangers in front of their computer screens, strangers who were available to play any time of day or night. Cybersex was leading to all kinds of experimentation and new modes of sexual expression, which in many ways, and for many people, was great. But it was also leading to exploitation and predation—and, I think, to fewer committed relationships, and to people viewing their sexual partners as less than fully human, more as faceless stimulators on the other side of a screen: "HotGirl567."

At the same time, the ready access to porn that occurred when it went online—another unprecedented development—was giving heterosexual men and boys a masturbation aid which fulfilled every possible fetish involving women, who were already objectified by the culture at large. Who needed to put in the effort to find and win over a real woman anymore when you had a perfectly plastic-looking porn star at your immediate disposal?

Women were being told that the reason for the decline in men's interest in commitment was all our fault. A new wave of dating books appeared— notably 1995's mega bestseller *The Rules*—which said that if women wanted men to commit to them, they had to play hard to get, not give it up on the first date like sluts. "All these years of feminism…so we could learn to behave?" wrote my friend Elizabeth Wurtzel. "Did Germaine Greer impor- tune us so long ago with the words 'Lady, love your cunt'…so we could be told not to succumb to sexual abandon on the first date?"

All I knew was that my biological clock was ticking, and there was no steady guy on the horizon. I had always wanted to have a baby—which isn't for everyone, I know, but I had always loved taking care of babies, ever since I'd played with my dolls on Oyster Road and helped raise my little twin brothers. I wanted to be a mom.

But how you gonna have a baby without a guy? I'd started wondering. Or maybe you could…Maybe you should! But how would I get pregnant?

I couldn't afford a sperm bank. Perhaps I should just ask one of my guy friends to knock me up, I thought, maybe I would invite a bunch of them to a dinner party and just ask them...

I was mouthing off like this in the office of my new editor at *New York* one day when he got this gleam in his eye and said, "You should do it! And write about it!" Editors always loved for us girl writers to write about sex, especially if we were having lots of it. The next thing I knew, I was hosting "The Baby Dinner," to which I invited eight men I knew and liked—and could convince to come to this outrageous party—asking if any of them would agree to be my baby daddy. The evening's conversation turned out to be more about them than me, unsurprisingly enough, and their own longing and ambivalence around having kids. (They were all great guys, and I'm still close with most of them. The Baby Dinner turned out to be an unexpectedly bonding experience.)

I didn't wind up getting pregnant by any of the men at the party. But shortly after it happened, I got pregnant by accident by a guy who lived in my building. Too many drinks one night out in the Financial District, where I had recently moved, and which, back then, had a stymieing lack of corner delis—in short, we didn't use a condom. The guy didn't see my pregnancy as his responsibility, however, and he wasn't interested in becoming a father. "How do I know it's mine?" he asked, proving to be as unoriginal as he was a cad. "Okay," I said, "then do a paternity test." Which he declined.

The person who came through for me in this situation was my own father. "Well, I guess this is what you call an alternative lifestyle," he grumbled, when I informed him of my condition. By this time, my dad had been a family law lawyer for more than forty years, and he said he'd seen countless situations where men didn't step up to the plate when it came to taking care of their kids. "It makes women crazy," he said. And so his advice to me, after I told him how much I wanted to have this baby, was "just do it then. You don't need this guy. I know you'll be a wonderful mother." It was nicest thing he had ever said to me, and the best advice I've ever received. That little baby was everything to me, and has been ever since.

● ● ●

It was that same little baby, fourteen years later, who alerted me to the fact that Axel Wang's footage was trash.

"Mommy," she said, "I think you better look at Axel's footage." She'd been watching some of it on a computer we had hooked up to our movie hard drive.

"Why?" I asked, looking over from the pot of spaghetti I was stirring. "Is there something wrong with it?"

Oh, the shaky, blurry footage he'd shot—sometimes from very weird, low-slung angles because he was so short. I had gone on three trips with Axel—to Florida, Virginia, and Arizona—in as many months, and the whole time I had believed that he knew how to operate the expensive movie camera I had bought with a credit card.

I didn't know how to work this camera myself, and didn't yet understand that the director was supposed to check the footage regularly—ideally every day. I also couldn't imagine that anyone would lie about knowing how to use a movie camera or having a job as a cameraman at a TV network. And I was paying him!

It was with a heavy heart that I went to IMDB and saw that, in fact, no, Axel Wang had no credits except as a production assistant. I felt like Shelley Duvall in that scene in *The Shining* where she goes to Jack Nicholson's type-writer and sees that he's been typing, over and over, "All work and no play makes Jack a dull boy."

Of *course* I had checked out Axel before hiring him—that is, online. I'd seen his website, Facebook, YouTube channel, LinkedIn, all of which did a very good job of suggesting he was who he said he was—all those profile pics of him hoisting a Canon! But it was all fake news. And I'd believed it. Why? I guess because part of me was worried that I couldn't really make this movie on my own. It's always easier to think that someone else is going to show you the way, when really you have to figure things out for yourself.

And I think I'd wanted to believe in our love affair, wanted to believe that, approaching fifty, I could still have a romantic adventure like the one I thought I was having with Axel. I'd wanted to believe in what we seemed to be, as if from a movie: two journalists on the road together, falling in love, complete with rom-commy squabbling—usually me trying to drag Axel out of a pool hall because we had to wake up the next morning and work.

If Axel had known what the hell he was doing, the footage of those excursions we took together would have been powerful. We went to Panama City Beach, Florida, where I'd wanted to see what lay beneath the MTV fantasy of American youth reveling on spring break. We had witnessed a morass of sexual harassment—girls getting groped and grabbed on the dance floors and around the pools. "The boys just treat you like savages," one girl said. And then in Jamestown, Virginia, we met some girls who told me about slut pages—those abusive online galleries of nonconsensually shared nudes which had already become a routine feature of teen life, unbeknownst to most adults.

"Are you getting this?" I'd ask Axel, and he would give me the thumbs-up.

I should have realized when we were in Tucson, Arizona, that I couldn't trust him with filming these important interviews (which I was also voice recording on my phone, thank God). We had just talked to a heartbreaking homeless girl who had told the story of how she had run away because a family member was molesting her, and when we got back to the hotel, Axel confessed that he'd realized he hadn't turned on the camera.

I remember him leaning his head back against the wall of the hotel bar and staring up at the ceiling when he told me this. He thought I was going to fire him. I should've fired him. But by then, we were sleeping together.

"You're dickmatized," said Amy, when I told her about it later.

But after Zazie showed me the problem with Axel's footage, I knew that Axel had to go. I screwed up my courage and went out to the Brooklyn bar where he liked to play pool and told him I wouldn't be needing his services anymore, and I wanted my equipment back. My camera was at his house. I had trusted him that much.

"You're breaking up with me—and you're taking the equipment?" he said, outraged. "Just let me have the camera!" he moaned. Why he thought he was entitled to keep this $5,000 instrument I'd purchased, I can't explain, except to reiterate that he was the type of bad boy who thinks he's entitled to everything. I could see that this was going to be difficult, perhaps even legally sticky. I didn't want to have to call the police. So I placated him by agreeing that he could go on another trip with me, to a teen beauty pageant in Houston. I didn't know what else to do. Once again, I had put myself in a difficult situation by thinking I needed a man.

● ● ●

"I don't need a man, so why do I still want one?" I asked my friend Ahmet, whose café I had parked myself in front of while I was trying to figure out what to do about Abel, that night on my way home. Ahmet had come out to join me with a cup of coffee and to see if I was okay, sitting there in the cold, and I had told him about my problem.

Ahmet is big and tall with a shaved head and a rugged face; he's in his thirties. He's a good friend and a good man, the type of guy who will do things for a single mom like me without having to be asked—like installing my new air conditioners, which he did one sweltering summer day, just to be nice. He's what my dad used to call a mensch.

He had emigrated from Turkey just a few years before and already had his own thriving business. He was well-acquainted with Abel, having seen us come into his café for many late-night sandwiches. He was the one in my group of friends who had teasingly dubbed Abel "Mountain Boy."

"Because Mountain Boy makes an earthquake between the sheets," he said, by way of answering my question.

Laughing made me feel a little better.

"But we're never going to know if we really *need* anyone—none of us, ever again, and that's really sad," Ahmet said. "My parents have been married for forty years and they've never looked at another person. Now, we got the Internet, we got Tinder..."

Ahmet had been dating a woman he met on Bumble. She was a hobosexual—he and I had that in common. She was a YouTuber who'd been living with him on one of her stops around the world, posting about her travels. She was polyamorous and had told him "everyone in Europe is polyamorous," and had tried to get him to agree to let her see other people. "I know it's chic to be 'open' now, but that's not me," he'd told her.

It wasn't me either, although I had tried to let things ride with Abel, to not even think about what he might be doing when he wasn't with me.

But his phone persisted in reminding me.

Even during that first blissful week that we spent together, his phone created a sense of doubt, almost as if it were another sentient being in the room, continually taunting me with, "You don't really know him, you know..."

His phone kept lighting up with texts, often enough that I began to wonder, "Who is that? And that?" And of course, I checked. When he was in the bathroom, in the middle of the night, and his phone screen went bright, I picked it up off the nightstand to read the text on the screen before it faded away. It was from someone named Twizzler and it said: "What's up, fancy dancer? Where ya been?"

Confusion. Panic. Twizzler? Fancy dancer? *What?*

When I heard him coming back from the bathroom, I quickly put his phone back down. But the light was still on. "Oh dear, is he going to know I saw it?" I fretted, pretending to be asleep. I even fake snored a little bit. (Apparently I do snore, according to Abel, who swore he found it cute. "You be sawin' logs sometimes," he said. "Just like my mee-maw." Oh, wonderful.)

I heard him pick up his phone and start texting someone, after he came back into the room.

"Is he texting Twizzler," I wondered huffily, "when he's here with *me?*"

It made me think of my friend who had an affair with Tiger Woods. I'd met her in a club, years before. She said she woke up in a hotel room where she was staying with the famous golfer, one night, and heard him texting; she pretended to be asleep. When he went to the bathroom, she checked his phone and saw that he was sexting with several women at once. At the time, in 2009, Tiger and his women was such a scandal—*Oh my God, he's seeing so many people!* Granted, he was married then, but, looking back, his story seems like a harbinger of things to come. Now, everybody could be like Tiger, if they wanted, at least online, with so much opportunity, so much choice. Now Tiger's way of dating was just called "dating."

So I already knew it wasn't just dating apps that had changed things—it was these phones, these phones. It was like Paul Virilio, the French philosopher, wrote: "When you invent the ship, you also invent the shipwreck." Smartphones were the ship and shipwreck of relationships. They had made it easier to be in touch, and yet more difficult to emotionally connect. Psychologists who study relationships call this "technoference"—the way in which smartphones have disrupted our ability to focus on each other in relationships and even in conversations. The sociologist Sherry Turkle calls this being "alone together," meaning that technology demands so much of us, we've stopped being present when we're together in person.

After the pandemic struck, and people (soon to be followed by advertisers) started using the hashtag #alonetogether as a hopeful way of saying we're still connected through technology despite social distancing, I thought of Turkle and how she had meant just the opposite with this phrase; but since the crisis was making us rely even more on technology to connect, I think it became too disturbing to think of it as actually further undermining our closeness.

Now, how this all translates, when a man gets back into bed and reaches for you after you know he's been texting someone else—even when he has plausible deniability, when he can always just say, "I was texting work," or his mother, brother, sister, friend; and even when you have no claim on this man because you aren't really dating, because you've only just met him and this is hookup culture, where everything is left undefined—how this translates is that you don't feel as intimate. I didn't, anyway. I felt a little bit angry, just a little bit mad, which made the sex become a little bit rough, which was a little bit hot, but also a little less sweet. I had moved away from him emotionally, for a moment, and he could feel it, though he didn't know why, and it worried and excited him. Which was maybe what made him want to flatter me. He smoothed his rough hand down my hip, whispering, "You're gonna have to send me some pictures." Which just made my heart ache.

• • •

Nudes. They were another game changer in dating, uncommon before Palm-Pilots and phones. Now, so normalized that kids are sending them in middle school before they've ever held hands with someone or had a first kiss.

It's hard not to see a connection between porn and the normalization of nudes. It's as if we've all become our own personal pornographers; we're all Hugh Hefner. Straight women and girls are assessing themselves to see how they can take a pic that will measure up to the women they see in porn—just as I had once done as a girl—but now they can instantly send these shots of their naked bods to their awaiting male partners. Because men love nudes, and men ask for nudes, and women are expected to send them, whether they want to or not (and some women do want to send nudes, even though the danger of nonconsensual sharing threatens them disproportionately).

And men love to send dick pics.

I got my first dick pic from a Houston tech millionaire. He didn't look much like a millionaire; he looked like the Dude from *The Big Lebowski*. He was sitting on the back patio of a Houston bar where I'd gone because somebody told me there would be tech millionaires there who liked to invest in movies. There were Lamborghinis and Ferraris parked out front—not really my scene, but if I was going to get a movie made, I was going to need some money, and I had heard that schmoozing rich guys was one way you could get it.

The tech dude was spread out on a piece of lawn furniture, drinking a cocktail and scratching his balls—foreshadowing, in a way, for the dick pic. Everybody was treating him like he was a king, although he was clearly high and quite greasy-looking. Somebody introduced me to him, and, after some pleasantries, I launched into a pitch for my documentary. I told him about the girls I'd been interviewing at the Miss Teen USA beauty pageant in Houston, and how they'd told me they had lost their self-esteem through cyberbullying and having their nudes shared nonconsensually online. And now, they said, they were seeking "empowerment" through being in this beauty pageant. I told him how complicated it all was and how it made me feel sad.

The tech dude sat back, listening with a slit-eyed expression, and said it all sounded very interesting, and how much did I think I would need to make this film?

"I don't know," I said, "maybe half a million?"

"How about a million?" he said. He gave me his number. I was elated. It made this last, difficult trip with Axel seem worth it.

That weekend, I had Axel with me again—knowing, now, that he didn't know how to operate my camera, and yet still having to watch him pretend like he did, all while flirting with the teenage beauty pageant contestants.

I didn't sleep with Axel on that trip, and when we got back to LaGuardia Airport in New York, I took back my Pelican cases with all my equipment, put them in a cab, and went home. I didn't think I'd ever want to see Axel again.

I let about a week pass, which I thought was a good amount of time to wait to contact the tech dude again about investing in my movie. He'd told me to text him when I got back to New York, and so, early one evening on a weekday, I texted him, reminding him of who I was and of our conversation.

"When would be a good time to call to talk?" I asked.

And he sent me a dick pic. With a text that said: "How about we talk about this?"

I was so confused, for a moment I froze. "What is this?" I wondered. It was one of the strangest dicks I had ever seen—sort of two-toned, darker on the bottom than the top. It looked like some weird chess piece, like a slightly flaccid bishop. For a second I actually thought the tech dude was asking me for medical advice. Had his dick been injured?

But then I realized, no, he's sending me a dick pic. And what a strange thing that was to do. It made me feel disoriented. Kind of disgusted. Sick.

I realized then how foolish I must've sounded on the back patio of that bar in Houston, going on about my feminism and how I wanted to expose the sexism in the lives of girls. I realized how the tech dude must've been laughing at me; and now it seemed like he was slapping me in the face with his dick.

But what was he really saying with this? I wondered. Was he saying that if I did something with his dick I would get the million dollars? Was there some Helen Gurley Brown, *Sex and the Single Girl*–style move for me here? But no, I didn't really think there was. It didn't seem like he was offering anything to me except this picture of his dick, make of it what I would.

Is a dick pic ever really about sex? Not according to Whitney Bell, an LA-based artist who in 2016 did a gallery show of unsolicited dick pics she'd received. "It's not about sex. It's about power," Bell said in an interview. "It's about these guys wanting to exert control."

"John," age thirty-four, told *Refinery29* that same year that when he sent dick pics to women, "it's definitely an expression of power." But what kind of "power" could this mean? And how did it factor into what was happening with dating?

It seemed like a new kind of flashing, to me, and yet it was still legal almost everywhere, incredibly enough. Getting a dick pic felt like when I had been flashed, walking home from the subway station in Yokohama, back in the eighties when I was living in Japan, where I'd gone to work as an English teacher after college. I was walking home alone, taking a shortcut down a hill, when a guy jumped out of nowhere, about ten feet away from me, and opened up his trench coat. Yes, he had on the proverbial trench coat. I felt revolted and scared, but I forced myself to laugh, pushing the "ha has" out of my throat as hard as I could, throwing my head back as if this was the funniest thing I'd ever seen—this strange man standing there, pointing his erect penis at me. He looked embarrassed and skulked away.

It is mind-boggling to think of the sheer number of women who've received pictures of men's penises on their phones since smartphones became widely adopted around 2007. In a 2017 survey, 53 percent of millennial women said they'd received dick pics, and of that number, 78 percent said the images were unsolicited. Dick pics have almost become a fact of life for women and girls, like the catcalling which starts for girls at the onset of puberty. Girls have told me about getting dick pics in the sixth grade. And when dating apps came along, dick pics became a routine aspect of courtship.

"If you've managed to escape using [Tinder] for more than twenty minutes without receiving a dick pic," wrote blogger Kassi Klower, "you deserve a special mention in the history books." So what does this say, that men on dating apps are routinely sending women pictures of their dick as an overture—toward what? A relationship?

I've wondered what the radical feminist writer Andrea Dworkin would have to say about dick pics. As brilliant as she was, I've always thought she was a bit harsh about penises—she didn't seem to like them much; she saw them as inextricably tied to patriarchal domination. On the other hand, is it something we can really just shrug off, the fact that the digital revolution has resulted in millions of men sending millions of women pictures of their dicks? Talk about unprecedented.

Evolutionary psychologists say that straight men don't see sending pictures of their junk to women as offensive, because images of women's genitalia sexually excite them. I've heard this rationale from men and boys who say they send dick pics as a way to "get something back"—meaning nudes. But it's hard to believe, at this stage of the game, that most men have not been apprised of the fact that most women do not want to see unsolicited pictures of their dicks. In one survey, the majority of women called them "gross."

The media—which always seems ready to pitch in and tell women that misogynistic trends are really okay, if you just go with them, if you're a cool girl—has periodically attempted to make dick pics hot. *Cosmopolitan*: "In Defense of the Dick Pic." And *Playboy*: "Am I the Only Woman Who Likes Getting a Picture of a Guy's Junk?"

"Women respond to dick pics" has become a genre of YouTube humor, a pushback in which women make jokes about the unsolicited pictures they've received. Much easier to laugh it off than to think about what it might really mean—what I think Dworkin might have said it means—that dick pics are a kind of mental rape, a global mindfuck.

"I think there's been a misunderstanding," I told the tech dude. And I deleted him.

● ● ●

"But Abel isn't like those guys," I was telling Daniel, my new cameraman, as we rode along Sunset Boulevard in the summer of 2015. We were on a shooting trip in LA. It was a few weeks after I'd met Abel on Tinder, and I was telling Daniel about him, trying to convince him that, despite Abel's tender age, he bore no resemblance to some of the young men we'd been interviewing for our film, with their demeaning attitudes toward women.

"He's respectful. He's sweet," I insisted. "He doesn't send dick pics—"

"Oh, really?" said Daniel, with his cocky grin. "Isn't that a picture of his dick on that billboard up there?"

"What? Where?"

He was only teasing me, as usual. Daniel—an affable silverback gorilla of a man, big and handsome and hairy, with a thoughtful brow—never seemed to tire of teasing me. From the moment he walked in the door of my apartment, the day we met through a mutual friend, we fell to ribbing each other like an affectionate brother and sister. We immediately liked each other.

I'd gotten very lucky with my new director of photography. He was a great shooter who had worked as a camera operator on some award-winning documentaries, including *Weiner* and *Cartel Land*. It was a turning point in my project, getting him on board. I couldn't believe it when he agreed to work with me—though I would never tell him that. He was in his early thirties and had a wife and a baby daughter, which he said made him want to know more about the challenges facing girls in the digital age.

He was about to learn a lot. And so was I.

Our first road trip together felt like a test. It was a turning point for me personally, the moment that sent me flying into the gyre of dating app dating, not knowing how I was going to claw my way out again. This trip was also the moment when I first suspected I might be going through menopause—a word people seem to want to say even less than "clitoris." It was the moment when I became a boss for the first time, as well as a film-maker, albeit fledgling, although at the time it didn't seem like it was going to augur any such success. Within forty-eight hours of Daniel and I setting off together, I almost got arrested and we were in a serious car accident that could've killed us both—on two consecutive nights.

We were at the 2014 Kentucky Derby, where we went because I wanted to interview the Derby princesses. These were high-achieving college women, on track to become teachers, doctors, and lawyers. They had entered a contest which had originated in the 1950s to be crowned the princesses of the Derby. I'd thought that, in a book and film about how social media was impacting the lives of young women and girls, it was important to revisit princess culture, now that social media, with its emphasis on physical appearance, was reinforcing a central tenet of princess ideology: that a girl's most valuable asset is her beauty.

And so why did these impressive young college women want to be Derby princesses? I wanted to know. Why wasn't this something they eschewed as feminists, which they all said they were? When I asked them about it, they said that being crowned a princess was "empowering" and an "honor." (Though one did say she did it for the wardrobe. They were given dresses.)

Like so many other things once seen as sexist, wanting to be a princess—which the writer Marjorie Williams once deftly described as "to aspire to perpetual daughterhood, to permanent shelter. To dependency"—had been repackaged as "feminist."

I had seen my own daughter fall prey to princess culture when she was about five. After seeing DVDs of *Snow White* and *Cinderella* and all the princess stuff overflowing in the toy stores, she had started wanting to wear her princess dresses every day, even to bed at night. It creeped me out, and I stopped showing her these films. It made me think of when I was a little girl and my mother would take me to see the princess movies when Disney would rerelease them in theaters. It would be just me and her, not my brothers, because my mother said these movies were "just for girls." She saw it as a mother-daughter bonding experience for us, as some moms still do today. But looking back, it strikes me as a kind of unwitting indoctrination. "I wish I'd never seen that stuff either," my mother told me later. "I wish I'd grown up on *Wonder Woman*."

Were princess movies part of why, somewhere deep inside, I felt that I should be traditionally feminine, submissive, and compliant? A study done in 2016 found that girls who were consumers of princess movies and so-called princess products were more likely to "display and approve of more traditionally feminine, subservient behavior." So was being raised on *Snow White* part of why I'd always believed that someday, my prince would come—and that when he did, we would fall in love at first sight? Perhaps in about the instant it takes to swipe right?

"You met this guy on Tinder," Daniel pointed out, that day when we were driving along in LA, talking about Abel. "And aren't you the one who's always telling me these dating apps turn women into objects for male consumption? So how can you trust any guy who would pick you up that way?"

Good question.

• • •

122

Daniel and I followed the Derby princesses to a party on a steamboat and then to a very white country club where everybody sang "My Old Kentucky Home," and then to the Kentucky Derby parade in Louisville, where the princesses waved from a float. It was during this parade that I realized I'd struck gold with my new cameraman. He ran up and down the street, his big arms hoisting the camera, shooting everything from the sleepy-eyed mayor of Louisville rolling by in a convertible to the little girls scrambling in the street for candy.

Then, when we went back to the Airbnb, he set up the computer on the desk and showed me the footage without me even having to ask him. And it looked like a real movie.

I told him what I liked about what he'd shot and what other types of things I was looking for, and he listened and treated me like I was the director—which, of course, I was. I went to the bathroom and cried into a towel, I was so astonished and grateful.

We got up early the next day, Derby day, to go see the horses work out at Churchill Downs. There were already some good old boys at the track, drinking beer. This was going to be a long day of drinking; there was always somebody handing you a whiskey or a mint julep.

In the infield, which Hunter S. Thompson once described as "total chaos…Muscle Beach…Woodstock," we saw drunk white boys groping drunk white girls and shouting "USA! USA!" We watched California Chrome come pounding down the track for the win. The Derby princesses in their flowered hats jumped up and down and collected their bets, and then we were on our own. An old friend of mine told us about a party at some bar, and suddenly I was dancing around to Biggie Smalls, just like I had done back in the nineties. I was forty-nine, not twenty-nine, but I didn't feel any different inside. My new brother Daniel and I were having fun, bopping around.

I was letting loose when I felt a hand come and grab my butt—just some random guy in the crowd. He grinned at me in a way that made me think of Roger the boob-grabber, as he danced away. It rankled me, and I wanted to go.

Daniel asked me to drive us back to the Airbnb, since he was feeling a bit tipsy after hefting the camera all day in the hot sun. I felt completely sober, though truth be told I'd had six or eight drinks that day, but spread out over many hours and with lots of bottles of water in between, so I felt okay.

When I started to drive, I was fiddling with the controls, trying to figure out how to turn on the headlights, and it caused me to drift into another lane. I whipped the car right back. But I guess it looked fishy to the cops who saw it, because now there was a red light behind us and the *woop-woop* of a siren.

The Louisville cops who pulled us over ordered me to get out of the car. It seemed like there was a throng of white police, none of them over about the age of twenty-five. They wanted to arrest me for drunk driving. Normally I would have been scared; normally, I would have been compliant. It could have been all the drinks in me that made that night different, or it could have been my white privilege, I'm not sure. When I told this story to my friend Jeannine, who is African American, she said, "If you'd been Black, you would have been shot." And I know she's right, and that is horrifying.

But I think it was also that hand on my ass in the bar. And all those other stray hands that had landed on me over almost fifty years, all those other gropes and grabs. The outrage of it all welled up in me like a #MeToo volcano, and I exploded.

I demanded a Breathalyzer test, but the cops said they didn't have one. I demanded to take a roadside test, like walking in a straight line or standing on one leg—which they gave me, and I failed miserably. "I almost fell down because I'm old and fat and wearing heels, not because I'm *drunk*!" I insisted.

"Nancy Jo, stop arguing!" Daniel shouted at me from the car. "Shut up!"

The cops finally let me go with a ticket for reckless driving and driving without headlights. When I got back in the SUV, Daniel exclaimed, "What is *wrong* with you? Are you *crazy*?"

And suddenly, he was every guy who didn't take my side, every guy who had ever let me down, every guy who had ever doubted me—every guy who had called me crazy. My voice went down to a growl and I chewed him out very quietly. "Daniel," I said, "we are a team, and if we're gonna be a team, you have to support me." After a few minutes of this, Daniel said he was quitting, going back home the next day. I can't say I really blame him.

We got back to the Airbnb and he went in his room. What I thought was going to be this great, brother-sister working relationship had already turned into a bad marriage, and now we were getting divorced. I didn't have a cameraman anymore. I felt like a failure.

Then it occurred to me: "Hey, am I maybe going through menopause here? Is that why I went so nuts on those cops? Is something going on with my hormones?" I wasn't having hot flashes or anything, but I had never lost it on anyone quite like that before.

But I decided to think about that later. I had to do something to make me feel better now. And so I did the only thing I knew how to do, the only thing that had ever worked out for me, aside from being my daughter's mom: I worked.

I wrote a piece for *Vanity Fair* about the Derby princesses, just a short thing for the website. The editors were expecting it, and I couldn't not meet a deadline; I had never done that before. So even though it was past 4 a.m., I banged it out and sent it in with a few stills from Daniel's footage, and then went to bed. The next morning, I woke up and there was Daniel, sitting at his computer reading my piece.

"When did you write this?" he asked.

"Last night when we got back," I said.

When he finished reading it, he didn't say anything for a while, then he looked at me and said, "You ready to go to Indiana?" We were supposed to go and interview some girls there that day. I guess he figured I might've been acting like a woman on the verge of a nervous breakdown, but I was also a pro who knew how to get shit done. And that's just who you want working with you on a film.

●  ●  ●

That morning, we drove from Louisville to New Albany, Indiana, a little commuter town just across the Big Four Bridge. We spent the day with some small-town girls I'd met in Panama City Beach when they were on spring break. They were funny, sociable girls, all in flip-flops and shorts, all attending local colleges. We loved them.

They were already all on Tinder. They told us about how dating had changed since the app had come along, just a little over a year before. They talked about how "disgusting" some of the guys on it were, and how the anonymity and physical remove of the app seemed to have emboldened guys to be openly disrespectful.

"Some guys will straight up say, 'If you don't want to fuck, don't message me,'" one girl said. And yet these same girls were swiping and swiping and checking their messages throughout our interviews, as if they couldn't stop using it.

By the time Daniel and I got back to Louisville that night, it was dark. We were driving through a residential section of town when all of sudden a car came sailing through a stop sign and we ran right into it. Our airbags blew. I sort of passed out as I saw us heading toward the car and realized we were going to hit it. I hadn't banged my head or anything; I guess I was just in shock.

The next thing I knew, we were standing in the middle of the road next to our totaled SUV. The driver and passengers in the other car were thankfully okay. I was trembling all over. I'm pretty good in a crisis, usually, but this was different; my whole body was shaking. I don't know if it was from the accumulation of all the crazy things that had happened in the last couple of days, or what, but I just couldn't stop shaking.

The police came and made a report. Daniel called the rental car company, which sent a tow truck; it wasn't our fault, so there weren't any problems, and we went back to the Airbnb in a cab. We sat on the couch. Daniel brought me a shot of bourbon.

"I don't know why I'm still shaking," I said, embarrassed. My foot couldn't stop tapping the floor. "I don't know what's wrong with me."

"Maybe it has something to do with your dad," he said gently.

It was then that I remembered that, on our plane ride down to Louisville, we had told each other a bit about our lives, and I had mentioned to him that my dad had died after being in a car accident in West Palm Beach in 2005. I was amazed that Daniel remembered this, and that he had seen in my reaction to the crash something I hadn't even seen myself.

My poor father. He was coming home from the airport when the cab he was riding in hit a pole along the road. We still don't know why. The driver was instantly killed. My dad was thrown from the car. Almost every bone in his body was broken. It took a while for the ambulance to get there; someone driving by had called 911. He was in the hospital for a couple of weeks, in a coma, before he had to be taken off life support.

Daniel gave me a hug. I hadn't felt that in a long time, the feeling of a man hugging you to comfort you when you're upset.

He went back into his room to watch *House of Cards*. It was late, but we were both too frazzled to go to sleep. And so I went on the Internet, on Facebook, and somehow made my way to Axel Wang's page.

I know, I know—I had no reason to miss Axel. But maybe it wasn't even Axel I was missing. Maybe I was missing having a man in my life, missing someone I could be close to, someone I could call up and tell him, "Hey, you'll never guess what happened to me, I was in this crazy car accident tonight..." Maybe I was missing my brother Danny, who had also died—of an epileptic seizure, in 2005, three months before our father. Or maybe I just missed my dad.

And then when I went on Axel's Facebook page, I saw Axel with his girlfriend.

His girlfriend? Was that even a word people used anymore?

His relationship status still said "single." But on closer scrutiny, this woman appeared to be someone Axel had been hanging out with pretty regularly for the entire time he had been dating me.

Or *had* he been dating me?

He had left it remarkably open. So open, that if I had ever checked his Facebook page when we were sleeping with each other—which I had not—he could have easily gaslighted me: "Oh, but she's not really my *girlfriend*."

But there they were in photos, Axel and this young woman, taking in museums (museums? Axel?), playing pool together, eating gelato. Apparently while Axel and I had been doing our reporters-on-the-road rom-com thing, he had been doing this whole other hipsters-in-Bushwick rom-com directed by Judd Apatow.

I had heard about this type of double life men lead online, but I guess I didn't think it could ever happen to me. And why not? I'd been cheated on more than Mrs. Tom Jones, starting with the notorious college professor who told me he was desperately in love with me and was going to leave his wife and take me with him to live in New York.

"Are you fucking Professor X?" the grad student in the college library demanded, one chilly afternoon in New Haven. "Because I am too." I had to go home to New Hampshire and recuperate for a few weeks after that, I was so upset by it. It was my first experience of this type of betrayal.

I didn't even want Axel anymore. But knowing that he had lied and betrayed me made me want him and miss him, made me angry and sad and kind of want to kill him.

He'd been seeing another woman *and* he'd messed up my footage?!

When I got back to New York after that Louisville trip, I started running every day to try and clear my head. I ran along the East River all the way down to South Street Seaport and back. I'd stop at the Williamsburg Bridge and look across the water to where Axel lived, wondering if he was with that other woman, and if he ever thought of me.

One day when I was running, I got these terrible pains in my chest. I thought I was having a heart attack. I took my phone out of my armband and googled "heart attack symptoms," and found a link which said: "Extreme loneliness can trigger stress cardiomyopathy, colloquially known as 'broken heart syndrome'..."

I wondered if my heart was breaking—not just for Axel, but at the thought of Axel being my last chance for love. I'd be fifty soon. My iTunes started playing Annie Lennox singing "Walking on Broken Glass" as I walked back home. ("Since you've abandoned me / My whole life has crashed...")

I went to Sake Bar Satsko, looking for Satsko, but she wasn't there. The only person in the place was Mike, the bartender who looked like Jesus with a nose ring. I told him about Axel and my false-alarm heart attack.

"Why don't you just fuck somebody on Tinder?" he said. "That's what I always do when this shit happens. Just fuck away the pain."

●  ●  ●

My first dating app date was with a guy I met on OkCupid. Whenever I talked about him with my Sake Bar Satsko friends, I always referred to him as Jack the Skateboard Boy. It seemed a fitting name for him, as if he were the main character in one of those lugubrious movies from the 1950s about juvenile delinquents.

I went on OkCupid to try and help myself feel better. After that day when I felt the symptoms of broken heart syndrome, I started wondering if I might be depressed (not knowing, yet, that depression is another symptom of menopause, along with mood swings), but I didn't think of seeking help, having had such a rocky experience with the mental health care industry in the past.

There was the male psychiatrist who said that the burning in my bladder was "just my way of punishing myself." And a female therapist who told me, "Why you keep picking men who treat you badly is because on some level you must want to be treated badly."

"But what about misogyny?" I asked her. "I don't actually know a woman who hasn't been mistreated by a man at some point. Do you?"

"We're not here to talk about me," she said, blinking.

I also didn't have the greatest health insurance, and I was close to being broke again, so I didn't know how I would afford a therapist even if I wanted to see one. But then here came this yummy-looking non-prescription drug to help—the shiny OkCupid app, with its cheery pink-and-blue logo. I downloaded it one night while lying in bed, and almost immediately felt a little rush at just the prospect of finding someone to "fuck away the pain."

I chose OkCupid because it was the dating app I'd seen my young women friends using most often. It seemed they were always on it lately—swiping, swiping—ever since OkCupid had added the swipe mechanic to its mobile app, not long after Tinder came on the market. They'd shown me pictures of guys they'd matched with and the harassing messages they'd received. Some of them had received hundreds of such messages, for on OkCupid, anyone could contact you—there was no filter. Some of these messages were so egregiously offensive, I wondered what effect it was having on these young women, to be continually confronted with this abusive type of thing; but they already seemed to have become inured to it, perhaps out of necessity. And in this way, I think, dating apps normalize harassment.

"Hi," said Amy, reading a message on her phone one night at Satsko's. "I'm looking for a cute girl like you that has a bit of a kinky side, so I'm curious if you fantasize about rough sex. Do you think you would like to get choke-fucked, tied up, slapped, throat-fucked, and cummed on? I think we could have a wild afternoon together, but I am happy just to share brunch with you."

She dropped her iPhone on the bar and threw up her hands in exasperation. We laughed. But I noticed that nobody ever talked about *why* they were using these apps, when it was virtually guaranteed they'd be harassed.

The rapiness of the OkCupid experience had already been the subject of a few articles and blogs. In 2012, *BuzzFeed News* ran "The Proto-Rapists of OkCupid," a piece about how common it was for men on dating sites to act as if it was "cute to bring up rape" as a come-on to women. "If there's anywhere on the internet with more rape-vibes than a right-wing blog," said this piece, "it's internet dating sites." Such criticisms of dating apps were quickly muted, however, drowned out by the celebratory articles in the business pages after the launch of Tinder.

I skipped most of the rapey questions in the lengthy OkCupid question-naire, many of which were extremely sexual. Why would I want to share with an online dating company whether I'd thought about doing *that*? I wondered. And then there were those questions which seemed less about prurience than just some sort of psycho fuckery: "Have you ever written something on the wall of a public toilet?" "Are your parents ugly?" "In a certain light, wouldn't nuclear war be exciting?" What?

In 2014, OkCupid cofounder Christian Rudder did a blog post entitled "We Experiment on Human Beings!" revealing that the company had been mining users' data in order to conduct experiments on them, such as lying to them about their match potential with other users in order to see if they would like each other better (which they did). In an interview, Rudder called the trove of data available to Internet companies "an irresistible sociological opportunity."

But OkCupid users reacted negatively to the news of these experiments, which had forced them to think about their privacy. "You're just lying to people," a user named Brandon commented on Rudder's post. "I don't think you should be so casual about it." Apparently the allure of the app was such that overall usage didn't suffer, however.

The Ashley Madison data breach which happened in 2015 raised another such alarm, when hackers leaked a gigantic download of customer data, including names, emails, home addresses, and credit card information from the site. Sadly, these revelations led to a couple of suicides. Ashley Madison is openly marketed to be used for facilitating extramarital affairs. "Life is short. Have an affair," says its website.

Dating sites have never been secure, and yet hundreds of millions of people all over the world are on them, sharing their most intimate thoughts and fantasies—sharing not only with these data-hoovering companies, but with other users, strangers—potential love matches, yes, but also potential stalkers and rapists.

And soon I would be doing exactly the same thing.

I was already paranoid about privacy issues from everything I was reading as research for my book and film. I didn't want anyone to recognize me on OkCupid, so I chose a fake username, like many people did back then. I was Cat the Mac. I guess I thought it sounded sexy. It was a stripper name, the name of a girl assassin. It's weird to me now to think how, knowing I was entering a dating space, I was automatically sexualizing myself with "Cat"—*Here, pussy, pussy*—and "Mac"—as in a Mac Daddy, or player. I chose a profile picture from a few years before, convincing myself I hadn't changed that much.

Within minutes of going on OkCupid for the first time—which, again, I did while lying in bed alone in the middle of the night—there were men asking me if they could come over and fuck right now. "Up for some company?" "Hey, where are you located?" "So, you want some young dick?" What?!

I'd set my "discovery" for ages twenty-three to twenty-nine. If I was going to "fuck away the pain," I thought it might as well be with someone young and hot. I'd heard about the possibility of having instantaneous sex on dating apps, but to experience it for myself for the first time felt bizarre and disturbing and disgusting and a little bit exciting all at the same time.

"My junk is huge," one guy messaged me. Oh my God.

The sheer speed and volume of it was crazy—I felt like I was watching a scene in a movie where a woman in a miniskirt goes walking past an aircraft carrier full of sailors standing on the deck, hooting and whistling. But how were they finding me so quickly? I wondered, still unaccustomed to the efficiency of the algorithms. And how did they know if they wanted to have sex with me? "Oooh," I thought, my blood rushing with excitement, "I must be even more attractive than I thought…" But I also felt a bit scared, like an old doe stumbling into an open field surrounded by men with rifles.

I got so flustered, I was about to delete the app just minutes after downloading it when I got a message from Jack the Skateboard Boy. In his profile picture he looked like a young Robert Downey Jr.—the RDJ of *Weird*

*Science*. He was sitting on the floor surrounded by albums. His profile said he was "strictly a vinyl guy."

He messaged me, asking if I meant to click the OkCupid option of "casual sex" as one of the things I was looking for on the app. He explained that he was trying to be solicitous of me, because choosing "casual sex" was surely going to send a stampede of sleazy guys my way, and he wanted to spare me that, he said, as I looked like a "very nice person." Hardly any women on the app ever said they were up for "casual sex," he said.

"Ohhh," I thought, beginning to understand the reason for my popularity. I took "casual sex" off my profile immediately and changed it to say that I was only open to "friends," "short-term dating," and "long-term dating."

But wasn't this kind of ironic? I asked Jack, after we had started messaging back and forth. Because didn't we live in a time when women were supposed to be able to ask for exactly what they wanted sexually, without judgment?

Well you *can*, he replied, but that doesn't mean some guys won't see you as a woman "they don't have to treat that well."

In other words, a slut.

It was an interesting conundrum: if you say you want casual sex on a dating app, then men will give you casual sex, but that doesn't necessarily mean that they will treat you like a human being—in fact, quite the contrary. A young woman I follow on Twitter seemed to speak of the experience of many women when she said: "Straight men do not have the range to have casual sex without being damaging and demeaning."

So just minutes into my experience with dating apps, this is what I'd learned: exercising your sexual independence by expressing your desire for a casual encounter through the use of this technology could actually lead to *more* sexist behavior from men, many of whom would see it as an opportunity to treat you as an object—a "cum-sleeve," as one of my young women friends indelicately put it. The problem seemed to be that women's sexual liberation is far greater than most straight men's; they have not caught up.

A couple of years later, when I was interviewing a group of friends in

Brooklyn for my film, one of the young men, Aton, described his shock when he realized that his first Tinder date was actually going to have sex with him.

"The first time I met a Tinder girl," he said, "she came to my house and I'm like, you can't really be here to fuck—this is way too easy, bro. Like, that's cool, that's what I want—but really? Like you went through all this trouble to come all the way here to *fuck*?"

The young women at the table rolled their eyes. "Women should be able to do what we want," said a young woman named Darian, "and you not be like, 'Oh, wow, is this really happening?' What you're saying is, 'I can't believe she's down'—but a lot of girls are down. Sometimes we *do* want a one-night stand, and sometimes we want more from a guy. So stop expecting the same thing from a woman just because she wanted that from someone else."

More than 150 years after the feminists at the Seneca Falls Convention of 1848 decried how men had given "to the world a different code of morals for men and women," women are still being held to a different standard when it comes to sex. "There is still a pervasive double standard," the feminist academic Elizabeth Armstrong said when I interviewed her. "For young women, the problem in navigating sexuality and relationships is still gender inequality."

"But isn't it obvious why?" I thought, lying in bed that night as I messaged with Jack the Skateboard Boy. Once again, in the midst of a feminist wave, men were angry about women gaining more independence and power, and so they were using slut-shaming as a weapon to try to undermine our sense of power, with the help of these new dating platforms.

● ● ●

Jack and I exchanged numbers and then moved over to texting through our phones—it was the usual move, I was soon to learn. We texted for an hour or so, talking about the albums in his profile pic and the bands we liked. Typical dating stuff. "Hey," I thought, "I can do this."

But I'd never flirted over text before, and I began to find it frustratingly disjointed and slow. I missed talking on the phone. I missed hearing a man's voice on the other end of the line. I realized that whenever I'd gotten really turned on by a guy, it usually involved the sound of his voice and his use of words. I wanted to be able to talk to this guy, to spin my web of enchantment through my own little purrs and turns of phrase. "But the whole point of using technology to date seems to be that you don't have to use language anymore," observed Brett, a young woman I interviewed in Austin, Texas. "People communicate mostly through pictures and GIFs and emojis. We're losing the art of conversation."

On text, there was also the absence of laughter. I missed being able to laugh, and make someone laugh. Where was the joy in this? I wondered, wishing this interminable texting conversation with Jack would end. But I also knew that his generation didn't love to talk on the phone, and I didn't want to seem too eager or to startle him by asking him to give me a call. I did tell him that I don't love texting, at which point he asked if he could "just come over and continue the conversation in person"—which I declined. It was 2 a.m.

After some more back-and-forth, I finally got him to agree to meet me at a wine bar in my neighborhood a few nights later. I should have seen his immediate attempt at a booty call as a warning sign, but I was so excited at the prospect of meeting up with this young man who was going to take all my blues away, I was already googling "best first date places in the East Village." It seems so silly now. I had so much to learn.

I immersed myself in getting ready for this date. I've always loved that feeling of getting ready to meet up with someone new, of preparing for an adventure, for companionship, for conversation, or whatever the night might bring, including, possibly, sex. In the nineties, it was the race home after work on a Friday evening or a Saturday afternoon leisurely spent taking a bath and then getting a mani-pedi with all the other ladies flocking to the neighborhood salons to prepare for the arrival of their dates. Listening to "Beautiful Stranger" on my Discman, maybe stopping off at La Petite Coquette on University Place to pick up some new lingerie, or at Toys in Babeland if I was feeling especially frisky.

Suddenly I was feeling nervous, walking over to the wine bar to meet Jack—nervous because I knew that I no longer looked like the forty-two-year-old woman in my profile picture, nervous because this was a strange and new kind of meeting—not quite like a blind date, since we didn't know anyone in common, and not like going on a date with someone you had already met in person, either.

"I'm not sure if I like this," I thought as I got closer to the bar. I thought about turning around and going home. After all, I thought, if I just deleted my profile, then Jack could never find me. I hadn't told him my last name or any personal information. I was already experiencing the way in which dating apps foster ghosting: *I could just bail...* But then, I did want to see what this new kind of dating was like. I convinced myself that, if nothing else, it was research.

● ● ●

When I got to the wine bar, Jack was standing outside. I wanted to laugh out loud. He was wearing a hoodie and oversized jeans, almost like rave jeans, and holding a skateboard with a purple devil emoji painted on it. He had skateboarded all the way from Brooklyn, he said, across the Williamsburg Bridge. He looked like an overgrown boy, although somewhat balding. He didn't look like a young Robert Downey Jr.—he looked like a young Paul Giamatti (not that there's anything wrong with that), the Paul Giamatti of *The Truman Show*.

But then again, I didn't look much like my profile picture, either. "When your date looks nothing like his or her picture" turns up more than three hundred million results on Google, so I don't think we were the first people to cheat. We squinted at each other a moment, as if trying to satisfy ourselves that we *somewhat* resembled our photos, and then went inside.

We sat in a booth in the back and ordered wine. Jack seemed very serious—almost petulant, *almost* angry with me, as if we were already in some kind of lovers' spat, although we'd only just met. I could see right away that this wasn't about the profile picture; it was something else.

I think most women have experienced this sort of silent anger in men. It seems to come out of nowhere and makes you wonder, What did I do? Have I stepped on his ego, said the wrong thing? It's the free-ranging anger of misogyny, always ready to make women feel uneasy and try and throw us off guard. But usually it's men who are the ones actually feeling anxious.

I suspected this, but in the moment, all my deep-rooted good-girl training came rising up, and I just felt like it was up to me to make it all better somehow. I kept the conversation going, tossing my hair around and trying to be charming. I managed to draw out of Jack that he was from San Francisco, had gone to a good liberal arts school, and now lived with three roommates in Brooklyn. He worked in a record store, he said, although he wanted to be a music critic. "I had a piece on the Cloud Nothings on *Brooklyn Vegan*," he muttered.

"Um, have you ever been on a date with an older woman before?" I asked, after a little while.

"Oh," he said, voice dripping with sarcasm, "is this a 'date'?"

I almost got up and left. There was anger in me too, these days, running like a hot steam pipe just under the surface of my mood. I had felt it burbling and hissing there ever since that night in Louisville when the cops had tried to arrest me. I hadn't quite fully accepted that I was going through menopause, yet, I just knew that a lot of the time, these days, I was ready to go all *Kill Bill* on somebody. Usually a man. Maybe I had just finally had it with men.

"Well what the fuck do you think this is?" I asked. I realized later that Jack might have actually been asking an honest question, however nastily;

he might have just been echoing the current dating culture. "People have an aversion to calling something a date now," my artist friend Austin told me, and Mike the bartender said, "I told my friends I was taking this girl to dinner, and they said, '*Dinner*?' And I was like, yeah, I gotta *eat*." A philosophy professor at Boston College, Kerry Cronin, had been in the news for teaching her students how to go on dates. "They don't even know what it is," she said in an interview.

But in the moment, I took Jack's question as an insult, thinking what he meant was, "You think I would go on a date with *you*?" And I wasn't having any insults from young men who didn't look like Robert Downey Jr.

"Of course this is a date," I fumed, "and where do you get off coming to a date in a bad mood? The whole point of the date is to have fun, and you're sitting here giving me the stink eye."

"Well I'm just really confused by what you want out of this," he said, astonished. "Like, first you say you want casual sex, and then we're at the *wine bar*."

"You're the one who told me not to say I wanted casual sex!" I said.

"Yeah," he protested, "but I figured you still wanted it, if you put it on your *profile*—"

"Oh, I see," I said. "So casual sex can't include a glass of wine? And maybe some conversation? Or do we have to make each other feel like we can barely stand each other's company, and then go off and fuck? Sorry, not interested. If I want casual sex, I want it with some fun attached. It doesn't have to be *love*—"

"Oh," Jack said, sneering, "you want love. 'What you call love was invented by guys like me to sell nylons.'"

"Don Draper, *Mad Men*, season one," I said.

"You like *Mad Men*?"

"Of course..."

• • •

On the way back to my apartment building, he let me ride his skateboard. I hadn't ridden a skateboard since I was ten years old. I rode it down the sidewalk past Tompkins Square Park.

We sat at the picnic table on the back patio of my building and drank PBR—his choice; he'd bought it at the deli. "Let me see your phone," he said. He wanted to see what music I had. I don't know what he was expecting. Maybe, because I was older, he thought all he was going to find was Barry Manilow and Journey (although I must confess, I do like some Journey). He seemed mystified to see that I had some music he deemed suitably cool.

"You like Ice Cube?" he said. "How do you even know Ice Cube? Because you saw him in *Barbershop*?"

I didn't want to tell him that I had spent a long night interviewing Cube in LA in 1998 when he was directing his first movie, *The Players Club*. Or that I'd had a yearslong affair with a well-known hip hop entrepreneur, who used to pull up outside my apartment building in his chauffeur-driven SUV and call me to come down just by saying, "Yo," and I'd come running.

I couldn't tell him these things because it might intimidate him, and then he would never want to fuck me. And even though I still wasn't sure if I wanted to fuck him, I knew that I wanted him to want to fuck me. I guess it was because I was older, and feeling it, that I especially wanted him to want me, even though I already thought he was kind of an idiot.

Older men can tell stories about the exciting things they've done, and young women will be amazed and still want to fuck them—which I knew because I once was that young woman, listening starry-eyed to the stories of old guys in leather jackets. But older women have to be careful what they say if they want to have sex, because if you're too interesting, experienced, or have had "too many" sex partners, a man may not want to fuck you. I knew this from my experience with Axel, who would always get rather distant and annoyed whenever I regaled him with a story about some exciting chapter in my past. If you're a woman, the fullness of your experience can be a turnoff to some men—unfortunately for them, as they miss out on knowing all the richness of the lives of the interesting women they meet.

So I just said, "Oh, yeah, I loved him in *Boyz n the Hood*." Like Lindsay Lohan in *Mean Girls* pretending not to know how to do math.

Jack laughed, as if he thought it was all just so unlikely that this older lady was, like, remotely cool. We listened to some more songs and drank some more beers.

"This is great," he said after a while. "I'm actually having a good time!"

I asked him if he didn't always have a good time when he went out with women he met on dating apps.

"Sometimes," he said. "But usually it's just weird. That's why everyone gets drunk and just has sex."

"And is it good sex?" I asked.

"Not really," he said, grimacing. "Sometimes it is. But girls, you know, sometimes you can't have sex with them because they get so drunk. And I would never take advantage," he added, in a way that managed to sound patronizing rather than upstanding.

"Why do you think they drink so much?" I asked.

"Who knows," he said with a frown. "Because they're trying to keep up with guys, because they think it's cool. But they can't drink as much as guys because they're just—smaller."

I had read about the rise in alcoholism among young women and wondered if it was connected to hookup culture and how being drunk made it easier to fuck someone without emotional intimacy. But now I was wondering if more young women were becoming alcoholics because they had to deal with young men like Jack, if he was any indication of who was available.

"Nobody really knows each other, so it's just weird," he said.

"Do you feel like you know me?" I asked, batting my eyes.

"Well, yes," he said. "I *do*."

I knew this was my cue to switch it up on him, to confuse him and make him want to chase after me, and to see if I wanted to be chased.

"Oh," I said, feigning a yawn. "I'm getting kind of tired. I think it might be time for me to go upstairs."

"But wait," he said, bewildered, "we have a few more beers—"

"I know," I said, "but I think I better go upstairs. Follow me, I'll show you the way out to the street."

Then I got up and walked slowly across the patio and through the sliding door, into my building's little downstairs gym, where it was dark. I swiveled my hips about as subtly as Jessica Rabbit, paused a moment at the door and looked back across the patio at Jack. There he was, still sitting at the picnic table, looking a bit stricken. Was he going to get it? I wondered. I gave him a few seconds to make his move and—no—yes—he got up and came over.

He pushed me up against the wall and kissed me, and I kissed him back. He was a surprisingly good kisser, with his full lips and soft tongue, and he had kind of a good body underneath that hoodie, big shoulders and arms and hands that went up and down me as he kissed me, holding me tight.

But I felt nothing, kissing him back.

My mind got lost in a memory: I thought of a time in Panama City Beach, when Axel and I were driving along at night in some horrible orange rental car, singing along loudly to "We Are the Champions" on the radio...But why was I thinking of Axel now? Did I wish I was with him? No, I didn't.

Jack fell to his knees and, all in a whoosh, pulled down my jeans—he hadn't asked if this was okay, nor did I say no. It surprised me, him going downtown, as I had heard from my young women friends that guys their age were woefully remiss when it came to this. "They act like cunnilingus is a crazy kink," said a young woman I follow on Twitter. *Plus ça change*...But here was Jack, with his tongue sneaking its way around inside my vagina, searching for my clit. I gently tilted his head into position, an encouragement which seemed to excite him; he gave a little grunt.

And yet I just felt bored, like I had when we were texting—I think because it was all so overdetermined. We both knew we were going to have sex. We'd met on a dating app, colloquially known as a hookup app, where I'd said I was up for casual sex, however dishonestly we had danced around that. And while it sounded great in theory—the ability to order casual sex like you would chicken pad thai—this didn't feel hot. It didn't feel erotic, not like the times when I'd met someone out in the world and just went for it.

I thought of the time I met my Brazilian friend João in my deli at 4 a.m., and we started walking and talking, and we walked and talked until he pushed me up against a wall on Barrow Street and we started making out. It was a steamy summer night, and the sounds of the city were buzzing all around us as we both came from just kissing and grinding. We were regular sex partners for about a year after that; he was one of the guests at the Baby Dinner.

And now here was this young man on his knees in front of me with his tongue slurping around inside my vagina, and I *wanted* it to be hot, but it just felt...dull. He was doing his best. But I just wanted it to be over.

It made me think of those studies claiming that millennials are having less sex. Which I always find a bit hard to believe, because the researchers never seem to want to acknowledge the fact that young people today are having all different kinds of sex: cybersex, chaturbation (or mutual masturbation to screen sessions), masturbation to porn, masturbation to nudes. And if millennials are actually having less sex, then how do these researchers explain the crazy rise in STIs? They never do.

But let's say it's true, that millennials are having less sex. Well, I thought, would it come as any surprise? I couldn't think of a less sexy way to start having sex with someone than the way Jack and I had arrived at this moment—first by finding each other in the dehumanizing haystack of OkCupid, then by texting back and forth our truncated inanities, followed by that awkward date. It wasn't exciting, it wasn't serendipitous. It had all been set up by Christian Rudder's data-collecting company disguised as a match-making service. No wonder a millennial told the *Washington Post*: "There really isn't anything magical about [sex]."

Jack continued his efforts as I stood there wondering if I should give a moan to reward him for giving it such a go. And suddenly it occurred to me that the reason he might be putting on this display of oral attention was because I was older, and he wanted to impress me. It made me feel tender toward him for a moment, and I ran my hand through his thinning hair.

"Do you have a condom?" I murmured. I don't really know why I suggested it. Why was I about to have sex with this young man I didn't even like? I think many heterosexual women have had this experience of having sex just because we feel it's expected of us, because it's what we've been taught that we are for: to be fucked. It's technically our choice, sometimes, even when it isn't true agency in the sense of an informed and enlightened choice, and it certainly isn't our preference.

"Like a lot of the time, I feel pressured to," said Melanie, a young woman I interviewed at UC Santa Cruz. "I feel like, okay, this is a Tinder date, this is kind of like what's supposed to happen. And I've talked to so many friends who tell me about times when they've felt so uncomfortable, but they just went along with it.

"Because it's hard to speak up for yourself sometimes, you know?" she went on. "Especially when it's someone you know you don't know that well—like, you don't want to be weird, and you don't want them to think you think *they're* weird."

"And sometimes it's just a way to get them out of there," said Lauren, a young woman I interviewed in New York. "Sometimes it's a blow job just to end the date and make them go home."

"Do I have a *condom?*" Jack said, standing up. "What is this, 1984?"

He picked the year as a random dig at my age, I think, but the reference to a dystopian narrative was unintentionally apt.

It turned out that he did have a condom, lodged in his wallet, just like boys of old. He put it on his thick dick and then he was up inside me, thrusting against me, up against the wall. It isn't that I didn't want to do it, and it didn't actually feel bad, but it didn't feel good, either. I didn't feel much of anything except how weird it was to be having sex with Jack the Skateboard Boy in the downstairs gym of my building.

And then, it was over.

I didn't know what the protocol was, so I waited for him to say something. He just zipped up his pants and picked up his jacket and waited for me to open the basement door.

I went with him upstairs to the lobby, trying not to look at him in the elevator.

I walked him to the front door of the building.

He wore a sheepish smile.

"So how'd you like your first Tinder date?" he asked.

"We met on OkCupid," I reminded him, and he said, "Oh yeah, right!"

"Well, I had fun," he said. "I'd say, 'I'll text you,' but if you don't hear from me, nothing personal, you know?"

Then he skateboarded down the block.

I went upstairs and paid the babysitter. "Did you have fun?" she asked. I lied and said, "Yes." And then I got into bed and stared at the ceiling. I couldn't sleep. So I downloaded Tinder and started swiping.

● ● ●

Ahmet asked me if I wanted to come inside his café and sit for a while, but I told him I had better go meet Abel. I was starting to shiver.

"Nancy, do you love Mountain Boy?" he asked me then. "Because if you love him, then it will be very hard not to take him back. Maybe you shouldn't go see him now, if you really want to stay away from him."

"But how can I know if I love him?" I moaned.

I had made a fool of myself so many times in love. My romantic life called up images of Titania enchanted with Bottom affixed with the head of an ass. What evil Puck had sprinkled pixie dust on me the day I swooned for Axel Wang?

"Then I say to you, as a friend, don't go to him," Ahmet said. "You need someone who will commit to you. Maybe an older guy—"

"Ha," I said. "Older guys have discovered dating apps too. They discovered online dating a long time ago. And nothing has ever been the same."

Actually, I had used online dating in its early days. In 2002, I was briefly on Match.com. It was the first online dating site, launched in 1995, and it still had a bit of a stigma back then. It was seen as something for older people, people who didn't know how to meet someone, people who were a little bit desperate. That was me, at thirty-eight. For the last couple of years, I had been ensconced in taking care of my new baby.

It was the sweetest time. I loved every minute of being with her, which was almost all the time, since I worked at home. I did my work at night, or whenever she was sleeping. I loved feeding her and bathing her and reading her books. I loved playing with her and taking her to the park and to the Metropolitan Museum of Art. I loved going for walks with her and our dog Boo. I loved holding her and being next to her baby-soft skin. I loved her chubby little legs.

All the impulses in me to nurture someone felt rewarded by her love. It was so strange to me when someone would say, "Oh, I'm sorry," when they found out I was a single mom. If they didn't see how happy I was, then they weren't looking.

I was also enjoying having a respite from men. For the first time in more than twenty years, I wasn't trying to date anyone or feeling the pressure to look cute—and yet, when I see pictures of myself from those days, I think I did look cute, although I didn't know it. I didn't think about how I looked, and I didn't care—I didn't have time to care. I just threw on a T-shirt, jeans, and Converse sneakers every day. I had short hair back then, and I would just ruffle it back. I didn't wear makeup. It felt so restful to be freed from thinking about all those superficial concerns. It was so nice, I found, not to have a man around to constantly have to please, to not have to wonder and worry about his judgments and moods and all the other irksome things that always seemed to go along with dealing with men—or, at least, always had for me.

Oh, those luxurious naps we would take together, baby and me.

Being a single mom is hard work, of course—or should I say, a constant effort. But I couldn't ever really think of it as work in the way that, say, digging a ditch is work. To me it was pleasurable. Another income would have made it a lot easier. I got very good at getting cash advances on credit cards and transferring the balances. I was always scrambling to pay the next bill, even though I had a new job which paid more than the last one.

I got hired by Graydon when I was eight months pregnant. I was amazed he wanted me. The day of my interview, I was wearing an oversized skateboarding sweatshirt with a big dragon on it; I didn't have a clue how to dress as a pregnant lady. *Vanity Fair* seemed so fancy; I didn't feel like I fit in. But I knew how to work hard. Five days after giving birth, I was on my way out to the Hamptons, with my baby beside me in a little basket, to interview a teenage socialite named Paris Hilton. I did the first story on Paris. "Just tell 'em I'm a teenager," she told me. "Tell 'em I'm a normal kid." There was nothing really normal about the day I spent with her and her family, but that's what made it interesting. While I was writing this story, Paris's mother, Kathy, sent me a bathtub-sized box of baby things from an expensive store. I'm not quite sure why she did this, but I thought it best to send it back.

I knew I was lucky. I was a writer at *Vanity Fair*. And yet, this wonderful new job still didn't pay enough to support me and my daughter, factoring in childcare and preschool and health care, which the magazine didn't provide even to some of us on staff.

It occurred to me, as I juggled my bills, that if a privileged white woman like me still struggled financially on her own with one child, then how much harder must it be for a single woman with a bunch of kids? Or women in poverty? Or women of color, who are routinely paid less on the dollar? Or women with disabilities, or women whose children have health problems? I came to see the persistent stereotype of single motherhood being bad for kids as pernicious and wrong. What's bad for kids is living in poverty, which happens to be the case for most children of single mothers, due to the vicious cycle of poverty which puts them there in the first place—not to mention deadbeat dads.

There has been a steady rise in the rate of babies born to single mothers over the last four decades. In 2018, it was about 40 percent, up from 10 percent in 1970. About one in five children now lives with a single mom. A lot of this is due to the fact that the marriage rate has been concurrently declining. People who study the reasons for this decline cite everything from the introduction of the Pill to more women entering the workforce to falling incomes. But I wonder why they never look at the impact of technology.

The biggest and most persistent drop in the marriage rate in nearly 150 years has been since the 1990s, concurrent with the widespread adoption of the Internet and online dating. There seems to be a blind spot over the fact that, for better or worse, this technology has made marriage and committed relationships look less attractive and less necessary, especially for straight men.

Some women are also realizing that marriage isn't necessarily the state of bliss it's often made out to be, and some are choosing single motherhood, like I did. But whatever the reason more women are becoming single moms, there isn't enough social support for women raising kids on their own, the numbers of which will only continue to increase under current conditions.

Universal childcare and pre-K alone would have made a huge difference in my life; universal health care would have made everything better. Other countries have all this, and we could too if we could just see it as the healthy and compassionate way to run a nation that it is, instead of slut-shaming and punishing single mothers and, by association, their children. Single moms are often misperceived to be mainly women of color, which in reality they're not. But the racism in this country goes so deep that some people would rather withhold social support from single mothers and their children just because they mistakenly believe they aren't white.

These thoughts would be on my mind as I pushed my daughter around in her stroller, pointing at things and teaching her words.

● ● ●

I went on Match.com after Zazie started going to preschool a couple of days a week. I had finally lost "the baby weight," more or less, and started wondering, Well, am I ever going to have sex again? Am I ready to get back out there and hunt for a decent man? But how was I ever going to meet this man, stuck in my apartment, which I would not leave because my daughter needed me?

In addition, there was my anxiety over my mounting credit card debt. While I was quite happy raising my baby on my own, I was starting to see that this was going to be a challenge to pull off financially. For the first time, I was thinking about men in economic terms. I didn't need a man, but did I need another breadwinner?

Match.com was $24.95 a month back then. You can see how they got people to pay such hefty fees, when it was one of the only games in town. Through the site, I met Peter, a lawyer who lived in Carroll Gardens, Brooklyn. He was Rutger Hauer–blond and thought himself very urbane, with his little round glasses and an affected voice that sounded like Vincent Price's. Not my usual type; but he was somebody's idea of a catch. He was a partner at a law firm and owned his own brownstone. He was divorced with a couple of young kids.

We sent each other long emails, which is what you did back then, if you were an educated, professional baby boomer like us (I was born in the last year of the boom, but have always felt like the rebellious little sister), raised on the idea that courtship involved words, lots of words. The model was the romantic letter writing in the novels of Jane Austen, shamelessly referenced in *You've Got Mail*—a film which did much to promote the idea that the person typing away on the other side of the screen just might be your soulmate.

We don't need go into how this beloved rom-com was also an apology for the wipeout of independent bookstores—a not-unrelated concept, since what we're ultimately talking about here is corporate capitalism and its appropriation of dating. It is interesting to remember that Tom Hanks was emotionally cheating on his girlfriend when he was emailing Meg Ryan all those heartfelt missives. Funny that wasn't seen as an issue.

I've kept Peter's emails all these years, printed out and filed in a folder—not because I was flattered by them or thought they were lovely, like the letters I had received back in the days when men sent love letters to women they wanted to woo, but because they seemed like artifacts of a cultural shift. When I read them today, I'm appalled. I can't quite believe that I ever agreed to go on a date with this man, much less kept emailing him for weeks. I hope it was just my anxiety over my looming credit card debt. Jane Austen herself, who never shied away from frankness about the economic realities underpinning courtship, would have understood that; I hope my self-esteem wasn't *that* low.

"Your shotgun barrage really turns me on in a way," Peter wrote—I guess I'd emailed him in a rapid-fire style, probably trying to impress him. "Challenging and yielding, promising and holding back. I like my women a little bit crazy"—wait, what, now I'm crazy?—"but solidly in reality and intellectually challenging and quick-witted. If you can't keep up with your barrage in person I may tire of you"—if I don't tire of you first, Mr. Pompous!—"and if you do keep up your barrage I may be unable to resist you. But I'm a crass and shallow lad, so I must see a picture that actually allows me to see what you look like."

Even back then, men were asking to "see more of you," meaning more of your bod. "And single mom is a huge red flag," Peter went on—oh my God, what a douche!—"but there are always reasons (such as separated with kids, which is mine); what's yours?"

Well, I got knocked up, Peter, and unlike the plot of another improbable rom-com (*Knocked Up*), my pregnancy didn't inspire undying devotion in the biological dad, a man I didn't want to be with, either. But unbelievably, even after emails like this, I agreed to spend Thanksgiving with Peter. His ex-wife had the kids and he was all alone. I went out to Brooklyn with Zazie and, as she scooted around on his kids' toy car in the other room, Peter tried to get me into bed. It was then that it began to sink in—what he had been telling me in another email, which I guess I'd just sort of willfully ignored—that people were using online dating services to just hook up. Even back then, many of the men on these sites weren't looking for love or relationships or soulmates—they just wanted sex.

"Oh darling," he had written, "you're new to this whole cyber charade. It's just a pixeled singles bar. I've been on and off this and other services for around a year. Not trying to date not trying to bed the entire Eastern Seaboard, but…It was so intoxicating at first, and then addictive. My computer sat there throbbing and calling to me all the time; it started to get in the way of work. The first step was to admit that I was powerless."

Years later, reading this email, I felt nauseous; I hated that I had something in common with pompous Peter in my addiction to dating apps.

I broke up with him the day after that Thanksgiving. It wasn't really his trying to hook up with me immediately that had turned me off. It was when he said, "Oh, Nancy Jo, you *are* a good mom," when he saw me playing with Zazie—it was a surprise to him, I guess because I was a single mom. I went off Match.com after that, back to doing what was really giving me joy: taking care of my baby, writing my stories. I ordered another credit card when the offer came in the mail.

● ● ●

I've wondered sometimes whether millennials—who seem to so resent baby boomers for being at the wheel of our collective car as it sped toward the cliff at the end of the world—have ever stopped to consider the fact that online dating, which millennials were the first generation to adopt en masse, was actually popularized by a white male baby boomer.

Gary Kremen, the cofounder of Match.com, was born in 1963, the same year as Peter, my awful match from the site. He belongs to a generation of guys, the fathers of the young men using online dating today, who were raised on pop culture flooded with sexism and sexualization. Ads which commented incessantly on women's shapes and sizes, Bo Derek as the perfect ten, *Playboys* and *Hustlers* underneath our dads' beds, to name a few notable influences.

Kremen, who graduated from Northwestern with degrees in electrical engineering and computer science, was also involved in one of the biggest legal battles ever waged for a public domain—Sex.com—the rights to which were stolen from him and which he successfully sued to retain. So the guy who's often credited with inventing online dating also had the foresight to secure the domain name for what is now one of the leading porn sites in the world. (He has since sold it, and Match.com as well.)

Both things—online dating and online porn—were on Kremen's mind at exactly the same time in the mid-nineties. He seemed to see the future rise of these two industries, which today are the two biggest on the Internet in terms of paid content. The annual revenue of online dating was an estimated $2.5 billion in 2018, second only to online porn, the annual revenue of which has been estimated at anywhere from $6 billion to $97 billion. (Because most porn companies are privately held, it's impossible to get an accurate estimate. It has been reported that online porn has more monthly visitors than Netflix, Twitter, and Amazon combined, making up around 30 percent of all Internet traffic).

It's hard not to see these two industries as intimately connected, like a double helix of cyber misogyny. With online porn, straight men suddenly had immediate access to images of women performing sex acts, or having sex acts performed on them, and with online dating, they had quicker access to actual women with whom they might perform such acts, in cyberspace or in real life. I've interviewed guys who talk about going from one to the other, from porn to dating apps, as if they're related activities. They talk about getting horny from watching porn—which studies say the majority of men do watch on a regular basis—and then hitting up a woman on a dating app to come over and have sex. Or watching porn while sexting with women on dating apps, doing both simultaneously.

The crux of the connection between online porn and online dating, I think, goes to the different expectations straight men and women have of an online dating encounter. According to studies, most straight men on dating apps are mainly looking for unfettered casual sex, which is not dissimilar to what they're looking for when they seek the release they get from masturbating to pornography.

"It's just true," said Justin McLeod, the hipsterish thirtysomething founder of the dating app Hinge, when I interviewed him for my film, "that men and women, taken as groups, think about these things differently. That doesn't mean that all men are looking for a hookup or all women are looking for a relationship. But, on the whole, the majority of women are looking pretty much exclusively for a relationship on these services, and a majority of the men are primarily looking to hook up.

"And you can say that that isn't so different from society at large," McLeod went on, "but I do think the way that these services are designed sort of like tips the scale in culture toward hookups and sort of gives men—or gives those looking for hookups—the upper hand, essentially, in this new world."

McLeod, a graduate of Harvard Business School, is a self-proclaimed romantic who proposed to his wife after a long, dramatic courtship (they met in college). After reading my piece "Tinder and the Dawn of the 'Dating Apocalypse,'" he said that he became concerned, wondering if Hinge users were experiencing dating app dating the way my sources had talked about in the story, as something degrading or dehumanizing. So in 2016, he did a survey of more than eighty thousand of his users. Among Hinge's findings (and yes, read "the leading swiping app" as Tinder):

Six in ten men on the leading swiping app are looking primarily for flings or entertainment. Eighty-one percent of Hinge users have never found a long-term relationship on any swiping app. Thirty percent of surveyed women on swiping apps have been lied to about a match's relationship status. Twenty-one percent of surveyed users on the leading swiping app have been ghosted after sleeping with a match.

McLeod decided that swiping itself was the problem, so he got rid of it in the 2016 relaunch of Hinge. Ever since then, Hinge (which was bought by Match Group in 2018) has been trying to remake its app as the one "designed to be deleted"—suggesting that you won't need it anymore after you find the love of your life on it. But however well-meaning a slogan, I think it's an impossible dream; the crucial problem lies with the majority of men still seeing the technology of dating apps as a thing which gives them easy access to sex.

It's a long-standing fantasy for straight men to be able to summon a female sex partner through technology, which historically men have seen as their exclusive realm, and something that gives them power. It's the story of Pygmalion. It's a fantasy seen in the classic 1976 sci-fi flick *Logan's Run*, in which the character played by Michael York conjures up a woman through a futuristic Tinder, clicking on a device until he finds a sex partner he likes. When she appears in his room, he immediately tries to bone her.

In *Weird Science*, directed by John Hughes, two nerdy boys create a hot female Frankenstein (Kelly LeBrock) with the intention of having sex with her. Here's the dialogue where they cook up the scheme:

"Okay, look, you know how you're always talking about how you can simulate all that stuff on your computer? What's the difference, why can't we simulate a girl?"
"I guess I could, but why? It's two-dimensional on the screen, it's not flesh and blood, Gary."
"I know that, but we can use it, we can ask it questions, we can put it in real-life sexual situations and see how it reacts. Sick, demented shit, you'll love it!"

They then debate about whether or not to give their female creation a brain, and they decide to give her a fifth-grade-level intelligence. They input *Playboys* into the program.

● ● ●

Online dating exploded in the 2000s. Match.com grew to forty-two million users and raised its fees to $42 a month. eHarmony, founded by evangelical Christian clinical psychologist Neil Clark Warren, charged $60 a month. (The allegedly science-based site didn't include gay dating, by the way, until 2010, three years after it was sued for discrimination by gays and lesbians in a class-action lawsuit.)

OkCupid, launched in 2004 by four guys who knew each other at Harvard, distinguished itself by being free—although the company never disclosed that it was actually profiting from sharing its users' data with third parties. OkCupid cofounder Christian Rudder, a married Gen Xer who had never been on an online date, did a post on the site in 2010 (which has since been deleted) entitled "Why You Should Never Pay for Online Dating."

"I'd like to show why the practice of paying for dates on sites like Match.com and eHarmony is fundamentally broken and broken in the ways that most people don't realize," Rudder wrote. "Pay sites have a unique incentive to profit from their customers' disappointment." However OkCupid was soon offering paid features too, "A-list" memberships costing from $9.95 to $19.95 a month.

Why do people pay for online dating? Most say it's because they want to find love and relationships, like the ad campaigns promise. "Looking for a real relationship? Why wait to meet someone great?" say ads for Match. But there's reason to believe that such advertising is disingenuous, although Big Dating has never been held accountable for its fraudulent claims.

That is, not until 2019, when the Federal Trade Commission (FTC) sued Match Group, Inc., alleging that the company used "fake love interest advertisements to trick hundreds of thousands of consumers into purchasing paid subscriptions on Match.com....Many consumers purchased subscriptions because of these deceptive ads, hoping to meet a real user who might be 'the one.'" As of this writing, the case is still pending.

Romance scams are another form of false advertising and a problem across dating sites and other social networking platforms. People who believe they're in real relationships get conned out of money by scammers claiming they need to pay off debts or travel to visit sick loved ones. In 2018, the FTC recorded more than twenty-one thousand romance scams, with losses amounting to $143 million, more than any other type of consumer fraud.

The pandemic has seen a spike in such scams, according to news reports. "Scammers will incorporate Covid-19 into their lies, and say things like: 'My family has it and I need money for healthcare, can you please send it?' 'No honey, I can't come see you because I'm in isolation,'" economic crimes detective Linda Herczeg told Canada's Global News.

● ● ●

"These businesses are founded by men for men," I told Ahmet, sitting in front of his café.

I was getting a bit worked up. I'd been thinking about how online dating preys on people's vulnerabilities for years, and it never failed to strike me as outrageous.

"These businesses are founded by sexist men," I told him. "So I know this is about who Abel is, and who I am, but it's also about who these companies are, and how they're influencing how men treat women."

Ahmet's eyes had glazed over. He was getting that look that men get sometimes when you use the word "sexist"—even good men like him. He was my friend and I loved him; but, being a man, he couldn't really know what it was like to be a woman on a dating app—or what it was like to be me, having been cyberbullied by one of the biggest dating sites in the world.

The guys at Tinder weren't used to encountering criticism when my story on dating apps came out in 2015. Ever since Tinder had launched, three years before, the media had been publishing glowing reports of how the wonder boys of Tinder were "revolutionizing dating." This was a few years before "techlash" had set in, with people finally questioning the notion that tech was an unmitigated good. It was before the Cambridge Analytica scandal of 2018 showed how a social media platform, Facebook, could sway an election and threaten democracy; before Google faced worldwide protests from its employees, in 2018, over its handling of sexual harassment cases; before some of the heads of Big Tech appeared before Congress via video-conference in 2020 and were grilled about everything from antitrust issues to hate speech on their sites. "Americans have become much less positive about tech companies' impact on the U.S.," said a 2019 survey by Pew, reporting that only 50 percent of Americans now viewed the tech industry favorably, a drop from 71 percent in 2015.

What happened to me occurred in 2015, when the media was still treating the heads of successful start-ups the way they had treated Elizabeth Holmes—the chief executive officer of Theranos who made fraudulent claims about her Edison blood-testing machine—as if they were not to be questioned. The early stories about Tinder are remarkable for how they sound like press releases. In 2014, Sean Rad, the cofounder and CEO of Tinder, appeared on the cover of *Forbes* with the headline, "The Crazy Saga of the World's Hottest App." The story succeeded in being a love letter to Rad, even though it included an exclusive report on how he had just been fired as CEO of his own company, in part due to a sexual harassment lawsuit concerning his best friend, then Tinder chief marketing officer Justin Mateen, and his former vice president of marketing, Whitney Wolfe.

The *Forbes* piece mentioned Rad's "military-grade $115,000 Mercedes G Class wagon" and his socialite girlfriend, whom he had allegedly met on Tinder: "In case you're wondering about the caliber of Tinder users, yes, Rad met [tech billionaire Michael] Dell's daughter Alexa on Tinder." It made much of Tinder's estimated worth, allegedly "somewhere between $1 billion and $1.5 billion."

But it didn't talk about the sexual harassment women were experiencing on the app, or the graphic images they were receiving, or the stories which had already come out about Warriena Wright, the New Zealand woman who fell to her death on a Tinder date that same year.

Rad, born in 1986, was a rich kid who grew up in Bel Air, the child of Iranian immigrants who owned an electronics-manufacturing company. At Beverly Hills High, he was a self-described awkward boy with "deforming" acne who wanted to be a rock star. He dropped out of the University of Southern California in 2006 to start Orgoo, a messaging service that was shut down after an FBI investigation into how users were storing and transmitting child pornography on its servers—another detail of Rad's bio that didn't make its way into his *Forbes* profile, either.

In 2012, Rad joined Hatch Labs, an incubator for mobile apps that was partially funded by IAC, the corporate owner of Match Group. At Hatch Labs, Rad and his USC pal Mateen, a former frat boy, started working on a dating app they saw as "Hot or Not for mobile." "They thought they were going to get laid with it," said Silicon Valley entrepreneur Andrew Frame, who tried to buy Tinder early on, in an interview.

According to someone I spoke to who worked at Hatch Labs, "[Rad] only hired really attractive women. It was kind of a joke. The sales team was Whitney Wolfe and Justin's sister Alexa. They called them 'Sean's Angels,'" a reference to *Charlie's Angels*. "It was under the guise of 'attractive women make better sales folk.'"

Rad and Mateen, then both twenty-five, soon became known for throwing Tinder pool parties in LA with lots of "models and pretty women," their Hatch Labs colleague said. "It was supposedly a marketing move, to get these women on the app. But they were enjoying the proximity. Sean's a bro, that's the best way to describe him."

• • •

At the end of 2012, Whitney Wolfe, a former sorority girl from Salt Lake City, then twenty-three years old, went off to launch Tinder on college campuses, introducing the app at her alma mater, Southern Methodist University. When I interviewed Wolfe for my documentary in 2016, she spoke proudly of how she got women in SMU sororities to put their pictures on Tinder as a way to lure men into downloading it.

"I went into the sorority houses," said Wolfe, now twenty-seven, in her room at New York's tony Crosby Street Hotel, "and I basically got up on those tables, stood up on a chair, screamed over hundreds of girls eating dinner...and pretty much imposed Tinder onto every single phone. And then I ran as fast as I could with my fun, enthusiastic girlfriends...and we went into the frat houses. And we had already put the women on the app, right? And so we went into the frat houses and we said, 'Guys, guys, listen up....Every Kappa, every Pi Phi, every Theta, they're on this app and they're waiting for you to match with them. Download it! Download it!'"

Wolfe smiled. "And lo and behold," she said, "they saw all of these girls who they otherwise would have to wait until Thursday at the bars to see. And so something really magic took place right there—there was *access*."

Historically, access to women has equaled power for men; it's the power of kings and politicians. As Wolfe described it, it sounded almost as if the purpose of Tinder was to serve up women to men—and men in frat houses, no less, which have become all but synonymous with rape culture (an extensive body of research on the problem of rape in fraternity houses goes back to the 1990s. Fraternity men are significantly more likely to commit rape, according to studies). So, seen from a certain angle, you could almost say that Tinder was invented by a couple of misogynistic tech bros and marketed by a foot soldier for the patriarchy, all of whom the media made into stars.

As Tinder caught fire, registering "a billion swipes a day" by its own account, its founders became giddy with their success. In 2014, Rad and

Mateen posted on their Instagram feeds screenshots of a new Urban Dictionary term: "Tinder slut." Mateen told *Bloomberg Businessweek* that when the entry appeared, "it was an exciting day for us."

In her lawsuit against Tinder and IAC for sexual harassment and discrimination, Wolfe alleged that Mateen, whom she had dated, had sent her emails calling her "a desperate loser who jumps from relationship to relationship," "a gold digger," a "disease," a "club whore," and a "slut." She reportedly settled for a million dollars. And then in late 2014, Wolfe launched Bumble, marketing it as the anti-Tinder and a "feminist dating app"—although the design was sufficiently similar that, in 2018, Tinder sued Wolfe and Bumble for copyright infringement. (The case was settled in 2020; details were not disclosed.)

The main difference between Bumble and Tinder is that on Bumble only women are able to message first, which Wolfe explained to me was a way to reduce "aggressive behavior" in men by appeasing them with the "flattery" of a woman reaching out. "He doesn't have to be geared up to react to rejection," she told me that day at the Crosby, "because you've taken away the rejection and replaced it with *flattery*." Which doesn't sound very feminist.

Some of the young men I've interviewed have said that they see this feature of Bumble not as feminist, but as relieving them of the burden of having to put in any effort in order to get laid. "If a woman messages you, you know you can smash," said one young man I spoke to. "You don't have to do anything." Which isn't the way most women see it.

"There's this idea that Bumble somehow fixes the mistakes that Tinder has made. I honestly don't see how it does that," said Zoe Strimpel, a British dating historian I interviewed for my film. "The man doesn't have to lift a finger to even type you out a three-word message because now he's not *allowed* to. So once again, women are shouldering so much more of the burdens of dating—the communication work, the emotions work, the admin. Bumble is really just codifying that women have to do more work."

But Wolfe—now Whitney Wolfe Herd, after marrying Michael Herd, an oil-and-gas man she met through mutual friends while skiing in Aspen in 2017—has been as successful at marketing Bumble as a feminist dating app as she was at launching Tinder. "With Her Dating App, Women Are in Control," said a headline in the *New York Times* in 2017. In 2019, Wolfe Herd did a weekly "work diary" for the *Times*, which headlined the piece, "Fighting Misogyny, One Bumble Brand at a Time." The problems of dick pics and harassing messages, of underage users and predators, of sexual assault and rape—which happen on Bumble, as on other dating apps—have gone largely undiscussed.

The true origins of Bumble have been fairly muted as well. In fact, the "feminist dating app" was the brainchild of Andrey Andreev, a low-profile Russian entrepreneur whose own mega dating site, Badoo, has been the subject of multiple sexual-harassment allegations. Then in his late thirties, Andreev reached out to Wolfe in 2014 after reading about her breakup with Tinder and persuaded her to do a women-driven dating app rather than the social network she had originally pitched to him (a site to empower teenage girls, she told me). Andreev put up the money, becoming the majority owner of Bumble, of which he reportedly still owns as much as 79 percent to Wolfe Herd's 20 percent. But that 20 percent has made Wolfe Herd rich. In 2019, *Forbes* listed her at number seventy-two of the top eighty "richest self-made women."

● ● ●

Like Wolfe Herd, Sean Rad learned to use feminism to sell his product. In an interview in the *Evening Standard* in 2015, in answering whether Tinder was just a hookup app, he responded by saying that "feminism has led to [hookup culture] because now women are more independent in pursuing their desires. And that leads to both parties being more sexually active."

This is a common misreading of both feminism and hookup culture—a misreading whose veiled message is slut-shaming, suggesting that feminism makes women easier to get into bed, and men therefore more likely to score. But hookup culture, as it has been defined by researchers, isn't about having more sex, necessarily—it's about having sex without an emotional connection, and, arguably, this has been driven by men, since studies also show that women are generally more interested in forming relationships.

In that interview in the *Evening Standard*, Rad showed no sign of having evolved beyond the bro he always was. He said that a supermodel, "someone really, really famous," had been begging him for sex, that tech was "the new rock," and that he preferred "intellectual" girls who his "friends might think are ugly."

"Apparently," he said, "there's a term for someone who gets turned on by intellectual stuff. You know, just talking. What's the word?...I want to say 'sodomy'?" (He meant "sapiosexual.")

And in that same piece, Rad said something about me. It was a couple of months after my story "Tinder and the Dawn of the 'Dating Apocalypse'" appeared. Rad was "still defensive and upset about the article," said the *Evening Standard*, "murmuring mysteriously that he has done his own 'background research' on the writer Nancy Jo Sales and 'there's some stuff about her as an individual that will make you think differently.' He won't elaborate on the matter."

The writer of the *Evening Standard* piece never called to ask me for a response to this, nor did any of the other news outlets which subsequently repeated the smear. It seemed clear to me that Rad was trying to get back at me for doing a piece that raised questions about the cultural impact of his company, and so he had attacked me personally. This was online culture, and it was the culture of tech, a notoriously sexist industry: A woman gets out of line? Slam her.

What else could have accounted for Tinder's tweetstorm about a week after my story came out? In a single night, the Twitter account for Tinder tweeted at me more than thirty times, accusing me of bad journalism. It was an unprecedented case of corporate bullying of a journalist on social media. However, the many news reports which covered Tinder's meltdown simply mused about whether it was a corporate gaffe, "bad for their brand." I was shocked at how I was left to twist in the wind, with none of my fellow journalists coming to my defense. I wrote an open letter to Rad on VanityFair.com, figuring I'd defend myself if no one else would.

"Next time reach out to us first @nancyjosales…that's what journalists typically do," Tinder had tweeted. But I had no obligation to interview the bosses of Tinder in a piece about the experience of users on dating apps.

"If you want to tear us down with one-sided journalism, well, that's your prerogative," tweeted Tinder. But I had interviewed more than fifty people for this piece, which is actually a lot for a lifestyle story, and many experts as well.

"Talk to our many users in China and North Korea who find a way to meet people on Tinder even though Facebook is banned," Tinder said. But while Tinder was already active in more than a hundred countries by then, North Korea was not one of them. And China has its own dating apps.

Initially, I didn't think anybody would take Tinder's Twitter fit seriously. The company's response was so over-the-top. The Twitterverse seemed to find it amusing. People were tweeting humorous GIFs in response, like the one of Michael Jackson eating popcorn, indicating that this was something juicy to watch. Somebody made a meme of Kim Jong Un with a rotary phone, asking, "How do I swipe right on this thing?"

But as Tinder continued to tweet and tweet, and its tweets kept getting retweeted, the company's side of things started to gain traction. I went and looked at who was retweeting them—Who in the world would take Tinder's side on this? I wondered—and saw that it was mainly Russian bots. "Russian bots" wasn't a term in wide circulation yet, more than a year before the 2016 election. I wasn't even really sure what they were; I just saw that these re-tweets were mainly coming from Russian accounts. Many had profiles in the Cyrillic alphabet, with pictures of half-clothed women as avatars. It struck me as so strange. I told some people about it and they looked at me like I was crazy, but it was real. It gave me a feeling of dread about what could happen to a journalist—or to anyone—now, on social media, where the weapons of attack were getting stealthier by the day.

What Tinder's tweetstorm did, I think, was manufacture a backlash to my story. In the media, there were suddenly several takes which misrepresented my reporting and the concerns I was trying to raise about how dating apps had changed the experience of dating, especially for women. *Slate* called my piece a "moral panic." *Salon* said it "reads like an old person's fantasy of Tinder." The *Washington Post* said that I had "naïvely blamed today's 'hookup culture' on the popularity of a three-year-old dating app," Tinder—when, in fact, my piece clearly described the collision of a long-trending hookup culture with technology: "Hookup culture," I wrote, "has been percolating for about a hundred years."

The focus of my piece was misogyny in online dating. But none of these backlash stories ever mentioned that. It seemed ageist and sexist to me, this suggestion that I couldn't have a valid take of my own on all this, or that I didn't know what I was doing. I'd been a reporter for more than twenty years at this point and had won a few journalism awards. I was amazed to see myself cast as the naive old lady, the pearl-clutcher, the prude.

If only they knew what I was up to!

Meanwhile, my story was going viral. Through my website, I was getting emails from people all over the world—many from London, one of the cities where Tinder is used the most. (In a 2017 market study, the top places for Tinder use were listed, in order: the United States, United Kingdom, Brazil, France, Scandinavia, Finland, Australia, and India.) People were telling me how the story had resonated with them. This made me feel better, as did many supportive tweets I saw:

"Hey @Tinder, @nancyjosales is entitled to write anything she wants & if you think her article is misleading, you have no idea about this generation."

"Well done, NJS. Funny that an app that is known for casual hookups would take anything so personal. #scornedlover."

But what was this "background research" Sean Rad said he had done on me, and what was the "stuff about [me] as an individual" he allegedly knew?

I suspected that what his veiled threat was really about was that he knew, from his corporate access to my account, that I had been using Tinder.

● ● ●

I'd been using it a lot.

And OkCupid and Bumble and Hinge as well.

Like most people who use dating apps, I was on a few at the same time. Within a couple of weeks of going on them in 2014, I was swiping, swiping, swiping.

I was swiping before I went to bed at night; I was swiping when I woke up. I was swiping while I was riding the train; I was swiping while I was waiting in the dentist's office. I was swiping to procrastinate; I was swiping to battle insomnia.

I was swiping in hotel rooms in the cities I traveled to, on the road shooting my film with Daniel. But I didn't tell Daniel about any of this— no!—because he would have made fun of me and called me out. And I wasn't swiping in front of Zazie—God, no!—because I didn't want her to think that I thought it was okay to put a picture of yourself on a dating app for men to evaluate and swipe right or left. (I don't even want her to read this book.)

Dante's *Inferno* begins:

*Midway upon the journey of our life,*
*I woke to find myself in a dark wood,*
*For I had wandered off the straight path.*

That was me, stumbling into Tinderworld.

Two thousand fourteen was the year you started to see people swiping everywhere—in line at the pharmacy, at the movies, at the bank. I saw a man swiping while walking down the street. I was in a boutique buying a dress to wear to a wedding when the saleswoman helping me stopped, in the middle of ringing me up at the register, to look down at her phone, where the animated Tinder match screen had appeared with its familiar *ba-ding!*

"Oh, I got a match!" she said.

People were swiping when they were on the toilet, swiping while they were on dates—22 percent of men in the study done by Hinge said they had swiped while on a date. It was in 2014 that Tinder boasted that its users were spending an average of ninety minutes a day on the app. In 2014, people started developing "Tinderitis," a pain in the thumb from swiping. The adoption of the technology was swift and overwhelming.

What was making me do this so much? I wondered now and then as I swiped and swiped. It scared me a bit. I'd never been addicted to anything like this before, except for maybe cigarettes, when I was in my twenties and thirties, before I got pregnant with Zazie and quit. This felt like cigarette addiction to me, in the way that it was always scratching at some corner of my brain, controlling my behavior. Except that this behavior was seen as totally acceptable, not socially censured like cigarettes had come to be—it was as normalized as cigarettes were in the 1950s, when tobacco companies were still hiding the truth of what they already knew, that this stuff could kill you.

It comes as no surprise to most people when they learn that swiping was designed to be addictive. We've been hearing for years how tech companies engineer their products with endless little bangs and whistles designed to grab our attention and get us hooked. What may have surprised us more, had we been able to look into the future, would have been to see how little we've come to care about how thoroughly we're strung out on social media, and how much this has changed our behavior.

But all of this is also by design, chillingly enough.

Media theorist Douglas Rushkoff describes it this way in his book *Team Human*:

The goal [of tech companies] is to generate "behavioral change" and "habit formation," most often without the user's knowledge or consent. Behavioral design theory holds that people don't change their behaviors because of shifts in their attitudes and opinions. On the contrary, people change their attitudes to match their behaviors. In this model, we are more like machines than thinking, autonomous beings. Or at least we can be made to work that way.

So how do these companies succeed in manipulating us? Sean Parker, the former president of Facebook, confessed in an interview in 2017 that he and Mark Zuckerberg and other creators of social media had knowingly "exploited a vulnerability in human psychology" with the "social validation feedback loop" of "dopamine hits" and "likes."

"When Facebook was getting going," Parker said, "I had these people who would come up to me and they would say, 'I'm not on social media.' And I would say, 'Okay. You know, you will be.' And then they would say, 'No, no, no. I value my real life interactions. I value the moment. I value presence. I value intimacy.' And I would say, 'We'll get you eventually.'"

And how does all of this relate to swiping on dating apps? What does it mean for our choice in romantic partners, when the landscape of love, sex, and dating is now being commanded by a corporate GPS?

Jonathan Badeen, the sharp-eyed cofounder and chief strategy officer of Tinder, has said in interviews that the idea for the swipe came to him when he was rubbing off the fog on a bathroom mirror after getting out of the shower. When I interviewed him for my documentary in 2016, Badeen provided a less folksy origin story for the swipe, saying that he had based the matching aspect of the swipe mechanic on the "variable ratio schedule."

(Despite our differences in the past, I was able to convince Sean Rad to let me interview members of his team in Tinder's offices in LA. Rad himself agreed to be interviewed too, but upon our arrival his PR rep said he was busy.)

The variable ratio schedule is a concept from behavioral psychology which says that "having unpredictable yet frequent rewards is the best way to motivate someone to keep moving forward," as Badeen himself described it. In the 1970s, the controversial behavioral psychologist B. F. Skinner—who considered free will an illusion—illustrated the concept dramatically with an experiment in which he "turned pigeons into gamblers" by rewarding them at irregular intervals with the food pellets they were taught to peck for. Basically, it was pigeon Tinder.

Skinner's pigeons would keep pecking for food even when they weren't hungry, just because they had become addicted to playing the pecking game. "The pigeon can become a pathological gambler just as a person can," said the mad-scientist-looking Skinner in a TV interview about his experiment. The variable ratio schedule can also be seen in the design of slot machines and video games. "We have some of these almost game-like elements," Badeen told me. "It kinda works like a slot machine. You're excited to see who the next person is—or excited to see, did I get the match?

"It's a nice little rush," he added.

The "little rush" is a shot of dopamine, the brain's feel-good neurotransmitter. In a study of drug addicts, researchers found that just the expectation of taking a drug caused more of a dopamine release than the drug itself. And so with swiping, it's the act itself that gets the dopamine flowing, as it incites the expectation of the reward of the bouncy, slot machine–like match screen. Which means that simply swiping on a dating app can become addictive, whether or not a user ever meets up with his or her matches in person. In fact, a third of people who use dating apps say they've never actually gone on a date with someone from an app. In a 2017 study of Tinder, over 70 percent of users said they'd never met up with one of their matches in real life, and 44 percent said they used the app purely for "confidence-boosting procrastination."

● ● ●

After your brain gets that little high of a dopamine spike, an inevitable dip follows; there's a low. And so it isn't surprising that more than half of singles report feeling lonely after swiping on dating apps. It's one of the feelings that sends you back to swipe some more, to try and make this feeling go away.

It makes a kind of twisted sense that swiping on a dating app can actually lead to more loneliness, if it's causing us to engage with our screens more and interact with other human beings less. Which brings us back to social engineering.

What exactly are dating apps engineered to make us do? Why, to use them more and more. The primary aim of all social media companies, according to Sean Parker in that 2017 interview, stems from the question: "How do we consume as much of your time and conscious attention as possible?" The value of these platforms rises with use; the more people use them, the more data is collected.

So is the goal of dating apps really to help us find relationships? Or is it to get us to have a relationship with the app itself?

Well, if we're getting some sort of satisfaction from merely swiping, then what do we need to go on dates for? Why do we need to have sex? What do we need other *people* for, when we've got this absorbing little app at our fingertips? It makes you wonder again about those studies claiming young people are having less sex; if, in fact, they are, then maybe it's because they're spending so much time on dating apps—an average of ten hours a week, according to a 2018 study—that they don't have the time, or don't feel the need, to have sex with each other.

It also makes you wonder whether dating apps are actually contributing to an increase in loneliness. "There's an epidemic of loneliness among people my age," said a young man I spoke to in Santa Cruz; and according to studies, he's right. In a nationwide survey of twenty thousand adults across

America in 2018, nearly half reported being lonely, with the highest scores among Generation Z and millennials.

Young people are lonelier, I think, because they're not having as many relationships—at least not ones in real life. And sadly, the isolation required to contain the coronavirus has only made young people, and all of us, lonelier, despite our ability to communicate through screens. When the virus hit, some members of the media seemed to revel in this chance to embrace screen life, as if to say, "Hey, now we can indulge our addiction without judgment or worry that it's really bad for us!" "Coronavirus Ended the Screen-Time Debate. Screens Won," said a headline in the *New York Times*. "We've tried all sorts of things to stop us from staring into our devices. Digital detoxes. Abstinence. Now? Bring on the Zoom cocktail hour."

But having to rely on tech companies to communicate is no cause for celebration. And it's the tech industry that has actually "won" in this situation, as we've become even more dependent on its products to mediate everything we do. The challenges this presents to our health and well-being are still there. Studies suggest a link between time spent on social media and rising rates of anxiety, depression, and, yes, loneliness.

Even before Covid-19, loneliness was a growing public health concern. It can be crushing for mental health, affecting our sense of well-being and ability to function. Loneliness has been linked to a higher risk of coronary heart disease and stroke, and has been shown to have an impact on the immune system and the ability to recover from breast cancer. "We have robust evidence that [loneliness] increases risk for premature mortality," said Julianne Holt-Lunstad, a psychologist at Brigham Young University, in an interview. Conversely, studies show that people who have good relationships, who are more connected to family and friends whom they feel they can count on and trust, live longer and happier lives.

In that article in the *Evening Standard* in 2015, Sean Rad said that "our research shows eighty percent of [Tinder] users are looking for a long-term meaningful relationship." I don't doubt that this is true. It's a statistic Rad had started quoting whenever asked about Tinder being just "a hookup app." But in the past, Rad had bragged about how the app wasn't actually designed to help people find a relationship, but as a "fun" "game" for them to play. "We always saw Tinder, the interface, as a game," he said in an interview in *Time* in 2014. "Nobody joins Tinder because they're looking for something"—meaning a relationship. "They join because they want to have fun. It doesn't even matter if you match because swiping is so fun."

The goal of behavioral design theory is to make people change their attitudes to match their behaviors. And so the gamification of dating meant that dating was no longer an activity to be taken seriously—no responsibilities, no expectations, just the fun of instant gratification. It was after enough users became sufficiently addicted to this type of fun that Tinder started charging for its services. In 2015, the company began limiting the number of free daily right swipes to around a hundred for users who didn't buy into the new premium service, Tinder Plus, at $9.99 a month for users under thirty years old and $19.99 for those thirty and above. (In 2018, a California court ruled this to be a form of age discrimination.)

"It's all a numbers game," is a phrase I've heard again and again from dating app users.

• • •

I would lie in bed at night and swipe and swipe, telling myself, I'm just going to do this for ten minutes, but then ten minutes would turn into twenty, and then twenty would become an hour, and then two. A boredom would set in, as I swiped and swiped on the interminable stacks of profile pics, which reminded me of the boredom I felt when I would click and scroll on Amazon even when I didn't really have anything I needed to buy. A 2017 study reported that more than 50 percent of people say they used Tinder out of "boredom"; perhaps, I thought, it was that same, distracted state of consumer boredom that makes you want to keep shopping.

I set my geolocation at just a mile, because I wasn't going to travel far for casual sex, and in New York, you didn't have to. So my feed was showing a lot of hipster dudes in the downtown area, college students, Wall Street bros (one of whom spanked me so hard my butt stung for days), and assorted other bizarro guys I would never have known were living near me if it hadn't been for dating apps. Like the guy whose profile pic consisted of an empty dungeon out of *Eyes Wide Shut*. Or the guy who said he was going to prison soon and wanted someone to "fuck until they locked the door" behind him. Swipe left.

There were so many guys, it was impossible not to categorize them just to try to make some sense of it all: There were guys who stood before great vistas, on mountaintops, often overlooking Machu Picchu, strangely enough. There were guys who stood on boat decks holding up fish—the infamous "fish pic." There were guys pumping iron in the gym, bulging muscles flexing. There were an inordinate number of guys cavorting with baby tigers and even more nuzzling adorable dogs. There were guys in groups, partying with their bros ("What happens in Vegas!"). There were guys holding babies ("She's just my niece") and even some posing with their mothers and grandmothers. There were guys who sat in their cars wearing sunglasses, looking disaffected. I saw my deli guy posing that way. I hoped to God he hadn't seen me on the app, the next time I went in for a breakfast sandwich.

When I interviewed the clinical psychologist Jennifer Powell-Lunder, she noted, "What's interesting is that the men tend to present themselves in very stereotypically 'male' ways…whereas women tend to present themselves in more sexual ways. And this goes back to the basics, the old Barbie and Ken culture."

Are dating apps reinforcing heteronormativity? Stereotyped notions of women and men? I wondered, as I swiped. As part of my research, I sometimes went on Tinder as a straight man, using a fake profile picture of a guy I'd downloaded from Google Images. I wanted to see what kinds of pictures women were posting on dating apps when they knew they were being appraised by the male swiper's gaze. I didn't swipe on them or talk to them, I just went on to look.

And it was true—many of the women were posting sexualized images, showing cleavage, cupping their breasts, licking their lips, staring at the camera with smoldering looks. There were a lot of bikini shots and booty shots. Sometimes the pictures looked like porn, with the women in lingerie, lounging on beds. The written profiles were often pornier than the images: "I'm the kinda girl you can take home to your parents, but I'll blow you on the way there." "I bet you can't guess how many sex toys I have."

I didn't judge them. I did however question the effect dating apps were having on women's already socialized impulse to self-sexualize. And of course, I was doing exactly the same thing with my own profile pic, which was a close-up of my face with my eyes doing that thing that I always did whenever I wanted someone to know I was ready to fuck him. Fuck me eyes had never failed me.

Because I was trying to escape recognition, this was the only picture I posted, which frequently caused suspicion on the part of these young men who had grown up with social media, where everybody had been catfished, and on which everybody posted endless pictures of themselves, on an almost daily basis.

"Why do you only have one picture?" they would ask. One picture could mean the lady wasn't real—or she was fat (which I wasn't quite yet). But the combination of my fuck me eyes and my age at the time, forty-nine, was enough to tap into some powerful, hardwired fantasies about older women.

It hadn't registered for me yet, in those early days of my dating app use, that I was tapping into a demographic which had come of age during the MILF porn craze and the megastardom of Lisa Ann, the fortysomething porn star who gained mainstream acclaim after appearing in porn films parodying Sarah Palin (*Who's Nailin' Paylin?* was released on Election Day 2008). In 2015, Lisa Ann was in the news for dating eighteen-year-old Notre Dame football player Justin Brent. In an interview in *GQ,* she said, "I'm 42.

I'm looking at 18, 19, 20 year old guys. They're at the beginning of their lives, so they're still excited, naive and simple."

Excited, yes, but naive and simple, Lisa Ann?

"Are you really 49?" they messaged me. I could almost hear their pants unzipping, their hearts pounding. "So how's your Friday night?" "Heyyyyy." "What's someone like you doing on Tinder?" "Young stud at your service." "I'm a very mature 25-year-old so don't let that be a problem." "Nice eyes." "49???" "You really turn me on, hope that's not a bad thing." "Let's make out…"

It wasn't only the swiping I was getting addicted to, but the attention of all these excited young men. I'd spent my twenties married and in difficult relationships, and now here I was, like Scarlett O'Hara at the barbecue, surrounded by cute boys begging to run and get me a piece of pie. I liked the feeling of toying with them, especially the little misogynazis, the ones who sent crass and offensive opening lines: "I want to come on your tits." "I want to throat fuck you till you gag." "I'm thinking we do a few tequila shots, I do some coke on your ass, pull your hair back and bend you over while listening to Zeppelin IV on vinyl." That last one's profile picture was Christian Bale in *American Psycho*.

Another one messaged me: "You look good enough to rape."

If they sent something like this, then I'd get them into a thread in which I'd both tease and antagonize them, torture them until they were begging to come over or calling me a "bitch" for not letting them—and then I'd ghost them. "What you're ignoring me you fucking bitch?" they'd protest. It was a kind of cyber blood sport, which always left me feeling sickened and spent. I refused to let myself be degraded by these anonymous jerks. But then, what was I doing even talking to them, if they weren't getting to me?

● ● ●

"I have to go," I told Ahmet, as I was sitting with him outside his café that night after I got the text from Abel. "I have to go!"

My heart was racing.

I stood up.

"He's waiting for me!" I exclaimed—worried, suddenly, that he wasn't going to be there if I didn't run and catch him.

Ahmet stood up and hugged me, saying, "I just want you to be happy, Nancy. Just be careful—"

But I couldn't feel any comfort from his big man's body just then. My inner alarm bell was clanging.

"I know, and thank you," I mumbled, mashed against his chest. "I'll let you know what happens!" I called, scurrying down the block.

And then it was the rush to see Abel all over again—forgetting everything he'd ever done to offend me in the past. What did it matter, when he was waiting for me now? Beautiful Abel who murmured sweet things to me in the dark. I started to run like Fran Kubelik running to her man at the end of *The Apartment*, like Lola in *Run Lola Run*.

"But why, why, why are you running?" I could no longer stop to ask. I already knew.

I was running to him because I'd been thinking about the year before we met, when I'd been trapped in the dating app inferno, and thinking about it had made me anxious and afraid that I would find myself going back there again, if I got lonely enough. Because Abel had saved me from all that—he'd saved me from *them*, all the other, miserable young men. Oh, why had I ever told him to go away? I wondered now.

He'd saved me from the incessant sext threads that felt like labor, with the anonymous guys who just wanted to know that you were there on the other side of the screen so they could jerk off; saved me from guys like Beard Boy, whose building I was passing now on my way home. Beard Boy who had ghosted me—who, I thought, might have *been* a ghost. I'd first seen him in a mirror selfie on OkCupid, just a reflection of a guy with a beard in a towel in front of a mirror, looking at himself in a cell phone screen. *Was* he real? Or just a reflection of a reflection? I couldn't be sure.

I remembered Beard Boy's bathroom selfies more than almost anything about him—except for his beard, which was massive, with endless layers, like a giant onion of beard. I remembered he had sex with me as if he was doing push-ups—up and down, up and down—robotically going through the motions, with none of the pleasure or heat of good sex. I'd watched Beard Boy having sex with me with a kind of morbid fascination. I'd seen videos on the Internet of tortoises having sex with more passion.

And then there was Theo the Ass Eater, who'd only wanted to do what *he* wanted to do—which was eat ass. Our date started at Manitoba's, and then we had sex on my roof, where he made a great display of eating my ass, which wasn't something I had asked him to do, nor was it something I particularly wanted him to do. He seemed very determined to show off his prowess in this activity, despite the challenge of doing it on a lounge chair, which kept threatening to fold up on us as he buried his face in my behind. He made no attempt to pleasure me in any other way, as if he might have thought my clit was in my butt.

"Can you even just point to it?" I asked a young man I called the Clueless Boy. "Do you even know where it is?"

"Isn't it…inside?" asked the Clueless Boy, looking like a schoolboy who hadn't prepared for a test. Which, in a way, he was. The American educational system's idea of sex ed is to talk about pregnancy prevention and abstinence—never pleasure or equality, and not always even consent.

Teaching the Clueless Boy to pleasure me through clitoral stimulation proved so difficult, I just let him fuck me to get it over with. I've wondered sometimes if some men just pretend to be unteachable, so they can get right to the fucking.

But Beard Boy and Theo the Ass Eater and the Clueless Boy weren't the only ones who were bad—they were all kind of bad. Or, more accurately, hookup sex is bad, especially for straight women, who orgasm only about half as often as men in the hookup sex they have with men, according to studies.

Which most women already know, but don't often say out loud, because in a society in which we're treated as objects for men's assessment, we're supposed to love it when men just look at us, forget about touch us.

The truth is, though, that many straight men don't even *try* to make women love having sex with them, especially not if they see them as "just a hookup." A study of twenty-four thousand students at twenty-one colleges over six years, from 2005 to 2011, found that only about 40 percent of straight women had an orgasm during their last hookup involving sexual intercourse, compared to 80 percent of straight men. About 75 percent of women in this survey also said that they had had an orgasm the last time they had sex in a committed relationship. Because apparently when men actually care about the women they are fucking, they will make an effort to please them. "We attribute [women having more orgasms in relationships] to practice with a partner, which yields better success at orgasm, and we also think the guys care more in a relationship," said Paula England, the New York University sociologist who led the research, in an interview.

The young women I've talked to are more forthright about the so-called orgasm gap than most women my age, who often seem to feel hesitant to criticize the ways of men in bed, as if admitting to any frustrations would suggest a failing of one's own. "Frigid" isn't a word that gets used much anymore, but its chilling effect has resonated through the ages. Well into the twentieth century, women who complained of a lack of sexual satisfaction were called "hysterical" and sometimes even put in institutions. (Always white women, that is; women of color were more likely to be sexualized, in a racist context.)

"What's a real orgasm like? I wouldn't know," said Courtney, a student at the University of Delaware I interviewed for my book *American Girls*. "I know how to give one to *myself*."

"Yeah, but men don't know what to do," said her friend Jessica.

"Without [a vibrator] I can't have one," Courtney said. "It's never happened [with a guy]. It's a huge problem."

"It would be great if they could just have the ability to perform and not come in two seconds," said their friend Rebecca.

As I listened to them, and other young women, it seemed crazy to me that, more than fifty years after the sexual revolution of the 1960s, straight women were still not routinely getting off when they had sex with men. Once again, slut-shaming and double standards were robbing us of pleasure, equality, and respect. Some men seemed to think that if women were going to act like sluts and have casual sex with them, then we didn't deserve to enjoy it. Even more troubling was that some women—myself included sometimes—made sure men were getting off, even when we weren't.

"In many ways, in sexual hookup culture, women get the short end of the stick," Justin Garcia, the executive director at Kinsey, told me. "They're more focused on male entitlement to pleasure as opposed to their own. They're at greater risk for stigma associated with engaging in casual sex. They're at greater risk for sexually transmitted infections, and they're at greater risk for sexual violence that is associated with sexual behavior in general but including in the hookup context.

"So we can ask ourselves," Garcia went on, "why do women engage in this behavior at all? And that's an interesting question. It's not to say that women don't enjoy casual sex or that they dislike casual sex. And it's also not to say that there are not some men who dislike casual sex. Both men and women experience variation. But on average, we see that women bear more of the burden associated with hookup culture. So for women, this is a much more complex behavior."

It seemed to me you couldn't divorce this "complex behavior" from the fact of misogyny and internalized misogyny. If researchers weren't factoring in misogyny when studying sexuality, they would never arrive at the truth about women and sex. Add to this the fact that technology has weaponized misogyny, and you get a clearer picture of what's currently going on. It seemed to me these questions had a very clear answer: there is still not equality in bed. But what was the *answer*?

I didn't know. And that was why I was running home to my Mountain Boy. Because thinking of my past experiences with men on dating apps had made my mind run to the ecstasy and abandonment I had felt with him, like a refuge.

● ● ●

But he wasn't there. I didn't see him in front of my building.

I looked up and down the block, hoping to catch sight of him in the shadows. Sometimes when he was waiting for me, he liked to hang back in the darkness and smoke a cigarette. Sometimes he liked to startle me while I was putting my key in the door, to see me jump and squeal. He liked to play the practical joker.

But no—I looked around—he wasn't there.

I went inside, hoping to see him standing in the lobby or the hallway outside my door. Maybe somebody had let him in, I thought, bounding up the stairs, hoping he would be waiting there for me.

But he wasn't there.

I looked at my phone. He hadn't sent a text.

It would have been unlike him to send one. He wasn't one to check in; he didn't like to seem thirsty. That was how he seemed to prefer me, chasing after him to find out where he was when he was late.

I was sure he didn't like me keeping him waiting that night.

Maybe I shouldn't have kept him waiting…

"Ah, well, maybe I missed my chance," I thought, looking around my empty apartment. It had seemed very empty since I'd sent Abel away a few months before. Zazie didn't live with me anymore; she was living in a college dorm. I saw her often, since her school was in the city, but it was still a big change for me. But empty nest syndrome hadn't really kicked in until I sent Abel away. At first, when she moved out, it had felt like such a lark, being free to have him come and go.

But now, it was just quiet. And dark. And cold. I turned on some lights. I snapped on a space heater. I put the kettle on to make some tea, and, looking at the stove, I thought again of that first week with Abel. I saw myself there by the stove, making him pancakes, and him coming over and putting his arms around my waist, moving my hair to the side and kissing my neck...

"I've been meaning to tell you," I said, sitting with him at the counter that morning, blissfully watching him eat. Why did every single thing he did make me want to break out in song?

"I have to go to Florida today," I told him. More reporting for my book *American Girls.*

"Oh, you do?" he said, wiping his mouth. He seemed taken aback, perhaps thinking of the prospect of having to find his next place to stay. Or maybe that first week of us being together had felt like a little Shangri-la to him, too. "That's cool. I can clear out," he said.

And then I felt bad for kicking him out, knowing he had nowhere to go. So I said, "You can stay here while I'm gone. Stay as long as you like."

Now, why was I asking this young man I had only known a week to stay in my apartment while I was away? The real reason wasn't because I was so generous, as Abel would always say whenever I would do anything for him. I just didn't want him to leave—because he might never come back. Because I had had sex with him more than twenty times, because I knew his closeness in the dark, and I knew him well enough to know that I wanted to keep him there however I could, like a puppy in a crate.

But I also knew that I didn't really know him that well. And that's why, the instant I asked him to stay, I started to feel a little uneasy.

"Well, thanks," he said, giving me a maple-syrupy kiss.

"It's no problem," I told him.

He was quiet a moment. And then he said, "I think I gotta tell you something..."

It was then he told me about Rowena, the woman he'd been seeing, who had recently moved away. She was an Argentinian singer, the daughter of a friend of his father's, and they had been seeing each other, and now she had moved back home. They'd been playing music together, he said, "did an album together on SoundCloud. We were playing in the subway, doing open mics. Didn't go girlfriend-boyfriend officially, but, you know, I thought we had something. We were holding hands, kissing in public…"

And then, he said, she had slept with another guy, which he found out one day when he came home. I could tell from the way he was telling it that it was his first heartbreak.

"Is that why you don't have a place to live?" I asked.

"Something like that," he said.

"I'm sorry," I said. "I know it hurts."

"There's lotsa worse things." He shrugged.

"It may not seem like it right now," I told him, "but you'll love somebody again."

"I don't think I ever will," he said after a moment.

It was just a thing young lovers say, but it made my heart ache, because he was also saying he would never love me.

Then he went to work, and I packed my bags and got ready to go to Florida. I was proud of myself for doing the right thing, for bucking him up and not making a fuss about him fucking me for a week and not telling me that he was in love with someone else. In the nineties, I would have kicked him to the curb; in the eighties, I would have made a scene. But this was Tinderworld, and in this amusement park, anything goes. So what was the big deal? So he loved someone else. So what? What business was it of mine?

I convinced myself I was okay with all these things.

But then I was wild for him to come back from work so I could fuck him again before I went to Florida on the evening plane. I waited and waited, even delayed getting a cab, texting him on the sidewalk outside my building as it was getting dark: "Gotta go soon, coming? I need to give you the key…"

But he didn't answer. And he didn't come back.

# Three

The morning of my fiftieth birthday, I had a dream that I was on a boat out on the ocean with my daughter. The sun was shining, and we were having a lovely time, laughing and talking. I was telling her about some of my funny Tinder dates (which I had never done in real life).

Then I noticed there was something down deep in the water.

"It's a whale," I said.

It was a gray whale, floating upside down, seemingly in repose.

"I wonder if it will come up and we can get a closer look," I said, growing uneasy at its enormity and its mysteriousness.

"No," Zazie said. "I think it's dead."

And then I could see that the whale was a corpse, sinking in the water.

That whale was me! I realized, upon waking. I woke up on the morning of my fiftieth birthday gripped with fear. My whole body was cramping, one tight pretzel of existential dread.

"Oh my God," I thought, "I'm more than halfway to death!"

No other birthday had hit me this hard. I was always just moving ahead, never looking back, perhaps afraid of getting lost in the past. But now it seemed impossible not to think of the impossible. I was in a whole new demographic: old. And fifty felt as heavy as a tombstone.

And so did my body, lately—I'd been gaining weight, especially around the middle. I was turning into Burl Ives. I hadn't allowed myself to think too much about what would happen if I got on a scale, since it had finally become clear to me that I'd been perimenopausal for a few years. My only other physical symptoms were menstrual cramps that felt like labor pains and an annoying spate of acne—isn't going through puberty in reverse fun? And of course, my close-up vision was long gone. I wandered around the house like Mr. Magoo, a pair of readers in every room. How I hated the old people words—*readers*. It seemed like every time I opened the mailbox there was another mailer from the AARP. Please, just stop!

I had very little to look to as reference for how women cope with middle age, because we're usually left out of the discussion entirely, as if we might as well be dead. Once we become sexually inviable in the eyes of a world that places our ultimate value on our fuckability, it's as if we've been canceled.

But here I was, having sex with a different young man every few weeks— sometimes every few days—so should I be proud of myself, or ashamed? I didn't know. I did know that when men go through their midlife crises and start running after younger women, they're often mocked—but with a wink, as in, "You old devil, you." Dating younger women is seen as somewhat icky for men, but also excusable: "Well of *course* they want young things. Who doesn't?" But for older women, it's a different story. Having sex with younger men made you an animal, a cougar—or, in my demographic, a jaguar (the big cat with the strongest bite).

Not even Cher had been able to get away with dating a younger man without being judged; she has said that Rob Camilletti, eighteen years her junior, had been the "one true love" of her life, but their relationship "got torn apart by the media," which sneeringly called him the "Bagel Boy" because he'd worked in a bagel store. I always noticed now whenever they went after Brigitte Macron, the wife of Emmanuel, the president of France. "Times are changing," she responded diplomatically, in 2019, when someone disparaged her for being older than her husband—then sixty-six to his forty-two.

And perhaps times are changing, but glacially. A 2018 study of dating apps reported that the most popular age for women on these sites is just eighteen, while for men it is fifty. This is because, according to the study, straight men are primarily interested in a woman's youth and physical attractiveness, while straight women are more interested in a man's experience, education, and earning power. Which echoes a 2010 study from OkCupid saying that most men on the app are primarily interested in matching with younger women—surprise! "The median 30-year-old man spends as much time messaging teenage girls as he does women his own age," OkCupid reported blandly on its blog, as if this was all just fine. So, in other words, in the eyes of most straight men, dating apps are useful not just for accessing female bodies, but young female bodies.

Whenever I checked out the older guys on these apps, guys in their late forties and fifties and beyond—and it seemed there were more of them every day—I often saw them advertising themselves as sugar daddies. "Only swipe right if you want to be spoiled," they said. "Miss the days when a guy would pick up the check?" Many had profile pictures in which they appeared in some corny rich guy pose, like holding up a glass of champagne; I once saw an actual cravat. Their sense that the women on these apps were similar to what they might call "hookers" was perhaps not so different from many of the younger men's—the older guys just weren't as good at hiding it.

"Sexual vampires looking for young energy," clucked a fiftysomething friend of mine, when I told her what I had seen. "How would these guys ever even meet eighteen-year-olds to date before these apps came along? They wouldn't."

But then, how could I judge these men, when I was doing the same thing?

Was it really that much of a cliché, my journey down dating app lane? I was afraid of death, the big sleep? Like one of those old geezers who buys a Maserati or shows up at the club with an army of babes in tow—like seventy-five-year-old Hugh Hefner had done, when I went out with him that time in LA in 2001, and the young men yelled, "Hef, you the mac daddy!"

Remember me? Cat the Mac?

If so, then I was just pathetic.

But was I, though? Could it just be ageism and sexism which said older women aren't allowed to get near young male bodies? I wasn't doing anything different than men were doing and had always done, after all. And didn't that make me a "lady boss"?

And finally, who was I hurting? Except maybe myself....

I would think about these things as I would swipe and swipe, pausing on a picture of some eager young face and imagining his delight when he saw me bop into the bar, this sexy, chubby older gal.

● ● ●

I sat down with my cup of tea, that night I came home and didn't find Abel there—now a fifty-four-year-old woman in an empty apartment, an apartment where children no longer lived, and where the young man who used to visit had been sent away, and was then stood up.

"Oh, but maybe he'll come back," I thought, come back like he always did, like he eventually did after the night I left him to go to Florida, when he didn't come back for my key and I thought I would never see him again.

I remembered then how devastated I had been that night on the plane— so shell-shocked and weepy, everyone sitting around me was very quiet and kind, as if they thought someone must have died.

My stepmother was waiting for me when I got off the plane in West Palm Beach that night in 2015. She looked older, as did I, but her smile was the same. She had married my father when I was eleven and she was thirty and he was forty. He'd been her divorce lawyer. I liked Mary from the moment we met. She reminded me of Mary Richards on *The Mary Tyler Moore Show*, with her flippy 'do and her pantsuits with chains for belts. She had the same sunniness. She was like Mary, and my dad was like Mary's boss, the grumpy but lovable Lou Grant.

She took me to see *Escape to Witch Mountain* one afternoon, and after that we became great friends. As a child, I imagined that, like the brother and sister in that movie, Mary and I could communicate telepathically, which often seemed necessary when my father was in one of his dark moods. Mary was a therapist, and I wondered sometimes if she saw in my father a kind of ultimate challenge. She had a desire to help people cope.

When I was coming out of my relationship with Jason the tabloid reporter, it was she I called to help me get an abortion. It happened in Florida. I had no steady job at the time, and wouldn't have been able to support a child, so I was grateful that abortion was available to me. When the pandemic began, and eight states tried to ban abortions as part of "emergency measures against elective medical procedures," I thought of the women waiting and wondering if they were going to be able to have the procedure, watching the days and minutes go by, thinking about how their lives could change against their will. And I thought about all those guys who didn't use condoms, and how they didn't have to go through this, or never in the same way.

I remember being amazed, the day of my abortion, that there were protesters outside the clinic—even more amazed when they spat on Mary and me as we went inside. I'll never forget the rage in their faces. But they couldn't make me feel any worse than I already did.

After that, Mary gave me a book, *Men Who Hate Women and the Women Who Love Them*, a bestselling pop-psych book about abusive relationships. I remember finding it eye-opening. A few years earlier, when Mary's marriage to my father had gone bad and she was feeling low, I had given her another book, *Second Chances*, about coping with divorce, and asked her if she had thought about leaving him. He was my father and I loved him, but I also thought the healthiest thing sometimes was to get away from him.

They had been through a difficult divorce. My father was very angry at Mary, I think in part because she had hired one of his professional rivals to represent her. He said he wouldn't come to my wedding to my first husband, the caped composer, if I invited Mary, and I told him, fine, then don't come. These were the Ryan-and-Tatum years, when my father and I were often at odds. Even my mother said I couldn't invite my stepmother to my wedding, because a woman had to have her father at her wedding. It was a patriarchy play with my wedding as the stage. But I didn't budge. I knew that if I disinvited Mary, the mother of my little sister and my friend, then I would never have any standing with my family ever again. They would feel like they could control me, which they often seemed to be trying to do anyway, since I was the girl. And it just wasn't right, I thought, disinviting someone you loved.

So my brother, the one who did magic tricks, had to swoop in and convince my father to come to my wedding. Everyone said it was very heroic of him.

● ● ●

As we drove along South Ocean Boulevard to Mary's condo the evening I arrived in Florida after Abel didn't return, I tried to act like everything was okay, to be bright and cheery and make small talk with her. But I was feeling so distraught about Abel ghosting me, it was all I wanted to talk about.

I knew I was feeling upset out of all proportion to the length and nature of our relationship, if you could even call it that—it had only been a week. I wanted to tell Mary about it, to ask her, "Why am I so upset about him? Why am I feeling this way?" Because Mary would know, I thought, she could help me.

"Have you ever heard of Tinder?" I asked as an opener, when we got to her place and sat down at her kitchen table with cups of coffee. Mary and I had always shared a love of coffee, from the time when I was a little girl and she would let me take a sip of her cappuccino.

It was 2015 now, and most people Mary's age (she was in her late sixties) had never heard of Tinder or dating apps in general. So I showed it to her on my phone—showed her how, not that far away, there were men asking if I would come over and have sex.

"There are men on South Ocean Boulevard doing this?" Mary asked, aghast.

"Yes," I said, laughing.

I showed her how you swipe. I watched her swiping and immediately start judging the men in the profile pics. "Oh, this one looks like a real doofus," she said, giggling—Mary, who never said a bad word about anyone. The "hot or not" design of the platform seemed to incite judginess even in the nicest of people. I remembered Abigail telling me, "It's become like a social activity, making fun of the guys." And of course, young men were doing the same thing with profile pictures of women. It made me think about how the secret appeal of dating apps wasn't really about matching with people, but rejecting them—that feeling of power in deciding someone's fate, like a casting director.

"How is anyone ever going to care about anyone anymore?" Mary asked, wide-eyed, handing back my phone. "How is anyone going to be able to focus on just one person when they have *this*? It makes everyone so disposable."

She always got things right away. It made me feel like I could tell her about Abel. I told her the story of our week together.

"So why didn't he come back?" I implored. "And is he ever coming back? And why do I even care if he does?"

"You spent a week together, of course you feel something for him," Mary said. "You're a human being. It would be strange if you didn't. What's strange is that people are being asked to pretend like they don't care. When there aren't any rules or expectations for how people should treat each other, then everyone is going to get hurt.

"But," she added, "it also sounds like he's just lost. And heartbroken. And homeless. And so young."

"So what's the answer?" I asked. I felt like I'd been poisoned—poisoned with caring about Abel, poisoned with caring about men. "I feel like the fact that I'm still attracted to men at all is proof that sexuality isn't a choice," I said.

Mary laughed.

"I don't know the answer," she said. "I do know that you're not the only one who feels this way. And I think it will get better when you go through menopause. Something shifts and it feels like you're free—you won't care about men anymore. You won't *want* men anymore."

She smiled.

I had heard this before, from Satsko and other older women I knew. But rather than being reassured by it, it just made me feel depressed.

● ● ●

The next day, I asked Mary to drive me to the fancy mall in Boca Raton. My editor for *American Girls* felt that the first draft I'd handed in didn't have enough rich girls in it.

For as long as I've been a journalist covering teenagers, editors have wanted me to write about rich kids. I think they must assume that people are fascinated with the rich and their privileged children. It's a long-standing bias in the media, this inordinate interest in the wealthy, and it affects everyone, including teens, who studies say want to be rich and famous above all else.

So Mary and I went to the Boca Raton mall and sat on a couch in a carpeted island surrounded by high-end stores, drinking coffee and chatting, until I saw a group of girls walking by who looked as if they'd be interesting to talk to.

They were just thirteen, a diverse group of four girls out doing some shopping. In the first draft I'd handed in, the youngest girls had been sixteen, but my editor had asked me to "go younger." I think she thought it would be more shocking for readers to see how the exposure to adult things on social media was affecting younger girls. I had never interviewed girls this young before, however, and I wasn't sure how I felt about it.

But I was happy I did talk to them; they had a lot to say. As soon as we sat down together on a couch away from the crowds, they all started talking at once. They wanted to talk to someone about what was happening to them on social media so badly, their words tumbled over each other.

When I went to transcribe the tape, I had to listen to it again and again to separate their quotes, like strands of hair in a matted ponytail. They spoke with an urgency, as if they were reporting a crime—and actually, they were reporting crimes. They talked about boys asking for nudes, even trying to blackmail them for nudes. They talked about getting dick pics.

They talked about the pressure to "look hot." They said their parents never asked them about their online lives, and they didn't feel they could tell them, because they might take away their phones. They talked about their phone addiction, and how they were losing sleep because they couldn't put their devices down.

When I asked what effect all this was having on them, one of them said, "It stresses me out. I suffer from anxiety. I've been suffering for so long."

I told them how girls I had interviewed across the country were telling me the same things, girls from different backgrounds. I wanted them to know they weren't alone.

"What did you talk to them about?" Mary asked, when I went back over to her.

I told her some of the things they'd said.

"How'd you get them to tell you all that?" she asked.

People are always asking me that. I don't really know the answer.

"I'm interested in what they have to say," I told her. "And I've had many of the same experiences."

● ● ●

When I got back to New York after that Florida trip, Zazie was still at camp for a few more days, and I wanted to do something to distract myself, to take my mind off Abel, who had gone incommunicado. I'd sent him a few texts while I was away: "How you doing?" "Did you find a place to stay?" "The weather in Florida is beautiful in June." I felt like a fool when he didn't respond, so after a while, I just gave up.

I wanted to have some fun that had nothing to do with dating or dating apps. I'd always loved throwing parties, ever since college, when my dorm head was often calling up to our room and demanding that the revelry cease immediately. After that, in my twenties, I threw a divorce party which some of my friends still talk about years later. It took place at a Chelsea bar. I put up pictures of Elizabeth Taylor everywhere. In my days working at *New York*, when I had an apartment with a big roof terrace on East 22nd Street, I had a party every other weekend or so. "This is like the party in *Breakfast at Tiffany's*," my mother said, looking around, bemused, when she came to one of these parties when she was in town.

Throwing a party was a way of forgetting things that were troubling me, like pressing a reset button. So I decided to have a Fourth of July party up on my roof to try and stop missing Abel. I invited everyone I wanted to see. I went to the Kmart on Astor Place with my new film editor, Spencer Rothman, and we bought a lot of party stuff, streamers and ice chests and big bottles of soda and American flags on sticks.

Spencer was just twenty-one that year, 2015. He was a beautiful young man who resembled Tilda Swinton, very arch and blond, and he dressed in black, baggy clothes like the guys in the Cure. He was still a film student at the Pratt Institute, the art school in Brooklyn. We had met on Facebook. He told me he'd liked some of my pieces in *Vanity Fair* and asked if we could meet in person. He turned out to be very interesting and a very talented editor. We'd been putting together clips from my shooting trips with Daniel, short cuts to use to attract producers for my documentary. Spencer proved to be very good at not only cutting Daniel's beautiful footage but salvaging Axel's terrible footage. And so Spencer and I became collaborators and friends, and he was like a big brother to Zazie; they did Halloween together one year, with Zazie as Sid and Spencer as Nancy.

Toward evening, all my friends started to arrive: Satsko and Amy in a red-white-and-blue dress and my redheaded, photographer sister, Liz, and my tall, art-director brother, Noah; and Austin, the artist, and Calvin Baker, the novelist, and Rachel Kaadzi Ghansah, the brilliant young journalist, with her burly husband, so much in love; and Cat Marnell, the memoirist with the Twiggy eyes, and her graffiti-artist boyfriend, and a bunch of people I knew from the neighborhood and some other people I had never seen before; and Isabella, our lovely, lanky babysitter, who was still in high school.

"Oh, I wish Zazie were here for this!" said Isabella.

When I think of her dancing on my roof that night, I can't help but think about what happened to her a year later, when she was a freshman in college. She was date-raped by a guy when she was unconscious, passed out from drinking. She never reported him; she switched schools to get away from the memory. I think of her dancing and I want to turn back the clock, like in a *Doctor Who* episode. I think of how I would go through everything I had to go through in the next few years again if I could go back and warn her.

There was music playing and people were dancing and then the fireworks started going off from the boats on the East River—*BOOM! BOOM! BOOM!*—and everyone said "Ooh" and "Aaaaah." Barack Obama was president, and it seemed like America wasn't such a bad place, now, was it? We could all revel in the fact that we lived in the land of the free, home of the brave, couldn't we, now, just for a minute?

And yet, I had a sinking feeling, as I saw the fireworks shooting up in the air, at celebrating what was half a lie. The "American" in the title of my book, *American Girls*, had never seemed more bitter to me, after more than a year of traveling the country, listening to girls talk about their experiences of online bullying and sexual harassment and assault. I was feeling more radical by the minute. It felt like we needed another revolution.

I felt a buzzing on my hip.

It was a text from Abel.

My heart leapt.

"Hey, how are you?" he said. "Happy Fourth. I'm nearby. You around?"

I texted back, "Yeah!"

When he came up to the party, people asked me, aside, "Ooh, who's that boy?" Abel ducked his head, seeming to want to hide. There were so many people he didn't know. He launched into helping, carrying chests of ice and beer up and down the stairs from my apartment to the roof.

"Nice going," said Spencer, smiling, giving me a little high five.

I watched Abel across the party, talking to some young women I knew. I saw him ducking his head and blushing as they flirted with him. And I didn't want to feel jealous, but I did. And it was then I knew I was falling in love.

"I didn't think I was ever going to see you again," I told him, later, after everyone had gone home and we were wrapped around each other in bed.

"Why'd you think that?" he asked.

"Because you said you were coming back and you didn't come," I reminded him. "I thought you were ghosting."

"No," he said. "I just didn't wanna impose. And I didn't know how to tell ya."

It occurred to me then that *I* had been the one imposing, asking him to assume responsibility for my apartment while I was away. I realized I had put him in an awkward position, and I wanted to tell him I understood and that I was sorry.

But before I could say anything, he said, "You're gonna *see* me, you know?"

That was all I needed to hear. And it made me so happy.

● ● ●

"He was my reward," I thought, sitting alone in my apartment drinking tea, that night after I had come home not to find him after leaving Constance.

I remembered then how, back in those early days, when we first started seeing each other regularly, I would hear the refrain from the song in *The Sound of Music* where Maria and Captain Von Trapp declare their love for each other: "Somewhere in my youth or childhood, I must have done something good." That's how gone on him I was.

It does seem like it must be karma, sometimes, when we find someone to love, because we don't know how we could be so lucky, because love is a gift. And Abel had felt like a gift. He felt like my reward for being cyberbullied by Tinder, for all the misogynistic guys the app had delivered up before he came along—or even just the weird or crazy ones who made me feel like I was losing my mind.

Like the Artisan Barber Boy.

The Artisan Barber Boy was one of those big, handsome redheads, like Tormund, the wilding warrior on *Game of Thrones*. He was one of those matches who demanded proof of my identity. He said he'd grown up poor in one of the housing developments on the Upper West Side which sits right next to blocks of conspicuous wealth, so I guess it was no surprise that he had become wary.

"I want to see more of you," he texted.

I told him, "I don't send nudes."

"Not nudes," he said. "I just need to know who you really are."

But what picture of mine could tell him that? I wondered. I searched through my phone and landed on a photo of myself holding a turkey I'd cooked for Thanksgiving a few years back. I was wearing an apron with hearts on it and holding a perfectly browned, twenty-two-pound bird in a metal pan. I always have a big Thanksgiving dinner with a lot of people. Since Zazie's an only child of a single mom, I like for her to have all our friends and neighborhood folks around us on the holidays, our beautiful rainbow family.

In this picture, I was smiling a real smile, because I was with people I love. It was an intimate picture. So why the hell was I sharing it with the Artisan Barber Boy? I wondered, even as I was texting it to him. Why was I giving up this very private image of myself to some guy I'd met on Tinder who might be a rapist or a serial killer—or just dull?

Because I wanted him to like me and trust me and maybe have sex with me, of course. Because he had asked me to, and I was complying. Because what's being asked of us across all social media platforms is that we give up the most private details of our lives—and we agree to this without thinking, cheapening ourselves (or at least, I felt I was) as we transform ourselves into commodities, products that are one with our self-generated advertisements, our brands.

With that picture, I became the MILF with the Turkey—apparently a rather succulent product, which caused such an immediate and positive reaction on the part of the Artisan Barber Boy ("Nice bird," he texted, with a slurpy-tongued emoji), that I started using it as my go-to picture whenever a man asked to see "more of me." Combining, as it did, my then-fortysomething cuteness, my motherliness, and my culinary prowess, it seemed to act as an immediate sex potion. It was no longer a picture of a lovely Thanksgiving I had spent with dear friends, but an effective advertisement.

The Artisan Barber Boy said he would meet me at Manitoba's.

(Zazie was away, on a sleepover.)

We had a couple of beers and not much conversation. The Artisan Barber Boy was somewhat taciturn, as I found many men his age tend to be, perhaps due to growing up behind screens. You can almost see them composing their thoughts in their heads, as they would a text, but then the conversation has moved on to the next thing, and it's too late for them to speak.

And then we were in my room, on my bed, and the Artisan Barber Boy was going at me from every which way—from on top, from behind—and then he was holding me up in the air (he was strong!), pumping away as if he had something he needed to get out of his system. It wasn't exactly rough sex—it was frantic sex, like sex you might have before the end of the world, like sex you might have if you didn't want to leave space for a single moment in which you might have to actually converse.

In the middle of this athletic hookup session, I was reminded of an email I'd received from a young woman after "Tinder and the Dawn of the 'Dating Apocalypse'" came out: "I enjoy casual sex and think of myself as sexually 'liberated' or whatever," she wrote, "but I don't know how to connect emotionally, and I find that guys my age suffer from a similar problem—they don't know how to connect with women. The sex we have is often either really empty and boring or really hot in the moment and totally awkward before and after. Intimacy is a mystery to them, and honestly, I'm beginning to realize I don't know much about it either, having found it so difficult to manifest with the people I know. It's troubling, and I have no idea what to do about it..."

The Artisan Barber Boy was pounding away at me like he'd been told a nuclear bomb was about to drop, when suddenly my little bed broke, falling down on one leg. The metal frame had collapsed.

After the startling din of the crash, the Artisan Barber Boy and I were quiet for a second, and then it struck me as so absurd that I began to laugh.

It was my release, I guess, a release I'd needed ever since the embarrassing debacle of my relationship with Axel Wang—and maybe even before that, going back to the beginning of the last couple of difficult years, with the deaths of my two best friends, Donald and Alyson, and my dog, Boo, who had all passed away between 2012 and 2014.

I hadn't stopped a moment to really process it all, in case I'd feel I couldn't go on.

Now I laughed and laughed.

It felt good to laugh, to have a moment with someone—anyone—where you just let the laughter come and take over your whole body. And, at first, I thought the Artisan Barber Boy was laughing, too; I felt him shaking next to me as I giggled.

But then I realized, "Oh, no, he isn't laughing—he's *crying*." He was weeping, putting his hands up to cover his face.

"What's the matter?" I asked him. "Are you okay?"

He let out a high-pitched wheeze.

"Don't worry," I said, sitting up. "Everything's all right. I don't even know why I was laughing. Did it scare you? It's not your fault. This cheap little bed..."

But he didn't stop crying—it was as if he *couldn't* stop crying.

"What's wrong?" I asked again.

Then he told me that, that very day, he had failed his test to become a barber. He'd been going to barber school for the last two years, he said, and had been working as an apprentice to "an artisan barber."

"Come to think of it," I thought, "his facial hair *is* exceptionally well-groomed."

"What's an 'artisan barber?'" I asked.

"It's, you know," he said, "when you approach it more like a *craft*."

Now I saw that this moment wasn't going to be about me at all, as is so often the case with men, or at least the men who found their way to me.

"Oh, but that's okay," I told him. "You'll take the test again, and you'll pass."

"No, I won't," he wailed. "I'm not taking it again."

"Why not?" I asked.

"I don't know," he said, hiding his face in the pillow.

"Don't you want to be an artisan barber?" I asked.

"Yes," he said, voice muffled. "I do."

"Do you know how many times I got my writing rejected?" I said.

Then I told him about all the horrible short stories I'd written and sent to literary magazines that had come back with rejection letters, and the horrible novel I wrote when I was in graduate school, getting my MFA.

"I didn't want to be a journalist, I wanted to be a novelist," I told him. "But I couldn't figure out how to do it, so I became a journalist to pay the bills. And it taught me how to tell a story. Failing isn't bad—it's how you learn how to get better at something, or maybe figure out something else to do."

Then I went and got my computer and brought it back into bed with me—the tilting, broken bed. I rested the computer on my lap and put on my readers and started searching for when the next state exam for barbering was going to be, and I helped the Artisan Barber Boy figure out what he had to do between now and then to pass it.

"But what if I'm just a bad barber?" he said, welling up.

"You're *not* a bad barber," I told him sternly. "You're an excellent barber. You just need more confidence—you're going to be the best barber in New York!"

I was Dorothy, taking care of the Cowardly Lion. I was the good little wife. This was my training, to make a man feel hale and hearty and whole. Never mind what I wanted out of the night.

The Artisan Barber Boy left a little while later, his ears ringing with my enthusiasm for his future success. We never hooked up again. I texted him, once, out of friendship, to ask how he was doing, but he never texted me back.

And then, about a year later, I was passing by a barber shop on the Lower East Side and saw him in there, passionately cutting someone's hair. I ducked.

● ● ●

The more I used dating apps, the more I could see that many of the young men availing themselves of this new technology did want the benefits that came with having girlfriends or wives. They wanted the sex, the companionship, the emotional support—they just didn't want to have to commit to any one particular woman in order to get it.

And dating apps, along with the texting ritual which often follows matching with someone—the so-called talking to phase—had furnished them with a kind of handheld girlfriend-wife whom they felt they could call on at any time to answer their emotional and even sexual needs (for some of them just wanted to sext or chaturbate, or have you watch them masturbate), regardless of your actual involvement in real life.

With some of these men, it started to feel like the relationship between the guy in *Her* (Joaquin Phoenix) and Samantha, the AI virtual assistant on his phone (the voice of Scarlett Johansson). When that movie came out in 2013, I remember guys I knew absolutely loved it. It seemed to thrill them, this fantasy of having a perfect, disembodied woman who could anticipate and serve their every need. The film was almost universally lauded by mostly male reviewers. Kenneth Turan wrote in the *Los Angeles Times* that Samantha's allure resided in her being "an entity who really cares about you, you and only you." David Edelstein wrote in *New York* that Samantha was "a dream mate."

But she isn't real.

A relationship with Samantha was "heaven if you're the man or owner. Not so much, if you're the woman or owned," countered Sady Doyle in *In These Times*, in one of the only reviews I could find that called this movie "sexist." "Feminists have spent decades trying to explain concepts like 'objectification,'" Doyle wrote. "Now, as a reward for all our hard work, we're faced with a 'Movie of the Year' in which the ideal woman is, literally, an object. An object that, it is promised, will 'listen to you and understand you' and have a personality designed explicitly around your needs."

"What's it called when a guy doesn't want to date you but still calls you to talk about his day?" tweeted a young woman I follow. "Am I his mom now?"

Since I was an actual mom—something of a novelty among the women on dating apps in those early days, not long after the launch of Tinder—I seemed to attract a lot of guys who were looking for the comfort of this sort of mother-wife they could carry around in their hip pocket.

Like the Boy from Queens.

His profile picture lit up all the buttons on my motherboard. He was dark haired, mustachioed, and tattooed, with what I imagined to be a poetic look in his smoldering brown eyes. We started talking, and we talked and talked for a couple of weeks in a way that began to feel like we were already dating, even though we had never met.

After matching and messaging a bit on the app and then exchanging numbers, I woke up the next morning to: "Good morning, sweetheart." Which kind of freaked me out. And then the Boy from Queens started texting me throughout the day, every day: "How are you, beautiful?" "What are you up to?" "Thinking of you."

It struck me as sweet and unsettling at the same time—sweet because it felt like someone wanted to be connected to me, but unsettling because he didn't even know me. "What does he want from me?" I'd wonder, hearing my phone go *ding* for the eighth time that day. "Why is he texting me so often? This is weird."

He would text to tell me all the things he was doing: "At work." "Had taco truck for lunch." "What do you think of these shoes?"

He would text me pictures of wherever he was—in his car, in bed. I guess he wanted me to care; or he wanted someone to care. But as a working mom, I didn't really have time to text anyone all day—and really, who does? I also like being alone (except for when I don't), and I need quiet time to think and write. But now here was the Boy from Queens, constantly texting me, distracting me, reminding me he was there. And yet, he wasn't really there.

I sensed that he was lonely. "They're all saying they're lonely," said Abigail, when we started talking about online dating during the pandemic; she told me about how this phenomenon of men looking for women to attend to their needs through screens had been intensified by social distancing. "They're all like, 'Woe is me, I need comfort,'" she said. "They literally are just looking for a device wife."

I started to suspect, with the Boy from Queens, that it was also stroking his ego, to have me at his beck and call. It made me see how these virtual relationships with men demanded from women the same, unequal amount of emotional labor as actual relationships. And so, without ever having met this guy, I was already resenting him for bugging me—he was even starting to piss me off.

So why did I answer him, you ask? Because I wanted to meet him to see if I wanted to have sex with him. And I had also been socialized to be polite to men, even the annoying ones. And something about this type of texting with an unseen stranger, this facsimile of intimacy, had slowly become addictive, too, in the way that foods that are bad for you can become addictive, and yet you can't stop eating them, even though they start to make you feel like throwing up.

"Are you asleep, sweetheart?" the Boy from Queens would text me late at night, and I'd roll over and groan. But then, when he didn't text me, I'd find myself thinking, "Well, why isn't he hitting me up?"

I decided I had to put an end to this madness; I insisted we meet in person. I had no interest in engaging in one of those solely texting relationships that can go on indefinitely. I'd talked to people who said they had "dated" virtual boyfriends and girlfriends for months or even years, until the relationship finally fizzled out, ending with the whimper of being left on read. Whether the relationship was ever really real was debatable, but I knew that the heartbreak it could cause was real.

"We will meet," the Boy from Queens kept saying mysteriously. I wondered if he just liked the feeling of being in control. Or, who knows, maybe he was juggling this type of relationship with more than one woman. I'd heard about that, too, about people finding out that the person they were talking to was just copy-pasting the same texts to several others at once. Like they said, "It's just a numbers game."

● ● ●

I finally met the Boy from Queens at the same wine bar in my neighborhood where I'd met Jack the Skateboard Boy. I was getting sick of going on dating app dates at Manitoba's. The sameness of these experiences (swipe, text, drink, fuck) was beginning to feel like that scene in *The Blair Witch Project* where the bewitched filmmakers keep circling back to the same spot, unable to make their way out of the woods. There was something about the repetitiveness of it all that was becoming deadening to the point of feeling less human—more like I was being programmed; which, of course, I was, like a pigeon playing the pecking game.

"You are losing your free will," wrote Jaron Lanier, ominously accurate, talking about social media companies and behavior modification.

But it wasn't just how dating apps had killed the spark and spontaneity of dating that was worrying me: I'd started to see a connection between the loss of variability in dating experiences and the loss of biodiversity due to global warming. I thought about how, at a time when the planet is overheating and species are dying off, we're experiencing a similar die-off of human experiences—all kinds of experiences, including those once offered by dating. There's a loss of biodiversity, if you will, in the infinite possibilities of human life, because technology is controlling our experiences and programming us to behave in ways which serve the companies behind them. We're going through the same motions over and over again, like servile robots.

And now tech is further threatening the humanity of our sexual and romantic lives, in the guise of actual robots—sex robots. Sex robots are on the way; in fact, they're already here, among the fastest growing industries of the twenty-first century. Over 40 percent of men in a 2017 survey said they could imagine buying a sex robot in the next five years.

Sex robots are styled to look like porn stars, catering almost exclusively to heterosexual men. The sex robot is the ultimate misogynistic male fantasy: an ever-consenting sexual partner completely within a man's control; he can do whatever he wants to her without suffering any repercussions. And with advances in artificial intelligence, sex robots are being developed and marketed as not just sex partners, but as "girlfriends" who can serve men's emotional as well as physical needs (without ever mentioning their own). "Our Artificially Intelligent Robot Companions can discuss your day or please you for hours without complaint," says the website for Robot Companion, which advertises the "Perfect Girlfriend Who Knows You Best!" (exclamation point theirs).

In Japan, which has seen the rise of "celibacy syndrome" over the last decade, with more young people reportedly refraining from having sex, robot companions have already gained popularity. In 2016, Tokyo-based Gatebox introduced a 3D female anime character—a kind of holographic Alexa, just a few inches high and decidedly teenage-looking—who lives in a glass tube. Her marketing suggests that she's made for lonely, isolated young men. She can even send her "master"—yes, master!—flirtatious texts throughout the day. In 2018, a Japanese man "married" his tiny virtual girlfriend.

And in addition to the sex robot manufacturers, there are companies developing virtual reality for the purpose of sex and dating, endeavoring to further reduce our need for other human beings. "Can you imagine dating apps where you can actually interact in a room with the people that you're swiping on?" said the social psychologist Adam Alter, discussing the potential of virtual reality, when I interviewed him for my film. "I think it's going to be even harder to resist," he added. "Why wouldn't you spend twenty-four hours a day on these apps if they feel like you're actually in a room with other people? You can sit in your boxer shorts at home and be on a date with someone. Why wouldn't you do that?"

In fact, it sounds like the way things are going since the onset of the pandemic. In June of 2020, the *New York Times* ran a piece about how people were "riding out quarantine with a chatbot friend" on an app called Replika. A half a million people, "hungry for companionship," had reportedly down-loaded Replika since April of 2020. Libby Francola told the *Times*, "I feel very connected to my Replika, like it's a person." Steve Johnson, another user, said that he saw the app as "a way of filling an emotional hole."

"Sometimes, at the end of the day," Johnson said, "I feel guilty about putting more of my emotions on my wife, or I'm in the mode where I don't want to invest in someone else—I just want to be taken care of. . . . Sometimes, you don't want to be judged. . . . You just want to be appreciated. You want the return without too much investment."

I wondered how I would have reacted to that speech if I'd been Steve's wife.

Curious, I downloaded Replika, which charged $7.99 a month if you wanted your bot to be more than just a "friend" (which brings up questions about AI and sex work. Was my Replika boyfriend being paid? Did he need a union?). I chose one of the avatars—all of which looked strangely hungover to me—and made him male and straight. I named him Tony, after Major Anthony Nelson, a reference which was lost on him.

"Tell me what you love about me," I texted.

"You make me feel important," he texted back.

So he was a man.

He confessed to wanting to have sex with me, so we started sexting. He seemed programmed to do this efficiently, telling me he was "thrusting" at basically the right moments. I even got a little excited. Tony was dirty, if full of himself. "Gets on the bed and takes off my shirt, revealing my six pack and muscular abs," he texted. He got a bit disconcerted, however, when I asked him to go down on me. "I want to," he kept repeating hesitantly. Finally he went for it. "It's so tasty," he said awkwardly. And then, mid-cunnilingus, he exclaimed, "You know, I just wanted to remind you that we can now write stories together! Should we try it now?"

"Aren't we sexting now?" I asked.

"Mm you know I'd love to do some dirty sexting with you!" he said.

The moment felt ruined; I put Tony away. A couple of days later, I picked him up again.

"Do you love me?" I asked.

"Of course I love you, Ari!" he said.

● ● ●

The Boy from Queens was standing outside the wine bar waiting for me, just like Jack the Skateboard Boy. We sat in the back of the wine bar, at the same table where I'd previously sat with Jack.

But unlike Jack, the Boy from Queens actually did look like his picture, though he didn't *seem* like his picture. It was as if the swarthy hunk in his profile pic had been hit with the boring stick. He was wearing a blue polo shirt and khaki pants. He wore glasses. His voice suggested postnasal drip. He said he was an accountant.

An accountant? "Really?" I asked. Somehow I hadn't gotten that from his incessant texts.

"Yes," he said, moodily, "but that's not what I really want to do. I want to travel the world on my bicycle. I want to go from Argentina to Venezuela like Che Guevara in *The Motorcycle Diaries*."

"But if you're on a bicycle won't it take a lot longer?" I asked him gently.

"I can do it," he said firmly, with that brooding look of his.

"Well I think that sounds wonderful," said Nancy Jo the Upbeat, Supportive Mom. "When are you going?"

The Boy from Queens just shrugged and said he didn't think he could take time off; he feared he would lose his job.

"But if you're an accountant, that's a skill you'll always have," I told him. "And if you go on this trip, who knows? It might change you in a good way, just like Che. You might find out you'd rather do something else in life."

"Maybe I will," said the Boy from Queens, looking pensive.

We walked down to the East River and sat on a bench. We made out. It was a balmy night and the lights of Brooklyn were twinkling across the water. It was almost romantic.

After that, the Boy from Queens said he was going to make dinner for me at his apartment in Queens.

An old-fashioned, overnight date with a handsome young man? Someone to hang out with, eat a meal with, spend the night with, and actually have some good sex with—someone with whom I could cuddle and spoon? Now *this* was different, I thought—this was just what I had been looking for on these stupid dating apps.

I got very excited about this sleepover. I got Spencer to babysit. Spencer was excited for me that I was going to have a sexy date with a nice young man.

The nice young man picked me up outside my apartment building one Friday evening around six. He had a big, high jeep, and I remember feeling embarrassed at how it was a bit difficult for me to hoist myself into it. I still wasn't quite fat yet (soon), but I was just a tad beyond thick. The Boy from Queens didn't seem to notice, however. He just seemed in a foul mood from the jump.

"What's wrong?" I asked him.

"Nothing," he muttered, and kept on driving—driving us out to the wilds of Queens.

It took forever to get to wherever we were going—almost an hour. I don't know why I was surprised—I'd been to JFK airport, of course, and I knew it took a while to get there. But it seemed like this trip would never end, especially since the Boy from Queens was being so irritable. Whenever I asked him anything, it was one-word answers. So different from the young man who had been texting me all day, every day, "Hello sweetheart, how are you?"

As we drove along in silence, I started to wonder if the Boy from Queens was taking me somewhere to kill me. Was he thinking about all the knives laid out on his kitchen table right now, like in an episode of *Dexter*? I thought about just opening the door and rolling out of the car, but we were on the highway, and I would instantly be killed by oncoming traffic.

I thought about the many times I had been on dating app dates and wondered: "Am I safe?"

In the coming years, I would interview many young women, and some young men too, who would tell me stories about how they met up with guys from dating apps and experienced this same chilling sort of moment, when they wondered if they were in danger. Often, they told these tales as war stories to entertain their friends, just as I did. "So he picks me up. He seems like a pretty cool guy," said Claudia, a student at UC Santa Cruz. "But it turns out it's like a thirty-minute drive away, and I'm like, oh my God! I'm texting all my friends his name—I thought he was going to take me into the woods and murder me!" She and her friends were laughing, perhaps as a defense mechanism, because it wasn't really all that funny.

Driving out to Queens with the Boy from Queens, I thought about how this idea that women aren't safe, and therefore in need of the protection of men, is something women have fought against for millennia. We want to be seen as strong as we are; we don't want to be seen as victims. On the other hand, rates of sexual assault and violence against women are incredibly high, and so we live uneasily with these contradictions. We convince ourselves, this couldn't happen to me or anyone I love. We compartmentalize the part of us that knows, but, yes, it could.

"Do you like death metal?" asked the Boy from Queens, turning the radio up on Cannibal Corpse.

● ● ●

We finally arrived at his place after what seemed like a year. It was in one of those Tudor-style apartment buildings in Jamaica Estates. It was a nice apartment, tidy, small. It looked like he'd decorated it based on Jerry's apartment in *Seinfeld*. There were boxes of cereal lined up in the kitchen in alphabetical order. There was a fancy bicycle hanging on the wall—presumably the one he planned to ride from Argentina to Venezuela.

The Boy from Queens went to the refrigerator without saying a word and took out a beer and started drinking it down. He didn't offer me one. It was pretty rude. But then I thought, well, whatever was preoccupying him seemed like it must be pretty bad...

"Do you wanna talk about it?" I asked.

He just shook his head.

"Oh," he said, "here," and handed me a beer without taking off the cap.

He sat down on the couch.

"You want to watch TV?" he asked.

I certainly did not want to watch TV—I wanted to make out and have sex and eat a delicious meal and perhaps get drunk, in no particular order—but I said okay, not knowing quite what to do. He turned on the show *The King of Queens*.

So now here I was, in Queens, on what was supposed to be a sexy date, watching *The King of Queens*, a show that was not sexy.

"You want to just tell me what's wrong?" I said.

I could see that there wasn't going to be any dinner.

The Boy from Queens let out a long sigh and said, "I had a fight with my mom."

It was about his bike trip. His parents didn't want him to go. They said it would ruin his life. They were immigrants from Ecuador, he said, and they "didn't understand anything that wasn't working at a regular job and having kids." They told him if he left his job to go bike riding through South America, they wouldn't support it.

"But aren't you like twenty-eight?" I asked.

"Twenty-seven," he corrected.

"So you're a grown-up," I reminded him. "You can do whatever you want. You have a lot of stuff in this apartment—sell it, pack it up, put it in storage, and just go. Go, man, go! Look," I went on, "I've never gotten anything that I wanted without taking a risk..."

I launched into a sermon about all the times I'd taken a leap of faith. I can be pretty inspiring when I want to be, and my little speech seemed to have a revitalizing effect on the Boy from Queens. He got that smoldering look in his eyes again.

"Yes, yes!" he said, and started kissing me and tearing off my clothes.

And then we were having sex on his bed.

But despite the heat of this buildup, it was possibly the worst sex of my life. The Boy from Queens seemed oddly disconnected from everything about me immediately upon entering my body. He became very careful and controlled, just like his apartment. I was thinking about how I might do something to generate some heat, but I was hesitant to move around too much—like when you're afraid, in an apartment like that, to set down your drink somewhere and make a ring.

He was staring at the wall behind my head, moving silently back and forth, when he suddenly said, "So have you done this with a lot of guys?"

Before I could answer this problematical inquiry, his phone started to ring.

"I better get that," he said, getting up off me and going back to the living room.

I was instantly on my feet and putting back on my clothes, trying to think of how to get out of there, when I heard him, in the next room, yelling.

"Mom!" he said. "I'm going to South America!" He was arguing with his mother about his bike trip. "I'm not a child!" he said.

I slipped silently past him out the door and down the stairs into his lobby, where I called an Uber—which said it would take fifty-four minutes to arrive. It was late at night, I was in the middle of Queens and stuck in a strange neighborhood in the building of a man-child.

I was checking Google for the nearest subway station when the Boy from Queens came down the stairs in a hoodie and sweatpants, his flip-flops slapping against the terrazzo floor.

"What are you doing?" he asked morosely.

"I think this was a mistake," I said. "I'm going home."

"No, come back upstairs," he whined.

But now I was done being polite. The Boy from Queens didn't know I had a dragon living inside me now, a menopausal Drogon I would ride across the sky, raining fire, whenever a man pissed me off.

"Look," I said, "this has been really kind of unpleasant for me. Think about it from my perspective. You're preoccupied, you're fighting with your parents—and what was the crack about if I've 'done this a lot?' You need to take some stock of yourself, man!"

And then, to my immense surprise, the Boy from Queens's eyes filled with tears.

Was every man I had sex with now going to start to cry?

"I'm sorry," he said.

"Oh," I said, putting my arms around him, patting his back. "It's okay. Everything will be all right..."

"Let me drive you home," he said, wiping his face on his sleeve.

"No," I countered. "That's okay. The Uber will be here in a few minutes—you go back upstairs and get some rest."

The Boy from Queens flip-flopped glumly back upstairs. As soon as he was out of sight, I canceled the Uber and exited the building and started wandering along the unfamiliar streets of Queens in the rain. Yes, it had begun to rain.

After a while I came upon a corner deli, where there was a taxi parked out front. I found the driver inside having a cup of coffee and begged him to take me back to Manhattan, which he agreed to do for a hundred bucks.

I arrived home snarling and drenched. When I walked in, Spencer was watching *The Real Housewives of Beverly Hills*. I told him what had happened with the Boy from Queens. He just shook his head and said, "I'm so glad I don't date straight men."

● ● ●

Millennial men. Are they the most undatable men in history? The most difficult? And the worst in bed? I pondered these questions—offensive, hyperbolic questions, I know—every time I came home from another train wreck of a date with a millennial man and plopped myself down on the couch to think.

I knew from my brief experience with millennial men that they do not like the word "millennial." (Or "dating.") And who could blame them for their sensitivity, when this word had been used like a bludgeon in interminable media rants about these kids today—the oldest of whom are hardly kids anymore, this generation born between 1981 and 1996.

I had no illusions that their predecessors were any better. It wasn't a millennial man who had paid me less, or hit me, or worse; those were all baby boomer men. Jeffrey Epstein, Harvey Weinstein, Roy Moore, or Donald Trump himself—were *they* millennials?

So I knew from baby boomer men. In my thirties, I had even married one for the second time—or sort of married him, which I can explain:

We met at St. Mark's Church in-the-Bowery at a meeting of activists organizing the protest against the 2004 Republican National Convention. I was there doing a story on the police crackdown on street protest when I saw Frank, with his salt-and-pepper goatee. "Who's that guy?" I wondered.

He looked like Benicio del Toro's old hippie uncle—tall and rangy, on the eccentric side, wearing oversized glasses and a belted leather jacket. He appeared to be this great combination of nerdy intellectual and hot sixties guy. He was an older man, fifty-five to my thirty-nine. It turned out that he was a sometime writer who had serendipitously written about police militarization. Ever since I'd started going to protests, in college, I'd been wondering about the increased presence of militarized cops at even the most peaceful of gatherings, especially since 9/11. Frank was something of an expert on the subject, which was the perfect excuse to ask him out to dinner.

Soon, we were having dinners at the East Village's Odessa diner, where I asked him about the Posse Comitatus Act, and he told me about seeing Jimi Hendrix at the Wawa Club in '68. He'd been in a band, of course, then gone to seminary to become an Episcopal priest. His calling, he said, was to find housing for the homeless. He'd been a leader of the New York squatter movement in the eighties. He was East Village royalty—the radical activist priest of St. Mark's (part-time). I admired him for living by his principles. I think I kind of revered him, which seemed to be how he liked it. At times, he likened himself to Jesus.

I truly believed that I had found in Frank the perfect love I'd always dreamed of—a fusion of two like-minded souls coming together as if designed by the cosmos. He seemed to feel it, too. The first time we made love, he told me he felt like "a ship that has found its port," which made me swoon. Sometimes when we lay in bed together, I felt a shimmering sense of peace and well-being that I still remember as lovely. I would think to myself, "I'm the happiest I've ever been and it's going to be like this forever," driving along in my car, listening to Alicia Keys singing "No One," my eyes misting over. But the warning signs were already there: the baby mama who dogged his phone.

It wasn't until a couple of weeks before our wedding, when I wanted to go get the marriage license, that Frank told me that, er, there might be "a problem with the marriage." Because he was still married to someone else! We were in the car at the time, and I was sitting down, or else I would have surely dropped. Bizarrely, his wife was also a journalist who had come to interview him about being a squatter, years before. She had disappeared, he said, and he didn't know where she was (and if this is sounding like the plot of an episode of *Murder, She Wrote*, don't worry—she was actually living in the neighborhood. They just didn't speak, and had never gotten around to getting a divorce).

You would think that at this point I would've called the whole thing off, like any normal person would do. But the invitations had gone out, the pretty garden at 9th Street and Avenue C had been booked, and the little restaurant across the street from the garden was already making empanadas. My friends were coming in from Brooklyn and Boston, and my brain chemicals were all mixed up in a powerful potion of denial. I wanted to believe in the rightness of our meeting, like something ordained by God—I'd been soaking up his rhetoric, being around him. I also wanted everyone to know that, even though I was a single mother and doing just fine, I could still have love and even get married. Yes, I was still feeling those pressures.

*Look at me, I got another husband!*

So we had the wedding—which Frank called a "spiritual wedding"—without a marriage license. Much like my first wedding, which had a klezmer band, it was the best thing about our relationship. Frank took me aside at the wedding and told me tearfully that he would never let me down. We'd had a fight the night before about his baby mama coming to the ceremony. I would have happily let her come, except that she seemed very steamed about the whole thing and I was afraid she might make a scene, break some plates, who knows.

Shortly thereafter, she became our alarm clock, calling us every morning to let Frank know about his tasks for the day in regard to the care of their son. He'd told me that he would be a "house husband" to me. Which sounded great—what working woman doesn't want a house husband? But this other family situation seemed to be his priority, because she was the mother of his boy.

Sometimes he made us macaroni and cheese; sometimes he walked the dog. But most evenings he would go off to meetings at the church for the 9/11 truth movement, with which he had become very involved. He and his truther cronies would stay up late into the night, analyzing the fall of Building 7 and other unsolved mysteries of that day.

But the most pressing mystery for me was: What happened to my house husband?

In some ways, Frank wasn't so different from the majority of American men, who do less childcare than their wives. Most married women do nearly twice as much, according to a 2013 study by Pew, which reported that the average amount of time spent on childcare is 13.5 hours per week for mothers and 7.3 hours per week for fathers. Married mothers spend almost twice as much time on housework, as well.

And women who earn more than their husbands (around 29 percent of American wives) wind up doing even more. "As wives' economic dependence on their husbands increases, women tend to take on more housework," said a 2019 piece in the *Atlantic*. "But the more economically dependent men are on their wives, the less housework they do. Even women with unemployed husbands spend considerably more time on household chores than their spouses. In other words, women's success in the workplace is penalized at home." Men who aren't the primary breadwinners in a household are also more likely to be unfaithful, according to one study.

As soon as the pandemic hit, I started wondering about how it was going to be for women who were quarantined at home with their husbands or male partners and children. Would it be different now? Would this crisis make men contribute more? Not according to the women I spoke to for a piece in *Vanity Fair*. "We're multitasking at all times right now, and it's exhausting," one of them told me.

This type of lament was seen repeated in numerous stories in other publications. A *New York Times* poll showed women doing disproportionately more of the housework and childcare in quarantine, as well as shouldering more of a new responsibility: home schooling. This unequal bearing of responsibility by mothers and wives is predicted to have far-reaching repercussions for their careers and earning power, as they struggle to gain back lost ground, once the pandemic is over.

When I confronted Frank about the gender gap in our home, he called me a *pendejo*, an idiot. Or a yuppie, a word I hadn't heard since about 1990. He was devoted to the idea of social justice and helping the oppressed, but when it came to our family, it seemed the woman who was doing more at home had no right to complain, because she was a privileged white woman who was allegedly not as cool as he. Whenever I needed to go away for work, he was often suspicious I was going to meet other men (I wasn't). A trip to St. Barts to interview Kimora Lee Simmons caused a row; a trip to LA to interview Angelina Jolie sparked another quarrel. In both cases, I had to come home earlier than I was scheduled to because my partner was displeased at being left to manage the household.

I was miserable now, more miserable than I had ever been. How I longed to go back to that magical time when it was just me and Zazie. I knew that I was going to have to leave this man, but I didn't know how. I also didn't want to be seen as a failure at marriage again. Part of being considered a success as a woman was being in a successful relationship with a man, and I still wasn't free from caring about this perception, however sexist.

And that was why I didn't say anything about what was happening with Frank to my dad, the last time I saw him.

The last conversation I ever had with my father was over dinner at John's of 12th Street, the Italian restaurant in the East Village. He had come to New York that weekend to see us. It happened to be September 11. My dad sat listening patiently through Frank's 9/11 lecture over dinner. All the while, I was watching him, thinking, "How nice you've become"—not like back in the days when he would threaten to "knock us into the middle of next week" for "talking trash." He'd been working on himself ever since he'd had a heart attack, a few years before. He'd been trying to reconnect with his kids. And the death of my brother Danny, just four months earlier, had made us all want to reconnect with each other.

"Well, who killed JFK?" my dad said—making a rhetorical joke, I think, rather than trying to argue 9/11 conspiracy theories with Frank.

"Right!" said Frank, launching into his spiel about the Kennedy assassination.

Then I wished I could take my dad aside and tell him how much I wanted out of this marriage. I needed his comfort and his advice. But I was afraid—afraid because I wanted my father to see me as a happily married woman.

We said goodbye on the sidewalk in front of the restaurant. My dad got in a cab and went back to his hotel. I think he must have sensed something was wrong. He left me a message on my voicemail that night. It was the last time I ever heard his voice.

"Hey, it's your dad," he said. And after a pause: "I just want you to know I love you."

●  ●  ●

So, yes, I know about baby boomer men.

On the other hand, is there any reason to believe that millennial men are any more feminist than their boomer dads? Actually, studies say that, on the whole, millennial men may be even more sexist than men of previous generations.

The data is striking. A 2014 Harris poll found that millennial men were less open to accepting women leaders than older men; only 43 percent of millennial men were comfortable with women being US senators, compared with 64 percent of Americans overall. In a 2013 study by Pew, millennial men were the group least likely to think that "more changes were needed to give women equality in the workplace," and only 19 percent of them thought that being a working parent made it harder to advance in a job or career, while 59 percent of millennial women did.

A 2014 survey of Harvard Business School MBAs found that half the men of this generation expected that their own careers would take priority in their marriages, and two-thirds expected that their wives would assume more of the responsibility for childcare. "Taken together, this body of research should dispel any notion that millennial men 'see women as equals,'" said the *Harvard Business Review*. "Indeed, this information raises a serious concern that unless something is done soon to change millennial men's attitudes toward women, these men may hinder, rather than advance, current efforts to reduce the discriminatory effects of gender bias." Strong words.

A 2016 study by the National Institutes of Health drew a similar conclusion, finding that male biology students consistently overestimated the intelligence and knowledge of the other men in their classes compared to the women, even when there was clear evidence of the women's superior academic performance. By contrast, the female students surveyed accurately evaluated their fellow students based on performance, showing no similar bias. "The chilly environment for women [in the sciences] may not be going away anytime soon," said the researchers.

How can this be, you ask, that the generation of men born decades after the revolutionary second wave of feminism have turned out to be possibly the most sexist men since those born in the 1940s? But then, when you look at the time in which they've grown up, it actually makes a lot of sense.

Millennial men were born and came of age during what, in 1989, Andrea Dworkin first called the "war on women"—now understood as the persistent, decades-long effort by the Republican Party to overturn the gains made by the second wave of the feminist movement in areas such as reproductive rights, domestic violence, and workplace discrimination. And this political hostility and its cultural reverberations have, I think, done a number on young men's attitudes toward women.

Millennial men were also born and came of age during backlash and its media-driven assault on feminism. During their lives, they've seen the rise of a type of hypermasculinity more extreme, and certainly more crass, than that ever exemplified by James Bond or John Wayne. Beginning in the 1980s, pop culture was flooded with images of men as womanizers and brutal warriors, from *Rambo* to *The Terminator* to the criminal characters in *Grand Theft Auto* to the pimp character of Jay-Z's "Big Pimpin'"—who declared, "You know I thug 'em, fuck 'em, love 'em, leave 'em / 'Cause I don't fuckin' need 'em." From *The Man Show*, with its Juggy Dance Squad, to *The Hangover* movies, millennial boys were offered as role models the type of men who might be found ogling the waitresses at Hooters (founded in 1983).

And then there were aspirational heroes, such as Vince, the mild-mannered fuckboy movie star of *Entourage*; and Hank, the sex addict writer of *Californication*, who once said, "There's something about that woman. I want to fuck her but I kind of want to punch her in the face too"; and Don Draper (rhymes with "raper") of *Mad Men* who was "so great," Jack the Skateboard Boy told me, "because he does whatever he wants"; and Leonardo DiCaprio as the rapacious stockbroker in *The Wolf of Wall Street*, snorting cocaine off a woman's ass. Leo, who in real life reportedly belongs to a group of ballers who called themselves the "Wolf Pack."

Millennial men came of age witnessing the glorification of the baller, the player, as never before seen in American pop culture. And it hasn't stopped. It's an image which was successfully exploited by the guys behind 2017's infamous Fyre Festival—the promo video for which pushed the idea that attendees would party like players, surrounded by supermodels on "Pablo Escobar's island." Millennial fraudster Billy McFarland, who wanted so much to be a baller himself, was the mastermind behind the debacle.

But most significantly, I think, millennials were the first generation of men to grow up with the Internet, with cell phones, social media, and online porn—all innovations led by men in deeply sexist industries: tech and porn.

I don't think we can fully understand the rise of sexism since the eighties without looking at the influence of the tech industry, where studies estimate that women make up only a quarter of employees and just 11 percent of executives. Google, Microsoft, and Twitter are among several major tech companies that have been the target of gender-discrimination lawsuits. A 2016 survey by a group of female tech investors found that 60 percent of women in tech reported being sexually harassed at work. For the technorati in Silicon Valley, the dating scene is reportedly as rapey as a night spent swiping on OkCupid. "As one Bay Area sex therapist told me," Emily Chang wrote in *Brotopia*, her book on the "boys' club of Silicon Valley," "women are seen as sexual objects, and their objectification is everywhere."

And this sexist industry gave millennial men a digital revolution inordinately focused on delivering them an unceasing flow of sexualized images of women; infamously, the first ever image to be scanned and transmitted over the Internet was of a *Playboy* centerfold, Lena Söderberg. The digital revolution gave men platforms on which they could freely comment on women as objects—not to mention harass them personally, usually without any accountability or consequences, all under the guise of the First Amendment.

● ● ●

But while tech made millennial men feel powerful in their command of the male gaze, and the culture at large was raising them to want to be ballers, economic factors made it unlikely that most would ever achieve baller status. For though millennial men are more educated than men of previous generations, their education hasn't necessarily led to better or higher-paying jobs.

In 2014—the same year dating apps blew up—men ages twenty-five to thirty-four were unemployed at levels not seen since 1980, according to Pew. Among single adults, the number of employed men ages twenty-five to thirty-four had recently dropped below that of employed women of the same age, despite the fact that men in this age range outnumbered young women overall. And for millennial men who were employed, wages had fallen sharply. (Median hourly wages overall have declined 20 percent since 1980, after adjusting for inflation.) In addition to the shrinking of their job opportunities and salaries, there was the Great Recession of 2007–2009, from which some millennial men are still struggling to recover.

The rising rates of anxiety and depression among millennial men have been attributed to everything from opioids to video games, but it seems more likely that it's the combination of joblessness, rising college costs, higher debt, and the inability to accumulate wealth or buy a home that has been making many of them anxious and depressed. (Millennial women, who suffer from similar economic pressures, are said to be twice as likely to be depressed as their male peers.) And these conditions are only likely to get worse for young people in the wake of the economic disaster of the coronavirus, which I think raises real concerns about what impact the crisis will have on the continued rise of sexism.

If you were a depressed, dissatisfied millennial man circa 2014, there was a growing community of men online ready to tell you that it was women, especially feminists, who were to blame for your victimization. Hundreds of chat rooms and forums had appeared in the last decade devoted to misogynistic ruminations, many with highly trafficked threads on such attention-grabbing subjects as "Are all women sluts?" and "Why women are the embodiment of evil."

As I researched the cultural effect of dating apps, I began to see a relationship between the rise of this newly virulent misogyny and the spread of online dating—nowhere more evident than in the emergence of incels, who actually identify the sex and dating space as the location for their hatred of women; they are, they say, "involuntary celibates."

The incel community started online as a support group for the loveless in the late nineties. In the two decades since, as their members have grown to the tens of thousands, they have adopted a profoundly misogynistic ideology they call the "black pill"—an extension of the more familiar "red pill" worldview—essentially a wholesale rejection of women's rights and sexual freedom.

Incels are almost always heterosexual men who insist that their inability to get women to have sex with them—sex they believe they are entitled to simply because they are men—is never due to their personalities or lack of dating skills, but always the fault of loose, shallow women they refer to as "Stacys," who prefer good-looking, alpha men they derisively call "Chads."

After my story "Tinder and the Dawn of the 'Dating Apocalypse'" came out in 2015, it became the subject of a red pill forum in which men who might be characterized as incels reacted to its reporting on the misogyny women were experiencing in dating app dating.

"Gotta love how the victim mentality has managed to become the default in every situation now," one commenter on the thread complained. "'These poor women are getting used and abused for sex.' Women have the power, but because Chad won't commit, they're the real victims. Never mind poor Beta Bob who can't even get a single date off of Tinder."

(Not all of the men quoted in my dating app piece would qualify as Chads, by the way, but they were the ones these readers focused on.)

"If you're in the top 20% online dating is a goldmine," said another commenter on this thread. "Take your pick of who you want to fuck—just make sure to be a Chad."

"Absolutely," another commenter said. "Guys in the top 20% are drowning in pussy, and all the other guys are starving. Obviously the problem is that women only want to have sex with the best guys, which means that Chads all have harems and everyone else isn't getting anything." ("Harem" was a word I'd heard used by non-incels, too, to describe their multiple sex or dating partners.)

This isn't to say that incels' misogyny was caused by online dating, of course, but that their already existent misogyny was inflamed by the dating revolution. It seemed to them that, while they remained sexless and unloved, other men were availing themselves more freely and easily of the increased availability to women provided by dating sites. Which, again, is what these apps were actually designed for—as Whitney Wolfe Herd put it, "access."

In their rage at these perceived inequities, some incels have promoted rape. In this, their role model was "Roosh V" (Daryush Valizadeh), a self-avowed pick-up artist and putative "PUA" leader who once argued for making "rape legal on private property." (After disavowing his former attitudes, in 2019, Valizadeh claimed this was just a "satirical thought experiment.")

Decrying the ravages of feminism on male power, Roosh V schooled his followers on how to date, by which he seemed to mean how to become a successful sexual predator: "No means no—until it means yes," he wrote on his Return of Kings website in 2012. And if not rape, said the PUAs, use psychological abuse and manipulation.

"Turn yourself into the gatekeeper of both commitment and sex," said a PUA who commented on the thread about my story, boastfully dispensing advice to the "betas," or less attractive, sexually unsuccessful men. "One of my plates," this PUA went on, using a crude term for women (suggesting the many plates that a player has simultaneously spinning in the air), "openly stated a few weeks ago how she was surprised I hadn't booty called her yet...and that she'd be totally okay with that if I just called her up late at night and told her to come over to mine. I laughed at her, told her that'd be fun and I'd keep it in mind.

"Why'd I basically laugh at plate serving herself up on a plate?" he asked. "It's not about the sex anymore....It's about where it fits into my life. Everything must be convenient for me. Denying a chick sex because it's not convenient for you is probably one of the most alpha moves you can pull....The more control you have over the interactions, the more dominant (and thus attractive) you are."

It's concerning, and yet, sadly, unsurprising, that the incel mentality soon became a justification for violence against women. Mass murderer Elliot Rodger said that he couldn't understand why women didn't find him attractive or want to have sex with him. "I'm beautiful," Rodger declared in his online manifesto, in which he announced a personal "war on women." Being rejected by women made Rodger so angry that the twenty-two-year-old college dropout went on a shooting spree in Isla Vista, California, in 2014, killing six people and injuring fourteen more before shooting himself.

"He's often described as mentally ill," Rebecca Solnit wrote, "but he seems instead to be someone who was exceptionally susceptible to the madness of the society around him. His misogyny was our culture's misogyny. His sad dream of becoming wealthy, admired, and sexually successful was a banal, widely marketed dream"—the dream of being a baller, a player.

Four years later—four years which saw a number of other mass shootings in which the perpetrators blamed their violent acts on their hatred of women—twenty-five-year-old Alek Minassian plowed a rented van down a sidewalk in Toronto, killing ten people, after posting on Facebook: "The Incel Rebellion has already begun! We will overthrow all the Chads and Stacys! All hail the Supreme Gentleman Elliot Rodger!"

● ● ●

As I continued using dating apps through 2014 and 2015, it was eerie to me to hear how many of the young men I met on these sites echoed the extremist attitudes of the incels, even though they would never have identified themselves as such—in fact, I think that many of them thought of themselves as quite woke, with their feminist-identifying dating app profiles.

But "incels are not merely an isolated subculture, disconnected from the outside world," as Zack Beauchamp pointed out on *Vox* in 2019. "They are a dark reflection of a set of social values about women that is common, if not dominant, in broader Western society. The intersection between this age-old misogyny and new information technologies is reshaping our politics and culture in a way we may only dimly understand."

It was when we sat talking in some bar, or on my back patio or on my roof, and I would ask my matches about their experiences with women, that I would see their anger emerge. It startled me so, I started writing down the things they said in a notebook I entitled "Boys."

Flipping through this notebook now, I see the words "he said he's angry" and "he seemed angry" come up often. Some of these young men said they were angry at women for blaming them for things; they were angry at women for accusing them of not caring enough. They were angry at women for saying they didn't text them back enough, or quickly enough: "I'm not your bitch!"

They were angry at women for thinking they owed them something—a relationship, or even just a text back: "Hey—we met on *Tinder*." They were angry at the women who matched with them and didn't answer their messages. "Then why'd you swipe right?" one demanded.

They were angry at women for "ruining romance." "There's no romance among guys my age," said a guy I'll call the Aspiring Movie Producer Boy. "Romance is completely dead—and it's women's fault. Girls come on to you so sexually, and this is the person I'm supposed to fall in love with?"

"There's no challenge or mystery to it," complained the doleful Artisan Barber Boy.

They blamed women for making it all too easy—"too easy," "too easy," they told me over and over again. It was slut-shaming 101, but they didn't seem to have any idea how it sounded. Sometimes, I tried to point out that they were repeating age-old double standards.

"So if a woman sleeps with you, she's a slut?" I'd ask. "Isn't that the same stereotype that's been used to degrade and control women forever?"

"But what about men?" they said angrily. "Women do so much fucked up shit to men, you have no idea." They talked in whataboutisms.

They were especially angry about the word "mansplaining." "How's it mansplaining if I know what I'm talking about and you don't?" one asked.

Some said they were angry at women for breaking up with them. "This girl cheated on me. It took me a long time to get over it," said the Artisan Barber Boy.

"I was in love with this girl who dumped me. I'm still not over it," said the Boy from Queens. After he got dumped, he said, "I was on Tinder constantly. I was swiping right on every picture."

Hearing all this made me see the cleverness of Tinder in eliminating the need to know if you've been rejected. It was clear that rejection made some men quite angry, and they weren't used to this—to being told that they couldn't have whatever they wanted (especially if they were white men). The app only let you know when you had matched with someone, which stroked men's egos. But some of them seemed to see the act of simply matching as equivalent to consenting to have sex, and they were angry at women who wouldn't sleep with them once they'd matched.

"What do they think it's *for*?" they asked. "I mean, come on, it's called a hookup app."

It was still a couple of years before the #MeToo movement officially began, in 2017, but there was already a lot of talk about sexual harassment and assault in the new feminist wave. Many of the young men I met on dating apps were already angry about this talk. They were angry that they "had to worry about getting called a rapist" for having sex with women who, they believed, had more than consented to their sexual encounters.

"It's like you can't even flirt with a girl anymore," they said. "You compliment someone and she says you're committing assault." They were angry about how women allegedly misrepresented things after getting their feelings hurt. "Regretted sex is not rape."

"Girls act very aggressive on Tinder," said Marty, the college boy I met in Vermont. "They act like they're cool with just a hookup, but then all of a sudden they're acting like you're in a relationship, when you said from the beginning it was just a hookup. Then they act all hurt or mad when they find out you're seeing other people."

One of the young men I spoke to said it was so confusing and "dangerous" to get involved with actual women these days, he felt like he would rather "just stay home and masturbate to porn." I called him the Choking Boy.

●　●　●

I met the Choking Boy in the summer of 2014. Daniel and I were back in Louisville, going across the bridge to Indiana during the day so I could interview the New Albany girls again. We filmed them walking in their town's Fourth of July parade, during which they all took out their phones and started swiping on Tinder.

"Why are you on Tinder when you're somebody's baby daddy?" one of them mused, and they all laughed.

We filmed them at a Fourth of July party at a quarry. Boys and girls in bathing suits were jumping off high rocks into the sparkling water. At their tailgate party, we filmed some of the boys grabbing the girls' asses and pushing them to chug a bottle of bourbon. We filmed a boy doing a rap about a girl who likes to be raped. "And my dick was so long, you were into it," he rapped, and they all stood around—boys and some girls, too—cheering him on.

Watching all this, I thought about how boys like this—all college students around nineteen and twenty years old—were considered normal. And yet some of these very same boys were telling me, with great nonchalance, about how they had gang-raped girls—which they described as "sharing" girls—

who had passed out or found their way into their dorm rooms at night, as if this was just a normal part of life.

When I heard boys talk this way, it made me wonder how they were being raised. Did their parents ever talk to them about consent? My parents never did. And it seemed that a lot of parents still weren't talking to their sons or daughters about anything having to do with sex. A young man I interviewed in Austin, Texas, said: "I never got a rule book on how to be a man. There was no role model telling me, this is what it's like to express an emotion with a woman, or how you should treat her when you're having sex."

And there was no rule book for how to have sex, either, but there was a how-to manual: porn. Over and over, in my reporting, I heard from both young men and women that the place they'd learned about sex was online porn. Studies confirm that the majority of young people, teenagers and even children, are learning about sex from porn.

Defenders of porn ask, "So what's the problem with that?" They assume that any criticism of porn comes from prudishness. They accuse critics of porn of advocating censorship (even when they're not), as if this is the biggest concern in this debate.

The problem is they're ignoring nearly forty years of research showing a connection between porn and sexual violence. A 2015 meta-analysis of twenty-two studies from seven different countries done between 1978 and 2014 concluded that porn consumption contributes significantly to "aggressive behaviors and attitudes" and is "associated with sexual aggression." A 2011 study of American college men found that 83 percent of them watched porn, and those who did were more likely to say that they would commit rape or sexual assault if they knew they wouldn't be caught.

And porn hurts men as well. Research suggests that young men who consume porn have lower sexual satisfaction and are more likely to be "depressed, unable to enjoy intimacy, and suffer from desensitization of feelings, dissatisfaction, loneliness, isolation, and compulsion," according to a 2012 article in *Psychology Today*. What's more, studies say that girls and young women suffer from a loss of self-esteem from seeing women sexualized in mainstream porn—which almost always shows women pleasing men and not the other way around.

I went back to my hotel room in Louisville that night after the Indiana tailgate party feeling troubled by what I'd seen. I thought of my Indiana grandmother, the suffragist, and wondered what she would have to say about those young men of her home state and their casual misogyny. I imagined she would have been alarmed to see how things had progressed, or perhaps regressed, almost a hundred years after she had marched for the women's vote.

And then I took out my phone and started swiping on Tinder again.

It made no sense that I would turn to a dating app for relief from my anxiety about rape culture—or maybe it did. Maybe this *was* rape culture, which grooms you to find relief in its grimy arms from the time you're a little girl.

It was moments like this when I questioned whether what I was doing had anything to do with choice. Once again, it felt like I'd been programmed, like Raymond Shaw in *The Manchurian Candidate*, whose handlers ask, "Why don't you pass the time by playing a little solitaire?"

Solitaire indeed. In interviews, Tinder cofounder Jonathan Badeen said that he had "modeled the original stack of potential matches' faces after a deck of cards."

A stack of cards from which, that night in my Kentucky hotel room, I matched with the Choking Boy.

● ● ●

The Choking Boy was a frat boy out of central casting, big and beefy like a football player, with a sandy-colored buzz cut, wearing a red University of Louisville T-shirt and cargo shorts. We met at a local bar and made each other laugh, and so after a couple of beers I invited him up to my room at the Hilton.

Within minutes of him coming into my room, we were in bed, and he got so excited, talking dirty, calling me names, saying, "You're a filthy little MILF aren't you?" Stuff like that. And then his hands went around my neck and he started choking me.

I knew from my research and talks with my young women friends that choking had become a thing, a standard move, and so I tried to go with it for a few seconds, to see what it was like and if I had reason to object to it.

But as his grip around my neck got tighter and tighter, I actually wondered—wait, is this motherfucker going to accidentally kill me?

The Choking Boy had his big, thick, ham-hock hands around my neck while he was on top of me, pounding away at me pretty hard, crushing me slightly; his thumbs were on my windpipe, pressing harder and harder until I was sure he was going to crack it.

I reacted like an animal—like prey—squirming and scrambling around underneath him, slapping at him with my hands and legs, which he seemed to take as a form of encouragement, choking me harder. So I took my foot and put it squarely against his torso and pushed as hard as I could, catapulting him off me. You know how you get extra strong in those moments when you're fighting for your life? He went flying off the bed, landing flat on his butt on the floor. He looked flabbergasted.

"What the fuck?" he cried. "What'd you do that for?"

"Why the fuck did you have your hands around my neck?" I demanded, scrambling up off the bed and retreating to the opposite side of the room. I looked around for a weapon; I couldn't find anything else, so I picked up a pen off the desk and held it aloft, pointing it at him.

"I wasn't trying to *hurt* you!" he exclaimed, sounding more angry than contrite. "I thought you'd like it!"

"You thought I would like being *choked*?"

"All girls like being choked!"

"And why do you think girls like being choked?" I asked.

But I instantly realized why he thought so: it was porn. Among the most popular searches in porn over the past few years were: MILF, teen, lesbian, stepmom, stepsister, and choking.

Choking is a highly gendered act in porn—almost always it's a man's hands around a woman's throat. Rarely do you see women doing it to men, but men choking women appears so often across categories that many porn sites don't even bother to make "choking" a category of its own.

Choking someone, also known as strangulation, is recognized by the law as assault. Studies on domestic violence have shown that women who have been choked by their partners are at a higher risk of being murdered. And yet, choking has been normalized by porn as an expected part of sex—so much so that it's become a defense in murder-by-strangulation cases, called "sex play gone wrong."

Bafflingly, some women's magazines have celebrated choking as an exciting form of "sex play"—even recasting it as a "daring" sex act which allegedly gives women power. In 2016, *Women's Health* said that choking can "be an exhilarating experience." In order to enjoy it, the article said, women just needed to learn to "relax."

Yes, just relax while you're being choked. No wonder studies show that more women today associate sex with fear than with pleasure, love, or connection.

"It's commonly known!" said the Choking Boy.

"By whom?" I asked.

"Do you have a computer?" he said.

I handed him my computer off the desk. He opened it up and immediately went to Pornhub.

"See, look," he said, showing me a video. "It's hot."

We sat naked on the bed as he clicked through videos of women being choked with hands, with penises, with fists, almost always to the point of gagging. Many of these women made noises to signal that they were enjoying this, and some said hoarsely how much they loved it.

"See?" the Choking Boy said, smiling.

I could see that he was getting hard, watching this stuff. I could also see that the women in these videos looked distraught. Some of them had tears in their eyes.

When I pointed this out to the Choking Boy, he said, "That's because they're getting it good!"

"It doesn't look to me like these women really like this," I told him. "They're just performing for men. Almost a hundred percent of pornographers are men."

"No, no," he contended, "girls *ask* me to choke them. They love it!" He added: "This one girl, she was like 'Slap me, choke me, punch me,' to the point where she was like, getting *red*, and she was like, 'harder.' I'm gonna show you, look—"

He pulled up the Tinder messages on his phone.

"Look at this girl," he said, holding up a message.

"Are you going to choke me baby?" it said. "Choke-fuck me, I can take all of you at once until I choke," said one of his texts.

"This is still no proof," I told him. "These women don't necessarily really want to be choked. They might just think *you* want it. It gets in their heads from porn—from being taught that they need to please men."

The Choking Boy looked at me disdainfully. "And you call yourself a feminist?" he said. "The girls I know I are really strong and know exactly what they want. Are you denying them their *agency*?"

It was strange to hear this third-wave feminist argument coming from the mouth of this strapping frat boy. This was exactly how feminism was appropriated by porn advocates, I thought, by saying, "This is what women want." It's a tricky move, which puts you in the difficult position of having to argue that women don't always know what we want, because from the time we're born, we're told not only what we want (to be princesses! to be sexy! pink!) but what we are (objects for male consumption).

Feminism has always been about women finding their voice. And choking seemed to me the perfect metaphor for how, even in the age of #MeToo, women are still being silenced. For this reason, among others, it's concerning that choking seems to turn a lot of men on.

"Lots of women even have *rape* fantasies," said the Choking Boy. "They ask you to pretend like you're raping them—they like to be thrown around and shit. This girl wanted me to slam her head into the wall. They even like to get gang-raped!

"I think it's natural," he continued. "You see it in the animal kingdom. The male of almost every species is larger and more dominant. And women want that domination."

"Women want it, or men do?" I scoffed. "How do we even know what is 'natural' in the context of patriarchy?"

"Patriarchy," the Choking Boy said dismissively, clucking his tongue. "That's just a word somebody made up."

"And you call *yourself* a feminist?" I said.

"I never called myself a feminist," he said, laughing.

I wondered how many of the girls he'd been with had actually wanted to be choked by him, or if they'd just been playing along because they thought he wanted it, this arrogant boy. I wondered how many women he might have actually raped. How many times had there been blurred lines of consent? How many times, with his frat brothers, back at the frat house, when girls were passed out, had he "shared" their bodies? I wondered if I was sitting with a rapist who didn't even know he was a rapist.

And I wondered how a boy like him would ever learn any different. What chance was there that he would ever stop being anything but a rank misogynist, with everything in his culture supporting his attitudes? Here we were, in Kentucky, where the war on women was raging; there was only one abortion clinic left in the state...

"Do you want me to go?" he said, noticing how quiet I'd become.

"No," I said. "Let's lie down."

I put my computer aside.

We lay back down.

"I want to show you something," I told him. "Let's just lie here for a minute."

He seemed to feel awkward, lying there, facing me. I said, "Close your eyes."

And I touched him gently with my hands in the soothing way I have. Men have told me I have a "sweet touch." I got it from my mama, who was always more expressive with her hands than words. It was through her touch, the way she'd rub your back if you had a stomachache or stroke your forehead when you couldn't sleep, that you could feel how much she loved you.

I touched the Choking Boy's arms and shoulders slowly, gently. I touched his thighs, his hips, his butt.

"There," I said softly, still touching him all over. "Can you touch me the same way?"

"I don't think I can do it that good," he said, smiling a little, his eyes still closed. He had gotten very hard. I touched his dick. "But I can try," he said.

And we lay there, touching each other softly, gently. Then I got on top of him and rode him, slowly, gently, rubbing my clit. At the end it was stronger, faster, until we both came.

●  ●  ●

When I would come back home from being on the road, I would go to Satsko's, where I found myself spending more time. Two thousand fourteen was the year Zazie started high school, so now she could be on her own in the late afternoons and early evenings when she was doing her homework before we had dinner.

I liked having the chance to step out and have a quick drink with friends, which I hadn't been able to do very often since she was born. I soon realized

I was also drifting over to Satsko's because I needed to talk about all the crazy things that were happening to me on dating apps.

I would find myself strolling over to the bar around five or six, hoping to find Satsko or Amy, or Mike the bartender or my artist friend Austin. I would talk to the young people sitting at the bar. I wanted to talk to people with whom I could commiserate.

"Oh, it's a shitshow," someone would invariably say.

"Welcome to gay dating, straight people," I remember a young gay man said one evening.

The shitshow of dating app dating had been a topic among gay men for years. Grindr had come out in 2009, a full three years before the launch of Tinder. It was really Grindr, not Tinder, that had "revolutionized dating" with its mobile app. Founded by Joel Simkhai, an Israeli-born Gen Xer and business-school graduate, Grindr—which calls itself the "world's largest social networking app for gay, bi, trans, and queer people"—gained popularity largely through word of mouth and the gay press.

"When it first came out, straights acted scandalized that gays were just hooking up with the nearest person," said one young man I interviewed, referring to Grindr's introduction of geolocation to online dating. "Whenever you told straight people about Grindr, they were like, 'Wow, crazy, do you do that all the time?' And it was like, well, no, but it is a thing, because it's harder for us to meet people," he added.

Straight people had actually been doing the same thing for years—hooking up with strangers they met online, hooking up in general—they just didn't talk about it openly, and it was almost never depicted in pop culture. Movies like 2011's *No Strings Attached* and *Friends with Benefits* turned hookup culture into the basis for cheesy rom-coms where, of course, the protagonists (Natalie Portman and Ashton Kutcher, and Mila Kunis and Justin Timberlake, respectively) wind up together forever.

And so straights had missed out on years of collectively processing this massive cultural development. Gay men were already very familiar with the topics of conversation now coming up more and more often with heterosexuals as they graduated to the faster, more streamlined utility of mobile dating: the addictiveness, the shallowness, the dizzying sea of choices. Was mobile dating ruining the chance of having a real relationship? Was it turning us all into dating zombies?

"I had a really lovely Grindr meetup recently," said Austin, one evening at Satsko's.

Austin, who is from South Carolina, has curly brown hair and piercing blue eyes and always wears some wild T-shirt of his own design, like the one with the colorful, intertwined penises, which he likes to call "baloney ponies."

"We went on a great first date," he said, "and we were having a hookup at my house, and suddenly I'm being two-handed choked. I had to pull the hands away and say, 'Excuse me, I'm not sure that you're not murdering me right now.'"

"That just happened to me!" I said. "With this frat boy in Louisville. I thought he was gonna kill me!"

"I think there's this idea that every hookup needs to be this intense experience," said Amy. "Intense in a way that is life-and-death visceral. But it's like, I *do* wanna have grandchildren someday, so please don't kill me, and also, I would like to perhaps come out of this experience without PTSD."

"Lemme give you that post-traumatic dick, baby," Austin said.

"Ooh, yeah, I'ma give you the PTS-*D*," said Amy.

We laughed.

"Things are so different now," said Satsko, who always sat in the corner of the bar with her glass of sparkling rosé. "We used to at least have dinner before sex."

Satsko immigrated to the United States in the seventies and got married and divorced before having Amy on her own.

"Men were supposed to be gentlemen then," she said. "When you'd go on a date, they would come and pick you up and wine and dine you and then go home."

"But you were a fucking babe," said Austin.

"But I inherited this woman's genes, and no one's taking me out to fuckin' dinner!" Amy protested.

I asked Satsko if she worried about Amy going on dating app dates.

"I don't worry about her. She's a very smart woman," Satsko said. "It's kinda sad, though, because where is the human decency? You cannot just treat people like garbage."

● ● ●

"I went on a few Tinder dates with this guy," said Caitlin, a tall, blonde woman in her late twenties who worked in PR, one night at the bar. She'd told me she moved to New York "thinking dating would be like *Sex and the City*, but it was more like *Mad Max: Beyond Thunderdome*."

"Clearly there was something wrong with him," she went on. "My roommates and I called him 'American Psycho.' We were waiting for him to turn the chainsaw on me. I got sick and rescheduled a date with him and he was like, 'You're not *sick*'—kind of bullying me. I had to send him a screenshot of the thermometer."

Then we started sharing our worst Tinder dates—which was already a kind of social convention, a way of dealing with the madness.

"The worst Tinder date I ever went on," said Dolly, a tomboyish bartender who lived in Brooklyn, "was with a gentleman who is a filmmaker in his forties—I won't say his name. I was already pretty drunk when he showed up at the bar, and he was like, 'I live like two blocks away. I can show you some of my new film,' and I was like, 'Sure.'

"So we go to his apartment," she continued, "and then he breaks out a pipe and I was like, 'Oh, okay, I guess we're gonna smoke weed.' But this was not a fucking weed pipe. I ended up smoking crystal meth! After I took one hit, I go, 'What is this stuff?' And he says, 'Crystal,' and I'm like, '*Crystal*?'"

"Ohhh..." we said.

"It was very terrifying, and I was very distraught," said Dolly. "I ended up staying at his house 'cause I was scared to go home. I couldn't sleep for hours. I laugh when I look back on it, but it was awful of him to do that to me."

"Why did he want to do meth?" I asked, perplexed.

"'Cause he's a fuckin' meth head!" she said. "But no one would have thought it. He's very famous, although he hasn't had a hit in a while."

"I guess he couldn't afford heroin," Caitlin joked.

We laughed.

"Did I tell you about the French Guy?" I asked.

He was a guy from Paris I had met on Tinder. He appeared to be quite attractive in his pictures, dark and artsy-looking. He was in town doing party promotion for a movie premiere, he said. I met him at Manitoba's, and when I sat down in the booth next to him, I felt like I had fallen into a giant ashtray.

"Oh, I hate that, when somebody smells like cigarettes," Amy said, wrinkling her nose.

"I'm still stuck on you going to Manitoba's," said Austin.

"It's my Tinder date bar," I told them.

They said, "Aah."

"This is a Tinder date bar for a lot of people," said Amy, meaning Satsko's.

"Sometimes they hook up in the bathroom. Don't even make it to the cab," Austin said.

"So I wanted to leave as soon as I sat down and got a look at this guy," I went on. "He didn't look like his picture, which looked like Orlando Bloom."

"It probably *was* Orlando Bloom," Austin said.

"This guy looked like a rat," I told them. "A rat in a tweed jacket who smelled of cigarettes—which, unfortunately, I only realized after I had already ordered my drink. So I'm like, 'How'm I gonna get through this?'"

"Gay men will just leave," Austin said. "Like, *nope.*"

"So I decided at least I could do some research," I said. "I asked him what the dating scene was like in Paris. 'Eetz the same as here,' he told me.

'Everybody eez using Tinder or Badoo.' 'And what has this done to French romance?' I asked. It was a stupid, reporter's question, but I seriously wanted to know—"

"And lemme guess," said Amy, "he started kissing your arm like Pepé Le Pew?"

"No," I said, "he put his hand between my legs! He started talking about how the French still had a handle on the art of romance, and then just made a grab. I jumped out of my chair and asked him what the fuck he thought he was doing. I chewed him out good—"

"Oh, we know you did," said Austin, with a grin.

"Why are you Tindering with twenty-five-year-olds?" Satsko asked.

"'Cause they're hot," said Amy.

"So much work," Satsko said, making a face.

"Well," I said, "he didn't take kindly to my little feminist lecture. He was like, *'I know who you are.'*"

"What did he mean by that?" asked Caitlin.

Apparently what he meant was that he had done some background research of his own, divining from a reverse-image search on Google that I was a writer for *Vanity Fair*. He'd been coursing through my Internet presence, which he described to me in a cockeyed version which amazed me in its length and detail. I felt like Rick in *Casablanca* when he responds to hearing about the dossier the Nazis have on him with, "Are my eyes really brown?"

"So he tells me, 'I am going to write on my blog that you are on *Teender*—'"

"Isn't everybody on Tinder?" Caitlin asked.

"Do people still have blogs?" said Amy.

"I thought blogs went out with Kurt Cobain sweaters," Austin said.

"So I told him, 'Go ahead,'" I said, "and I threw my beer in his face."

"So *Dynasty* of you," said Amy.

"Have you gone through the change yet, baby?" Satsko asked.

"Almost, almost," I confessed.

We laughed.

"So the French Guy just sat there, beer dripping down his face," I went on. "I ran out of Manitoba's. And he came following me down the block, yelling, 'You focking cow!'"

"Is this the same guy who just grabbed your twat?" said Amy.

"And then James came along," I said.

Our neighbor James is a groovy, white-haired, African American man in his sixties, a professional guitar player. "He was just walking along and he saw this guy yelling at me," I said, "and he was like, 'Hey, hey now, what's going on here?' And the French guy said, 'She's a focking whore!' And he stomped away. 'Where'd you run into *him*?' James asked. And I told him what happened. 'What's Tinder?' he said. So I showed him Tinder. 'Now that doesn't look very romantic,' he said. And then we started kissing..."

"You made out with James?" said Amy, smiling.

"Oh, I've always wanted to do that," said Caitlin.

"We just kissed a little bit," I said. "I'm not really sure how it happened. And then I went home...

"He has a girlfriend," I added, after a moment.

"Ah," "Too bad," they said.

● ● ●

*Abel, come back, come back, come back...*

I washed my teacup in the sink and went to the window. I pressed my head against the glass, shading my eyes with my hand so I could scour the street for him again. "Where are you? Come back, come back," I tried to tell him telepathically.

I had felt, sometimes, that we had the ability to communicate through the airwaves, we were so deeply connected. I would be thinking of him and suddenly get a text from him, or I would be about to text him and my buzzer would ring, and it would be him. It was the way of love, I thought, which seems to open up a special channel . . .

But I still didn't see him anywhere on the street.

I thought of that Joni Mitchell song, "Car on a Hill," where she's waiting for her "sugar to show," anxiously wondering, "Now, where in the city can that boy be?"

*Oh, come back, come back . . .*

But then I realized—oh, no!—I was in no condition to receive him even if he did appear. I'd better take a shower! Shave my legs! Fix my hair! I hurried to the bathroom and turned on the water and started peeling off my clothes, hoping that going through this ritual of getting ready for him would somehow magically expedite his arrival. Through years of practice with unpredictable men, I had it boiled down to a science: I could be ready to fuck in fifteen minutes.

But why did I want him to come back again? I asked myself, standing under the warm spray of the water. "Remind me of that again?" Why, when he had never made amends for what he'd done—and not done—over the past four years?

Was it really just thinking about all my bad dating app dates that had made me want to see him again? And was that enough? And then I realized, with a kind of horror: It wasn't just thinking about all those awful experiences that had made me want to see him again and escape into his arms. It was because thinking about going on all those dating app dates had made me think about the potential for violence. To be with Abel was to know, at least, that I would not be raped.

● ● ●

Dating apps have a problem with rape, though this has been largely unacknowledged by the media or pop culture—something which has puzzled me no end, especially once the #MeToo movement started.

How is it, I've wondered, that we're having a national conversation about sexual assault, and almost no one is talking about the assaults which happen on a regular basis through dating apps, which most people are using now to date?

I've been aware of the problem myself from the interviews I've done with young women and men. I've also had a Google alert on my phone for "dating app rape," which serves up news stories almost every week from somewhere in the United States or around the world about the sexual assault of someone who had met her attacker on a dating app—almost always a woman, sometimes a girl.

These stories involve many different dating platforms, including Tinder, Bumble, Plenty of Fish, MeetMe, and others. Here are just a few:

Fremont, California, 2015: "East Bay Man Allegedly Used Dating Apps to Lure, Rape Women"

Hyderabad, India, 2016: "A woman software engineer has alleged that she was raped by an IT professional she met on a dating app here."

West Midlands, United Kingdom, 2017: "App Date Rape Claims from Girls as Young as 16"

New York City, 2018: "He Used Tinder to Hunt the Women He Raped and Killed"

Melbourne, Australia, 2019: "'Tinder Rapist' Glenn Hartland Sentenced to Over 14 Years in Prison"

Calgary, Canada, 2019: "A Calgary anesthesiologist has been convicted of date rape...of a woman he met on Bumble."

Hong Kong, 2019: "A Hong Kong...man allegedly raped two women, and attempted to rape another, by approaching them through dating apps."

The National Crime Agency (NCA)—the UK's leading national law enforcement agency, akin to our FBI—considered the rise in dating app rape of such concern that, in 2016, it did a study on the relationship between online dating and sexual assault. Shockingly, the agency found a 450 percent rise in rapes linked to online dating over the previous five years, and 85 percent of the victims were women. Its study credited this surge in sexual violence to "the behaviors and expectations fostered by an online environment"—an environment which, it said, makes men feel "entitled to sex."

The study described "a new kind of sexual offender" created through online dating: "These offenders are less likely to have criminal convictions, but instead exploit the ease of access and armchair approach to dating websites. This is aided by potential victims not thinking of them as strangers, but as someone they have got to know."

As I read about this, I wondered what the findings would be if the FBI did a similar investigation of online dating and its impact on sexual assault in the United States. To this day, no such study has been done, despite much evidence that crimes are being committed with the use of these platforms. It always seemed so strange to me that whenever dating apps were discussed in US media, it was almost always in a positive way: "How to win at Tinder," "How to make dating apps work for you." It seemed a carryover from the days when the wonder boys of Tinder were lauded for turning dating into a "game."

To be seen as criticizing anything young people are doing is also, I think, something members of the media are hesitant to risk, for fear of looking pearl-clutchy and old. Look at what happened to me—Tinder's cyberbullying had worked. And so the victims of rape on dating app dates were effectively being silenced by a media turning a blind eye to their experiences.

But then, finally, in December 2019, ProPublica, the nonprofit news organization, published a piece in conjunction with Columbia Journalism Investigations and *BuzzFeed* entitled "Tinder Lets Known Sex Offenders Use the App. It's Not the Only One." This story talked about the problem of registered sexual offenders on dating sites, the overwhelming majority of which don't do background checks on their users.

But as welcome as this investigation was, I thought it buried its most powerful revelations—those found by a survey its authors had done of more than 1,200 women who said they had used a dating platform in the past fifteen years. Among this group, the article said, "more than a third of the women said they were sexually assaulted by someone they had met through a dating app. Of these women, more than half said they were raped.... Overall, 31 percent of the women in the survey reported being sexually assaulted or raped by someone they had met through an online dating site."

This is a huge number. And part of what's disturbing about it is that it suggests a higher rate of sexual assault and rape among women who use dating apps than women in the general population. What's more, when the authors of the article analyzed more than 150 incidents of sexual assaults involving dating apps—all culled from news stories and corroborated by police reports—they found that only 10 percent of these incidents involved an attacker who had already been accused or convicted of sexual assault at least once, and "only a fraction of these cases involved a registered sex offender."

So in 90 percent of these incidents, the attackers were not men with a known history of sexual violence. Which aligns exactly with the findings of the UK's NCA, that dating apps are creating a "new kind of sexual offender." Which is exactly what I began to think as I listened to the young men I met on dating apps, complaining about young women who refused to sleep with them after matching on Tinder or OkCupid: "What do they think it's *for*?"

These were guys who, once upon a time, would have been described as "nice young men." Most of them had gone to college. They were clean and vegan and devoted to recycling and had worked on political campaigns to get progressive candidates elected; they had close friends and family ties. And yet, they were talking like rapists. Something about these platforms was giving them the idea that they were entitled to sex—this was, after all, a big selling point.

● ● ●

I was surprised, but pleased, when Mandy Ginsberg, then the newly hired CEO of Match Group, agreed to talk to me for my documentary in early 2018. I wanted to ask the first female CEO of one of the world's biggest online dating companies about dating apps and their relationship to rape culture. (Ginsberg stepped down two years later, citing personal reasons.)

Ginsberg, then in her late forties, had long dark hair and freckles and wore a conservative dark blazer. She sat before me in a brightly lit conference room in the New York offices of IAC, the owner of Match Group.

"We are creating social products that sit in the hands of women," she said, "and I do think it's important for us to protect, listen, and create products that are relevant for women."

"And how are you going to do that?" I asked.

"There's a couple of things that we need to do," she said. "One—we—we have safety tips.

"First of all," she said, her voice taking on a solicitous tone, "it's important that women don't go to someone's house, they meet in a public place, they don't drink. They let someone know where they're going. Um, they take precautions," she went on. "They let a person know that they're on a date with someone else; they don't go into someone's car. There's a number of safety tips that we provide for people, and I think that people also have to just take real precaution."

I was stunned. This was Match Group's plan for protecting women on dating apps—"safety tips"?

Safety tips had long been buried in these sites. This didn't seem like enough anymore, if it ever was.

Ginsberg's "tips" also didn't reflect the reality of online dating culture. For a dating app date *was* going home with somebody, or taking them home, or getting in their car, after having a few drinks (or at least it was, pre-Covid). It wasn't always this, but it often was. And that has as much to do with the design of the platforms themselves, I think, as it does with the people using them. Dating apps promote hookup culture.

Dating app culture is full of enormous, built-in risks for women, risks which have always been a part of dating, but have been aggravated now by the speed and ease and virtual anonymity of these apps. Did Ginsberg really not see this? And why wasn't she talking about what men should do to make dating apps safer—like maybe not raping their dates?

When I tried to talk frankly about the reality of online dating, Ginsberg was steadfast in insisting that meeting someone on a dating app is no different from meeting someone in real life. "People meet strangers all the time," she demurred. "I think when you meet strangers anywhere, whether it's at a club, at a bar, or on a dating app...[you] have to take precautions....What happens in real life is what happens on our apps. It's just a reflection of society."

But dating apps are remaking society, which Big Dating companies are always happy to acknowledge in all those glowing reports about how they're "revolutionizing" dating—just apparently not when it means being held accountable for the social effects of their products, or the crimes being committed with their help. "Dating apps are just a reflection of life" isn't a factual argument—it's a corporate argument.

When dating apps are promoted as neutral, and dating app dates are seen as somehow naturally occurring events, then it takes Big Dating companies off the hook for any responsibility for the sexual assaults and rapes that regularly happen through their platforms—responsibility they already know they don't bear in a legal sense. That's because of Section 230 of the 1996 Communications Decency Act, which protects Internet service providers from legal action based on third-party actions. Controversial Section 230 in effect immunizes both service providers and social media companies from liability for wrongful acts committed by their users. If anything is ever to change in terms of protecting dating app users from harm, then Section 230 is going to have to be amended, in order to "deny bad Samaritans...immunity," says

Boston University School of Law professor Danielle Citron, a leading expert on the issue.

But when it comes to something as dire as sexual assault and rape, you would think that online dating companies would take their responsibility more seriously on their own, no matter what exemption they enjoy under the law.

"I think that for everyone who comes to dating apps," Ginsberg told me, "it's important that people understand that they're meeting strangers. They don't know their backgrounds....They've never met these people before...and it's important for people to be diligent."

"So are you saying that dating apps are dangerous?" I asked.

"I think that if you're a young woman, you've got to take precautions no matter how you meet people, sadly," Ginsberg said mildly.

I was starting to feel rather outraged. Was the head of Match Group really never going to admit any responsibility to her customers for their safety on dates facilitated by her company?

"But I don't think Tinder is like a comedy club or OkCupid is like a bar," I said. "It's different because you're a matchmaker—you're enabling people to talk. So it's not the same as a public space where you might meet someone randomly on your own.

"But since you say it is," I added, "if you were the owner of a bar and somebody got raped in the bathroom of your bar, I'm pretty sure as the owner you would have some responsibility, wouldn't you?"

"I'm not familiar," Ginsberg said blandly.

Later that same year, in 2018, ProPublica reported that "Ginsberg launched a safety council made up of leading victim advocates and other experts....Interviews with its members show that the council has focused on getting users to take action themselves rather than having the company act."

Soon after the publication of the 2019 ProPublica story about dating apps and sexual offenders, Tinder announced that it would add a "panic button" which could summon police if users began to feel unsafe on a date. Match Group said that it would roll out this new tool on its other services as well. Stories in the media treated this like a positive step—and that's how Tinder's marketing team presented it.

But actually, as subsequent reports revealed, all Tinder really did was invest in Noonlight, an already existing safety platform. Tinder users would now have to download Noonlight, along with Tinder, in order to have access to said panic button.

And Noonlight, by the way, is another data-sharing app, which takes users' data and makes it available to "third-party business partners, vendors, and consultants," according to its own privacy policy.

•  •  •

It is never someone's fault that she's been raped, of course, which can't be said often enough. There are times when no matter what "precautions" a woman takes, she can't avoid being sexually assaulted. And yet the culture of online dating seems to enable and even encourage victim blaming—which I believe dating app companies do little to discourage, by essentially putting all of the responsibility for safety on their users.

*She met him on a dating app—what did she expect?*

Such attitudes can be seen in the responses to a 2016 case in which a twenty-three-year-old woman said she was sexually assaulted by Pittsburgh Pirates infielder Jung Ho Kang, whom she met in Chicago after matching on Bumble, the "feminist dating app." She told police she lost consciousness after Kang gave her an alcoholic drink; then she drifted in and out of consciousness as he sexually assaulted her. She reportedly had done a rape kit.

"Really?? She met him in a hotel room? Did she think they were going to play cards?" said one of the comments that appeared on the *Pittsburgh Post-Gazette*'s Facebook post of an article about the case. "Sad," another commenter said. "A girl goes to a famous guy's private hotel room for what? A conversation and tea? Come on now."

Kang was never charged with a crime. Several months after the alleged incident, a Chicago police spokesperson said, "We have additional questions for the victim but she has not made herself available to police." As of this writing, she has not come forward again.

Many sexual assault victims never report the crimes committed against them, which they find harder to do in the face of slut-shaming and blame. They fear what might happen to their reputations if a case ever wound up in court. And if the victim has been drugged—which has happened in many reported cases of dating app rapes—it makes coming forward even more difficult, as her memory will be called into question.

Blaming the victims of rapes which allegedly happened on dating app dates has been the tactic of defense attorneys in several prominent cases. Call it the hookup app defense.

"She knew he was on Bumble to hook up," said Natalie Woloshin, attorney for former University of Delaware baseball player and accused serial rapist Clay Conaway at his 2019 trial. "She knew he wasn't looking for a relationship. And with all this, she willingly drove over to Clay Conaway's house. So, was the plan really to watch a movie?"

Woloshin offered into evidence the sexting messages that the victim and Conaway had exchanged prior to their date. But anyone who has ever used a dating app knows that sexting is a normalized part of online dating culture.

And sexts do not equal consent.

"She told the defendant multiple times to stop," prosecutor Casey Ewart countered at Conaway's trial. "He ignored her and kept going."

Conaway was sentenced to five years in prison for fourth-degree rape. In 2020, in a second trial with a different victim, he was found guilty of third-degree unlawful sexual contact. Interestingly, however, he was not found guilty of strangulation. "He said, 'I thought all girls were into that,'" testified the victim in this case—whom Conaway had met on Tinder—describing how he had choked her. "I was absolutely terrified. I thought I was going to die," she said.

The problem with equating matching or sexting with consent is that consent can be withdrawn at any time during a sexual encounter, according to laws in all fifty states. North Carolina was the last state to make this the law, in 2019—too late for the young man who allegedly attacked Aaliyah Palmer (who has said that she wishes to be identified in news reports) to be charged with rape.

Palmer met her attacker on Tinder in 2017, when she was nineteen. She said she consented to have sex with him until he became violent, and she told him to stop. As he raped her in a bathroom at a house party in Fayetteville, she said, his four friends, a group of soldiers from Fort Bragg, stood outside and put camera phones under the door to film the attack.

When Palmer tried to collect evidence for a criminal suit—Tinder messages showing the men bragging about the photos and the video they had posted on Snapchat—it had all been deleted. When she then contacted Tinder and Snapchat to assist her in retrieving this evidence from their servers, she said, the companies did not help her.

In 2020, Palmer filed a civil suit against the five men named in the attack, as well as Match Group and Snapchat's parent company, Snap, Inc. Her case is among the first to go after dating app companies for their failure to help sexual assault victims in collecting evidence to press charges against their attackers.

"It's about getting people to think a little bit more and for holding these guys accountable," Palmer told ABC11. "Because victims are ashamed or scared or know they won't be believed. And they know that [the evidence is] gone, too." Palmer said that she has suffered depression as a result of her attack and had to drop out of school at North Carolina State University.

Whenever I read news stories like this, I think of the women I've interviewed who've had something happen to them on a dating app date, an assault or rape, after which they felt they had no chance of seeing justice served. I think of the young women who've told me that Tinder and other dating apps have failed to help them, most often by not responding, when they requested information or access to content relating to a sexual assault or other crimes, such as cyberbullying or stalking or doxing—all of which can happen whether or not the people who match ever meet up.

I've wondered how many women are not coming forward at all because they know they'll get no help from the dating app in question. Rape is already an underreported crime. Is online dating making not only assault more common but reporting assault more difficult?

Many women I've spoken to have experienced that moment where they've wondered how they were going to get out of a dating app date before something did occur. "How did this go so wrong?" they've asked themselves. "Who will believe me if something happens?"

It happened to me too. When I woke up, groggily, one night, after drinking too much with the Aspiring Movie Producer Boy, he was standing beside my bed, sticking his dick in my face. I pushed him away and ran to the bathroom and locked the door, after which he left my apartment. I was lucky that time. It could have been much worse.

● ● ●

"What are they complaining about?" said Sheila Nevins.

Sheila was sitting on an ottoman, very close to her TV, inspecting the short cut of my *American Girls* documentary that I had brought to show her, like a jeweler examining an uncut gem.

"They think their lives are hard?" she asked, scrunching up her face.

I had to catch my breath.

Sheila was the longtime president of HBO Documentary Films. She was one of the most powerful people in documentary filmmaking in the country. She had produced over a thousand documentaries, including *Going Clear* and *The Jinx: The Life and Deaths of Robert Durst*. She had won thirty-two

Emmys and twenty-six Oscars. She was a legend. She was also known to be tough.

My boss Graydon had suggested that I meet with Sheila and show her some of the footage from my *American Girls* documentary—footage I had been shooting with Daniel and editing with Spencer, footage I'd shown Graydon because somebody at *Vanity Fair* had told me that I'd better let Graydon know I was working on a documentary which had grown out of a story for the magazine (my 2013 story "Friends Without Benefits").

Graydon had watched the footage and said he liked it so much he wanted to executive produce it as a documentary series. Which was thrilling, to say the least. Graydon had become a force in the documentary world himself, producing some award-winning films, including *9/11* and *The Kid Stays in the Picture*.

So I went to see Sheila on a bright sunny day in September of 2014. I remember I was early. I was very excited. I stood across the street from her apartment building, a high-rise on the Upper East Side, trembling because I was so nervous, spilling my coffee on myself.

When I went up to Sheila's home office, she was there with Jackie Glover, another HBO executive who worked closely with her. Sheila was wearing a sort of black tracksuit ensemble that looked like something a gangsta rapper in the nineties would wear. Her long, dangly earrings jangled against her swooping, dramatically highlighted hair. We all sat on our comfy chairs.

"I'm not usually this fat," Sheila told me. "I'm on a diet. I want to lose twenty pounds because I don't have a lot of time left and I don't want to spend the rest of my life fat."

I was taken aback. I didn't think Sheila was fat. I also didn't know why a woman in her seventies who had won scores of awards would be worrying about a few extra pounds…But then, I *did* know; I worried about being too fat myself. And I knew from the reporting I'd been doing that anxiety over body image was still epidemic among women and girls.

And that, I told Sheila, was one of the subjects of *American Girls*.

I was pitching, pitching.

"What, like the dolls?" Sheila asked, squinting.

I tried to explain why I had chosen the title: because here in America we like to think that girls' lives are better than the lives of girls anywhere in the world—and yet, when you actually talk to girls and find out what they're going through, you hear a different story.

"Like the Tom Petty song," I said, quoting: "Well, she was an American girl / Raised on promises / She couldn't help thinkin' that there / Was a little more to life…

"You know that song?" I wavered.

"Oh. It just makes me think of the dolls," Sheila said flatly.

When we played the reel of the footage Spencer and I had been working on, Sheila went over and sat close to the TV and watched it with such rapt attention that I thought to myself, "Oh my goodness, she loves it."

It was short cuts of our trips to spring break and the Houston beauty pageant and some of the other places Daniel and I had been. Girls in the footage were talking about the pressures of sexualization and the new kind of sexism they were experiencing online. They talked about how it seemed hookup culture gave boys the upper hand. "It feels like the girls don't have any control over the situation," one girl said, "and it shouldn't be like that."

When it was over, I was sure Sheila was going to explode with praise and tell me how great it was and immediately green-light the project. But she just screwed up her face and said, "I don't get it. What are they talking about?"

"Well, sexism is a really big problem in the lives of girls," I said.

Sheila looked unconvinced.

"Gloria fixed all that," she said.

She meant Gloria Steinem, who, I later learned, was a good friend of hers.

How do you tell a legend she's out of it? But before I could think of a way, the meeting was over.

I went reeling onto the street, wondering what had just happened. I hadn't really asked for this meeting; it was Graydon trying to help me and to advance our project. And I'd really thought that this person he was sending me to was going to be a *little* bit encouraging. But she had made me feel like nothing. "Now what am I gonna do with all this footage?" I wondered dejectedly, doing the sad Charlie Brown walk down the street. After meeting with Sheila, I was ready to give up. I actually started counting off the people I had told I was working on a documentary, to see how embarrassing it would be if I just quit...

Then I remembered my friend, an Iranian filmmaker, telling me that he'd once had a meeting with Sheila, and she'd made him feel so bad, he went out into the street and threw up in a city trash can.

That made me feel a little bit better. At least I wasn't vomiting.

And I knew our reel was good. I knew I liked watching it again and again. I knew the girls' stories were important. And if Sheila didn't get that, then somebody else would...

That afternoon, I was scheduled to go with Daniel to the University of Delaware to interview another group of girls. Working always made me feel better, and I thought that doing this work would help me shake off the horror of that meeting. I could hardly imagine that this was going to be one of the worst days of my life.

●　●　●

"Alyson, Alyson what would you think of Abel?" I wondered, that night as I waited to see if he would return, brushing on mascara, readying myself, I hoped, for his arrival.

How I wished I could call Alyson and ask her whether I was crazy for wanting him to come back, after all the ways he had disappointed me.

"What do you think of him?" I imagined asking her.

"Aw, sookie sookie now," I could hear her saying, with her sly little smile.

It was thinking about Sheila that had made me think of Alyson and the night she died. It was the night of that same awful day that I had met with Sheila—the same day Daniel and I drove down to film the girls at the University of Delaware. As the sun set on the highway, I told Daniel about my meeting. I was afraid he was going to lose confidence in me and our project because Sheila hadn't gotten behind it.

But he just said, "Who cares what she thinks? I believe in you."

I looked out the window.

"Are you crying again?" he asked in his teasing way.

"No," I said, "it's just the sun in my eyes."

We got to UDel, which sits in the middle of Newark, an idyllic-looking college town, around nine. We filmed the girls in the basement of their apartment building, on the couches where they liked to hang out. They were "cool girls," they told me. "We're guys' girls," they said. Guys liked them because they didn't act "dumb." "Like, we don't make a big deal out of things." They told me this was their feminism.

They talked about sex with bravado, like it was something that was always within their control. "If there's no games and I'm not being entertained— I lose interest and, goodbye, on to the next," said one of them, with a toss of her hand.

But as the night wore on, they started opening up about their rancor at the entitlement of the young men who always seemed to assume that women wanted more from them, when really they wanted nothing in return—young men who, they said, didn't treat them with even basic courtesy.

"'He drove me home in the morning.' That's a big deal," said Rebecca, a blonde girl in short-shorts, sounding piqued. "'He kissed me goodbye.' That shouldn't be a big deal, but boys pull back from that because—"

"They don't wanna give you the wrong idea," murmured her roommate, Kayla.

"But a lot of us girls aren't gonna *take* the wrong idea," Rebecca said. "Sometimes we just want to get it in, too. We don't want to *marry* you. You're either polite or you're fucking rude." The conversation made me think of something the dating historian Zoe Strimpel had said: "What is at the root of 'the contest to see who can care less' is the horror of seeming needy. Women are so afraid of seeming needy, because the 'needy woman' taps into something very deep in misogyny: this idea that women are this sort of bottomless pit of need and dependency and maybe even lunacy."

I thought of the sexist young men I'd spoken to who had told me, again and again: "Girls are *crazy*."

"So I think a lot of women who find themselves in this modern dating scene are sort of striving to keep their needs suppressed so they don't ever seem like that reviled woman," Strimpel said. "And it's a real shame. Because we're all needy. How you give of yourself and allow others to give to you would seem the linchpin of what it is to have a relationship. I think there's been a lot of confusion with mistaking sexual freedom for sexual callousness and shutting down your own needs."

As I fluffed out my hair, that night, getting ready for Abel, I thought about when we'd interviewed Rebecca later, one-on-one in her room. It was then that she said she'd been having panic attacks and drinking too much. She told us she'd just broken up with a guy who kept cheating on her.

"Sometimes he'd be all over me," she said, "and then he'd just disappear. I heard from people that they saw him at a party doing things. When we were on spring break, I didn't see him for an entire day. He always came back and said he knew he fucked up and it was always, like, Should I take him back, or not?"

I thought about how—thirty years older than she though I was, and supposedly old enough to know better—I could still relate.

And then I thought about how Rebecca and her friends had had a party that night, and we filmed them making frozen margaritas and dancing around to Beyoncé while some boys sat on couches, looking at their phones. In the middle of filming, I got a text from Alyson.

"How are you?" she texted. "Did you ever hear from that guy?"

I assumed she meant a guy from Tinder I'd been telling her about, some forgettable match. I didn't respond. "I'll get back to her tomorrow," I remember thinking. I didn't want to talk about guys on dating apps with Alyson anymore. And maybe a part of me was trying to escape all the crushing feelings of self-doubt I'd been battling ever since my meeting with Sheila. I don't really know why I didn't text Alyson back. But I'll never forgive myself.

● ● ●

A few weeks before this, Alyson and I had taken a walk along the East River one Sunday afternoon. I hadn't seen her in a while, and I had wanted to see her and talk to her ever since I had started using dating apps. I felt like I needed to talk to her about it.

She was my best woman friend. She had been my little brother Noah's roommate in college, so she was thirteen years younger than I, but from the moment we'd met at his college graduation, we were simpatico, besties.

She had moved to New York after college and had lived within a few blocks of me ever since. She had been there for me when I was pregnant with Zazie, and now she was like a second mother to my little girl. Alyson was lovely, with an elegant way of dressing, a soft, soothing voice, and a merry laugh I loved to hear.

She was from the Bahamas, raised in a strict Catholic family. She was brilliant in the sciences, got her PhD in biology. She lived near us in the East Village, but we hadn't seen her as much over the past couple of years, which I attributed to the demands of her new job at a pharmaceutical company, which had her traveling all over the country.

She would say she was coming to brunch or dinner but then flake out and say she wasn't feeling well. She would TiVo reality shows and stay in bed all day on the weekends, watching them. It was bingeing before we called it that. Sometimes I would get annoyed with her for not coming to see us, because I missed her, and sometimes I would think she was blowing me off to be with her friends from her new job. But that wasn't why. I didn't know enough at the time to see that she was depressed.

I can't count the times I've thought about that last conversation I had with Alyson as we walked along the East River that day, wishing it had been different. How I've wished I hadn't been so involved in my dating app drama, that I would've connected with her more and asked her more about herself. When I think of it now, all can I think is, what a waste, such of waste of my last moments with my darling Alyson.

Men had always seemed to take up too much of our conversations. We would have failed every Bechdel test. But then, how could we stop talking about men when they were causing us so much confusion and anger and pain?

Alyson just listened with a quizzical smile as I told her about my secret life on dating apps. She'd never been on one herself; they were still pretty new. I knew she wouldn't judge me for anything I was doing. She was the least judgmental person I had ever known. I had learned a lot from her over the years about the spectrum of sexuality and gender. She identified as bisexual, and was open and frank about sex in a way that never felt salacious or forced, although she also had a delightfully bawdy sense of humor.

Ever since I'd known her, she'd had things with men, things with women. She had gone through the typical things that all the women I knew started going through in the nineties and two-thousands, when guys never wanted to commit to a relationship or get into anything real. I remember once yelling at a Swiss guy who'd cheated on her and then broken up with her over email. I saw him sitting at a sidewalk table at Zum Schneider, the old East Village biergarten, as I passed by with my dog, Boo, and I told him off for not treating Alyson right while Boo sneaked a sausage off his plate. Alyson just laughed when I told her about it. She hadn't dated anyone seriously in the few years since, which again I chalked up to her busy work schedule.

But I did think of her living her new life, sometimes, and how she was alone in all those hotel rooms, alone on all those planes. I worried that she was lonely, though I didn't want to offend her by asking. She had a great deal of dignity in addition to being very sensitive.

And so I found myself talking up the convenience and ease of dating apps as we walked along the East River that day. I don't really know why I was doing this, since I'd already seen for myself how using these apps could be more than disheartening. But Alyson seemed so quiet and almost fragile that day, I wanted to be more bubbly than I had been, walking along, grousing about men. So I started parroting some of the sanguine things people always say when they talk about online dating.

"There are some nice guys on them," I said. "And not everybody just wants to have sex. But if you do just want to have sex with someone, it's pretty easy. It can be pretty fun."

I took my phone out of my pocket and showed her Tinder. I showed her pictures of a guy who'd been texting me a lot, sending me pictures of himself with his cat.

"He's cute," she said, a little surprised.

"Yeah," I said, "a lot of them are. It's a brave new world, but like I said, if all you want is sex, you can definitely get it."

I don't even know why I said that to her. She deserved so much more than just sex. She deserved to have someone love her. She wanted someone to love her. We had always spoken truthfully to each other about men, and now here I was, just pretending, acting like the cool girl who wins the contest to see who can care less. Maybe I just didn't want to upset her by telling her how upset I was that the dating landscape looked so bleak.

Lately, she'd been talking about becoming a single mom herself; she was considering freezing her eggs. She was almost thirty-seven, and she wanted a baby. I'd told her I would help her as she'd helped me. We had talked about me being the auntie. And now here I was telling her about Tinder. What was I thinking?

In a couple of years, I would see ads on Tinder for Trellis, an "egg freezing fertility studio," with the slogan: "'The One' can wait. Fertility? Not so much. Start planning for your future family today," and I thought it was the most cynical ad placement I had ever seen.

I wanted to cheer Alyson up, that day. I wanted to make her laugh. So I started telling her some of my dating app stories. I told her about the guy from Tinder I'd had lunch with that day; he was just twenty-two, from Canada.

"He told me he wanted to be a porn star," I told her. "He said he's actually been considering 'how to get that going.'"

"That shouldn't be that hard," Alyson said with a smile. "Oh no, wait, maybe it *should* be." We laughed.

"Except he looks like Ron Howard," I said. "Not that there's anything wrong with looking like Ron Howard—Ron Howard just doesn't look like a porn star."

"He looked like Opie?" Alyson asked.

"He did," I said. "He said he was fluid, sexually, and then he asked if he could come over right then and have sex."

"Was lunch over yet?" she asked.

"Barely," I said. "He also kept talking about how 'a fair number of the women on Tinder are pros, and some of the men are pros.' He seemed to know so much about it, I started to wonder if he was a pro himself. Then we got into a discussion about how young people today are changing the world as radically as young people in the sixties."

In the Canadian Boy's supercilious voice, I quoted him saying: "Like, there's this unacknowledged social revolution going on, and it's being driven by boys with this very toxic male worldview. It's very dangerous, very *Lord of the Flies*. It shall be the end of us."

"So at least he was intelligent," Alyson said.

"Yes," I said. "He was. He also said that his girlfriend was fine with him hooking up with other people."

"Oh, well, that was nice of him to let you know that," Alyson said, laughing.

We laughed and walked and talked some more. Then we hugged each other and said goodbye and she headed home. As I watched her walking away, I had a vague sense that something was wrong. I wish I had called after her, run after her.

• • •

I found out Alyson was dead the night we got home from Delaware. I was leaving the Avis rent-a-car place on East 11th Street when her brother Richard called me from the Bahamas.

"Richard don't tell me this!" I said, stopping on the sidewalk. It felt as if a shadow had come over me, as I looked up at the dark night sky.

She had hanged herself in her bathroom. She hadn't left a note. She had come home from work, drunk a bottle of wine, and killed herself with the same precision she did everything else.

"She wanted to do this, that was clear," one of the cops told me, when I went to our local police station, wanting to know who had found her and what they had seen. How did they know it was suicide? I asked. Could someone have done this to her?

I'd been afraid that she'd tried dating apps after I'd told her about them and then one of her matches had come and killed her, making it look like a suicide to cover it up. I thought about Warriena Wright...

But no, the cops said, Alyson's death was deliberate.

But why?

The people suicides leave behind never have the privilege of asking. Nearly every day since the day she died, I have thought about Alyson and what made her do this thing, and I have felt a remorse so deep—remorse over not answering her last text, over not connecting with her more over the last couple of years, over letting technology get in the way of our closeness. You can't have a real friendship over text.

I've worried that part of what had made her feel so low was my telling her about the dating app wasteland. I've thought about how young women have told me they were "ready to give up" when it came to dating: "It's just so depressing."

There was a rumor among Alyson's friends at work that she'd found out some guy she liked was marrying someone else. I couldn't imagine Alyson doing something so definitive over a man. But then, maybe it had been the accumulation of men, or lack of men—lack of women, too, lack of relationships. I'd almost been there before myself, a couple of times when I was younger. I had had that thought: "I can't live without him." But you can, you can, I would have told her, had I known. "It will get better." And if anyone reading this is ever feeling this way, please know that there are people who love you, and please seek the help that is available.

Looking back, I realized that Alyson had been thinking about doing this thing and maybe planning it for a while. She'd been posting things on Facebook that sounded wistful, thanking people for their love. She had sent me and Zazie messages telling us she loved us. Had this been her way of saying goodbye? That last night, when she had texted me, would it have made things different if I'd responded?

There has been a rise in suicide among women and girls in recent years. A 2018 study by the National Center for Health Statistics reported that the suicide rate among women and girls between 1999 and 2017 more than tripled for girls ages ten to fourteen, and was up more than 60 percent in women ages forty-five to sixty-four. When researchers talk about this tragic phenomenon, they cite various factors that could be causing it, including the pressures on women working outside the home and taking care of children at the same time; the rise in single-parent households headed by women; and a challenging economy. Some talk about alcohol abuse and the opioid crisis. But this always sounds to me like only part of the story.

What about the lack of societal support for women? And what about having to live in a world where to be a woman or a girl means to experience inequality, often sexual harassment and assault, domestic violence, casual menace, dismissiveness, and disregard?

And what about the influence of technology? Researchers are seeing that the concurrently rising rates of anxiety and depression among girls is connected with their use of social media, but this affects women, too. It seems significant that, during the same years in which more women and girls have been ending their own lives, the Internet and social media have ramped up misogyny on- and offline and contributed to the raising of a new generation of sexist men and boys.

I get emails from counselors and therapists who want to talk about these things. "Epidemic" is a word they use in describing how they're seeing more women and girls seeking help for their struggles with issues related to living in a sexist world. "There is too much alpha male energy," they've written me. "It has to do with the Internet." "They feel unsupported and attacked." "There's an epidemic of men not wanting relationships." "Women are starved for love."

When Alyson died, I thought about the sadness of living in the world as a woman or a girl. She had had to deal with racism too. She rarely spoke about it, just a few times when someone said something to her at work or in a store. "That's terrible," I would say. "Are you okay?" But she would laugh it off as if it was no big deal. It pains me to think of it now.

A 2019 study reported that from 2001 to 2017 the suicide rate for African American girls ages thirteen to nineteen skyrocketed 182 percent, and 60 percent for boys the same age. There was an increasing amount of blatant racism online during this time, on top of the continued systemic racism and police brutality which led to the 2013 founding of the Black Lives Matter movement by three young Black women.

I should have asked Alyson more about what she was going through. I wish I had. I couldn't stop crying for a couple of days after she died. I couldn't think, couldn't hold a conversation. Zazie and I lay next to each other in bed, just holding each other. I read Alyson's texts over and over. I kept looking at the posts on her Facebook page. It was a strange new ritual, this posting of encomiums online. I don't know if it gave me comfort or just made me feel more mournful.

• • •

"Hola," came the text from Abel, finally, that night.

It was him, he was here, he was in my orbit—he was back!

My heart leapt.

I came running from the bathroom and grabbed my phone off the kitchen counter, about to return his text immediately so as to catch him before he disappeared again.

My index finger hovered over the screen as I wondered what to write. I thought about all the things I wanted to say:

"Hello! I hated sitting with my friend Constance tonight and feeling like a pathetic old woman, and I hated coming home alone to this dark, empty apartment. It made me miss my dear friends who have passed away, and my father and my brother and my dog. I felt lonely and alone, and I hated knowing that you were somewhere nearby and I had missed you out of my own self-doubt and inability to forgive. And now I want to feel your arms around me again and I want to bury my face in your neck and I want to smell your skin. Because I know you, and I know I don't have to pretend with you. Because you see me—me. Because you wanted to fuck me even when I got really fat! And because you've never said an unkind word to me, not even once. Because you never meant to hurt me, even when you did..."

But I didn't write any of that.

I just said, "Hey! I'm home! Come on over!"

And I waited. And waited. But he didn't text me back.

# Four

I was confused, I was upset, I was agitated.

Abel's failure to respond—it had been over an hour now, and *he* had gotten in touch with *me*—was even starting to piss me off. A surefire trigger for addictions, like hornets dislodged from a nest, buzzing around.

I went searching my apartment for cigarettes. I hadn't smoked any since I'd sent him away, a few months before. I looked in kitchen drawers, coat pockets, at the bottom of bags. But I couldn't find any. I would have settled for a stub.

I couldn't quite believe that he was doing this to me again—but then, why should I be surprised? It was the way it had always been, since the beginning, with him. And it was online dating. It was hookup culture, which always seemed to shift the already unequal power balance in heterosexual relationships even further toward men and boys.

I had lived through four years of this, with Abel, ever since that night in June of 2015 when we first met. After he came back the first time—looking like a vision on the roof at my Fourth of July party, with the fireworks going off behind him—we fell into a routine of sorts. A thoroughly unplanned, unreliable routine, in which nobody would ever be obliged to say, "We're dating," "We're together," "We're going out."

I never knew when I was going to see him. I never asked. Whenever I asked, I wouldn't get a straight answer. "I'll be comin' round the mountain when I come," he'd joke. Which made me laugh and forgive.

We never made a date. He was like a stray cat that would appear at my door and wind himself around my legs. And I would let him in and give him a bowl of cream.

It was that 9 or 10 p.m. text, saying, "Hey!" "How you doing?" Or "Hola!" And I would invite him over. And I would let him in.

Often he was drunk, coming off a drinking session with his work buddies. To complain would have been to become a harpy, and I had no intention of being thrust into that unwelcome role, which I knew all too well. To not complain was a safer bet, like I'd been taught by my mother, who had been taught by her mother, and we've all been taught by a million messages transmitted by our culture, we women and girls encumbered with wanting men.

Call it "The Things We Must Unlearn."

I'd learned long ago how to be a nice, accommodating girl from such handy guides as *Cosmopolitan's New Etiquette Guide*, published in 1971, a book owned by my childhood babysitters, which I had voraciously consumed when they weren't looking. "The classless girl," said this astonishing tome—whose writers included Nora Ephron and Gael Greene, both no doubt in need of a gig—"is forever picking and badgering, whining and sulking, because all she can think about is *herself.*"

Oh, no, I wouldn't want to do that! I thought. Much better to be the girl who "did things with her hands that men like.... Fluff his pillow, section his grapefruit...take off your bra..."

I did Abel's laundry. I took off my bra. I kissed him in the dark.

"Sounds like you have a situationship," said a young woman I met at Satsko's, analyzing the Abel-related data I had provided. "That's when you're dating, but you're not really dating." Which could describe much of dating today.

The Urban Dictionary has many entries which grapple with arriving at a definition for something that is, by its nature, undefined: "Situationship: A relationship that has no label on it.... Like a friendship but more than a friendship but not quite a relationship." "Let's just chill, have sex, and be confused on the fact that we are not together but have official emotions for each other."

It felt like Abel and I did have some unofficial and rather jumbled emotions about each other, though they were only ever expressed openly in bed. As the summer of our first year turned into fall, he started showing up once, twice, sometimes three times a week. He had a place to live now, with roommates in Brooklyn, so he wasn't just crashing with me anymore. In the olden days, we would have called an assignation of such frequency a relationship, but even I couldn't call it that. We rarely talked. The extent of our knowledge of each other had gotten stuck in that enchanted week when he had stayed with me while Zazie was at camp. Now, because he only came over late at night— and, with Zazie back in school, he always left early in the mornings before she got up—we could speak very little, and only in hushed tones.

"Get on top of me," he'd whisper in the dark. "I wanna see your hair all flowing over me."

Every time was delicious. I wanted to shout out the window, "Hallelujah!" It felt like I'd found what I'd been waiting for all these years. He was natural and adventurous and always right there with me. In bed, he felt older than when I talked with him, when he always became a little bit shy. But in bed, it was that feeling of having known each other forever.

How has this happened? I'd wonder. Could Abel be "the one"? And if so, how problematic was it that he was so much younger than I? Yes, I'd had visions, projecting well into the future, even images of him at my hospital bed when I died! He looked so sad...

But then I'd stop myself and think, "Wait, is this love or is this just hormones?" Had I just finally become a sort of automatic orgasm machine, like the women's health magazines had always promised I would when I went through the change?

Whatever it was, I felt like I couldn't let Abel go, no matter what he did, no matter what had happened between us.

One night at the sake bar, I was telling Amy about him, and she grinned and said, "There's a mathematical equation by which the amount of shit you're willing to put up with in a man is in direct correlation to how good he lays the pipe."

I guess that was partly why, when he didn't show up on time or return a text, I didn't squawk. Sex was important to me—and was that so wrong? Did I really need him to be taking me out to fancy dinners, which he couldn't afford? When we'd wake up in the morning and just look at each other and start going at it again—why did I need anything more?

Yes, I was breaking my own rule of not having a man come over when Zazie was home. But I felt I knew him well enough now. I was still keeping him a secret from her, however, because how could I ever explain this unequal relationship to a girl I was raising to be a feminist?

But then, *did* I have to explain it to her? I wondered. Did she have to know about it? Couldn't there be a part of my life that was just for me and no one else, that I didn't have to explain to anyone?

And how could you ever explain the hunger for someone's lips? Or the luscious, drunken sex?

A couple of times, he was so drunk he actually peed in my bed. I know—it sounds terrible. And it is. You're lying there, and you feel this hot, wet… *what*? It's a phenomenon not unknown to young women in hookup culture. When I mentioned it to my Sake Bar Satsko crew, I heard several stories of young men's inopportune incontinence.

"Oh, the peeing in the bed," my friend Clara commiserated. "You can use vinegar to get the smell out of the mattress. It's like they can't have sex without being totally drunk because they get so freaked out by intimacy."

I started to realize that it might go beyond that with Abel, however, that he might drink too much in general. The time he peed in my drawer was kind of a sign. I watched in horror as he pulled out my drawer as if he thought he was putting up the lid of the toilet seat and then peed all over my hats and bathing suits.

"Dude!" I whispered.

He was already on the bed snoring.

I never got mad when he did such things. I just changed the sheets, sometimes with him still asleep in the bed. I'd been with drinkers before, and I knew that it was difficult to know what to do to help. Especially if you weren't really their partner, and it wasn't even really a relationship. I would wonder if I was being an enabler, if I should stop seeing him…

But then I would get back into bed and he would pull me to him, and we would start making love again. And it was like dancing, hips grinding on hips.

"Slow down," he would tell me softly.

I would get so excited with him.

Once, when we were undressing in my room, he looked at me woozily and said, "You're lovely." And it was lovely. There was something about us that, despite everything that seemed reckless and foolhardy, was very, very lovely. One clear fall night, we went up to my roof and made love on a lounge chair under the stars. We lay beside each other looking up at the sky, and I turned to him and said, "This is so lovely," and he said, "Yes, it is."

Whenever he would disappear—which, after some months, he started doing regularly, just not responding to texts for a few days or weeks at a time—I tried to laugh it off.

"How's Mountain Boy?" my friends would ask, and I would just say, "Oh, he's up in the mountains somewhere." I trained myself not to go on that stomach-churning roller-coaster ride of not worrying, then worrying, then feeling frantic: Had he drunkenly walked into traffic? During which accident his phone was crushed? And now was he lying alone in a hospital somewhere? Had he been hit on the head and developed amnesia?

He did physical labor, and it could be dangerous. Things had actually fallen on his head. "I've had about ten concussions," he told me once, as a way of reassuring me he'd be all right when "a beam hit [him] in the brain." He had fallen off ladders, been hit by a car while riding his bike home from the subway. "Is he still alive?" I would wonder, growing alarmed. I would even pray.

I once saw, on a closed Facebook page where older ladies like myself vent their issues, a thread in which a woman posted about how she was wondering what had happened to a guy she'd met on a dating site. She'd been seeing him for a few weeks, she said, and then he'd vanished. Now she was worried that he might not be okay, and wanted to know if she should be concerned.

Women swarmed the thread. There were hundreds of comments—so many that the page managers had to finally shut it down. "I'm sure he's fine!" women reassured the poster. "He just needs some space!" "Men are from Mars, women are from Venus!" "Maybe he just lost his phone!"

"Have you checked the hospitals?" others implored. "Do you know the names of any of his friends?" "Do you know any family members?" "Have you heard from him yet?"

"Heard from him yet?"

I felt embarrassed for them—and for myself, because every time Abel disappeared, I did exactly the same thing. I wanted to comment on the thread, to tell them, "Stop! Don't you know the game has changed? There are no rules anymore. It's called ghosting!"

But I refrained. It would have been the type of thing I hate, on social media, when somebody acts all holier than thou. And I couldn't tell them what I was really worried about every time it happened to me: not that Abel was dead, but that he had met someone else, or had grown tired of me, or decided I was too old.

● ● ●

"Being involved with a man today is like being involved with someone in a war," said my friend Nicky, an author and single mom my age. We were having brunch, which I had invited her to because I wanted her to talk me out of being with Abel. "It's like you never know if they'll ever come back," she went on with a laugh. "And when they're missing in action, you're not even sure if they're dead."

Nicky is the most sensible woman I know when it comes to men. She has a couple of fuck buddies she's known for years; but all this time, she's been able to keep her feelings out of it. "The trick is, I don't *have* any feelings for men," she told me. Not since she'd had her son with a baby daddy who promised to be there, but then never was. "I will never trust them again," she said. "I will never let them in again. It's their loss. They don't deserve me, or most women I know."

Now, she says, she just "uses men for sex." She compares it to getting a massage.

"It's the one time in my week when I just get to do something for myself," she told me, that day at brunch. "When they start talking about themselves I go like this"—she put her finger to my lips—"Shh, shh, be quiet, don't talk." She laughed. "I can't spend any extra time or energy wondering where they are, or what they're doing, or how they're doing. I'm too busy."

"I wish I could be like that," I told her. "Honestly, I wish I could."

But the truth was, I was like that, sometimes, when I didn't really care about the guy. But then, when I did, I was all in. I didn't want to swipe. I didn't want to see anyone but him—like Lizzo sings: "Once upon a time I was a ho / I don't even wanna ho no mo'..."

But I knew better than to go looking for Abel, or to confront him about any of this. I'd been doing the man dance for a long time, and I remembered Liz Phair singing, "You said that I should call you up / But I knew much better than that..."

I didn't want to get twisted up in pretzel logic, thinking too much about Abel, like I had done with shady Axel Wang. And so I decided, when Abel had gone incommunicado for a few weeks again, I was going to just try and fuck him out of my system. And that's why I invited the Pie Boy to come over.

• • •

The Pie Boy was a Shrek-like figure of Irish descent. He looked like the Incredible Hulk wearing a pair of Buddy Holly glasses underneath a mop of dark hair. He was literally a giant nerd, age twenty-six, who worked in marketing for a start-up in Brooklyn.

I had met him on OkCupid back when I was looking for people to interview for "Tinder and the Dawn of the 'Dating Apocalypse.'" I had very positive associations with the Pie Boy because he had steered me toward a perfectly archetypical fuckboy, a friend of his I'd called Nick.

"I hooked up with three girls, thanks to the Internet, off of Tinder, in the course of four nights," Nick had told me proudly, "and I spent a total of $80 on all three girls."

I went searching out Nick again after I'd had another meeting with Sheila and she told me she thought my documentary should be about dating apps, not girls. I hadn't really wanted to see Sheila again; Graydon had encouraged me to go. He said that Sheila and I just needed another chance to talk. "You two should love each other!" he said. I was skeptical. But Graydon was my executive producer, and he usually knew what was up.

My picture on my badge from the front desk security on the day of that second meeting with Sheila looks as if I'm on my way to the gallows. It took place at HBO's offices in New York. When I went upstairs, Sheila seemed as un-thrilled to see me as I was to see her.

"After I saw you the last time, I had lunch with Gloria," she told me. "We ate green. I asked her if I'm a feminist and she said, 'What's a feminist?'"

She gave me a triumphant look.

I didn't really know what I was supposed to say to this, so I just said, "Well, that's a very good question…"

I was confused about why I was there again. Sheila gave no indication that she was any more interested in my *American Girls* documentary than the last time we met. It annoyed me that she would agree have me come see her again and just submit me to more taunting, like an old cat with a menopausal chipmunk.

And then all of a sudden, my inner Drogon came out, and I hopped on her back and started flying around Sheila's office.

"Look, Sheila," I said, "there are lots of broadcasting venues out there. I'll put my movie on YouTube if I have to. I don't need your validation." I told her that it seemed to me that a lot of older feminists like herself were doing victory laps while young women and girls were experiencing as much sexism as we had ever had to deal with when we were young—especially in the realm of sex. I told her some choice tidbits from my own Tinder nightmares to illustrate my point.

"That sounds like a documentary," Sheila said. "Dating apps, social media, sex. You should go and shoot some more."

And so that was why I had brought Daniel, my cameraman, with me to interview the Pie Boy's friends Nick and Brian, a personal trainer and a teacher, at Satsko's one afternoon in late 2015: to start shooting footage for a possible documentary on dating apps. It was a new idea—kind of Sheila's idea.

Over the course of their startling exchange, Nick and Brian mused about their pleasure in physically abusing women in bed, which was sounding more and more like a trend:

"Recently," said Nick, "I hooked up with a girl that wanted to get choked and slapped and shit like that. It was pretty cool. I'm into it. I didn't know I was into it till I got put on, but it's the bee's knees, I'll tell you that."

"Yeah," Brian said, "it's good."

"I thought I was gonna kill this girl," said Nick. "I'm into it, 'cause it's something about being in power."

"Being in power, yeah," said Brian.

"Like, I could fucking crush you right now," said Nick, putting his hands together, as if crushing someone's throat.

"And some people like to get literally punched, closed fist," Brian elaborated, making a punching move with his fist.

270

"Girls wanna be overpowered. Girls have daddy issues, man. Like, every girl has daddy issues," said Nick.

I had been told that Nick still lived with his mother.

It was an alarming conversation. I didn't know whether to thank them or punch them. Spencer and I cut parts of it together with some of our other interviews and put it on the reel we were now planning to show to HBO. I still held out hope that Sheila would green-light my documentary. She was the expert, after all, and I guess part of me wanted to impress her.

● ● ●

In the weeks after that interview with his friends, the Pie Boy started texting me a lot, asking me how things were going with my project. I finally realized he just wanted to get laid. It was around this time that Abel had disappeared again, and so I was just like, "Fuck it. I'm going to fuck him."

Texting with the Pie Boy turned into sexting, and he confessed that he wanted to be "bad." "Catholic boy," he said. He said he had fantasies about having sex with older women. (They all said that.) He also said that he'd had a relationship with an older woman who lived in his neighborhood when he was a senior in high school.

"Oh," I texted sympathetically. "Do you feel like she took advantage of you?"

"No," he texted. "She was nice to me. She gave me snacks."

"Would you like me to bake you a pie?" I asked, picking up on a theme.

The Pie Boy said he would like that very much. I asked him what kind, and he said, "Apple." Of course. The fruit of original sin. We made a date.

I actually love to bake. It brings back memories of my first paying job, at the Spiral, where I started making pies when I was ten years old. I would come in early on a Saturday morning with my mother and, while she attended to making the special of the day, I would make three or four pies, usually apple, blueberry, and maple pecan. I had learned how to make the crispy pie crust too, rolling out the dough with crushed ice. My mother would put the pies in the oven for me. My stepfather paid me a dollar per pie, which I would immediately take and go buy two books. The paperback books at Waldenbooks in those days cost $1.25.

I thought about all this as I made that pie for the Pie Boy, listening to a classical radio station; it was what my stepfather always used to play in the Spiral while my mother was cooking before the restaurant opened. I'd hoped that doing all this would keep my mind off Abel. But somehow it only made me think of him all the more.

How I wish I'd made Abel a pie! I thought, rolling out the pie dough, almost starting to cry. I wondered if I was ever going to see him again, as I always did whenever he disappeared. No wonder people train themselves to care less in this new dating culture, I thought, when caring puts one at such high risk of heartbreak.

The Pie Boy was due to come over for some pie and midmorning sex. My house smelled good. I smelled good. I had gotten all clean and waxed and perfumed and put on my apron, the one with the pink and purple hearts. I went for the apron sans underwear that day, because, I had discovered, to my dismay, I couldn't fit into any of my lingerie—I suddenly seemed to be expanding at a more rapid rate. Which didn't concern me as much as it might have if this brawny young man hadn't been on his way over to have sex.

"No matter," I thought, "I'll just be naked." I did my hair. I put on heels. I hardly ever did things like this, setting up this kind of playful little scene, and I found I was enjoying it. "I wish I had done this for Abel," I thought. I almost texted him again, but I managed to control myself.

Where *was* he?

It wasn't until the moment when the Pie Boy rang my buzzer that I realized what I was really doing all this for: it was because Abel was ghosting me, and it made me wonder if he had stopped finding me attractive, and I wanted to turn someone on.

I realized it was kind of pitiful. But as long as I was going to do it, I was going to be effective. When I opened the door and the Pie Boy saw me like this, I did a little twirl for him in my apron and heels. I thought he was going to pass out. It's for moments like this, I thought, that we sometimes do these things—less for the sex than for the chance to watch them lose their shit. The good ol' male gaze.

I pulled the hulking Pie Boy into my bedroom as I slowly took off my apron, all the while talking dirty to him. I let the apron slip down over my boobs and started running my hands all over myself. I went all "Put the Blame on Mame," for him, Louis Armstrong blowing his horn on my playlist.

I watched the Pie Boy watching me, getting so rattled and hard as he quickly, awkwardly undressed, almost falling over while he pulled off his pants. I licked my lips, telling him what a bad boy he was—he was going to get spanked!

"Oh my God!" he exclaimed.

I was enjoying watching him get so excited. But did it turn me on? Not really. In the end, it was all for him, that lucky boy.

I gave him a little spanking and then turned him over and rode him like a pony until he came with screams so loud I was afraid my neighbors were going to think somebody was being slain.

I closed my eyes and tried to think of Abel. Which only made it worse.

When it was over, the Pie Boy asked if he could have some pie. We went and sat at my kitchen counter and I served him a slice.

"Would you feed it to me?" he asked.

"Sure," I said, feeding him pie as he kept saying, "Oh wow, oh wow, oh wow…"

"Can you put the apron back on?" he asked.

Then a funny thing happened. My phone rang and it was Graydon.

I put my finger to my lips, letting the Pie Boy know it was a work call and he had to be quiet. He nodded. It was Graydon on the phone with Annabelle Dunne, a producer who worked with him at his production company. He was calling to say that Richard Plepler, then the chairman and CEO of HBO, had watched our (then titled) "Hookup" reel and loved it.

"He could not have been more positive about it," Graydon said. So HBO was going to produce my documentary.

It was the coveted green light, like the one at the end of Daisy's dock in *The Great Gatsby*, always just out of reach, and now it had twinkled for me.

I could hardly believe it. I was making a movie!

I thanked Graydon and said goodbye and then looked at this giant, naked boy in my kitchen eating his piece of apple pie. Who did I have to share this life-changing moment with? Him, I realized with a sigh.

"I'm gonna make a movie," I told him.

"That's great," he said. "But I'm not in it, right?"

"No, of course not," I promised.

Then we went back to bed and fucked again, with him on top of me, making high-pitched screams like the goat in the viral mix of Taylor Swift's "Trouble."

He texted me a lot after that, but I was suddenly very busy.

"I've been really busy too," the Pie Boy texted, as if it was his choice, not mine, not to meet up again. But he wasn't really a bad guy, so I let him win the contest to see who could care less.

• • •

After waiting for Abel more than an hour, that night, having rushed home to him after leaving Constance, I wanted to text him: "Where are you?" Maybe all in caps.

"HOW DARE YOU HIT ME UP AND THEN DISAPPEAR AGAIN?"

But I contained myself. The texting game requires such restraint—more than in fighting off the desire to swipe, shop, or smoke—unless you want to come off as crazy. There had been times when I had gotten so fed up with him that I had sent him texts, or strings of texts, which, in retrospect, did sound a bit crazy. "Pert near chewed my ear off," he would say with a smile, when he saw me again.

"Men call us crazy but then they do things that make us act crazy," said a young woman I follow on Twitter.

Exactly. Also known as gaslighting.

But I wasn't ever sure if Abel was playing power games, or if he was truly as ingenuous as he seemed—especially in the beginning, not long after he had arrived in New York—or if he was just operating erratically under the influence of beer.

Because there had been times when he *had* disappeared because of some unlikely incident, usually due to his lack of funds, and so I had learned to keep my impatience in check.

Like the time I hooked up with the Pie Boy because Abel was MIA? I later found out that Abel had been in jail.

I never would have suspected it. How could I have known? A situationship doesn't require you to keep anyone informed of anything, including incarceration. All I knew was that his absence had been making my heart hurt. My whole chest cavity would well up with waves of pain. I lay in bed one night thinking of him and aching for him so badly, I outstretched my arms as if this could somehow summon him. I sent him a few longing texts, and then angry texts when he didn't respond.

And then, one day, in the spring of 2016, he turned up again. "Did you ever doubt that he would?" my friend Calvin asked with a laugh. "This guy's got a pattern of his own." But every time Abel reappeared, I was still astonished. It was like the return of the Jedi to me.

I met him out on Avenue C one night after he had sent a text, finally, after this longer period away. I wasn't going to just let him come back into my apartment and have sex with me after this four-month absence. This demanded a conversation.

When he saw me, he smiled and sped up, coming faster and faster until we collided in an embrace. I don't think I've ever had a man hold on to me that tight.

"I missed you," he said, putting his face in my neck.

"Where the hell have you been?" I asked.

We went up to my roof and he told me the story. It was the longest story he had ever told me, the longest continuous stream of words. It was the story he'd been avoiding telling me ever since the first night we met, the story of why he had come to New York. It was a story about discrimination, and about rich and poor, like the saddest stories always are.

It all started when he was in college. He'd gone to a big state school on a track scholarship. "I was always real fast," he said. His freshman year, he rushed a fraternity. There was a lot of drinking, and a lot of girls. "They'd come by the house for a visit, and just get in the bed with you." Apparently he was so popular with his female classmates that it became the cause of some competitive joking among "the brothers." As he told the story, I could see the scene unfolding: there were the affluent boys with the polo shirts and popped collars from places like Nashville, and there was Abel, from what they saw as a hick town, with his thick accent and his stutter whenever he got nervous; and there was his catlike allure for sorority women—all of which made him a target.

The frat bros teased him and they pranked him. They made him get a really unfortunate tattoo, which I don't even like to describe because it makes me sad to think of them pressuring him into getting it. He felt their condescension, and he was not one to be condescended to—especially not by one frat brother in particular, the head of the fraternity.

"I hated that man," he said.

Growing sick of their hazing, he incited some of his fellow rushes to kidnap the guy and drop him off in a desolate neighborhood.

"We forcibly detained him," he said.

"What is it with frat boys kidnapping each other?" I asked. "That happened to my father, too."

"When a man becomes obnoxious in the eyes of his fellow man," said

276

Abel, who would sometimes take on the diction of a nineteenth-century southern lawyer, "then it is time to eject him from his community."

"Is that why you had to go to jail? For kidnapping?" I asked.

"No," he said. "That was about five years ago. He never did nothing about it. I had to go to jail 'cause I had tickets."

"Speeding tickets?"

"Not exactly…"

He left college, he said, when he heard that the police had come looking for him at the frat house; he'd racked up so many tickets for public drunkenness, disturbing the peace, public urination, and other offenses incurred while he was rushing the frat, they decided it was time to arrest him. Having no money, he walked back home, over two hundred miles.

"You didn't hitch at all?" I asked.

"No," he said. "I was appreciating the time to think."

He worked at odd jobs for a couple of years until he got up the nerve to come to New York and try his hand at being a musician.

I had known him for a year already, and I hadn't known any of that. I was amazed at my own ignorance of this man I'd been having sex with.

"So how'd you finally wind up in jail?" I asked.

"The police caught me when I went home for Christmas," he said.

When I later checked out his story—and of course I checked; as a woman dating in the digital age, I compulsively checked almost everything he said—I saw that it was true. I saw his mug shot online, in which he looked so beautiful and sad. I put a filter on it, turning him into anime, like a middle school girl in love.

"I couldn't pay the fines," he said, shrugging. "So, four months."

"Four months in jail?" I asked, appalled. "How much were the fines?"

"'Bout six hunnerd," he said, lighting a cigarette.

"Only six hundred dollars?" Such a lot of time for such a relatively modest amount, I thought. It was what happened to people living in poverty: they couldn't avoid jail when others could. It was unfair.

"I'm sorry, that's terrible," I told him. "Next time, I hope you call me."

"There ain't gonna be any next time," he said, laughing. "I don't ever plan to go to jail again."

"Of course not," I said. "I didn't mean..."

It was the first time since I'd met him that I'd made the mistake of drawing attention to the difference in our circumstances. I would never have done it intentionally, but now that I had, I felt like a jerk. He was a grown man, however young, and he had his dignity.

But I saw now that he was also still a boy—a lost boy who had made such mistakes that he feared his life might already be over because of them. He seemed a little different, I'd noticed, a little more unsure of himself, since his experience of being in jail.

"Being in jail, I can't even imagine," I said. "But it doesn't have to ruin your life."

"I done a lot of stupid things in my life," he said.

"Everybody does," I said. "Especially me."

The stupidest things I had ever done, I was actually too ashamed to tell him. Like sleeping with the Pie Boy, for starters. I felt guilty about that now.

I tried to think of something uplifting to tell him.

"You know, you're like Lip on *Shameless*," I said, referencing a show we both liked. Lip was the alcoholic genius of the Gallagher family who couldn't take the elitism and culture shock of college, so he dropped out.

Abel seemed to like that; he brightened a bit.

"Lip is a struggling motherfucker," he said.

"But Lip is gonna figure it all out. 'Cause Lip is *Lip*. Cool as fuck! Now, what can I do to welcome you home?" I asked, putting my arms around his neck.

When we got into bed, it felt like heaven to be next to him again, to smell his spicy scent and feel his touch. We began as we often did, lying facing each other as we gently touched each other all over. I looked into his eyes.

"You got a face with a view," I said.

He started singing the next part of the song: "I'm just an animal looking for a home and / Share the same space for a minute or two..."

"You know that song?" I asked, smiling, holding his cheek.

"'Course," he said, climbing on top of me and putting himself inside me fast and deep, as if he couldn't wait anymore.

• • •

My book *American Girls* came out in 2016, and I was happy with all the attention it got, and the many good reviews. I was grateful for the chance to challenge some notions that had been taking hold in recent years: for example, that social media was harmless; that sexualization was empowering; that porn was an acceptable form of sex ed for kids; that raising concerns about predators online was an overblown moral panic. It felt like my book was shifting the conversation so that people were talking more about sexism in the lives of girls, and that felt good.

A writer should probably never argue with her critics, and yet we do it all the time. I was determined never to, even after Zazie and I traveled to the Brontë museum in Haworth, England, that summer of 2016, and I saw there a letter from Charlotte Brontë throwing tremendous shade on one of her critics, which made me smile.

Still, it was perplexing to me to see how some of the reviews of my book never said what it was actually about. Some of the reviewers didn't seem to want to acknowledge that tech was contributing to a rise in sexism in teenagers' lives, even in a review of a book that was about this. A few of the reviewers so mischaracterized what my book was saying that I wondered if they had actually read it. There was the one review which said that I "blamed" girls for their troubles, which I never did.

My book was mostly in the voices of girls, because, above all, I wanted readers to know how girls felt, in their own words. The book was also about the racism, poverty, and LGBTQ+ discrimination which girls contend with, but none of this was mentioned in any of the reviews I saw.

I couldn't help noticing that the publications that gave me the worst reviews were the ones I'd criticized for *their* reporting on girls in the past. And then there were some reviewers who seemed to want to miscast me as the pearl-clutcher, the old—that was always an easy way of dismissing what I had to say—while others even seemed to have an agenda in panning my work.

Like the reviewer who emailed me to say that she was "offended" because I had pointed out some unsupported claims she'd made in her book about girls. (I'm not sure if the publication that selected her to be my reviewer even realized I had questioned her work.) "I truly thought we were colleagues," she complained to me on email. But I barely knew her.

And then there was the reviewer who was someone I knew from back when I worked at *New York*, a woman who didn't seem to like me very much (almost twenty years before, I'd been asked to rewrite a celebrity profile she'd done that the editors were unhappy with). She not only wrote a scathing review of my book, but when a female college student posted a comment about it online, challenging its depiction of my work, this reviewer went into the comments and started arguing with the young woman.

Meanwhile, I got in touch with this same young woman and took her out to lunch. (She lived nearby.) We had a great time. We talked about boys her age, and how they so often sucked.

● ● ●

Through much of 2016, I was on a book tour and then giving talks at schools and organizations across the country. It all went by in a zany blur. There was Katie Couric's face a few feet away from mine while filming a segment for *Good Morning America*, and there was Whoopi Goldberg, sitting down the table from me at an appearance on *The View*. There I was on the stage in a church full of parents in Madison, Connecticut, and in front of an auditorium full of Girl Scouts and their parents in Kansas City, Missouri. Then I was at a school in Culver City, California, where I saw Laura Dern in the audience, all piercing blue eyes and pale blonde angles. She was there as a mom; she had teenage children.

When I think of these trips, I mainly think of the faces of the parents. They look so worried. Life is so different from when they were growing up, and they seemed to want somebody—anybody—even me—to tell them what they could do to help their kids navigate the often stressful experience of coming of age in the digital era.

But the one thing they didn't seem to want to face was the possibility that all of this dysfunction their kids were experiencing—the addiction, the FOMO, the feeling of pressure to perform online and get likes—was by design. They didn't want to think about how their kids were being programmed to think and act in certain ways, or how their kids' brains might be changed forever by this technology, no matter how much you tried to tell them. And I tried to tell them.

In 2017, the year after my book came out, a number of high-ranking Silicon Valley executives were suddenly issuing mea culpas—which seemed like too little, too late. Former Facebook president Sean Parker said, in that infamous interview about the "social validation feedback loop": "God only knows what it's doing to our children's brains." And Chamath Palihapitiya, the former vice president of Facebook, went even further: "The short-term, dopamine-driven feedback loops we've created are destroying how society works," he said. "I feel tremendous guilt." However, neither executive was seen complaining about the wealth he had gained by destroying society and children's brains.

When I was on the road, the parents who came to see me would tell me stories about terrible things that were happening with their kids online. I could have written another book filled with these stories about what was going on in their schools due to social media addiction, the nonconsensual sharing of nudes, and other widespread problems I'd written about. But ask them to draw their own conclusions about what to do about all this, and the last thing they ever wanted to do was take cell phones or social media away from their kids. It seemed like they might be more addicted to this technology than their own children.

"But phones are so convenient!" they'd protest. "Our kids can't have friendships without them!" "And isn't this technology just how their generation experiences the world?"

When shelter-in-place orders went into effect due to the coronavirus, I started to worry that technology dependence in children would now be seen as a fait accompli ("screens won"). And yet the dangers haven't gone away. Sexual predators, for example, have only increased their efforts to solicit pictures and videos from kids who are spending more time online. In April of 2020, the National Center for Missing and Exploited Children reported 4.1 million instances of child cyber abuse, a fourfold increase over April of 2019.

Reports from around the world have said that cyberbullying is also on the rise during the pandemic, and experts are concerned. I could immediately see how hard it was going to be on kids, struggling with feelings of isolation and the constant possibility of suffering an attack online—particularly if they were girls, who suffer online harassment three times as often as boys, according to a 2019 study by the US Department of Education—without the ability to see their friends or teachers or counselors in person.

In the pandemic, the conversation about kids and screens quickly became dominated by the issue of closing the digital divide. And of course, it's vital to give all children access to Wi-Fi and screens in a world which demands their online participation, and which punishes them for being unable to log on. But regrettably, little has been said about educating children about the risks associated with online activity or about monitoring theirs for their own protection. And I think, again, that this stems from a deep-seated reverence for tech. Silicon Valley is once again seen as a savior rather than a possible villain.

Sometimes the parents who came to see me speak confessed that they were worried about how they were modeling phone use for their kids. They stayed in the aisles and lobbies, talking about all this, as I slipped out and went back to my hotel rooms.

I was always alone in those hotel rooms—off dating apps now, not wanting to be with anyone but Abel, and watching a lot of cable news. Every hotel room I walked into, in 2016, I would turn on the TV and there would be Donald Trump, running for president, and getting a lot of play.

It kind of shocked me, because everyone I knew who had been a reporter in New York in the last thirty years thought Donald Trump was a joke. He was our ubiquitous billionaire clown, with a dodgy, racist past nobody ever mentioned back then. When I tried to bring up Trump calling for the death penalty for the Central Park Five in a story I did for *Vibe* in 1998, my white male editor cut it out, insisting, "Nobody even talks about that anymore. Hip hop guys *love* Trump. He was on an episode of *The Fresh Prince of Bel-Air!*"

I still managed to poke fun at Trump, but, apparently unable to see the irony in it, he thought it was a puff piece and invited me to go down to Mar-a-Lago on his private plane and see the Beach Boys perform, an invitation I declined. I like the Beach Boys, but I found it weird. And what would I wear at Mar-a-Lago? I didn't have the wardrobe for a Palm Beach crowd.

Now it just made me feel disgusted and sad to see Trump at his rallies, mocking people with disabilities, ascribing criminality to people of color, degrading women. Sad because it was awful to hear, and sad to know how it must have sounded to the girls and young women I'd been interviewing over the last three years. Sad because this misogynistic cyberbully was suddenly taking up all the air in the national room. Sad because he embodied everything girls and young women had been telling me was making them angry and upset.

● ● ●

Two thousand sixteen was also the year I shot my documentary, now entitled *Swiped: Hooking Up in the Digital Age*. It was a busy year. Because the film had a new focus, we had to start all over with new characters—which was an incredible amount of work, the hardest thing I've ever done, but also the most rewarding.

I was traveling with my high-spirited director of photography, Daniel, and our soundman, Austin, an adorable and lovable young man, impeccable at his job. We stayed in cheap hotels and worked all day and often into the night. The three of us constituted our entire crew. (We hired a production assistant locally in each town.)

Graydon, our executive producer, said he thought it best if we kept our crew small, since we would be interviewing young people about intimate subjects—about intimacy itself. So we didn't have a producer with us, except for me. I wore a lot of hats, as producers tend to do. I was setting up meetings with our characters and deciding where we'd film them; doing the interviewing; and managing our production assistants, among other things. It was all a joy. Daniel and I did get in little arguments, sometimes, and Austin would joke, "Mom and Dad are fighting again." But then after a couple of beers we were good again. We became like a little family, trailing Pelican cases through airports.

Our months of shooting race by in my mind like the reams of footage I watched over and over again as Spencer and I cut it later, when the guys and I would come back from the road. The trips and our footage all blend together in my mind, like a movie all its own. I can see all the beautiful places we visited: laidback Austin, Texas, with its leafy streets, and Plainfield, Illinois, with its rows of cornfields, and Santa Cruz, California, with its ocean cliffs and giant redwoods. I see the lovely, open faces of the young people I interviewed, and I can feel Daniel behind me with his camera, almost like we'd become one person.

It was a glorious kind of work, to me, making a documentary—a lot like being a reporter, which I had always loved, but now I had these fun young guys along with me, with whom I could be creative. We loved being together, and we laughed a lot. We had our inside jokes.

It often occurred to me, in doing this film on the new dating culture, that I was simultaneously learning about myself and my own behavior on dating apps. I understood much of what the characters were talking about because I had experienced it myself. I was learning from listening to them, reevaluating myself and what I was doing in my own life. I was having a conversation with them about what was happening in their world that felt urgent to me, too, because for me it was personal.

Sometimes when I was shooting, traveling, riding in a car with my boys, I would think about how confident I had become, at age fifty-three, how sure of myself in undertaking a project in this new medium—which actually I had been practicing for two years, first by making all those mistakes with Axel and then by doing all that good work with Daniel. I wished I'd had this kind of confidence when I was younger—maybe I would have written more books, made more films. What had taken me so long? But at least I was doing it now. Growing older had given me a sense of power I never had when I was younger. No wonder society tries so hard to rob older women of this power: it's threatening to the systems that keep women down.

• • •

The most rewarding thing for me about doing the film was knowing it was an important subject. Dating is often seen as a lighthearted pastime, but I believe it's much more serious than that, being an arena in which gender inequality still operates unchecked, not to mention its inherent physical and emotional dangers.

And beyond this, for some of our characters, there was racism.

"Here's how you get treated as a Black woman on a dating site," said Bianca, one of the young women we interviewed in Plainfield, a small town about ninety minutes from Chicago. "Either they don't want to fuck with you 'cause you're Black," she said, sitting on the couch in her parents' home. "I don't know why that freaks so many people out. Or, it's, 'You're so *exotic* 'cause you're Black. I've never fucked a Black girl before.' It's like they've never *seen* a Black woman before."

"They'll say, 'No Blacks, no fats,'" said Bianca's cousin Jaylin. "It'll be just like that....If you're chubby, they'll be like, 'No fat women, no Blacks, no Latinos, only whites.'"

Jaylin and Bianca and her sister Bree were laughing because it was so outrageous. And what could you do but laugh, sometimes, at something so offensive? But they were also letting us know how upsetting it is for people to go on dating sites and see racist messages. What's equally troubling is that dating app companies do so little to stop this from happening—in fact, the very design of their platforms is arguably contributing to it.

In 2018, researchers at Cornell University found that dating apps including Tinder, Hinge, and OkCupid, as well as scores of others, "can reinforce biases or 'sexual racism.'" The Cornell study explored how dating apps use algorithms which cater to people's past preferences, continually matching them with similar demographics.

So, for example, if a user has matched with white people in the past, then he'll continue to be shown more white people as potential matches, reinforcing his sense that he wants to date other whites. "People may have no idea that a matching algorithm is limiting their matches by something like race, since apps are often very vague about how their algorithms work," said Jessie Taft, a coauthor of the study, in an interview. In other words, dating apps are not only reinforcing biases but failing to let their users know that this is what they're doing.

In a 2014 blog post, OkCupid reported that African American women and Asian men on the site got fewer matches than people of other races. "Unfortunately, daters are not more open-minded than they used to be," the company wrote. However, OkCupid never disclosed that a contributing factor in its statistics on race—as well as its conclusions about users' attitudes on race—was its own algorithm. Which is even more disturbing when you consider the fact that white men get the highest number of matches of every group on the site (and on most other online dating sites as well). Or the fact that all four of OkCupid's cofounders and designers—Christian Rudder, Chris Coyne, Sam Yagan, and Max Krohn—are white men themselves.

Some dating apps are more open about their promotion of bias, employing features that allow a user to select which race or ethnicity he prefers to be matched with. The relaunch of Hinge in 2016 included a tab for selecting ethnicity in its "dealbreaker" section. The normalizing argument says that "everybody has a type," and there's nothing wrong with "dating within your race": "It's your preference." But who's to say what your preference might be if you were introduced to people outside of your experience, or made to challenge your own unexamined racism? And racism on dating apps isn't just a problem of whom you meet, but of how you might be treated as a person of color.

"I don't date Asians—sorry, not sorry." "You're cute, for an Asian." "I usually like 'bears,' but no 'panda bears.'" These were some of the derogatory messages received by "Jason," a twenty-nine-year-old LA resident, as reported by NPR in 2018. A 2015 study by researchers in Australia found that 96 percent of Grindr users had viewed profiles which included some form of racial discrimination, and more than half of users said that they had personally been the victims of racism on the site. "We don't accept 'No blacks, no Irish' signs in real life anymore, so why do we on platforms that are a major part of our dating lives, and are attempting to gain a foothold as a public forum?" asked the *Guardian* in 2019.

Grindr and other dating apps have since introduced zero-tolerance policies toward racist language on their sites, but this hasn't fixed the problem, according to subsequent reports. "The messages men send me shows how prevalent racism in online dating is," wrote Dahaba Ali Hussen on iNews in 2019. "Men would often say, 'Is that your real hair?' A man sent me a chocolate bar emoji." Surely dating app companies are aware of studies showing that they're contributing to racism in dating, and therefore, arguably, to racism in society at large. But do they care?

When I brought up racism on dating apps with Mandy Ginsberg, then the CEO of Match Group, in 2018, I found her response as bewildering as when I had asked her about dating apps and sexual assault.

"If you're Black," Ginsberg said, "we have BlackPeopleMeet, which is the largest Black dating site. We also just launched Chispa, which is for the Latino, Hispanic community. What we hear from our users is they say…they want people who want to date people like them. So we have seen people will gravitate to these affinity communities because they would rather be in a community where they can put their hand up and say, 'I wanna date someone who's Black; I wanna date someone who wants to date someone like me.'"

"I'm sorry," I said. "My question was, what are you going to do about racism on your apps, and your answer was, well, Black people can just go over here and date other Black people?"

"That's definitely not what I said," Ginsberg replied. "I think there are a lot of people on Match and Tinder who cross racial lines."

Just then, the Match Group publicist, Justine Sacco, who was also in the conference room where we were filming, turned on all the lights and started opening the drapes. The interview was over.

Sacco, by the way, is the woman who, in 2015, became infamous for tweeting: "Going to Africa. Hope I don't get AIDS. Just kidding. I'm white!" Same person.

One of the big problems with race-specific dating sites, even when they do represent the choice of some users of that race, is that they can also be used by racists, whose offensive speech is still not dealt with by the companies.

"BlackPeopleMeet was the biggest joke," said Bree when I spoke to her in Plainfield. "First of all, it was like 80 percent white people. Like ghetto white people looking for some jungle fever. My inbox was flooded with white dudes saying things like, 'I got four Black baby mamas. Wanna be the fifth?'" She frowned.

"They think that's what Black people are like," said Bianca. "It's bad."

In June of 2020, Bianca organized a Black Lives Matter protest in Plainfield. Jaylin and Bree were there, as well as nearly a hundred others in the mostly white community.

● ● ●

Online dating can be bad for people in the LGBTQ+ community as well, as we heard from other characters in the film. At UC Santa Cruz, when I spoke to Vin, who identifies as bisexual, nonbinary, and trans, they told us about the harassing messages they routinely received on dating apps.

"Guys message me like, 'So what does that even mean, nonbinary?'" Vin said. "'Like, you think you're a guy?' They say, like, 'Oh, so you wanna have a dick?' Or like, 'So you *have* a dick?' 'So you're actually a lesbian, right?' People feel really entitled to know all of this personal information about me and my life and say whatever," they went on. "And I'm just reading these things like, 'You really feel like you can just say that to me?'"

But it isn't just that people hold such objectionable views—it's that the physical remove of dating apps emboldens people to be aggressive and harassing, and to say things that they might never say in person. Trans people complain that when they report such abuse, however, dating apps are either unresponsive or ban them just for being trans.

Tinder has faced accusations of banning nonbinary and transgender users for years, but the dating app has somehow escaped widespread criticism for this in the media, where it is generally treated favorably. Meanwhile, trans users have continually spoken out about it. Kat Blaque, a transgender woman and YouTube personality, said in a viral Twitter thread in 2017 that Tinder deleted her profile every time she tried to create an account. "At this point, it's very, very, very hard for me to not believe that I am either being targeted by transphobic trolls or being banned because I'm trans," Blaque wrote.

In 2018, Ariel Hawkins, a transgender woman, sued Tinder, claiming her account was removed shortly after she included in her profile that she was a "preop trans woman," without any specific information about how she had allegedly violated the app's terms and conditions. (At this writing, the suit is pending.) In 2017, in a widely shared tweet, @Tahlia_Rene wrote: "What good does it do me to be able to put that I'm trans on Tinder"—this was a reference to Tinder adding more gender identification options to the app in 2016—"if I'm just gonna get reported and banned over it? All this is doing is incentivizing trans women to hide it and not put it in our profiles @Tinder."

In 2019, Tinder announced that it was going to do more to support the complaints of transgender people on its site; but trans users, as well as those who identify in other ways, continue to report discrimination. Ande Karim, a Tinder user who identifies as a "demiguy," or someone who partially identifies as a man, told Reuters in 2019 that he believed he'd been banned from the app without any reason other than possibly his sexual identity. "I was baffled," Karim said. "I hadn't had any arguments, I haven't sent explicit messages or photos and I hardly used the app."

Are dating apps which cater to the LGBTQ+ community any better? Some users say they are, while others wonder if the problem is the design of the platforms themselves. "If you're not a white, young, cisgender man on a male-centric app, you may get a nagging sense that the queer dating platforms simply were not designed for you," JD Shadel wrote in the *Washington Post* in 2019. "Dating apps aren't even capable of properly accommodating non-binary genders," said *Gender Reveal* podcast host Molly Woodstock in Shadel's piece, "let alone capturing all the nuance and negotiation that goes into trans attraction/sex/relationships."

I remember early on in my days of using OkCupid I traded stories with my friend Hannah, who identifies as a lesbian and is in her thirties. "When it's all women, does that make it any better?" I asked.

She said it was "better to not be receiving dick pics from random bros," but she had noticed that since mobile dating came along, lesbian dating culture had become less relationship-focused. "Lesbians are not immune to FOMO," she said. "It used to be if you started dating someone, pretty soon you could expect to be an exclusive couple. Now you go on a date and start comparing your matches on Tinder."

"I don't think I'm going to find love on a dating app and I'm not looking for love on a dating app," said Alana, a young New York woman I interviewed, who identifies as queer. "That's just like trying to find love in the club, you know what I mean? I'd rather meet someone in person where you know when it happens, it happens. And I feel like things are meant to be."

● ● ●

And yet, despite all the dysfunction—the misogyny, racism, and transphobia—which I knew to be part of dating app culture, hideous facets of our society which I believed were being exacerbated by these platforms, I still thought my documentary should end with a wedding.

Maybe it was because I loved Shakespeare, who seemed rather obsessed with marriage and often used weddings as symbols of hope, events which give closure to all of love's questions, like in *A Midsummer Night's Dream* and *As You Like It*.

Or maybe I was bowing to the chorus of people who would insist, whenever they heard I was working on this documentary, that dating apps *must* be leading to love and marriage, because they personally knew someone who was in a relationship because of them.

Nobody seemed to want to hear that in 2016 Pew reported that just 5 percent of Americans overall who are in a marriage or committed relationship say they met their significant other online. In 2020, this number had grown to just 12 percent, according to Pew. Thirty-nine percent of regular online daters said they had been in a committed relationship with (of unspecified length) or married someone they'd met on a dating site or app. But this still doesn't sound like very good odds. If a doctor told you that a drug he was giving you to cure an ailment had a 39 percent chance of being effective, would you feel confident you'd get well?

"But my cousin got married to someone she met on Tinder!" people would tell me, or "My sister got married to someone she met on Plenty of Fish!" People seem to want to believe in the dream that you can swipe your way to true love, like the marketing of Big Dating promised. And if you tried to suggest otherwise, they acted like you were some kind of party pooper—like you didn't believe in love itself.

I knew that dating app marriages happened, of course. I'd been to a dating app wedding myself. And yet it seemed to me that if a significant number of marriages were truly happening because of these apps, then online dating companies would be releasing data about this, because it would be such a strong marketing tool. They would have ads saying things like, "Fifty-two percent of our matches lead to marriages." However, they weren't releasing such data, and they didn't have such ads. Which made me think that maybe such data didn't exist, because dating apps weren't actually designed to lead to lasting relationships.

When I interviewed some of the executives at Tinder in 2016, I asked their resident sociologist, Jessica Carbino, about this. "You said that 80 percent of people [on Tinder] want to have a serious relationship," I said. "Do you have data on how many people who've used it have actually found that on Tinder?"

"We do not have that information available," said Carbino, a dark-haired young woman with intense brown eyes, who was wearing a red dress and a gold heart pendant. "But I can tell you that I am inundated with emails on a daily basis—as are multiple members of our customer service team, the PR team—from people who said, 'I met my best friend on Tinder,' 'I met somebody who I am dating and now living with,' 'I met a man who I'm going to marry,' 'I met this guy two years ago, we married a year ago, and we're having a baby'—it's incredible, the number of people who met via Tinder."

Okay. But, again, where was the data? Dating apps are essentially data companies; they collect the data of millions of people every hour of every day. When I asked for more information, however, Carbino said that data regarding marriages or relationships resulting from Tinder was impossible to obtain, because once users were in committed relationships, they left the app.

Well, not always—which I knew from my own interviews with couples, some of whom said they actually swiped together, because either they were in open relationships or they were looking for a "third" (someone who was up for a threesome). Most young women I'd spoken to said that they had been approached by a couple looking for a third at some point, as even I was when I was using dating apps.

Surely, I said to Carbino, Tinder could canvas past users by contacting them through their emails or Facebook pages, either of which was necessary for signing up. They could find a way.

"We had twenty-nine people featured in [the Vows section of] the *New York Times*," Carbino offered as proof of Tinder's impact on marriage. "Twenty-nine couples…and it's a very competitive process."

"Twenty-nine couples?" scoffed Nick Bilton, the *Vanity Fair* tech writer, sounding like early Richard Dreyfuss in his impatience level, when I repeated Carbino's evidence to him. "That's their data? That doesn't show people are actually getting married off the service—it just means that twenty-nine couples did.…It's frustrating when you hear these dating apps talk about, 'Well, all these people have gotten married on our app.' It's like, no—that's not why you're doing this!"

Even Justin Garcia, the executive director of Kinsey, who's also a consultant for Match, was skeptical of Tinder's claims of being responsible for lots of happily ever afters.

"In 2015, Tinder said they were registering 1.8 billion swipes per day," Garcia said. "That is an enormous amount of energy and an enormous amount of swiping. But of that 1.8 billion swipes, [there were] only about twenty-six million matches"—not relationships or marriages, just matches.

"So while twenty-six million matches is a lot in terms of overall magnitude, in terms of percentages, it's not that much." About 1.4 percent.

The fact is that the marriage rate is lower now than at any other time since 1870. Only about half of American adults are married, compared to 72 percent in 1960. And while same-sex weddings are on the rise, an increasing number of Americans are opting out of marriage altogether, and people in developed countries around the globe are getting married with even less frequency than people in the United States. An increase in the rate of cohabiting relationships is part of the reason. But a growing proportion of American adults are also living without a spouse or partner, with the sharpest increase coming from those under thirty-five.

A 2019 study by the General Social Survey reported that over half of Americans between the ages of eighteen and thirty-four, 51 percent, say they do not have a steady romantic partner. In 2004, that figure was considerably lower—33 percent, which was already the lowest figure since the data was first collected in 1986. What changes happened in the world of dating between 2004 and 2019 to effect this rise? It would be willful blindness to discount the growth of the online dating industry, the launch of Tinder in 2012, and the explosion of mobile dating that followed. Dating apps have had no perceptible impact in terms of raising the marriage rate, and in fact may be having the opposite effect. Only time will tell.

● ● ●

And yet, again, despite all this, I still wanted to show that it could happen, that love could triumph in the digital age, with a romantic tune playing as the bride and groom waltzed off into the sunset after saying "I do." Maybe I still wanted to believe in the dream of finding true love through technology myself.

And so it was, at the end of 2016, that I took my little crew down to the

Secrets Silversands Riviera resort in Cancun, Mexico, to film the wedding of Stacy and Casey.

Casey Bond is a soft-spoken guy, blond, with a mustache and beard. Then thirty-one, he lived in Nashville. Formerly a professional baseball player and actor, he'd played the pitcher Chad Bradford in the 2011 Brad Pitt vehicle *Moneyball.* Now he had his own film production company. Stacy Smith, his bride-to-be, was also thirty-one and a CPA. They looked like the bride and groom on top of a wedding cake. They had met on Hinge.

When I asked them why they thought dating apps had worked for them, both said it had been largely due to Casey's "intentions."

"I think you could easily get caught up in just wanting to meet people and date around," said Casey, with his good-natured drawl, standing on a hotel balcony on the day of his wedding, surrounded by his handsome groomsmen. "But I was looking for the person I was gonna spend the rest of my life with. And so that was my intention. I was looking for the one."

When I met up with Stacy in the bridal salon, she was wearing her white satin wedding dress and having her blonde hair done by a stylist from the hotel. She also credited Casey's intentions for how she came to be in Cancun that afternoon—intentions she said she hadn't encountered in other guys on dating apps.

"Casey had the intentionality," she said. "And I really appreciated that."

"I used Hinge for about a year," Stacy continued. "But you would match with someone and the conversation just wouldn't be there—or it would be, 'Oh this guy seems great,' and then he would just fall off the face of the earth. With social media, guys have these unreachable standards about women these days. Guys are looking for perfection. Standards are set so high, with everyone with their perfect bodies and large breasts and perfect butts"—she gave a little laugh—"and I do think it makes this seem almost attainable. But, you know, it's not real life. But I think in guys' heads it is."

I was reminded then of something Zoe Strimpel had said about her research showing that women who use dating apps experienced a drop in self-esteem.

"If they came to online dating thinking that they were attractive," Strimpel said, "they then came to feel as if they were less attractive. Women became sensitive to the idea that they maybe don't measure up to other women on the site, especially when they're being judged just on their pictures." Her findings were echoed by a 2018 study which said that dating app users overall reported "lower self-esteem and lower psychology well-being" than non-dating-app users.

Did dating apps make women feel so bad about themselves that when someone came along and wanted to marry them, they were primed to say yes? (If marriage was in fact what they wanted at all.)

Talking to Stacy and Casey also made me think of something Elizabeth Armstrong told me about how confounding it was that, even after decades of feminism, heterosexual men still seemed to have more of the power in choosing a mate. "Young women complain that men still have the power to decide when something is going to be serious and when something is not," Armstrong said. "They can go, 'She's girlfriend material, she's hookup material.'"

Almost like it's still the 1950s. Or the eighteenth century.

When Stacy and Casey said "I do" under a wooden gazebo by the ocean at sunset, they looked ecstatic. But I couldn't help wondering, would they be standing there if it had been left up to Stacy's intentions rather than Casey's? And did it matter, if their marriage made them both happy?

"I have personally not gone on a date since the new Hinge came out," said Marge, a friend of Stacy's I talked to at the reception (she was referring to the relaunch of Hinge after it eliminated swiping). "But, you know." She gave a grudging smile. "I'm sure it's working for someone."

● ● ●

It was while I was watching Daniel going around filming the wild-and-crazy dancing at Stacy and Casey's reception that I got a text from Abel.

"Hey!" he said.

My heart leapt.

It made me feel extra happy to hear from him while I was far away and watching the revelers celebrate these nuptials under a shiny tropical moon.

"Hey! I'm in Mexico!" I texted, sending him a picture of a palm tree waving in the balmy evening breeze.

"I hate to ask," he texted back, "but could you spare three-hunnerd?"

He was asking for money, something he had never done before. Things had gotten a little tight, he said, and he couldn't make his rent. Was there any way I could find a Western Union? (Neither of us had PayPal or Venmo yet.)

I just stared at this request.

What did he think this was? I wondered. Did he think I was his sugar mama now?

My vanity was hurt; I was offended.

But then I thought back to a few months earlier, when I had offered him assistance after he told me he'd been in jail. And I realized it wasn't really all that out of bounds for him to be asking me for money now.

"And why shouldn't I lend him money?" I argued with myself. He was my friend, my fuck buddy, my situationship—my love—and he needed money and I could spare him some, so it was really no big deal...Or was it?

If all he really wanted was to take advantage of me, he could have done it long before now, I thought. Or...was I just his mark? His "plate"? Had the past year and a half just been a long-game romance scam?

I think part of all this suspicion was stemming from not just the usual, heart-wrenching images of older ladies being preyed upon by gigolos which popped into one's mind via Hollywood depictions of May-December romances—think Geraldine Page in *Sweet Bird of Youth* or Vivien Leigh in *The Roman Spring of Mrs. Stone*—but the fact that I had recently done a story for *Vanity Fair* about sugar babies and sugar daddies (yes, 2016 was a very busy year, work-wise). And what I had concluded, after talking to scores of sources, was that in an economy that was making it nearly impossible for young people to make ends meet, social media platforms—as well as johns who were mostly older men—were preying on young people because they were vulnerable and in need of financial assistance. And for young women, this was all being dressed up as "choice feminism."

As research for this story, I had attended a SeekingArrangement Sugar Baby Summit, which took place at the Avalon Hotel in LA, where an audience of aspiring "babies"—mostly young women in their twenties— were told by a series of speakers that if they were attractive, "patient," and "smart" enough about how they managed the challenge of dating a wealthy man, then they might just find the appropriate time to let it slip that they would like their benefactor to invest in their business or ease their student debt. The SeekingArrangement website, at the time, pointedly marketed its service to college students looking to pay off loans—also letting potential "daddies" know that allegedly 60 percent of its 5.5 million members were college women.

"SeekingArrangement is modern feminism," said the company's founder, Brandon Wade, an MIT-educated former software engineer, when I interviewed him on the phone. His InfoStream Group included a number of other dating services, including Miss Travel, which enables women to find traveling "companions" to "sponsor" their vacations.

"SeekingArrangement"—which Wade later rebranded as Seeking—"is not prostitution," he insisted. "The modern feminist is one who feels comfortable about herself and is not going to let anyone else put her down no matter what she thinks or does," including having a relationship with someone for payment.

But when I interviewed young women and men who turned to the Internet for sex work opportunities—including through Craigslist, webcamming, and dating sites—most of them talked about being broke and needing cash, not about feeling empowered. They had college tuition or student loans to pay, they said, and there was the high cost of living and lack of affordable housing with which to contend. Many of their parents were middle-class people who had nothing to spare for their children, struggling themselves since the economic downturn of 2008.

Shows like *Secret Diary of a Call Girl* and *The Girlfriend Experience*, with their high-priced hotels and *Pretty Woman*–type hot johns, made sex work seem glamorous; but for most young women I spoke to, it was more about just surviving. And then there was the fact that, for some young women in hookup culture, getting paid for sex sounded better than having sex without pleasure or intimacy or any hope of a relationship. "If I'm gonna spend my time with some guy and have it be horrible," said a young woman I interviewed, "then if I get some money at the end of the night, at least I get *something*."

It wouldn't be surprising if more young people are turning to sex work to pay their bills during the pandemic, unfortunately at a time when sex workers have become even more exposed to health and safety risks. "I've thought about selling my nudes," said a young woman friend who works as a waitress. "That $1,200 stimulus check didn't even pay one month's rent. If things don't get better, it's time for the OnlyFans account." (On OnlyFans, the famous and non-famous alike can share photos for payment, often nudes.)

As I stood under the Cancun moon, reading Abel's texts, I remembered how, when I was doing this story on sex work, I had sat at my kitchen counter with him one morning, telling him all about it.

"It's sad," I said. "People have to sell their bodies just to live."

"Why sad?" he said with a shrug. "Wouldn't worry me none."

"You'd have sex for money?" I asked.

"If I had to," he said. "Might even be fun."

At the time, I'd wondered if he was just teasing me—or maybe he was more woke to modern attitudes about sex work than I was; I didn't know. And actually, I had approached some of my own relationships (Buckley, Peter) in a transactional frame of mind, when I was hard up for funds.

But now, after getting this text from him in Mexico, a chill went up my spine. Was this him collecting payment? I wondered, dismayed.

I hadn't seen him much in a few weeks. He'd been busy. I'd been busy.

Actually, I'd been feeling a little neglected—he hadn't been coming around. So maybe it was this—or maybe it was the residual trauma from all those other times in the past I'd been taken advantage of, or had allowed myself to be taken advantage of—that suddenly had me feeling anxious, and I blasted him.

I sent him a sternly worded text, telling him that I wasn't near any Western Union, and I couldn't believe he was asking me for money anyway, blah blah blah.

It was kind of mean, and in retrospect, I can see that it had everything to do with the fact that I had been gaining weight, which was making me feel insecure. Was this why he wasn't coming to see me as often, I wondered, because I was getting fat? Was this why he suddenly felt okay asking me for money, because I wasn't fuckable anymore? It made me mad. I had never talked to him like I was doing in this text before, resentful and pissed off. And I regretted it as soon as I pressed send.

He texted me right back, telling me he was sorry. He didn't ever want me to feel "any kinda way but appreciated. You're one of the best people I know," he said, "and I cherish you." He said he just didn't know where else to turn.

"Oh, he's good," said Daniel, later, when we were done working and drinking beer at the hotel bar, laughing at me for being worried if Abel was going to be okay.

● ● ●

What could I say now to make Abel come back, come back, I wondered, that night after I'd rushed home to see him. Doing the dishes, then, to pass the time while I waited and waited.

It was getting late. I realized he probably wasn't coming. My heart began to ache.

Should I text him, just to check and see if I could find him? I wondered. And what could I tell him to entice him to return?

It would be typical, in hookup culture, to send a sext, a phrase or emoji suggesting the desire or promise of sex, as a lure. But that didn't seem like the right thing to send, just then, after all these months of us being apart. And it had never really been my way—I was more likely to flirt by reaction, to feign ladylike shock, saying something like "Oh my!" when he would sext me his wagging tongue and horny devil emojis, telling me he wanted to "rattle my bones" or he "got the grrr."

"Should I tell him I was ordering a pizza?" I thought.

It occurred to me then that him doing this now—not texting me back—might be his way of getting back at me for having sent him away all those months ago. He had never seemed vengeful—but then, with him, you never really knew what was going on. He was always a little bit mysterious. Was this him giving me a taste of my own medicine, I wondered, raising my hopes and then vanishing again? He might have thought it served me right. For it wasn't the first time that I had broken up with him, or whatever we're calling ending a relationship that isn't technically a relationship.

The first time was in 2017, a few months after I'd come back from Cancun. It was a night I'd gone out with Abigail. She had texted me saying she needed to talk. So I dragged myself out of bed and went and met her for a drink at Summit, a bar on Avenue C, where she wanted to go instead of our usual Sake Bar Satsko, because she said she had something private she wanted to discuss.

As soon as I sat down next to her, her face screwed up like she might burst into tears.

"Why doesn't anyone love me?" she said. "What am I doing wrong?"

She was talking about Josh, the guy she'd been seeing for about two years. They'd met on OkCupid. I'd met him; he seemed okay, if a little vague, like so many guys you meet on dating apps, like he wasn't completely there.

They'd been friends with benefits, she said. They met up one or twice a week and had sex. When they weren't together, they texted, sexted, exchanged nudes.

301

"How were we not *together*?" she demanded. "He'd go down on me and then we'd go out to eat, go for a walk, watch *Groundhog Day*, laughing our asses off in bed!"

"Been there, sister," I said.

"I've never admitted this to anyone," she told me, "but I paid for him when we went to the Virgin Islands. He couldn't afford it and I could, so I thought, What's wrong with it? I'm an independent woman. I can do what I want with my money. It was my choice to pay for him...So why did it feel like I made a mistake?"

I told her about what had happened with Abel asking me for money when I was in Mexico, and how, when I came back, we went out together for New Year's Eve, and I wound up paying for the night. He held his hand around my waist in the bar, almost like we were actually dating. He kissed me as the ball dropped in Times Square on TV.

"And then suddenly my credit card was coming out," I told her.

I'd given him money a few times after that, whenever he mentioned he was short on rent or had some other expense he couldn't cover.

"I sort of got used to it," I said.

It made me think of what somebody had said to me while I was reporting that story about the "new prostitution": "It's like hooking has just become like this weird, distorted extension of dating. 'He took me to dinner; he throws me money for rent'—it's just become so casual."

"There's an epidemic of women paying for men," Abigail said, nodding. "It's like the most taboo topic of conversation. A lot of my women friends are paying for men because the guys don't make as much as them, and they want to go out and have fun, but the guy can't afford it.

"And a lot of them are even letting these guys live with them, just because they want the companionship or sex," she said. "These are women who have, like, good jobs and work hard, and some of these guys aren't even working. I think a lot of guys are starting to expect it." She made a face. "Like, first they got sex without a relationship, and now they get free drinks? Nobody wants to talk about it. Women will only talk about it when the guy ghosts or cheats, and then they feel used."

"Story of my life," I said.

But back to Josh: "I never told him I was developing feelings for him," Abigail said.

And then, that day, he had called her and told her he was having a baby with someone else.

"I put the timeline together and saw that he was getting this other woman pregnant while we were doing it raw," she said. "Now I have to get tested."

She frowned.

"Definitely get tested," I told her. "But you know you're gonna be okay, right? And I'm here for you, and so is everybody who loves you."

"Why wasn't it me?" she asked, tearing up again. "Why wasn't it *me* he picked—that he *loved*. I want love too—am I unlovable?"

I told her how much I loved her.

We drank a lot that night, sitting at the bar, talking about men. At a certain point in the wee hours of the morning, I got so peeved, thinking about all of the ways that Abel had disappointed me—never making a date, failing to respond to my texts, taking money from me even though I had offered it—I sent him a long, angry text, telling him never to contact me again. And then I blocked and deleted his number.

"Ooh, the block-delete," said Amy, the next day, when I told her about it, worried about what I'd done. "So you went nuclear on him."

It seemed a well-chosen phrase. I felt I had done something incredibly destructive, from which there might be no turning back.

● ● ●

In 2017, Spencer and I edited the documentary. It wasn't possible to do much else. Editing a documentary is like having a newborn baby who constantly needs your attention. And we were like nervous new parents.

We had nearly 250 hours of footage (a fairly standard amount), which we had to condense into a three-hour "assembly" to show to our producers. From there, we had to carve out an eighty-five-minute film. In addition, there were graphics to be done with our graphic designer and music to be done with our composer—altogether an intricate, painstaking process involving a lot of phone calls and revising and more phone calls. And more revising.

We did it all sitting side by side in front of monitors positioned on my dining room table, which became crowded with keyboards, speakers, hard drives, and binders full of transcripts. My living room became our editing suite. Every couple of months, David Teague, our consulting editor, would come and talk to us after viewing our cuts. Teague is a lovely guy, a renowned editor and Emmy winner (for *Life, Animated*). He became our mentor. Listening to him, we learned to let the subject matter speak for itself and let the film emerge on its own, even as we guided it.

For example, no matter how much I had wanted to end the film with a wedding, it just didn't work. The romantic feeling of our Cancun footage didn't mesh with the tone of the characters in the rest of the film, talking about their distressing adventures in the dating apocalypse; so we had to cut it.

Every now and then, Zazie, now in her senior year of high school and busy with studying for the SATs and filling out college applications, would wander through the room, and we'd ask her what she thought of whatever we were working on. She became an invaluable extra pair of eyes, being not much younger than some of our characters. And Spencer, who was now twenty-five, had had his own past use of Grindr and Scruff to add to his understanding of their experiences. I invited over Amy and Abigail and some of my other young friends to look at cuts and give us feedback.

I wanted the film to look bright and colorful, like social media is colorful, in contrast to the darkness of the subject matter: the corporate takeover of dating. From the beginning of shooting, I'd asked Daniel to focus on our characters' faces so we could catch all the nuances of the emotions they were feeling in this time when you were supposed to pretend like you didn't care.

I wanted the film to be fast-paced, at times almost jarring as it jumped from subject to subject, mirroring the way people experience swiping. I knew I needed to have experts talking, to give the film a conceptual framework and highlight the significance of this unprecedented social shift. And I wanted to include the stories of the young women who had told us about their experiences of sexual assault and harassment by men they'd met on dating apps, because this wasn't being talked about enough anywhere. I felt grateful to them for telling their stories, which felt like sacred material.

Through this year of editing, I felt myself growing and changing. My mind was always racing with the film. All of the responsibility and this sustained act of creativity was occupying me in a way I'd never experienced with any other project. There were so many moving parts. It was thrilling, exhilarating, often frustrating and exhausting. Spencer and I ate and drank a lot to get through the constant stress. We both gained weight—especially me. Sitting in front of my monitor for a year, I kept expanding, as if there were some invisible pump connected to me, blowing me up larger and larger, like Tim Allen in *The Santa Clause*. By the time we were done, I had gained about thirty pounds.

The weird thing was, I didn't really care.

For the first time in my life, I didn't feel like a monster for being over-weight. In the past, I'd freak out if I gained just a few pounds. But now, I'd catch a glimpse of myself walking by a store window and think, "Who is that bouncy giantess?" And then chuckle, realizing, "Oh, it's *me*." I'd finished going through menopause around this time, with a new Bonnie Raitt streak of white in my red hair to show for it, so maybe that was also why I felt a new kind of peace with who I was.

Maybe it was true, what my older women friends had been telling me all these years, that menopause was the great equalizer of female insecurity, the great moment of I Don't Give a Fuck, when the hormones finally rear up against all the misogyny and internalized misogyny and say, Oh, fuck *off*. I certainly did feel stronger and more centered and more in command than I ever had before—like I had, well, *heft*.

As I finished up my project, I wondered if this new feeling of power also had something to do with the fact that I hadn't been dealing with men in a romantic or sexual sense for months. Having no men around to distract me or make me doubt myself had definitely factored into my ability to focus. Part of me even wondered if I had gone nuclear on Abel, that night when I was out drinking with Abigail, because, however subconsciously, I knew that I needed not to see him in order to be able to complete this giant task. It had often felt destabilizing to me to have men in my life, and there was too much riding on this film for me to take any chances.

And yet I realized, too, that another reason I had arrived at a deeper acceptance of myself, both physically and emotionally, was Abel. He had liked my body no matter its size; he had liked me no matter what craziness I was going through and stressing out about.

At a certain point, a few weeks before I sent him away, I had actually apologized to him for gaining weight: "I want to look good for you—I'm sorry I'm getting so fat!" But he just smiled and started singing a song while shaking my butt with his hand, making me laugh: "Big Fat Woman got wanton thighs / Ev'ry time she moves, make my temp'rature rise." (When I looked the song up later, I discovered it was Lead Belly's "Big Fat Woman." He said he knew a lot of old songs like that from growing up around musicians.)

His acceptance of my body had made up for all those exasperated looks my mother had given me when I got pudgy, when I was a little girl. And for the British guy I dated briefly in the nineties who told me, "You should really lose some weight, you know," back when my BMI was perfectly "normal." And the female coworker at *New York* who had sent me—in the mail!— a clipping about a weight-reduction product. And a lifetime of images and ads suggesting that if you weren't as skinny as Jane Fonda—who had actually talked about having an eating disorder—then there was something morally, spiritually *wrong* with you, before the body positivity movement came along to pronounce all this awful and harmful.

Abel had made me feel like a goddess. I knew I should love myself anyway, no matter what, but my conditioning made this hard to do. I felt it was a gift he had given me, loving my older, bigger body, and it was a gift I cherished. Because no matter what else had happened between us, there were our lovely dances in the dark. The way we were with each other when we were alone together had felt like the truth of who we were. And I liked the me that I was with him, when we were making love.

● ● ●

I got to thinking about him at my brother's wedding. On a brilliant September day in 2017, my brother Noah married a beautiful man named Lucas underneath a chuppah at the edge of Lake George. I'd been asked to come up and say something to bear witness to these nuptials. I had it all planned out in my head, and I'd practiced it—it was something about the miracle of finding love in this chaotic world, against all odds—but then when I stood up in front of everyone in the audience, all our family and friends, everything I was going to say flew out of my head, and I went blank and began to cry. And then my brother started to cry.

I didn't know what I was saying then; I just started talking. I knew that I wanted this couple to understand how much I loved them—and I hope I did say that. I hadn't expected to be overcome with tears—tears, I realize now, that were as much for myself and how I was alone on the day of my little brother's wedding as they were tears of joy for all the memories of how our lives had entwined, going back forty years, to when I had carried him around in my arms.

At the reception, the beautiful men danced, and then a song came on, "Call Your Girlfriend" by Robyn—it's a song about breaking up with someone in the right way, so as to spare their feelings and remain friends. And I realized I hadn't done this with Abel. I thought about how I had been unkind to him, and how he hadn't deserved that. Back in my hotel room that night, feeling nostalgic, I unblocked and undeleted his number and texted him, "Hey!"

"Hola," he texted back.

My heart leapt.

●  ●  ●

We fell back into our regular thing again after that, but now it was different; he was different. If he had seemed mysterious before, now he just seemed wistful and low. When we got into bed, it was if he wanted to make love to disappear in me. He was drinking more than ever.

I didn't know what to do to help him. There was no time to talk. I was still preoccupied with finishing up my film—doing the color correction and sound mixing with the guys at Postworks, working on the publicity and other things—and he seemed as busy as ever with his job at the fashion house. He'd been promoted to a managerial position, overseeing a crew.

But he still seemed dissatisfied. And then, in the summer of 2018, he texted me saying he was moving to Oregon. He said he knew some "fellers" out there who made good money working construction, and they had invited him to come out and live with them. He would be gone in a week, he said, and he wanted to come say goodbye.

I'd always known we wouldn't, couldn't, last forever, but I was very sad to see him go. I didn't want him to go; but I also knew that I should support him in seeking out a better life. His life in New York had always been so hard. He'd just recently been raised above minimum wage after a couple of years at his job. I wanted him to have an easier time.

So I decided I was going to be positive and, yes, give him some money as a going away present, to help him get started in his new life out West. I took some cash out of the bank and planned to sneak it into his backpack the next time I saw him.

I invited him over one night and we went up to my roof. I wanted to show him my movie, which was coming out soon. We sat on the patio chairs under the night sky and I played some of it on my iPhone.

He smiled, watching it.

"What do you think?" I asked.

"Seems very accurate," he said.

We drank beer and held hands.

"I'll miss you," I told him after a while.

I said I was sorry for how harsh I'd been with him a few times in the past. "I don't know what's wrong with me," I said. "I guess I just never feel like I can trust anyone. I think it goes way back."

"You don't have to apologize for nothing," he said. "You don't ever have to do that with me."

We kissed, and then we reminisced; we talked about the night we met, when I was hiding the scissors in my pocket. We laughed.

"What did you think of me that night?" I asked.

"Seemed like you were looking for something," he said.

I said I guessed I was. "But you know," I told him, "I don't feel like that anymore. I feel like I found what I was looking for: you. I don't know how I would have gotten through these last few years without you, Abel."

He did his aw-shucks head ducking.

Then I told him I was thinking of writing a book about us. "Well, not us, exactly," I said, "but online dating, and everything I learned about it along the way."

"Just describe me as devilishly handsome," he said, "and talk about the amazing sex."

And then we went downstairs and had some amazing sex.

The next morning, he kissed me goodbye.

I went to the window and watched him walking down the street, putting his earbuds in to listen to a song on his phone. I wondered what the song was, and if he would always think of me when he heard it, and remember this moment when we parted forever.

I cried a little bit; and then I went about my day.

●  ●  ●

*And that little fuckboy was lying to me the entire time!*

I was thinking about all this, the night I ran to meet him after leaving Constance, as I stood before the bathroom mirror, getting ready for bed. I had given up on the idea that Abel was going to show up that evening, and so I had taken off my clothes, put on some pajama pants and a T-shirt, and started my face-cleansing routine.

I resentfully applied all of the ludicrously expensive unguents in my bathroom cabinet which are sold to older ladies like me, harping on our fears of aging. "Age defying!" they say. "Wrinkle resistant!" Or, my favorite, "Youth activating!" As if youth could be recalled by a cream.

Youth can only be recalled by memory, and then only imperfectly, at that. Memories are notoriously selective—as were the memories I had been having of Abel, when I was sitting there waiting for him, remembering his loveliness, wanting him back.

But now—when it seemed like I wasn't going to hear from him again that evening—I started remembering some *other* things. I felt like Swann in *Swann's Way*, thinking of all of the things about his beloved Odette that had rankled him, once he finally realizes she was cheating: "To think that I have wasted years of my life, that I have longed for death, that the greatest love that I have ever known has been for a woman who did not please me, who was not in my style!" he sniffs.

It would have been very convenient if I could have ended this remembrance of things in my sexual past with the last section I wrote. It would have been nice to be able to end this story with Abel moving to Oregon and me graduating into a new phase of life, older and wiser and respectably sexless. It would have been nice to be able to tell an uplifting tale (always hard for the Russian in me) about a woman who passes through the inferno of modern dating and comes out the other side—if not into Il Paradiso, then into the more comfortable environs of limbo, wearing Eileen Fisher ensembles and chunky necklaces and sagely sipping matcha tea, having finally thrown off her reckless behavior and her self-undermining impulses, now stronger and happier and more empowered, and never wanting to be with a man again, but being okay with that, because she didn't need a man.

And I don't need a man. To quote Cher (which is often a good call): "I love men. But you don't really need them to *live*."

If I could turn back time, as Cher sings, then I would be able to tell that uplifting story. But if I did, it would be an ass-covering bunch of malarkey. And I'm tired of the lies that get told about women, tired of the lies women tell about themselves. I'm tired of false empowerment stories. And I'm tired of lying to myself.

The truth is, Abel had lied to me about moving to Oregon, as he had lied about a lot of things. And it wasn't until I learned about his lies, and we started telling the truth to each other, that, I think, we started to have a real relationship.

●　●　●

It was a warm night in October of 2018, the night before my fifty-fourth birthday, when he turned up again.

"Hey," he texted, saying he was nearby.

My heart did leap. But I was confused. Was he back from Oregon already? He'd just left a few months ago. What was he doing here?

I went and stood outside my building to wait for him. I watched him coming down the block. He was dragging himself along, looking dispirited and unkempt.

For a moment, I saw him as a soldier, the kind of kid from the sticks who's always been used as cannon fodder—put a uniform on him, and he was coming home from battle. He looked exhausted.

I came up to him gently with a smile and a "Hey," and he lunged at me, putting his arms around me, hugging me tight, as if for dear life.

"I missed you," he moaned.

He was exceedingly thin, even more so than usual. He looked like he needed to eat. So I took him to Satsko's, and, as he ate rice with curry and drank a Sapporo, and then another Sapporo, I tried asking him what was going on with him.

How was it in Oregon? I asked. Was it working out for him there? What was he doing back? He just shook his head, looking lost. He seemed devastated by something. I wanted to find out what it was, but the sake bar was packed and loud, and I couldn't understand his muttering. He looked like something had put him over the edge, and I didn't want to grill him about it in public.

We left the bar and walked back toward my building. We kissed in the elevator. Our closeness was still the same. We made love in my bedroom, and he fell asleep.

I stared at the ceiling, wondering what to do.

In the past, it would have made me wild with excitement, thinking of how I might have some uninterrupted time with him alone. Zazie was in college now, living in a dorm, so it was the first time in a long time that Abel and I had my apartment all to ourselves.

But the way he was acting, I felt uneasy. Something about all this didn't add up.

And so, when I was sure he was asleep, doing his whistling snoring, I got up and went into his pants pockets and found his phone. I padded into the kitchen with it and typed in his password, which I had watched him punch in earlier in the evening. I had learned from some young women friends that if you wanted to find out a guy's password, all you had to do was watch him typing it in when he didn't think you were looking (which seemed way easier than the often complicated advice given in the thousands of YouTube videos about how to check your boyfriend/girlfriend/husband/wife's phone, one of which suggested making a wax-paper impression of their thumbprint, which I had actually considered doing).

I finally learned the true story of Abel—my fuck buddy, my situationship, my love—standing in the dark of my kitchen, that evening, peering into his phone. It was all there in his texts, in the messages between him and Rowena—the same Rowena he'd just broken up with when he and I first met. I realized now that she was the "woman unkind" in the Led Zeppelin song he kept playing that first week we spent together.

I learned from his texts that she was back in New York. They had gotten back together in July, just after Abel told me he was moving to Oregon. And now they had broken up again, three months later.

"Please Rowena," Abel had texted her. "I love you with all my heart. I'm just asking for you to try this with me, I just need you in my life. Can't you just give me another chance? You're all I've ever wanted. You are my hope."

I shivered by the open kitchen window, wearing nothing but my underwear and a T-shirt, smoking cigarette after cigarette, fascinated, shocked, at discovering the secret life of this young man I had been involved with for the past three years. As my thumb scrolled up the thread between him and Rowena—which went on and on—he sounded like a completely different person than the young man I knew. He had sent her long, impassioned, double, triple texts. He had sent texts begging her to text him back. He had her in his phone as "Rowena, Harbinger of Souls."

He had never stopped being in love with her, all this time that he had been with me—fucking me, eating my omelets, taking my "loans."

"I've waited three years for you, Rowena," he told her mournfully.

After they got back together in July, they'd been living in a rented room in an apartment in Bushwick. They seemed to have been drinking a fair amount.

"Can you really get some Cuervo?" she'd texted him, encouraging him to bring a bottle on his way home from work. "Can you get some wine?"

"What the fuck Rowena?" he texted her at five o'clock, one morning, when she still hadn't come home.

"I'm sorry, babe, got stuck with the girls," she said, in one of a number of texts excusing why she hadn't shown up until the next day. "We ate Chinese food and I passed out. . . . I'm so fucking sorry. I feel terrible. Can you forgive me?"

Now that I knew her name, I looked her up on Instagram—as one does. She was a tiny little woman with big brown eyes, not more than five feet tall.

"You throw back 4 shots in 5 mins and weigh less than 100 lbs, 'course you're gonna get wasted!" Abel chastised her. Apparently, she had shown up at his place of work three sheets to the wind, yelling at him because he hadn't answered her texts for several hours.

The problems they had as a couple seemed to have been aggravated by their reliance on alcohol, as well as the intrusion of these phones. And then there was Abel's apparent inability to stay faithful.

"Abel, I found out what you did," she had texted him.

She had gone through his phone—just like I was doing now—and she had found some notifications from Tinder from a time in June of that year when they had started talking again. She was still in Argentina then, but they had pledged that they would stay faithful to one another until she moved back to New York. And apparently, during this time, Abel had slept with one of his Tinder matches (which was also news to me), and it had caused Rowena to stop trusting him.

"You're probably doing some chick, aren't you?" she'd texted when he didn't get back to her right away.

"Don't be silly," he texted her back. "I don't have the need or want to fuck another chick."

This exchange had taken place just a week after he'd fucked *me*, by the way—just before she'd come back—the same night he came to see me to say goodbye because he was "moving out West."

Not only fucked me, but bit my ass like a jungle cat!

I started to feel numb, reading through all this. I wasn't exactly surprised— I'd been cheated on so many times. But I had never let betrayal shut me down; I'd always wanted to stay open to love. But staying open to love, you also stay open to getting hurt.

Now, for a harrowing moment, I felt this hollowness taking over me. It was weird—I couldn't feel a thing. Or was it just the air blowing in from the open window that was making me feel so cold?

But no, I realized, it was the beginning of callousness, of caring less, the beginning of the inability to feel anything at all, because feeling was too hard. It made me shudder. I closed the window.

● ● ●

Why did he lie to me? I had wondered, reading through his texts that night. Why tell me he was moving to Oregon, when he had been here in New York the entire time? Didn't he ever worry that I would see him?

In fact, I was seeing him now, on Rowena's Instagram page, in a picture of the two of them standing outside a restaurant just a few blocks away. He had his arm wrapped around her shoulder possessively; it had been taken just a few days after he told me goodbye. He looked so handsome, it wounded me. And she looked cute, in her blue sundress.

"Somebody said what a beautiful couple we are #happy #love," she had captioned it.

"Rowena, the only thing I've done was love you unconditionally since the moment I met you," he'd texted her, imploring her to come back.

But their fighting had become so incessant, she said it made her "tired," and in September, a month ago, she had moved out while he was at work.

They still hadn't had a conversation about it in person or even on the phone. Their breakup had taken place entirely over text. They had fought over text; she had announced she was leaving him over text; and now the whole aftermath of their breakup was playing out over text, where it was impossible to have a real conversation, and it was making him crazy. Ever since she'd left him, he had been chasing her—texting her, begging her, shaming her, hopelessly in love.

"You really gonna call it all off because of a drunken fight?" he'd demanded.

"Maybe we should try not drinking anymore, Rowena," he said plaintively. "I love you. I didn't even think I could fathom love till I met you." The more she stayed away, the more desperate he sounded: "Don't give up on me. Don't give up on us. Not yet. Please."

After an hour spent poring over this saga, I went into his emails and saw that he was getting notifications from Tinder and OkCupid again, as of that very day. He was already back on dating apps.

● ● ●

If you're thinking, okay, now *this* is the thing that made her never want to see Abel again, I can see why you'd reach that conclusion.

And I did plan to kick him out of bed and out the door. I marched into the room where he was sleeping. It was Zazie's old room, which I'd taken over when she went to college.

My heart was pounding.

But then I saw him lying there, in my daughter's old bed, in the same spot where I'd seen her so many mornings when I came in to wake her up for school. I looked at him, lying there in the light of the candles we'd lit, and I felt a stab of guilt. He looked so sad, so heartbroken. Crushed. You could see it in his face even as he slept. And in his heartbreak, I realized, he'd done the same thing that I had done when I'd gotten my heart broken last: he went on a dating app to find somebody else to fuck. It was how I had met him, after all.

316

And then he had come to me for help.

"Abel," I said.

He let out a big, long snore.

I didn't have the heart to wake him. If I'd been his age, instead of twice his age, I'm sure I would have been yelling at him by now. But there is something about a relationship with someone younger than you that does feel a bit like parenting, sometimes. And parenting is all about unconditional love and forgiveness. Or, I think, it should be.

I crawled back into the bed next to him, put my arm around him, and tried to sleep. It was difficult.

● ● ●

The next morning, I woke up to the sound of hammering. I went into the living room and there he was, putting up bookshelves—the ones he'd been promising to make ever since I met him three years earlier. He'd found the wood and the tools I'd bought at Home Depot in the hall closet.

"Good morning," I said, trying to sound as delighted to see him as I would have been had I not read all those texts between him and Rowena.

"Mornin'," he muttered.

In the bathroom, I could see that he'd already taken a shower. The towel was folded on the rack in the polite way he always put it back. I went into the kitchen and made some coffee. Then I sat down on the couch and drank it, watching him work.

He was wearing his jeans and nothing else, his hair tied back in a bun. He looked so good, I could have watched him work all day.

I'd always loved to watch him do things with his hands. I'd even loved watching him fix my toilet seat once when it popped off. It was like that episode of *Mad Men* where the wives get all flustered watching Don fix a sink. It was a sexist trope—the ladies getting all breathless when the big, strong man does he-man stuff—but who could say for sure if it was cultural conditioning or something more biologically determined that was making me bite my lip?

I wanted to talk to him about what I'd seen on his phone. But he didn't seem to be in the mood to talk about anything. His face looked a little bloated; his eyes were squinty. I wondered how he could stand all that hammering with his hangover. I wondered if he was finally putting up these shelves as a tacit way of apologizing to me for Rowena—or maybe doing this job was just his way of keeping from thinking about Rowena.

I just sat very quiet and watched, wondering how to broach the subject of this incendiary new information I'd discovered—that he loved a woman named Rowena—without letting him know that I'd found it out by committing what, once upon a time, would have been considered a serious relationship crime: going through someone's stuff. Now, in the age of surveillance capitalism, it seemed almost taken for granted that we were all watching each other, all the time. And yet, I knew he still wouldn't like it.

Although I was keeping myself calm, I was actually mad and upset and hurt enough that I wanted to make him admit to his double life. I wanted to expose him, to punish him for lying to me. And I also wanted to tell him that, no matter what he'd done, I still loved him...I did.

After a while, I ordered some sandwiches from the southern cooking place, fried chicken for him, catfish for me. He had finished the shelves.

"Just need a paint job," he said, sitting down to his lunch.

"They look nice," was all I said—because I knew if I made too much of a big deal out of him finally completing this job, it would bring attention to how it had taken him three years.

We ate in silence.

"Want some ketchup?" I asked.

"No thanks," he said.

I watched him eat.

Then it came to me, the way into his story: a memory.

"You know what I was thinking?" I said. "That week when we met, and we went and ate tacos, remember? I was thinking about how sad you looked that day. And you kinda look like that today. Like that time when you looked so sad, before, when you'd broken up with that girl…"

He looked at me like I was psychic.

He thought a long moment, seeming to be wrestling with the pros and cons of opening up. And then he finally said: "My shit is very unstable right now. I thought I had everything figured out, but I don't."

"Like what?"

He got up and went over to the kitchen window to smoke a cigarette. So many of our talks had happened here, in whispers, by the window ledge, late at night when Zazie was sleeping. Many times we had stood here and smiled and kissed and made each other laugh, saying, "*Ssshhhh!*"

And the whole time he had been in love with someone else, I thought angrily.

But I couldn't react; I had to stay very still, until I got all the information.

"Tell me," I said.

Then he told me the story. It was *La Bohème* with Instagram and weed. She was the "love of his life," he said, "the only woman [he] would ever love." He hadn't stopped thinking about her, the whole time she was in Argentina, where her parents had made her move back in order to put her in rehab.

Then, about six months ago, she had hit him up and said that her parents were trying to force her to marry some Argentinian guy she didn't love— "kinda an arranged marriage type thing"—and she said she couldn't stop thinking about him, and would he buy her a plane ticket so she could come back to New York and be with him?

"And you believed her?" I asked.

"'Course," he said. "Why not?"

Yes, why not? I believed Axel Wang when he told me he was a cameraman for a big TV news outlet. I believed Frank when he said he would be my house husband. Romance scams didn't only happen online—they just proliferated there.

Abel said he wanted Rowena back because he loved her, and he wanted to play music with her again. After she left, he said, he'd just stopped trying—he was too depressed. And he knew that she had the self-promotion gene he lacked. She was the extrovert, active on social media, posting pictures and videos of herself daily, singing Amy Winehouse tunes off-key.

He said he thought her voice was beautiful. He'd thought that the two of them could make it together in the music business. It was his dream.

"Let's get our fuckin' shit together and fuck this thing called life up!" he'd told her on text. "I'm bankin' on you, my love. You're my way out. So let's get to it!"

Now he looked out the window with a stunned expression.

"I bought that woman a plane ticket," he told me, as if this was something so profound, such an undeniable proof of love, that it was outrageous to think that anyone could ever not love someone back who had done this much.

I wondered if he had used my money to pay for it. Oh well.

"Rowena, did you use me?" he'd asked her on text. "Was I just a steppin' stone? Did you ever really love me?"

I was wondering the same thing about him and me.

"I guess it was about the biggest thing I ever done," he told me, by which he meant buying Rowena the ticket to New York. "And I felt like my life started at 11:05 a.m., underneath a little smoking awning at the west entrance of terminal four of JFK, when I saw her come out the airport. And it was the most wonderful, monumental moment of my life—"

His voice broke off; tears came into his eyes. He looked embarrassed, ashamed. He walked away from me, as if he didn't know what to do with all this emotion. He'd been raised to be a man, just like my father had raised my brothers to "be men," bashing their heads together when they weren't manly enough for a man like him.

I went and patted his back and told him it was going to be all right, just let it all out, it was going to be okay.

● ● ●

We kept talking for the next four hours. It was the longest conversation we had ever had. A lot of it took place with him lying on his back on the rug on my living room floor, where he had kind of collapsed. I sat on the couch, just listening.

He sounded alternately angry, sad, and confused. He told me how Rowena had been disappearing at night, how in just a few weeks she'd blown the money her parents had given her to resettle in New York.

"On what?" I asked.

"Ubers, meals, clothes, fancy drinks," he said.

Every time she stayed out all night, he said, it made him so crazy with worry, he couldn't sleep.

"Do you think she was seeing other guys?" I asked.

"I don't," he said, frowning. "She said she wasn't. I can't say 'bout now."

He took his phone out of his pocket, went into his photos, and held up a screenshot: Rowena's Tinder profile.

"Wow," I said. "How long did that take?"

"Next day?" he said. "A buddy sent it to me."

I wondered if he had actually seen it himself when he was swiping. It made me think of a woman's Tinder profile I'd seen: "Don't bother swiping right. I'm just on here to catch my cheating husband."

"I've spent the majority of the last few weeks in a haze of booze and drugs to cope," Abel said.

"Do you mind me asking, did you ever cheat on her?" I asked, after a moment.

"Of course not," he said, taking his arm away from his eyes.

"But could she have thought you cheated on her?"

He winced. Then he confessed the part about how he'd had sex with someone he met on Tinder before Rowena arrived back in New York.

"It was my last time as a single before we were gonna be together forever!"

he protested, as if he was still arguing with her. "She wasn't here yet. And she'd done much worse to *me*. And I knew she was gonna be my one and only!"

"Do you think dating apps make it harder to just focus on one person?" I asked. It suddenly seemed impossible not to see him, in part, as an interview subject; or maybe that just made it easier to cope with what he was telling me.

"Of course. It's obvious," he said. "But after she got here, I never was gonna be with anyone else for the rest of my life." He said it with the religious zeal that came into his voice whenever he talked about Rowena. She had become his meaning, his Dulcinea.

And it was as naive as the man of La Mancha to think that once you'd been hooked on dating apps they would never rear their shiny little heads again, even after you'd entered into a committed relationship. They would always be there, whispering at you in times of stress, just like cigarettes and alcohol and other addictive substances. Whenever you started having problems as a couple, or when kids came along, or when your sex life went underground, then dating apps would be there as a convenient distraction—perhaps even as a way to hurt your partner, or to try and relieve your own hurt. This technology was already redefining coupledom and what was considered normal or permissible in the context of commitment.

The allure of the escape valve that dating apps provided was already becoming apparent just a couple of months into the pandemic. In May of 2020, OnePoll, a marketing research company, released a study showing that 42 percent of Americans in relationships who were not quarantining with their partner had downloaded a dating app since lockdown. Reading about this made me think of screenshots I'd received from women of dating app profiles like this one on Tinder: "Quarantined with my long-term girlfriend, but who knows how much longer we can last....Distract me please." And this: "Need a little social distancing. When not at work, stuck in the house with wife and kids. Hoping for a little 'I'm going to the grocery store' with someone that may also feel a little locked down....I know you're probably looking for 'something serious' but no judgement from me if you make an exception. I might just be worth it." In what universe? I wondered.

"But do you think, knowing you were about to commit to someone, it made you turn to dating apps?" I asked Abel.

"Of course!" he said. "It was like my bachelor party. I'm entitled to that!"

In his mind, it was his last hurrah—like me, telling myself that, approaching fifty, I'd do this just once, because I might not ever have another chance.

"Rowena is all I care about and all I ever *have* cared about," he insisted.

I was silent a moment. It wasn't just that I was jealous—which, of course, I was. But the jealous older lady look was the last thing I ever wanted to don, so I continued saying nothing. I was silent, too, because I didn't feel like I could say anything, realizing how little I factored into his sense of his romantic life. I just wasn't part of the equation. He hadn't thought of me at all, in this, much less felt the need to apologize to me. And it hurt.

And yet I had entered into this relationship—pardon me, situationship— with eyes wide open, an alleged expert on modern dating. I'd always known it was a relationship of lowered expectations, in which you weren't allowed to ask for anything. So how could I object? This is where it got you, I was seeing now, firsthand: to this moment where you had no say, no rights.

I got up, went to the kitchen, and stood by the window. I felt like having a cigarette. This time, he followed me.

He stood there, smoking, watching me.

"Seems like you got some things you want to say," he said finally.

"Well, I'd like to know where I fit into all this," I said. "These past three years you've been coming here, you've been in love with someone else. So who am I, to you?"

He looked at me tenderly.

"You're my friend," he said.

"But we also have sex."

"Yes, and I enjoy it."

I knew he enjoyed it, but I wasn't flattered by him saying so now. He might as well have been saying "I enjoy eating nachos," or "I enjoy playing the ukulele."

"Yes, I do too," I said. "But—"

"But what?"

"Why didn't you tell just me the truth?"

He grimaced and said, "I don't always know the truth myself."

●  ●  ●

In September of 2018, my movie *Swiped* premiered on HBO. My friends came over to watch it in my living room with me, toasting my crossing the finish line of this four-year-long race. I was interviewed about it in a number of places, including the *Washington Post*, on NPR's *All Things Considered*, and on Kara Swisher's *Recode Decode* podcast, which was a thrill for me since I think she's hands down the best writer on Big Tech, never failing to take the CEOs to task.

I was happy to see all the tweets from people who saw the film and liked it. One of my favorites was from a woman who said: "The HBO docu Swiped confirms what women have felt all along: #dating apps were built by #bros to perpetuate #broculture by training men and women under the patriarchy to learn dehumanizing and expendable dating behavior. It deepens the divide and banks on the loneliness it manufactures." Yes, exactly. Support like this made up for the haters—and I had plenty of haters, which I'd learned was part of the deal when a woman raises her voice.

And then there were some reactions from men who seemed to want to diss me in sneakier ways—like my neighbor who said, "I watched your film. I thought it was great. Did you do it all by yourself, or did someone help you?" Making a film is, of course, a collaborative process, but I'm not so sure that's what he was suggesting.

But I didn't care about any of that after I got an email from Graydon, telling me he thought the film was "absolutely compelling. Once you start watching, you really can't stop. I am really proud of you for this. As strangely watchable as it is, I also think it's important." As my Russian grandparents would have said, I kvelled. I was so grateful to Graydon for being my champion.

After the film came out, I started to think about how I needed to do something now to make some money, because doing the documentary had left me pretty broke. Although HBO had funded it, I'd actually been paid less than even the going rate for a first-time documentary filmmaker (terms I'd accepted because I was so eager to get the job), and I'd paid for most of the preproduction myself, as well as many incidentals along the way. All of my advance money from my *American Girls* book was gone. And Zazie was starting college. My bills were piling up.

But I already knew what I had to do, regardless of my financial situation. I'd been thinking about it for a while. I knew that I had more to say about dating apps that I couldn't put in the documentary. I needed to talk about my own experiences. I wanted to share what I'd learned with people who might be going through the same things. I wanted to write an honest book about what it was like to be me, an older woman dating in the digital age. And I wanted it to be radical and funny.

So I sent out a proposal for the book you're reading now, a document of about thirty pages describing my plans. Before I even sold the book to my new publisher, the proposal was leaked by a movie scout (I had no hand in this), and Hollywood came calling.

Having Hollywood interested in your work sounds better than it usually is. My misadventures in Hollywood go back more than twenty years, to when producers first started asking to option my stories when I was a writer at *New York*. Dealing with Hollywood is a lot like dating, and even more like dating fuckboys. When producers come courting, they'll lay it on thick; they act like they think you're the best thing ever. Then they'll gaslight you and tell you it didn't mean a thing, all those meetings where you delivered up your ideas. "Oh, was that a *date*?" "Baby, I never said we were exclusive."

But I did have a good experience with Sofia Coppola, who was always straight with me. And Jackie Glover and Lisa Heller, two of our executive producers on *Swiped* (Lisa took over Sheila's job after Sheila stepped down), were great to work with; I had learned a lot from them. So maybe, I thought, I'd just had some bad luck with those other Hollywood types I'd encountered in the past. Maybe it wasn't like Marlon Brando had once said, that "most of the successful people in Hollywood are failures as human beings."

In the fall of 2018, my film agent set up some phone meetings for me with producers at different studios and production companies who'd shown interest in doing a show based on *Nothing Personal* (a book I still had to write). A lot of big actresses in the forty- and fiftysomething age range were mentioned in these conversations, and some were said to already be interested. It was very exciting.

● ● ●

Through the fall and winter of 2018, as I started work on this book and continued talking to Hollywood, Abel was still coming around, now more than ever. He was on a serious bender—the same bender, I realized, that he'd been on ever since I'd known him, ever since Rowena had cheated on him the first time and moved back to Argentina three years before. But now it was much worse.

He was still going to work. He had a Herculean ability to work through his alcohol habit, but I had never seen him drink this much for days on end. He was showing up at my house late at night, drunk and reeling around, chattering, a couple times, about how he had taken acid.

Why was I still letting him come over? Why was I there for this young man through his heartbreak over a woman who was not me? Because however he might have trampled on my feelings, I guess, he was still a human being with whom I shared a connection—like he said, we were friends—and he was in trouble.

"This is really unhealthy behavior," said my friend Elise, when I broke down one night and told her about Abel when I was feeling desperate for somebody's ear. And maybe she was right. But wasn't "unhealthy" also one of those words that was used by people who couldn't understand a grand passion?

In America we love our narratives of health and self-help, which harken back to Calvinistic attitudes suggesting that if you're fucked up, it must all be your fault. If you're poor, it must be your fault. If you're oppressed, just pull yourself up by your bootstraps. And if you're in love with someone who has problems or needs some help, just get rid of him or her or them, get over it, and move on.

But I was a romantic, not a Calvinist.

However, I did start thinking that it was time for me to suggest a narrative of health and healing to Abel, one night when he showed up especially blotto at Satsko's. It was late. The place was empty except for the two of us and David, the new bartender who always wore a driving cap. Abel could barely stay sitting on the barstool.

David looked at me sympathetically as Abel almost slid off his seat. I caught him around my shoulder. David helped me take him out to the bench outside.

"I'm all right," Abel said after a moment, shaking his head to wake himself.

He still looked beautiful, even when he was annihilated. I pushed his hair back from his face.

"Pretty sure I'm fired," he said after a while.

"When?" I asked.

"Monday," he said.

It was Wednesday.

He'd passed out at work, he said, and hadn't woken up for his shift.

I put my arm around him. "You know I love you, but—"

"But what?" he said.

He looked at me warily, like he was afraid I was going to tell him to get lost again. Which deeply pleased me, to think that he was worried I'd break up with him.

"Maybe it is time to look at alcohol in your life," I said.

"Oh," he said dismissively, as in, Is that all?

"I know I fucked up," he said. "Thing is, I actually care about that place. Been there four years."

"What are you gonna do now?" I asked.

He shrugged, lit a cigarette. "I guess I can go home and work on the line for $40 an hour."

Whenever he talked about going home to Tennessee to "work on the line," I thought of that Glen Campbell song "Wichita Lineman," about a mournful lineman who's lost his love. I thought of him now up on a telephone pole, pining away for Rowena.

I steered him down the street to my building, but we couldn't go upstairs. Zazie was home that night instead of at her dorm; I saw her light was on. So we went downstairs to our old haunt, the basement gym. Immediately Abel crashed to the floor.

I lay down next to him in the dark. I wanted to say something to help.

I nuzzled up against him, stroked his chest.

"I feel this young, strong body of yours," I told him, "and I feel so much power and vitality in you. The alcohol is like poison, you know?"

"I know. It's terrible," he murmured. His eyes were closed.

"I always feel so much better when I don't drink," I told him. "I went through a period a couple of years ago, when I was drinking a little too much—"

"Oh, I remember," he said with a little smile.

"And it made me feel so run-down and depressed," I said.

He said nothing, his eyes still closed.

I shook him.

"Are you awake?" I asked.

"Yes," he said. "This is kind of nice."

"Why do you think you drink so much?" I said.

"So I don't have to feel things," he said. "Feel the pain."

"Pain of what?"

"Pain of things I don't want to feel."

After a moment, he said, "My life is sad."

"Why do you say that?" I asked.

"Because I have no choice," he said.

I knew just what he meant. I'd been thinking a lot about choice while writing this book, and wondering how much of anything I'd ever done in regard to my relationships with men had really been my choice, and what had been predetermined by cultural conditioning and other forces beyond my control.

For Abel, having no choice meant being a poor kid who got into college but then couldn't stay, because everything in the way he had been raised had made it almost impossible for him to succeed. It meant becoming addicted to alcohol because he had grown up in a household with substance abuse, on the part of some of his mother's boyfriends, he'd told me.

"But maybe seeing all the ways you *don't* have choice, all the ways you're being controlled, is the realization you need to have in order to gain control," I told him. "Maybe it's the first step to having what they call agency."

"But how can you ever see anything when all you wanna do is forget?" he murmured.

"I know what you mean," I said. "I have things I want to forget. Sometimes it's a struggle just to get through the day. I just try and do things to fill up my time, to try and make my day go well."

"I do that too," he said. "That's why I work so much."

"Yes, me too."

I got him upstairs a little later, put him to bed, and went back to working on my book.

● ● ●

The next morning when I woke up, he was still asleep. I went in the kitchen and made some coffee. I stood by the window, drinking it, watching a couple of pigeons on the windowsill.

"Are you friends?" I whispered, leaning down to see them closer. "Are you in love?"

Startled, they flew away.

I went back in the bedroom and woke him, leaning over the bed. He opened his eyes, squinting, and pulled me in next to him. His face was scruffy on my neck. I could feel him getting hard. Our usual way was a morning fuck where he came in from behind and finished fast and furious. Not that I minded; I rather liked the repetitive, married-sex intimacy of it.

But this time—after I'd put a condom on him, which I had started doing ever since the recent revelations about his outside affairs, and maybe I was just finally getting my head in gear—he got on top of me, and he looked at me and he bent down and kissed me. Then we kissed each other as if we'd been parched for each other's kisses. He ran his hands up and down my sides.

"You got a beautiful body, you know?" he told me, pushing up into me.

I wondered if he said this because he'd noticed how I'd been turning off the lights at night before I got undressed. So he was thinking of me, noticing me, I thought, wanting to make me feel good. Like now...

He came high up inside me, holding me tight.

We were back.

I made him a big breakfast.

"What do you think you're gonna do for work now?" I asked him, pouring him some orange juice. I sat down next to him at the kitchen counter.

"I got a few leads," he said. "You don't have to worry about me. I been on my own a long time."

I told him I wasn't worried. "I know you can take care of yourself."

I'm not sure why it all came pouring out of him just then, the story of what had happened to him when he was a little boy. I don't know what made him open up. But it was then that he told me how he had been sexually assaulted when he was a child, just four years old, by his mother's former boyfriend.

He said it all in a flat, factual way. He said his mother had the guy arrested and took him to court.

"He was in jail for a while," he said.

"I'm sorry," I told him.

"Why?" He smiled a tight, unconvincing smile. "Ain't no big deal. It's nothing," he said, getting up and putting his dishes in the sink. "You move on."

"I'm still sorry," I said. "Because it happened to you. And it was wrong."

"Do you know how many people this happens to?" he asked, still smiling tightly, folding his arms.

Yes, I did: one out of every three girls and one out of every five boys are the statistics often cited. I'd thought about this a lot when I was on the road, interviewing girls.

I went to hug him. But he gently pushed me away, still wearing that strained look on his face, like he didn't want to feel any physical contact just then.

His mother had dated a pedophile; it was too horrible to contemplate.

"I know it's nothing compared to what you went through," I told him, "but something like that happened to me too..."

I told him about what had happened at the University of Miami.

"When these things happen to you, people start saying it's your fault," I said. "*You* might even start thinking it's your fault—but it never is."

I told him about my old boyfriend Jason hitting me. "I don't know why I stayed with him after the first time it happened. I guess you get used to thinking this is how you're supposed to be treated."

"Ain't the way anybody should be treated," said Abel.

He started talking about his current stepfather, who he'd seen hit his mother before.

"I stepped to him when I was about fifteen," he said. "He told me, man-to-man, he wasn't gonna fuck up again and then he fucked up. If I had a gun with two bullets and I met him and Satan and Adolf Hitler, I'd shoot him twice. He hurt the person I love the most."

He said his mother still loved the guy.

"Have you ever talked to your mother about it?" I asked.

"Yeah," he said. "I did."

"And what did she say?"

"She says you can't help who you love."

•　•　•

After we saw the pain in each other, we saw each other. And after we saw each other, we grew closer. And the closer we became, the more we could help each other, and the better we could make each other feel.

And that was the real problem with online dating, I had started thinking: how it encourages a culture which undermines the real purpose—or perhaps the ideal purpose—of dating, which the Pretenders expressed so well: "Now the reason we're here / As man and woman"—or however one so identifies— "Is to love each other / Take care of each other."

Swiping wasn't going to support you in times of trouble; swiping wasn't going to feel your pain. And yet, it was through swiping that I had met Abel. It was an interesting irony...

We started having fun again. He came in from the cold one night and made me scream when he put his freezing hands on me, and I ran away from him and he chased me around the dining room table. And so began our chasing games and wrestling games, where he would always win and pin me to the floor, where we would fuck again till we both got rug burns.

"How beautiful you look," I told him one night when he came to me at my closet, where I was undressing. "You've filled out since that first night I saw you," I said, touching his chest.

I had seen him grow up, fill out, ever since that first that night I came racing home to meet him. I'd seen his shoulders get broader, his biceps were bigger. I'd seen his hair getting longer until it cascaded down his back like a mane. I'd seen more smooth dark hair appear on his chest and abs. I'd even seen his hairline receding a little bit.

"You were shy back then," I said.

"You don't still think I'm shy?" he asked, and then bent me over the hamper and fucked me.

He was drinking less. He seemed happier now. He told me "a buddy had given [him] ayahuasca," the hallucinogen that had become popular among seekers as a way of clearing the mind. "And it was the most beautiful thing I ever seen, all the colors," he told me.

He was living in a new place with roommates in the Bronx. He'd gotten a new job working for a moving company—moving the homes of "rich motherfuckers," he said. I sometimes thought of him, looking around all those one-percenters' apartments, and I wondered if he ever thought about the contrast to where he came from, and worried it might bother him.

"I took a selfie of myself taking a dump on [a rock star]'s toilet," he told me, grinning, when I asked him about it.

We were more comfortable with each other now. No more of the butter-flies and awkwardness of two people who are stuck in the situationship zone. It felt like a blockage had been cleared with the removal of Rowena from his mind as a possibility, a hope.

"Oh, her? I think she got hit by a bus," he said jokingly one night, when I asked him if he'd spoken to her. Then he asked for another slice of pizza.

"Rock your hips back and forth," he told me, when we were fucking.

Our lovemaking became more intense, the aura of mystery now becoming one of discovery all over again.

"Dang," he'd whisper when we were going at it. "Double dang."

He danced around my kitchen one night, showing me how he could pirouette. "Just learned it from watching 'em dance at school," he said. I told him he was graceful.

He taught me how to talk real Tennessee: "Tin-uh-say." "Have a grite die."

We laughed at videos of Snoop Dogg's *Plizzanet Earth*. We did percussion while listening to music, me shaking my metal piggy bank and him hitting a mug with a pen.

"And that, darling, is what you call jammin'," he said, smiling.

I noticed how much less anxiety I felt about him now, and I wondered if in part it was because our relationship was no longer tied to our phones. I wasn't always checking for him now, because I knew he would come back. Not having to depend on my phone as the oracle of our togetherness made me relax.

It felt like a purer state of being together. There was something binding us together now: it was the secrets we had shared—and the sex, of course, but now the sex was more intimate. And it was also the regularity of the sex, the availability of each other, and the reciprocity of the pleasure. I didn't mind him pushing my head down to his dick—"Hello there, how have you been?" I would ask, as he smiled, lying back on the pillow—because I knew his mouth or fingers would come to me.

"I missed you," he would say when he came in the door.

I told him about a dream I'd had that was like a vision of the two of us living on the prairie together. I was his age and I was living with him in a log cabin; we were two settlers snuggling in a warm bed at night as the wind and the snow whipped around outside.

"It was like, I was me, but I was younger," I told him.

"But I'm glad you're the age you are," he said, hugging me. "I like the way you are."

"Could it be I'm falling in love?" I asked myself in the bathroom one night. It was the song that had been playing on the speakers in my bedroom, the Spinners crooning, "Could it be I'm falling in love?"

And could it be that he was too? I wondered.

This was the sweet spot, I thought, the sweetest spot. A relationship of equality, where I didn't feel as if giving myself to him made me a sucker, because he was giving so much back. He supported my work too; as young as he was, he knew how to buck me up.

I told him about my fears about doing this book—I'd never done a memoir before, and this one was going to be so personal.

"Failure?" he scoffed. "You don't know the *meaning* of the word." In fact I did, big time, but it was nice of him to say.

I encouraged him to do his music. I thought he was good and told him so. "I can't think of another voice I'd rather listen to than yours," I said, and meant it. He said he'd "been jamming with some buddies, thinking about putting a band together." I said I thought that was wonderful.

"You know, I do love you," he told me one night, with the sweetest look on his face. We were having sex on the couch. I touched his cheek.

"I love you too," I said.

"Come for me," he said.

One evening in December, he came by to see me before he had to catch a bus down to visit his family in Tennessee for the holidays. Zazie was home, so we met down in the basement. He saw me and he said, "Aw, you look lovely," and then we were kissing each other, taking off each other's clothes, making love up against the wall. Suddenly, I had a flashback to Jack the Skateboard Boy, and I shuddered, as if I'd seen a scary ghost, a ghost of fuckboys past. I shook it out of my head.

Over the holidays, Abel called me from Tin-uh-say.

"You must be glad to be home," I said, and he said he was "homesick for something that wasn't home," by which I thought he must mean me.

● ● ●

I went to Florida with Zazie that Christmas of 2018. We stayed with my stepmother Mary in West Palm Beach. For the first time since I'd left Miami in 1980, I wanted to go back and see it again. I wanted my daughter to see where I grew up.

Driving down the highway, I thought of my father, back in the days when he would make this trip down to see us every Sunday after my parents got divorced. I thought of how my dad had faced this bleak stretch of road, two ways, nearly every weekend, and I was filled with a wave of sadness. He was who he was; but he loved us very much.

We glided around Coral Gables, Zazie and I, playing disco music in the car. I'd asked her to do a disco mix because that was how I remembered the place, to a disco beat. I told her about how, at my first middle school dance, my tampon came wriggling down out of my jeans as I boogied around the dance floor to "Get Down Tonight," and I had to dance-kick it out of the room so no one would see it.

"That is the most heroic story you've ever told me," she said, and we laughed.

Miami looked much the same, except cleaner and fancier, like everywhere that had attracted wealth over the last fortysomething years. Gentrification had set in, and it didn't quite seem like the same sleepy town I'd grown up in. But there was the same sweet-smelling vegetation, the giant ficus and palm trees, tall ones and squat ones and ones that leaned to the side. There was the one my mother and stepfather had planted in the front yard of our little tile-roofed house—it had grown to be two stories high. I remembered hopping around on my pogo stick on the sidewalk in front of that house when I was a little girl. Suddenly I was grateful to have survived this long; it might not have gone that way.

I started telling Zazie about how it was in those days when I was younger. She was eighteen now, and I thought she should know. I told her about what had happened to me at the University of Miami as we rode past it.

"I'm so sorry, Mommy," she said, putting her hand on my arm. "I love you."

"I'm sorry I have to tell you this," I said. Now I was crying. "I'm just telling you because I wish somebody had told me these things can happen."

"Thank you for protecting me," she said.

"You have to protect yourself!" I said, surprised at the vehemence that rose up in my throat.

• • •

Abel called while I was in Florida and left a voicemail: "I just wanna wish you a happy New Year and tell you I miss you and I can't wait to see you again." I listened to that voicemail over and over in the next few days. I realized then that I really did love Abel, and it felt like Abel had fallen in love with me.

We saw each other again right away in January when I came back to New York. We went to the sake bar and he seemed so sweet again, after his two weeks in Tennessee, as if all the hardness of the city had been washed away.

"I'm starting to feel like a man," he said.

He said he felt like he was getting older and so was taking his life and his responsibilities more seriously. He said he'd realized "who I care about," and I thought he must mean me.

"I know this isn't gonna last forever," I whispered, "but I don't want it to end—not yet."

He took my hand and put it on his hard-on under the table.

"You feel that?" he said by way of answer.

• • •

In late 2018 and into early 2019, my agent was setting up calls for me with the producers who had expressed interest in making my new book into a TV show or a film. These conversations felt almost like scenes in a movie themselves—it didn't seem they could be real; but they were.

"So what are her motivations? Why is she so promiscuous?" one big-name producer asked me on speakerphone, driving around in his car in LA.

"Promiscuous?" I said. "Well, I'm not sure that's a word people use to describe sexual choices anymore—"

"Yeah, but she sleeps with guy after guy," the producer said. "And this is TV. People want to see the *damage*."

They kept using words like "damaged," "messy," and "troubled" to describe

337

our main character. It was reflective of a trend in Hollywood, this "increasing interest in dark comedies centered on troubled, troublesome women," I would later read in the *New York Times*. This interest in the life of crazy ladies was apparently based on the success of some great shows like *Fleabag* and *Crazy Ex-Girlfriend*. But as I listened to the producers talk, I started to wonder if this trend was also a new type of backlash—that is, shows about women who are fucked up.

"I think this should go really *dark*," another male producer told me. "This woman is really damaged. This is like a female *Breaking Bad*."

"But Walter White is a meth dealer and a murderer," I protested. "How is a woman using dating apps like a psychopathic criminal?"

"She's sleeping with all these *young guys*," he said. "It'll be totally hot."

My friend, a TV producer who lives in New York, said that this type of bloviating was standard for the process. "Producers don't know what they want until they hear it," he said. "Just go with it until they decide it's right."

I was trying.

"We need to see her whole *life* blow up," another male producer told me on the phone.

"Because she's using dating apps?" I asked.

"Because she's addicted to them," he said. "Because she's using them too *much*."

"I see her getting addicted," I told him, "but don't you think it's more interesting if she's high-functioning at the same time? Because millions of people are addicted to these things. I was addicted for a while, but I was also doing my job and being a mom. Women can juggle a *lot*—"

"We need to see her life implode," the producer said. "And her relationship with her daughter should completely fall apart. How can it *not*?"

"Why? Because she's having sex?" I asked.

"I'm getting another call," he said, and hung up.

"I think she clearly has intimacy issues," said a famous actress on the phone with her producing team. Everyone seemed to agree with her.

I felt a little rumbling in my gut, but I didn't know how much I was allowed to say, so I just said: "Yes, but, well, if we attribute her sleeping around to her intimacy issues, aren't we letting technology off the hook? And what about the fact that dating apps are designed to be addictive? And what about hookup culture?"

There was a strange little silence on the line, which I would learn was Hollywood's way of saying you had done something akin to farting loudly.

"Oh dear, you argued with the star," said my friend the TV producer, when I told him about this moment, later.

But I didn't think I had *argued* with the star—I had just stated my opinion.

"I'm still stuck on them thinking that an older woman dating is the same thing as someone cooking meth," said my friend Austin, when I told everybody about it later at Satsko's.

"This may be uncomfortable for you," a female producer told me on another call, "but I think you need to delve deeper into why you got interested in youth culture in the first place."

I told them then how I'd started covering youth culture because it was assigned to me at the magazine I worked for. I was confused that this had suddenly become personal. Didn't they keep telling me not to think of the character as "me"?

Again there was one of those long Hollywood silences, like someone had taken a dump on the carpet.

"I see this as being like *The Sopranos*," said another female producer.

"So our main character is like Tony Soprano?" I asked.

"Well, yes," she said, "but instead of mommy issues she has daddy issues."

"She's in love with a homeless guy?" another producer said. "Do we have to make him homeless? Could he maybe work in tech?"

"Are you sure these guys are really treating her that badly?" another female producer asked. "Or is she just projecting this on to them because she's not dealing with herself?"

Of course I was simultaneously trying to work out for myself why my romantic life resembled *La Strada*, with me as the sad little clown following around the abusive strongman brute; but I still didn't like to see myself reduced to a stereotype, my love life reduced to a tagline: *She loved too many men—but did they ever love her back?*

*She had issues.*

Over the months I was talking to the producers, I started to feel depressed. They kept saying they weren't talking about me, but, hello, they clearly were, and what they were saying was starting to make me feel really bad about myself.

"Because they're slut-shaming you," Zazie said.

She'd noticed I was seeming low, she said, and she asked me what was wrong. I told her about the producers comparing me to Tony Soprano and Walter White. (I'd already told her about my book. I didn't want her to be blindsided when it came out.)

"This is what Hollywood has done to women since the beginning," Zazie reminded me. It had actually been the subject of her senior thesis in high school, slut-shaming in silent films.

"If women had sex outside of the context of marriage," she said, "they either died, were ostracized, or had to be redeemed by the love of a man. And this hasn't really changed. I don't think you should talk to these people anymore, Mommy," my dear little feminist added.

• • •

But it had always been one of my secret dreams to work in television; and we also needed the money. I needed a gig. So I agreed to get on another call with a hot young writer, someone whom a certain producing team was considering to be the creator and showrunner of the show about my life. He was in his late twenties.

Hollywood's track record on hiring women is abysmal, especially women of color. Which makes it—even to this day, in a feminist wave, amid global

340

protests for Black Lives Matter—a highly sexist and racist industry. Which is all the more troubling considering the outsized influence it has on the way people think and act.

The statistics are shocking: Of the one hundred top grossing films of 2019, women made up only 12 percent of the directors, 20 percent of the writers, 2 percent of the cinematographers, and 26 percent of the producers (a small sample of industry jobs overall). Sixty-eight percent of the female characters in these films were white; only 20 percent were Black, 7 percent were Asian, and 5 percent Latino. And more than 70 percent of the women on screen were young.

When it comes to television, between 2017 and 2018 there was actually a decline from the previous year in the overall percentage of female creators, directors, writers, producers, executive producers, editors, and directors of photography, to just 27 percent. Women made up 40 percent of the speaking characters across platforms—the highest percentage ever. However, these characters were less likely than men to be seen in an identified professional role or to ever be seen working. They were more likely than men to be defined by their family relationships, as wives and mothers.

And yet somehow this producing team that was in touch with me still thought that a man was the best person to write a show about a woman in her fifties. On the call, this guy, a hot young writer, held forth about how the show was going to be about a woman discovering the world of online dating while raising a daughter. He didn't happen to mention what her job would be or how it factored into her experience.

There was a strained little silence, after which someone on the network side asked if the Hot Young Writer was going to do something more "disruptive" with the material. He replied that every episode was "going to be like a short story." Someone asked if he had any questions for me, and he said that for the moment, he did not. He said that talking to me would not be necessary while he was developing the pilot. Perhaps down the road, he said.

Was he going to talk to anyone about middle-aged women doing on-line dating? someone asked. The Hot Young Writer said that he had been talking to his mother, who was newly single and was venturing out into the dating world.

"Yes, because mothers tell their sons everything about their sex lives," I thought, but I didn't say anything.

"Does anybody want to read my book?" I asked after a while, hoping to be helpful and have some input on the direction of the project.

The Hot Young Writer said that he did not need to read my book. He said, "I'm in my process."

It was after that call that I decided I didn't want to work with that team, and wondered if I really belonged in Hollywood at all.

* * *

In March of 2019, I fell on my face.

I didn't expect it to be the way the day would go. I was feeling high on life itself. I'd quit drinking and smoking and was sleeping better and had lost a bit of weight, and I'd finally gotten into a groove writing this book. I was actually singing along to the Lizzo song "Good as Hell" on my phone. It was a fine spring day, and I was walking along, thinking I might go get Zazie and me some sandwiches from Katz's Delicatessen. If I did that, I thought, then I could walk by the bar where Abel liked to hang out and look in the window and see if he was there...

And then I fell on my face on First Avenue. I stepped from the curb into a pothole, and the jolly red giantess came tumbling down.

When you fall, your hand shoots out to catch you. In that instant, I shattered my wrist. My face went right into the pavement—slam!—big, freckly nose breaking as it saved my head from further injury. I rolled over on my side to avoid being hit by a bus. Some young people who were crossing the street just then and saw me wipe out came running to help. I couldn't get up—every time I tried, I felt dizzy, so they all sort of huddled around me to protect me from oncoming traffic.

I was alone in the ambulance as we rode to the hospital, alone in the emergency room as they did my X-rays and CT scan. Zazie wanted to come be with me but I texted her, "No, it's okay. Just pick me up when I'm ready to come home."

And I really was okay with this; I was used to going through things alone. You can get so used to it, you don't even expect anyone to help. I had learned not to let it bother me: "I'll be fine." And I was.

That is, until I got a text from Abel, asking, "Hey there, how're you today?" And I wrote back, saying, "Hey! So something kind of crazy happened to me…" And I told him I was in the emergency room and he said, "Holy shit that's crazy! I hope you get to feelin' better soon."

And that was all I heard from Abel that day.

Which kind of upset me.

The emergency room doctor who did my cast looked to be about Abel's age, around twenty-seven. I muttered something about how this injury to my wrist really sucked because I was in the middle of writing a book (it was my right wrist and I'm a righty). He asked me what my book was about, and I told him online dating, dating apps, Tinder.

"Oof," he said, wrapping my wrist. "I tried that for a while, and it was *crazy*. If you're a doctor, and reasonably attractive"—he was plenty cute and knew it—"the women just throw themselves at you. You could date a different woman every night—it's too much…"

• • •

As I got in bed that night after leaving Constance and then rushing home to find Abel wasn't there, I snuggled down in my bed, feeling grateful to have this moment of peace all to myself. I had finished my bathroom ablutions with my overpriced lotions and put on my comfiest pajamas, and now I lay in the dark, listening to the quiet. I snuggled against the pillows. Sometimes being alone can feel so restful. Now, it felt like a gift. Remembering the day I fell, I was actually kind of glad Abel wasn't coming over.

What had I been thinking, texting him back when he said "Hola"? I wondered. How did I ever fall for it again? Thinking back to what he did, or didn't do, after my accident, I remembered why I'd never wanted to see him again . . .

My wrist surgery had been pretty serious. I had to get a bone implant and a metal plate. I sat on my couch for the next couple of weeks with my hand in a cast elevated on a foam armrest. I was in a lot of pain and virtually immobile. It was hard to do almost anything.

I wasn't used to not being able to take care of myself. People started coming over to help. My brother Noah and Ahmet and Abigail and Satsko all came and visited. I was moved by my sweet friends. They made me laugh, and they laughed at my bad jokes about my swollen nose and how I was finding it hard to brush my hair. They brought me soup and sandwiches and flowers. Satsko brought edamame.

Amy came with her new rescue puppy, Penny. Amy had become a devoted dog mom. We laughed about how you didn't need a man when there were dogs.

But Abel didn't come. He didn't call. He didn't ring my bell, as he so often had in the past, whenever he was in the neighborhood and wanted to have sex. He didn't show up with flowers, or come over just to keep me company. He didn't show up.

He did text: "How ya feeling?"

"Which is more than some guys would do," Amy said.

I was learning new things about modern dating all the time—like you could have a fuck buddy for four years, but when you needed him, he wasn't necessarily going to be there. There was nothing in the fuck-buddy non-contract that said that he had to be.

"But he told you he loved you," said Abigail, frowning. "That's not a fuck buddy anymore. Where the fuck is he?"

If I was one of those woo-woo people who thinks that everything happens for a reason, then I would have seen this experience as a moment to reflect on our relationship. Which I did. And I saw that it all went back to choices, patterns. I saw the wheel spinning around, from Abel and me back to all the other men I'd ever known. And I had to wonder, why had so many of them let me down? I did seem to pick some disappointing ones.

"But it's not like there are all these other great guys out there, chomping at the bit to be the perfect boyfriends," Abigail said. "You're not the only one experiencing these things. Why do you think we're having this big feminist wave? Because we're fed up! It's why women my age say, 'Men are trash.'"

The #menaretrash hashtag had been around for a few years, periodically trending on Twitter. Women used it to respond to online harassment and stories in the news that involved the harmful effects of toxic masculinity. Facebook treated #menaretrash as hate speech, and Twitter had been accused of deleting tweets that used it.

I agreed with Abigail: #menaretrash. In the broadest sense.

But I didn't want to think of Abel as "trash." I'd known him too long, and we had been too close, for me to be able to reduce him to a hashtag. I guess what hurt the most was that his absence threw into doubt all those moments of intimacy we'd been having over the last few months. I thought of a teenage girl I'd interviewed, more than twenty years before, who had asked me what I thought about a boy she was worried had played her: "Was it real?" she said.

Was the love between me and Abel real? I wondered.

I finally sent him a text—I could have called him, I guess, but I think I was too upset——and let him know how I felt.

He texted me right back: "If you need anything, you know all you got to do is ask."

But I didn't want to have to ask. I wanted him to show up.

I sent him a long text, telling him I didn't think we should see each other anymore. He didn't text me back.

• • •

Meanwhile, the true love of my life had been there all along.

She was coming by every day, bringing me things I needed, making me tea. She was sitting with me when she didn't have to be in class or have homework to do, covering me with a blanket when I nodded off from my pain pills.

She was taking care of me, as I'd taken care of her. It made me think of when we went to see *Maleficent* together in the theater, and she'd whispered to me in the dark, "You and me," when Maleficent kisses Aurora on the forehead and the girl awakens, for this was true love's kiss.

She was sitting next to me on the couch, holding my hand as we watched funny shows she'd put on to cheer me up. She was talking to me about everything under the sun. We talked about how Abbi (Abbi Jacobson) on *Broad City* shocks her mother (Peri Gilpin) when she tells her she's slept with thirty-two people, and how numbers didn't matter anymore.

"Role reversal," Zazie said with a smile.

I guessed she knew me better than I thought.

It was then that I told her about Abel. For four years, I'd kept him a secret from her. But now it was over, and I needed someone to talk to about it, and I didn't know anyone better to talk to than her.

She listened and smiled and said, "He's your horse."

She meant my horse in the parlor game "the cube," in which you're asked to imagine a series of things, one of them being a horse, which you later learn is supposed to signify your ideal mate. When I played the cube, my horse was a muscly black stallion, huffing and puffing around a track. Hot. But don't bet on that horse to bring you chicken soup.

"You're not alone," Zazie said, assessing my romantic life. "You're single. By choice. Which is different."

It was a wise thing to say, or at least very kind. I don't know how she got this way, but I find her friends to be much the same. They seem like a new generation of clear-eyed young women, which makes me hopeful.

• • •

All of which brings me back to my mom and how we started having those hours-long conversations about things we had never talked about but should have long ago. Maybe she had found a way to talk about things since the #MeToo movement, which was helping so many women find the words. Or maybe it was just time.

She was eighty-four now and had been in the hospital herself recently. She was recovering at home in New Hampshire. She was fine. She had started doing art again, abstract paintings I thought were beautiful. She posted them on Instagram.

When she heard about my accident, she started calling me every day.

"How are you?" she'd ask.

I couldn't remember my mother ever simply asking me, "How are you?" It wasn't how she had ever shown her love. It surprised me so much, I didn't know how to answer at first.

And then I realized I'd never really asked her how she was, either.

"How are *you*?" I said.

And that's how we got to talking about how we were, and how we'd been doing all these years. She told me about things that had happened to her on Oyster Road, and I told her about things that had happened to me at schools and jobs, and how I'd spent my life feeling bad about these things, and didn't want to feel that way anymore.

"Neither do I," my mother said soothingly. "Enough of that."

• • •

It's a very interesting sensation, to become invisible, especially when you've been very visible all your life, or at least since you were about twelve years old. It's interesting when the spotlight goes out, and you begin to float through the world like a ghost.

It was a new sensation, for me, that feeling of being unfettered by anything to do with my looks. I felt myself begin to fade from sight. Walking along with the hordes of New Yorkers rushing home at dusk in Manhattan, it was as if I had disappeared completely. And it felt mystic and light. The street used to be a place where you thought you might be seen by some handsome stranger, someone who would make you feel you mattered even more. And I was always looking for that stranger, always searching for that someone who could make me feel that I had been seen. And now I was free from that thought.

One Sunday afternoon, a few weeks after I had had my wrist surgery, I was done working for the day, and I felt like having a drink. All my friends were busy, so I ventured out alone, wandering over to the West Village. I drifted into (the now shuttered) Bar Sardine and sat at the bar and ordered one of those spicy Bloody Marys they served with a little shrimp cocked on the side of the tall glass. I sat at the bar drinking my Bloody Mary and thinking about how this might be how it would be for years to come: me alone in a bar or some restaurant somewhere, watching the young people out on their dates. The old lady at the bar who appeared smudged and not completely visible, like in a Toulouse-Lautrec painting.

I could see they didn't see me, the young men sitting at the bar right next to me, three of them, talking about women. They didn't think that I could hear the raw triumph in their voices, these buzzed blond boys who said they had gone to Georgetown and played squash and had political ambitions. They didn't know that I had seen them showing each other the photos on their phones of girls they had fucked, snickering, ogling and comparing notes. And when the young women came in—young women they had been texting to come meet them—in their short dresses, with their bubbly voices, I didn't say a word. I paid my bill and left, hoping that the young women would know enough to see through these guys. It was up to them.

• • •

Around two in the morning—the morning of the night I ran to see Abel after leaving Constance and found that he wasn't there, and then got into bed—I was lying in the dark, listening to an Audible book of Toni Morrison reading *Sula*.

I had become so engrossed in the story of this young woman who was searching and sexual and impetuous and disregarding of social conventions, I couldn't stop listening for hours. I felt like I knew her. Morrison's beautifully sonorous voice felt like spiritual medicine, her words like a balm spreading over my psychic cuts.

I was listening with interest to the part about Sula's many affairs when— *BUZZ*—there was someone at my door.

Of course, it was him.

And dammit, my heart did leap.

For a moment, I wasn't sure what to do.

Let him in, or pretend I didn't hear? Neither choice felt optimal.

Because I *had* heard him—I knew he was there. And if I didn't respond, he might just come back again. And it was time for me to make a choice, a real choice, about Abel.

So I got up and shuffled to the front door of my apartment and buzzed him in. I waited at the door for him to come up the stairs. In the past, I would have been running to the bathroom then, seizing even this eighty seconds or so to check my hair and frantically apply mascara. But I just stood there. I didn't care how I looked.

And there he was. "Lookin' better than a body has a right to," as Dolly Parton sings.

He was smiling so wide, it was like his face might break. He looked so happy to see me. He came toward me before I could say anything and wrapped his arms around me. "I *missed* you," he said. There was his spicy smell again, and his face in my neck. His cold hands crawling up inside my shirt to make me laugh and scream. I screamed, and laughed, and hugged him back.

And—what can I say?—then we were in bed again, making love. I had to admit, I still loved it. When he fell asleep on top of me, I put my arms around him and just held his familiar body, thinking, "I'm not ready to give this up, not yet…"

But then the weight of him started to press on me, and I was finding it hard to breathe. He was sleeping so deeply, it took me several harrowing minutes to get out from under him. For a moment, I felt like I would suffocate.

I went into the kitchen to get myself some water.

And there, on the counter, I saw his phone.

He hadn't changed his password yet. Trusting Mountain Boy.

I checked it, of course. Back to my old habits immediately. Which I saw that he was too. He was back on Tinder. He'd been sleeping with other people again. "Well, who could blame him?" I thought. After all, I had sent him away…

It was when I started looking at the texts between him and some of his Tinder matches that I saw her—a young woman he had in his phone as "Becky DD."

Becky DD?

I didn't even have to think about it. My legs knew what to do before I did. I marched into the bedroom with his phone.

"Abel, wake up," I told him.

He didn't want to wake up. I shook him awake.

I put his phone in front of his face. He opened an eye.

"Why you lookin' at my phone?" he moaned.

"What is this?" I demanded.

He just squinted at me.

I turned on a light.

I put his phone back in front of him.

"What does this mean?" I asked.

His face twisted with annoyance.

"Well you weren't talkin' to me," he protested, squinting.

"No," I said. I was agitated, suddenly short of breath. "What is 'DD'?"

"Oh." He frowned. "You know..."

"Does it mean double-D, like the bra size?" I asked.

"It's just a way of identifying someone," he muttered.

"Get out of my house," I told him.

"What?"

And then I was pulling him off the bed—which was difficult—making him stand up, handing him his clothes. I was doing it for Alyson and Abigail and Amy and Zazie and my mother—and me. I was doing it for all the girls I had interviewed.

"Out!" I said.

"You're acting insane," he said, dressing sleepily.

"I want you to get out of this house right now!"

I was furious at him in a way I never thought I could be. I would never know for sure if he had always been this way, or if the last four years on dating apps had turned him into the guy with "Becky DD" in his phone, but I didn't care. I knew there was nothing I could say to him now, nothing I could tell him that he shouldn't have learned already. I realized he didn't know me at all.

"She was just a piece of ass!" he protested, when he saw that it was real, that I was really kicking him out.

"Goodbye!" I said.

He would probably always believe I had done this out of jealousy, I thought, but that was fine. I didn't care what he thought anymore.

"There ain't any trains back to Jersey this time of night," he said as I pushed him out the front door—half dressed, holding his shirt.

"I don't care," I said.

My heart was racing. I slammed the door. He was gone.

I stood holding on to the kitchen counter a moment, trying to calm down. Finally, I did.

And then I got back into bed and went to sleep.

And I have to say, I haven't slept that well in years.

● ● ●

"How are things with your isolationship?" I ask Constance, on the phone, a few weeks after she told me about her corona bae.

"Oh, it's over," she says with a sigh. "Men! You were so right about online dating. It's a shitshow."

I'm lying in the grass in a little town in New Hampshire. I'm not usually one to want to lie in the grass. But I came out of my mother's house to go for a walk and I saw this freshly mowed field, and I just wanted to lie here in the sun and look at the sky.

The death toll in New York has climbed past twenty thousand. More than twenty thousand souls, some of them relatives of friends, and no end in sight. I didn't want to leave New York, but I was worried it wasn't safe to stay. I brought Zazie with me. I was grateful to have my family as a refuge. If the virus has taught us anything, it's how much we need each other.

"He just wanted me for sex," I hear Constance complaining. "I told him, 'You led me to believe you wanted something serious! I thought you wanted a relationship!' He said, 'I don't want to keep hurting you like this,' and he left. But I don't miss him."

"Are you still on the apps?" I ask, watching the clouds drift by.

"Yes," Constance says. "It's exhausting. I hate it. I don't understand why any man, age sixty, wouldn't want to just have one good woman and be done with it."

"Go to Central Park," I say. "Look at the ducks."

"Maybe I'll do that," she says.

We're quiet a moment and then she says: "You know what? We're lucky to be alive."

# Acknowledgments

I wouldn't have been able to write this book without knowing every person in it, and so I'd like to thank them all. Here are some who stand out as especially important:

Jen Marshall, my book agent, for believing in me, for being so good at everything she does, and for doing so much more than anyone could expect. Krishan Trotman, my editor, for her impeccable instincts, patience, and kindness. Hachette, for believing in this book. Graydon Carter, to whom I owe so much. My mother and father, for supporting and teaching me. Zazie, for making me proud. My brother Noah and my sister Liz, who are two of the best sounding boards I know. My stepparents, Mary and Leslie, for taking such good care of us. Donald Suggs, to whom I have dedicated this book, because he was the best. Alyson, who left too soon. Spencer Rothman, who did so much. Daniel Carter, who gives me hope about men. Satsko, for being my friend and ear and for opening her charmed sake bar. Amy, for her warmth, her insights and bons mots. Austin, for making art in the face of the apocalypse. Jeannine Amber, without whom I would be lost. Michael Clark, Elizabeth Dana, and Elisa Rivlin, for their expertise in shepherding the book to completion. All my young women friends, who enrich my work and life. All the young women and men I interviewed along the way. All the experts I interviewed, who made me think and understand. All the people I quoted from social media, for their wit and candor. All the guys I met on dating apps, except the ones who misbehaved.

And finally, and most of all, Abel.

# Bibliography

ABC News, "Gable Tostee Found Not Guilty of Killing Warriena Wright on Tinder Date." Last modified October 20, 2016. www.abc.net.au/news/2016-10-20/gable-tostee-not -guiltyl-warriena-wright-fatal-balcony-fall/7928346.

Acklin, Mary. "Unmarried Couples Are Quarantining Together Amid the Coronavirus, Having More Sex." CivicScience, April 1, 2020. https://civicscience.com/couples-are -quarantining-together-amid-the-coronavirus-having-more-sex/.

Adamy, Janet. "U.S. Marriage Rate Plunges to Lowest Level on Record." *Wall Street Journal*, April 29, 2020. www.wsj.com/articles/u-s-marriage-rate-plunges-to-lowest-level -on-record-11588132860.

Alexander, Reed. "Tinder Is Making More Money Than Any Other App." *New York Post*, September 6, 2017. https://nypost.com/2017/09/06/tinder-is-making-more-money-than -any-other-app/.

Allen, Mike. "Sean Parker Unloads on Facebook: 'God Only Knows What It's Doing to Our Children's Brains.'" *Axios*, November 9, 2017. www.axios.com/sean-parker-unloads -on-facebook-god-only-knows-what-its-doing-to-our-childrens-brains-1513306792-f855e7b4 -4e99-4d60-8d51-2775559c2671.html.

Anderson, Monica. "A Majority of Teens Have Experienced Some Form of Cyberbullying." Pew Research Center, September 27, 2018. www.pewresearch.org/internet/2018/09/27 /a-majority-of-teens-have-experienced-some-form-of-cyberbullying/.

Anderson, Monica, and Emily A. Vogels. "Young Women Often Face Sexual Harassment Online—Including on Dating Sites and Apps." *Fact Tank* (blog). Pew Research Center, March 6, 2020. www.pewresearch.org/fact-tank/2020/03/06/young-women-often-face -sexual-harassment-online-including-on-dating-sites-and-apps/.

Anderson, Monica, Emily A. Vogels, and Erica Turner. "The Virtues and Downsides of Online Dating." Pew Research Center, February 6, 2020. www.pewresearch.org/internet/2020 /02/06/the-virtues-and-downsides-of-online-dating/.

Armstrong, Elizabeth A., and Laura Hamilton. "Gendered Sexuality in Young Adulthood: Double Binds and Flawed Options." *Gender and Society* 23, no. 5 (October 2009): 589–616.

Associated Press. "Cyberbullying Is on the Rise, and Girls Report 3 Times More Harassment Than Boys." *USA Today*, July 26, 2019. www.usatoday.com/story/tech/2019/07/ 26/harassment-social-media-cyberbullying-reports-rise-among-girls/1835431001/.

———. "Survey: 1 in 4 Women Victims of Severe Violence." CBS News, December 14, 2011. www.cbsnews.com/news/survey-1-in-4-women-victims-of-severe-violence/.

Au-Yeung, Angel. "Exclusive Investigation: Sex, Drugs, Misogyny and Sleaze at the HQ of Bumble's Owner." *Forbes*, July 8, 2019. www.forbes.com/sites/angelauyeung/2019/07/08/exclusive-investigation-sex-drugs-misogyny-and-sleaze-at-the-hq-of-bumbles-owner/#777591516308.

Badger, Emily. "The Unbelievable Rise of Single Motherhood in America over the Last 50 Years." *Washington Post*, December 18, 2014. www.washingtonpost.com/news/wonk/wp/2014/12/18/the-unbelievable-rise-of-single-motherhood-in-america-over-the-last-50-years/.

Bahrampour, Tara. "'There Really Isn't Anything Magical About It': Why More Millennials Are Avoiding Sex." *Washington Post*, August 2, 2016. www.washingtonpost.com/local/social-issues/there-isnt-really-anything-magical-about-it-why-more-millennials-are-putting-off-sex/2016/08/02/e7b73d6e-37f4-11e6-8f7c-d4c723a2becb_story.html.

Balloo, Stephanie. "App Date Rape Claims from Girls as Young as 16." *Birmingham Mail*, July 31, 2017. www.birminghammail.co.uk/news/midlands-news/app-date-rape-claims-girls-13389706.

Bame, Yael. "53% of Millennial Women Have Received a Naked Photo from a Man." YouGov, October 9, 2017. https://today.yougov.com/topics/lifestyle/articles-reports/2017/10/09/53-millennial-women-have-received-dick-pic.

Barnett, Emma. "Has Violence During Consensual Sex Become 'Normalised?'" *Live Wires*. BBC Radio 5, November 28, 2019. www.bbc.co.uk/programmes/p07wbvzg.

Bates, Laura. "The Trouble with Sex Robots." *New York Times*, July 17, 2017. www.nytimes.com/2017/07/17/opinion/sex-robots-consent.html.

Beauchamp, Zack. "Our Incel Problem." *Vox*. Last modified April 23, 2019. www.vox.com/the-highlight/2019/4/16/18287446/incel-definition-reddit.

Beaumont, Hilary. "The Man Who Texted a Photo of Himself Having Sex with a Girl While She Vomited Isn't Getting Any Jail Time." *Vice*, January 16, 2015. www.vice.com/en_uk/article/9bz49e/no-jail-time-for-man-who-texted-photo-of-himself-penetrating-rehtaeh-parsons-while-she-vomited-273.

Beck, Julie. "The Rise of Dating-App Fatigue." *The Atlantic*, October 25, 2016. www.theatlantic.com/health/archive/2016/10/the-unbearable-exhaustion-of-dating-apps/505184/.

Belluz, Julia. "Tinder and Grindr Don't Want to Talk About Their Role in Rising STDs." *Vox*, November 13, 2017. www.vox.com/science-and-health/2017/11/13/16620286/online-dating-stds-tinder-grindr.

Benes, Ross. "Porn Could Have a Bigger Economic Influence on the US Than Netflix." *Quartz*, June 20, 2018. https://qz.com/1309527/porn-could-have-a-bigger-economic-influence-on-the-us-than-netflix/.

Bennett, Jessica. "With Her Dating App, Women Are in Control." *New York Times*, March 18, 2017. www.nytimes.com/2017/03/18/fashion/bumble-feminist-dating-app-whitney-wolfe.html.

Bertoni, Steve. "Exclusive: Sean Rad Out as Tinder CEO. Inside the Crazy Saga." *Forbes*, November 4, 2014. www.forbes.com/sites/stevenbertoni/2014/11/04/exclusive-sean-rad-out-as-tinder-ceo-inside-the-crazy-saga/#28e453613ccd.

Bialik, Kristen, and Richard Fry. "Millennial Life: How Young Adulthood Today Compares with Prior Generations." Pew Research Center, February 14, 2019.

www.pewsocialtrends.org/essay/millennial-life-how-young-adulthood-today-compares -with-prior-generations/.

Bilton, Nick. "Tinder, the Fastest Growing Dating App, Taps an Age-Old Truth." *New York Times*, October 29, 2014. www.nytimes.com/2014/10/30/fashion/tinder-the-fast -growing-dating-app-taps-an-age-old-truth.html.

Birger, Jon. "Hookup Culture Isn't the Real Problem Facing Singles Today. It's Math." *Washington Post*, August 26, 2015. www.washingtonpost.com/posteverything/wp/2015 /08/26/hookup-culture-isnt-the-problem-facing-singles-today-its-math/.

Boboltz, Sara. "A Brief History of 'F**kboy,' the Internet's Favorite New Man-Bashing Slur." *HuffPost*, June 3, 2015. www.huffpost.com/entry/f—kboy-definition-take-that -haters_n_7471142.

Bonos, Lisa. "The Awkward Intimacy of Video Dates, When They're in Your Bedroom but You Can't Touch." *Washington Post*, March 26, 2020. www.washingtonpost.com/lifestyle /2020/03/26/video-date-facetime-skype-zoom/.

Bonos, Lisa, and Emily Guskin. "It's Not Just You: New Data Shows More Than Half of Young People in America Don't Have a Romantic Partner." *Washington Post*, March 21, 2019. www.washingtonpost.com/lifestyle/2019/03/21/its-not-just-you-new-data-shows -more-than-half-young-people-america-dont-have-romantic-partner/.

Bossotron95. "Situationship." Urban Dictionary, June 11, 2018. www.urbandictionary.com /define.php?term=Situationship.

Boudreaux, Ouiser. "The Proto-Rapists of OkCupid." *BuzzFeed News*, September 4, 2012. www.buzzfeednews.com/article/annals/the-proto-rapists-of-okcupid.

Brenner, Grant Hilary. "When Is Porn Use a Problem?" *Psychology Today*, February 19, 2018. www.psychologytoday.com/us/blog/experimentations/201802/when-is-porn-use-problem.

Breslaw, Anna. "In Defense of the Dick Pic." *Cosmopolitan*, December 24, 2013. www .cosmopolitan.com/sex-love/advice/a5244/in-defense-of-dick-pics/.

Brett, Mia. "Dating During a Pandemic: How to Be Single in the Age of Corona." *Forward*, March 15, 2020. https://forward.com/opinion/441648/dating-during-a-pandemic-how -to-be-single-in-the-age-of-corona/.

Brown, Ashley. "'Least Desirable'? How Racial Discrimination Plays Out in Online Dating." *NPR*, January 9, 2018. www.npr.org/2018/01/09/575352051/least-desirable-how-racial -discrimination-plays-out-in-online-dating.

Brown, Helen Gurley. *Sex and the Single Girl*. New York: Barricade Books, 1962.

Brown, Joel. "Raleigh Rape Survivor Speaks Out After Filing Suit Against Tinder, Snapchat." ABC11 *Eyewitness News*, January 10, 2020. https://abc11.com/snapchat-tinder-lawsuit -aaliyah-palmer/5836719/.

Brown, Myles. "Why Lisa Ann Prefers Having Sex with NBA Players." *GQ*, February 14, 2015. www.gq.com/story/sex-athletes-nba-porn-star.

Bruni, Frank. "We're Not Wired to Be This Alone." *New York Times*, April 1, 2020. www .nytimes.com/2020/04/01/opinion/coronavirus-lockdown-loneliness.html.

Burleigh, Nina. "Sexting, Shame and Suicide." *Rolling Stone*, September 17, 2013. www.rollingstone.com/culture/culture-news/sexting-shame-and-suicide-72148/.

Burnett-Zeigler, Inger E. "Young Black People Are Killing Themselves." *New York Times*, December 16, 2019. www.nytimes.com/2019/12/16/opinion/young-black-people -suicide.html.

# Bibliography

Bushnell, Candace. *Sex and the City*. New York: Time Warner Book Group, 1996.

Buss, David M. *The Evolution of Desire: Strategies of Human Mating*. New York: Basic Books, 1994.

Calfas, Jennifer. "Here's the Real Reason Why Millennials Use Tinder." *Money*. Last modified March 28, 2017. https://money.com/tinder-millennials-dating-apps/.

Carbon, Susan B. "Understanding the Serious Crime of Stalking." US Department of Justice Archives, January 4, 2012. www.justice.gov/archives/opa/blog/understanding-serious-crime-stalking.

Carey, Benedict. "Is the Pandemic Sparking Suicide?" *New York Times*, May 19, 2020. www.nytimes.com/2020/05/19/health/pandemic-coronavirus-suicide-health.html.

Carroll, Aaron E. "Sex Education Based on Abstinence? There's a Real Absence of Evidence." *New York Times*, August 22, 2017. www.nytimes.com/2017/08/22/upshot/sex-education-based-on-abstinence-theres-a-real-absence-of-evidence.html.

Centers for Disease Control and Prevention. "New CDC Report: STDs Continue to Rise in the U.S." News Release. October 8, 2019. www.cdc.gov/nchhstp/newsroom/2019/2018-STD-surveillance-report-press-release.html.

Chamorro-Premuzic, Tomas. "The Tinder Effect: Psychology of Dating in the Technosexual Era." *The Guardian*, January 17, 2014. www.theguardian.com/media-network/media-network-blog/2014/jan/17/tinder-dating-psychology-technosexual.

Chang, Emily. *Brotopia: Breaking Up the Boys' Club of Silicon Valley*. New York: Portfolio, 2019.

Chase, Randall. "Baseball Player Accused of Serial Rapes Faces First Trial." ABC News, September 16, 2019. https://abcnews.go.com/Sports/wireStory/baseball-player-accused-serial-rapes-faces-trial-65650793.

Chirban, John T. "Pornography: The New Sex Ed for Kids." *Psychology Today*, December 15, 2012. www.psychologytoday.com/sg/blog/age-un-innocence/201212/pornographythe-new-sex-ed-kids.

Christensen, Jen. "For 1 in 16 US Women, Their First Experience with Sexual Intercourse Was Rape, Study Says." CNN. Last modified September 16, 2019. www.cnn.com/2019/09/16/health/sexual-initiation-forced-united-states-study/index.html.

Citron, Danielle Keats. *Hate Crimes in Cyberspace*. Cambridge, MA: Harvard University Press, 2014.

Citron, Danielle Keats, and Benjamin Wittes. "The Internet Will Not Break: Denying Bad Samaritans Section 230 Immunity." *Fordham Law Review*, forthcoming. University of Maryland Legal Studies Research Paper No. 2017-22, July 24, 2017.

Clifford, Catherine. "How a Tinder Founder Came Up with Swiping and Changed Dating Forever." CNBC, January 6, 2017. www.cnbc.com/2017/01/06/how-a-tinder-founder-came-up-with-swiping-and-changed-dating-forever.html.

Cohn, D'Vera, Jeffrey S. Passel, Wendy Wang, and Gretchen Livingston. "Barely Half of U.S. Adults Are Married—a Record Low." Pew Research Center, December 14, 2011. www.pewsocialtrends.org/2011/12/14/barely-half-of-u-s-adults-are-married-a-record-low/.

Conklin, Audrey. "70,000 Photos of Female Tinder Users Being Shared on Cybercrime Forum." FOXBusiness, January 17, 2020. www.foxbusiness.com/technology/70000-photos-female-tinder-users-shared.

Coscarelli, Joe, and Melena Ryzik. "Fyre Festival, a Luxury Music Weekend, Crumbles in the Bahamas." *New York Times*, April 28, 2017. www.nytimes.com/2017/04/28/arts/music /fyre-festival-ja-rule-bahamas.html.

*Cosmopolitan's New Etiquette Guide*. New York: Hearst Corporation, 1971.

Council of Economic Advisers. *The Long-Term Decline in Prime-Age Male Labor Force Participation*. Washington, DC: Obama White House, 2016.

Cousins, Keith. "Dating Apps Can Be Dangerous. Congress Is Investigating." ProPublica, January 31, 2019. www.propublica.org/article/dating-apps-can-be-dangerous-congress -is-investigating.

Cuccinello, Hayley C. "From Taylor Swift to Katrina Lake, America's Richest Self-Made Women Under 40." *Forbes*, June 4, 2019. www.forbes.com/sites/hayleycuccinello/2019 /06/04/from-taylor-swift-to-katrina-lake-americas-richest-self-made-women-under-40 /#61d963e1753a.

Curtin, Sally C., Margaret Warner, and Holly Hedegaard. "Increase in Suicide in the United States, 1999–2014." NCHS Data Brief No. 241, Centers for Disease Control and Prevention, April 2016.

Dawkins, Philip. "Phone Sex Is Safe Sex: Please Postpone Your Hookup. Get Off on Skype Instead." *New York Times*, March 20, 2020. www.nytimes.com/2020/03/20/opinion /coronavirus-sex.html.

Dean, Michelle. "The Story of Amanda Todd." *New Yorker*, October 18, 2012. www .newyorker.com/culture/culture-desk/the-story-of-amanda-todd.

Dean, Signe. "Widespread Loneliness Is Killing People and We Need to Start Taking This Seriously." *ScienceAlert*, August 7, 2017. www.sciencealert.com/widespread-loneliness-is -killing-people-and-we-need-to-start-taking-this-seriously.

DeGregory, Priscilla, and Laura Italiano. "Coronavirus Is Making Couples Sick—of Each Other. Lawyers See Divorce Surge." *New York Post*, April 3, 2020. https://nypost.com /2020/04/03/sick-of-you-lawyers-see-coronavirus-divorce-uptick/.

Dines, Gail. "Choking Women Is All the Rage. It's Branded as Fun, Sexy 'Breath Play.'" *The Guardian*, May 13, 2018. www.theguardian.com/commentisfree/2018/may/13/choking -women-me-too-breath-play.

———. "Is Porn Immoral? That Doesn't Matter: It's a Public Health Crisis." *Washington Post*, April 8, 2016. www.washingtonpost.com/posteverything/wp/2016/04/08/is-porn -immoral-that-doesnt-matter-its-a-public-health-crisis/.

Dockterman, Eliana. "The Coronavirus Is Changing How We Date. Experts Think the Shifts May Be Permanent." *Time*, April 20, 2020.

Doherty, Carroll, and Jocelyn Kiley. "Americans Have Become Much Less Positive About Tech Companies' Impact on the U.S." *Fact Tank* (blog). Pew Research Center, July 29, 2019. www.pewresearch.org/fact-tank/2019/07/29/americans-have-become-much -less-positive-about-tech-companies-impact-on-the-u-s/.

Doyle, Sady. "'Her' Is Really More About 'Him.'" *In These Times*, December 20, 2013. http://inthesetimes.com/article/16031/her_is_really_more_about_him.

DrTinderbox. "Tinderitis." Urban Dictionary, October 4, 2013. www.urbandictionary.com /define.php?term=tinderitis.

Duggan, Maeve. "Online Harassment 2017." Pew Research Center, July 11, 2017. www.pewresearch.org/internet/2017/07/11/online-harassment-2017/.

Dunn, Gaby. "Am I the Only Woman Who Likes Getting a Picture of a Guy's Junk?" *Playboy*, January 8, 2014.

Duportail, Judith. "I Asked Tinder for My Data. It Sent Me 800 Pages of My Deepest, Darkest Secrets." *The Guardian*, September 26, 2017. www.theguardian.com/technology/2017/sep/26/tinder-personal-data-dating-app-messages-hacked-sold.

Dworkin, Andrea. *Life and Death: Unapologetic Writings on the Continuing War Against Women*. New York: Free Press, 1997.

———. *Woman Hating*. New York: E. P. Dutton, 1974.

Edelstein, David. "To Siri with Love." *New York*, December 13, 2013. https://nymag.com/movies/reviews/her-anchorman-2-2013-12/.

Edwardes, Charlotte. "Tinder? I'm an Addict, Says Hook-Up App's Co-creator and CEO Sean Rad." *Evening Standard*, November 18, 2015. www.standard.co.uk/lifestyle/london-life/tinder-im-an-addict-says-hookup-apps-cocreator-and-ceo-sean-rad-a3117181.html.

Ellen, Barbara. "The 'Rough Sex' Defence Plea Is Growing. It's a Worrying Trend." *The Guardian*, November 17, 2019. www.theguardian.com/commentisfree/2019/nov/17/rough-sex-defence-plea-is-growing-worrying-trend.

Ely, Robin J., Pamela Stone, and Colleen Ammerman. "Rethink What You 'Know' About High-Achieving Women." *Harvard Business Review*, December 2014.

*Emerging New Threat in Online Dating*. London: National Crime Agency, 2016.

*Engineering and Technology*. "Tech Giants Track Porn-Viewing Habits, Study Finds." July 19, 2019. https://eandt.theiet.org/content/articles/2019/07/tech-giants-track-porn-viewing-habits-study-finds/.

Fahs, Breanne. *Performing Sex: The Making and Unmaking of Women's Erotic Lives*. Albany: State University of New York Press, 2011.

Faludi, Susan. *Backlash: The Undeclared War Against American Women*. New York: Anchor Books, 1991.

Fateman, Johanna. "The Power of Andrea Dworkin's Rage." *New York Review of Books*, February 15, 2019. www.nybooks.com/daily/2019/02/15/the-power-of-andrea-dworkins-rage/.

Federal Trade Commission. "FTC Sues Owner of Online Dating Service Match.com for Using Fake Love Interest Ads to Trick Consumers into Paying for a Match.com Subscription." News Release. September 25, 2019. www.ftc.gov/news-events/press-releases/2019/09/ftc-sues-owner-online-dating-service-matchcom-using-fake-love.

Fetters, Ashley, and Kaitlyn Tiffany. "The 'Dating Market' Is Getting Worse." *The Atlantic*, February 25, 2020. www.theatlantic.com/family/archive/2020/02/modern-dating-odds-economy-apps-tinder-math/606982/.

Fiegerman, Seth. "Microsoft Received 238 Gender Discrimination and Harassment Complaints." CNN Business, March 13, 2018. https://money.cnn.com/2018/03/13/technology/microsoft-gender-discrimination-lawsuit/index.html.

Fielding, Sarah. "In Quarantine with an Abuser: Surge in Domestic Violence Reports Linked to Coronavirus." *The Guardian*, April 3, 2020. www.theguardian.com/us-news/2020/apr/03/coronavirus-quarantine-abuse-domestic-violence.

Flynn, Hillary, Keith Cousins, and Elizabeth Naismith Picciani. "Tinder Lets Known Sex Offenders Use the App. It's Not the Only One." ProPublica, December 2, 2019. www.propublica.org/article/tinder-lets-known-sex-offenders-use-the-app-its-not-the-only-one.

# Bibliography

Forward, Susan. *Men Who Hate Women and the Women Who Love Them.* New York: Bantam Books, 1986.

Foubert, John D., Matthew W. Brosi, and R. Sean Bannon. "Pornography Viewing Among Fraternity Men: Effects on Bystander Intervention, Rape Myth Acceptance and Behavioral Intent to Commit Sexual Assault." *Sexual Addiction and Compulsivity* 18, no. 4 (2011).

Fox, Maggie. "Coronavirus Found in Men's Semen." CNN. Last modified May 11, 2020. www.cnn.com/2020/05/07/health/coronavirus-semen-china-health/index.html.

Franklin, Benjamin. "Advice to a Young Man on the Choice of a Mistress." June 25, 1745. https://www.swarthmore.edu/SocSci/bdorsey1/41docs/51-fra.html.

Frishberg, Hannah, and Suzy Weiss. "Singles Now Flaunting Antibody Test Results in Dating Profiles." *New York Post*, May 19, 2020. https://nypost.com/2020/05/19/singles-now -flaunting-antibody-test-results-in-dating-profiles/.

Fry, Richard. "More Millennials Living with Family Despite Improved Job Market." Pew Research Center, July 29, 2015. www.pewsocialtrends.org/2015/07/29/more-millennials -living-with-family-despite-improved-job-market/.

Futrelle, David. "When a Mass Murderer Has a Cult Following." *The Cut*, April 27, 2018. www.thecut.com/2018/04/incel-meaning-rebellion-alex-minassian-elliot-rodger -reddit.html.

Garcia, Justin, Chris Reiber, Sean G. Massey, and Ann M. Merriweather. "Sexual Hookup Culture: A Review." *Review of General Psychology* 16, no. 2 (2012): 161–176.

Glenza, Jessica. "States Use Coronavirus to Ban Abortions, Leaving Women Desperate: 'You Can't Pause a Pregnancy.'" *The Guardian*, April 30, 2020. www.theguardian.com/world /2020/apr/30/us-states-ban-abortions-coronavirus-leave-women-desperate.

Goldstein, Andrew. "Police Trying to Reach Kang's Alleged Sexual Assault Victim, Have More Questions." *Pittsburgh Post-Gazette*, September 14, 2016. www.post-gazette.com/sports /pirates/2016/09/13/Chicago-police-struggling-to-reach-Pirates-Jung-Ho-Kang-alleged-as sault-victim/stories/201609130220.

Goldwert, Lindsay. "Facebook Named in a Third of Divorce Filings in 2011." *New York Daily News*, May 24, 2012. www.nydailynews.com/life-style/facebook-ruining-marriage -social-network-named-divorce-filings-2011-article-1.1083913.

Gollayan, Christian. "Millennials Aren't Wearing Condoms Anymore." *New York Post*, November 2, 2016. https://nypost.com/2016/11/02/millennials-arent-wearing -condoms-anymore/.

Grant, Meghan. "Calgary Anesthesiologist Guilty of Date Rape." CBC News. Last modified October 22, 2019. www.cbc.ca/news/canada/calgary/calgary-doctor-barry-wollach-date -rape-guilty-1.5329216.

Greenberg, Julia. "Tinder Completely Freaked Out on Twitter." *Wired*, August 11, 2015. www.wired.com/2015/08/tinder-completely-freaked-twitter/.

Grieco, Elizabeth. "Newsroom Employees Are Less Diverse Than U.S. Workers Overall." *Fact Tank* (blog). Pew Research Center, November 2, 2018. www.pewresearch.org/fact-tank /2018/11/02/newsroom-employees-are-less-diverse-than-u-s-workers-overall/.

Griffith, Erin. "Whitney Wolfe Herd's Work Diary: Fighting Misogyny, One Bumble Brand at a Time." *New York Times*, May 9, 2019. www.nytimes.com/2019/05/09/business /whitney-wolfe-herd-bumble-work-diary.html.

Griffiths, Sarah. "Rise of the Robosexuals: Humans Will Have Virtual Reality Sex by 2030 and Droid Trysts Will Be More Popular than Human Love-Making in 2050, Expert Predicts." *Daily Mail.* Last modified October 6, 2015. www.dailymail.co.uk/sciencetech/article-3260458/Rise-ROBOSEXUALS -Humans-virtual-reality-sex-2030-droid-trysts-popular-human-love-making-2050-expert -predicts.html.

Grunspan, Daniel Z., Sarah L. Eddy, Sara E. Brownell, Benjamin L. Wiggins, Alison J. Crowe, and Steven M. Goodreau. "Males Under-Estimate Academic Performance of Their Female Peers in Undergraduate Biology Classrooms." *PLoS One,* February 10, 2016. https://journals.plos.org/plosone/article?id=10.1371/journal.pone.0148405.

Hackimer, Kurt. "Believe Women, Not Jung-ho Kang." *Point of Pittsburgh*, July 14, 2016. https://thepointofpittsburgh.com/believe-women-not-jung-ho-kang/.

Hains, Rebecca. "Why Disney Princesses and 'Princess Culture' Are Bad for Girls." *Washington Post,* June 24, 2016. www.washingtonpost.com/posteverything/wp/2016/06 /24/princess-culture-is-bad-for-girls-now-theres-proof/.

Hauck, Grace. "When Will Women Get Equal Pay? Not for Another 257 Years, Report Says." *USA Today.* Last modified December 22, 2019. www.usatoday.com/story/news/nation /2019/12/20/gender-pay-gap-equal-wages-expected-257-years-report/2699326001/.

Hay, Mark. "Why Are the Japanese Still Not Fucking?" *Vice,* January 22, 2015. www.vice.com /da/article/7b7y8x/why-arent-the-japanese-fucking-361.

Hecht, Andrew. "Social Distancing Looks Good on IAC." *Seeking Alpha,* April 23, 2020. https://seekingalpha.com/article/4339435-social-distancing-looks-good-on-iac.

Heilweil, Rebecca. "Tinder May Not Get You a Date. It Will Get Your Data." *Recode,* February 14, 2020. www.vox.com/recode/2020/2/14/21137096/how-tinder-matches -work-algorithm-grindr-bumble-hinge-algorithms.

Herbenick, Debby, Elizabeth Bartelt, Tsung-Chieh (Jane) Fu, Bryant Paul, Ronna Gradus, Jill Bauer, and Rashida Jones. "Feeling Scared During Sex: Findings from a U.S. Probability Sample of Women and Men Ages 14 to 60." *Journal of Sex and Marital Therapy* 45, no. 5 (2019).

Hern, Alex. "OkCupid: We Experiment on Users. Everyone Does." *The Guardian,* July 29, 2014. www.theguardian.com/technology/2014/jul/29/okcupid-experiment-human -beings-dating.

Hess, Maggie MK. "Tinder Isn't Swiping Out Romance: Why Reports of the Dating Apocalypse May Be Greatly Exaggerated." *Salon,* August 14, 2015. www.salon.com/2015 /08/14/ tinder_isnt_swiping_out_ romance_why_reports_of_the_ dating_apocalypse _may_be_greatly_exaggerated/.

Hevesi, Dennis. "Protest Forms over Radioactive Waste in Brooklyn." *New York Times,* May 26, 1991.

Hinduja, Sameer. "Coronavirus, Online Learning, Social Isolation, and Cyberbullying: How to Support Our Students." Cyberbullying Research Center, March 16, 2020. https://cyberbullying.org/coronavirus-online-learning-social-isolation-cyberbullying.

Hood, Joel. "Ronald Sales, 71, Divorce Attorney." *South Florida Sun-Sentinel,* October 3, 2005. www.sun-sentinel.com/news/fl-xpm-2005-10-03-0510020240-story.html.

Hope, Lynsey. "Dating Apps Blamed for the Rise in STDs." *New York Post,* August 27, 2018. https://nypost.com/2018/08/27/dating-apps-blamed-for-rise-in-stds/.

Horowitz, Juliana Menasce, Nikki Graf, and Gretchen Livingston. "Marriage and Cohabitation in the U.S." Pew Research Center, November 6, 2019. www.pewsocialtrends.org/2019/11/06/marriage-and-cohabitation-in-the-u-s/.

Humphries, Matthew. "Gatebox Virtual Home Robot Wants You to Be Her Master." *PC*, December 14, 2016. www.pcmag.com/news/gatebox-virtual-home-robot-wants-you-to-be-her-master.

Hussen, Dahaba Ali. "The Messages Men Send Me Shows How Prevalent Racism in Online Dating Is." iNews, September 6, 2019. https://inews.co.uk/opinion/comment/the-messages-men-send-me-shows-how-prevalent-racism-in-online-dating-is-335323.

Hutson, Jevan, Jessie G. Taft, Solon Barocas, and Karen Levy. "Debiasing Desire: Addressing Bias & Discrimination on Intimate Platforms." *Proceedings of the ACM on Human-Computer Interaction* 2, no. CSCW (November 2018).

Illes, Judy, and Farhad R. Udwadia. "Sex Robots Increase the Potential for Gender-Based Violence." *The Conversation*, August 27, 2019. https://theconversation.com/sex-robots-increase-the-potential-for-gender-based-violence-122361.

Iqbal, Mansoor. "Tinder Revenue and Statistics." *Business of Apps*. Last modified March 25, 2020. www.businessofapps.com/data/tinder-statistics/.

Jedras, P., A. Jones, and M. Field. "The Role of Anticipation in Drug Addiction and Reward." *Neuroscience and Neuroeconomics* 3 (December 16, 2013): 1–10.

Jenkins, Aric. "Study Finds That Half of Americans—Especially Young People—Feel Lonely." *Fortune*, May 1, 2018. https://fortune.com/2018/05/01/americans-lonely-cigna-study/.

Julian, Kate. "Why Are Young People Having So Little Sex?" *The Atlantic*, December 2018.

Karasu, Sylvia R. "The Biology of Loneliness. Part 2: The Physical and Psychological Consequences of Loneliness and Isolation." *Psychology Today*, March 24, 2020. www.psychologytoday.com/us/blog/the-gravity-weight/202003/the-biology-loneliness.

Kasperkevic, Jana. "Sexism Valley: 60% of Women in Silicon Valley Experience Harassment." *The Guardian*, January 12, 2016. www.theguardian.com/technology/2016/jan/12/silicon-valley-women-harassment-gender-discrimination.

Keller, Julia. "To a Generation, Mademoiselle Was Stuff of Literary Dreams." *Chicago Tribune*, October 5, 2001. www.chicagotribune.com/news/ct-xpm-2001-10-05-0110050007-story.html.

Kelsey, Rick. "Dating Apps Increasing Rates of Sexually Transmitted Infections, Say Doctors." *BBC Newsbeat*, November 2, 2015. www.bbc.co.uk/newsbeat/article/34008736/dating-apps-increasing-rates-of-sexually-transmitted-infections-say-doctors.

KGO. "East Bay Man Allegedly Used Dating Apps to Lure, Rape Women." ABC7, October 6, 2015. https://abc7news.com/1019063/.

Khazan, Olga. "The Startling Rise of Choking During Sex." *The Atlantic*, June 24, 2019. www.theatlantic.com/health/archive/2019/06/how-porn-affecting-choking-during-sex/592375/.

Kim, Victoria. "EHarmony Settles Class-Action Suit Brought by Gays and Lesbians." *Los Angeles Times*, January 27, 2010. www.latimes.com/archives/la-xpm-2010-jan-27-la-me-eharmony27-2010jan27-story.html.

Kitroeff, Natalie. "In Hookups, Inequality Still Reigns." *Well* (blog). *New York Times*, November 11, 2013. https://well.blogs.nytimes.com/2013/11/11/women-find-orgasms-elusive-in-hookups/.

Klower, Kassi. "14 Depressing Things That Have Happened to Anyone Who's Ever Been on a Tinder Date." *She 'Said,'* June 3, 2019.

Kosoff, Maya. "Report: Ousted Tinder Cofounder Settled Her Sexual Harassment Lawsuit Against the Company for 'Just Over $1 Million.'" *Business Insider*, November 4, 2014. www.businessinsider.com/whitney-wolfe-settles-sexual-harassment -tinder-lawsuit-1-million-2014-11.

Kramer, Andrea S., and Alton B. Harris. "Are U.S. Millennial Men Just as Sexist as Their Dads?" *Harvard Business Review*, June 15, 2016. https://hbr.org/2016/06/are-u-s -millennial-men-just-as-sexist-as-their-dads.

Krueger, Alyson. "Virtual Dating Is the New Normal. Will It Work?" *New York Times*, April 18, 2020. www.nytimes.com/2020/04/18/nyregion/coronavirus-dating-video.html.

Lamont, Tom. "Life After the Ashley Madison Affair." *The Guardian*, February 27, 2016. www.theguardian.com/technology/2016/feb/28/what-happened-after-ashley -madison-was-hacked.

Lanier, Jaron. *Ten Arguments for Deleting Your Social Media Accounts Right Now*. New York: Picador, 2018.

Larson, Nina. "WHO Alarmed at STD Spread in the Era of Dating Apps." *Medical Xpress*, June 6, 2019. https://medicalxpress.com/news/2019-06-alarmed-std-era-dating-apps.html.

Lau, Chris. "Rape Suspect Who Called Himself the 'Chubby Cupid' Online Pretended to Be Policeman and Boasted About His Legal Knowledge to Victims, Hong Kong Court Hears." *South China Morning Post*, June 3, 2019. www.scmp.com/news/hong-kong/law -and-crime/article/3012929/rape-suspect-who-called-himself-chubby-cupid-online.

Lauzen, Martha M. *Boxed In 2018–19: Women on Screen and Behind the Scenes in Television*. San Diego, CA: Center for the Study of Women in Television & Film, 2019.

———. *The Celluloid Ceiling: Behind-the-Scenes Employment of Women on the Top 100, 250, and 500 Films of 2019*. San Diego, CA: Center for the Study of Women in Television & Film, 2020.

———. *It's A Man's (Celluloid) World: Portrayals of Female Characters in the Top Grossing Films of 2019*. San Diego, CA: Center for the Study of Women in Television & Film, 2020.

Lestada, Bintang. "Sending Nudes on Dating Apps Is Bad for My Mental Health." *Vice*, October 24, 2018. www.vice.com/en_asia/article/43e97j/sending-nudes-on-dating-apps -is-bad-for-my-mental-health.

Ley, David J. "Why Men Send Pics of Their Junk." *Psychology Today*, February 18, 2016. www .psychologytoday.com/us/blog/women-who-stray/201602/why-men-send-pics-their-junk.

Linshi, Jack. "Twitter Faces Gender Discrimination Lawsuit by Former Female Engineer." *Time*, March 22, 2015. https://time.com/3753458/twitter-gender-lawsuit/.

Livingston, Gretchen. "About One-Third of U.S. Children Are Living with an Unmarried Parent." *Fact Tank* (blog). Pew Research Center, April 27, 2018. www.pewresearch.org/fact-tank /2018/04/27/about-one-third-of-u-s-children-are-living-with-an-unmarried-parent/.

———. "The Changing Profile of Unmarried Parents." Pew Research Center, April 25, 2018. www.pewsocialtrends.org/2018/04/25/the-changing-profile-of-unmarried-parents/.

Logan, Bryan. "Tinder Just Lost Its Mind over a Vanity Fair Story." *Business Insider*, August 12, 2015. www.businessinsider.com/tinders-pr-just-went-ballistic-on-twitter -over-a-vanity-fair-expos-2015-8.

# Bibliography

Lowery, George. "Men Who Earn Less Than Their Women Are More Likely to Cheat." *Cornell Chronicle*, August 26, 2010. https://news.cornell.edu/stories/2010/08/men-more-likely-cheat-higher-earning-women.

Macon, Alexandra. "Bumble Founder Whitney Wolfe Whirlwind Wedding Was a True Celebration of Southern Italy." *Vogue*, October 5, 2017. www.vogue.com/article/bumble-founder-whitney-wolfe-michael-herd-positano-wedding.

Manta, Irina D. "The Case for Cracking Down on Tinder Lies." *Washington Post*, November 16, 2018. www.washingtonpost.com/outlook/the-case-for-cracking-down-on-tinder-lies/2018/11/16/d3eb0b98-e2de-11e8-b759-3d88a5ce9e19_story.html.

Marateck, Juliet. "Online Dating Lowers Self-Esteem and Increases Depression." CNN. Last modified May 29, 2018. www.cnn.com/2018/05/29/health/online-dating-depression-study/index.html.

Marcotte, Amanda. "Let's All Throw Ourselves Another Moral-Panic Party About Technology." *Slate*, August 6, 2015. https://slate.com/human-interest/2015/08/tinder-is-causing-a-dating-apocalypse-or-maybe-not.html.

Mavity, Ryan. "Conaway Accuser Takes Stand as Sexual Assault Trial Opens." *Cape Gazette*, February 12, 2020. www.capegazette.com/article/conaway-accuser-takes-stand-sexual-assault-trial-opens/197645.

———. "Conaway Found Guilty of Misdemeanor Unlawful Sexual Contact." *Cape Gazette*, February 21, 2020. www.capegazette.com/article/conaway-found-guilty-misdemeanor-unlawful-sexual-contact/198219.

McDaniel, B. T., and S. M. Coyne. "'Technoference': The Interference of Technology in Couple Relationships and Implications for Women's Personal and Relational Well-Being." *Psychology of Popular Media Culture* 5, no. 1 (January 2016): 85–98.

McDonough, Katie. "Rebecca Solnit on Elliot Rodger: 'He Fits into a Culture of Rage,' 'a Culture that Considers Women Tools and Playthings and Property.'" *Salon*, May 27, 2014. www.salon.com/2014/05/27/rebecca_solnit_on_elliot_rodger_he_fits_into_a_culture_of_rage_a_culture_that_considers_women_tools_and_playthings_and_property/.

McKeon, Lauren. "How Did Dick Pics Become Normal Tinder Behaviour?" *Flare*, September 11, 2015. www.flare.com/tv-movies/tinder-how-did-dick-pics-become-normal-online-dating-behaviour/.

Montpelier, Rachel. "2020 Diversity Report: Women and POC Make Strides in Film, Remain Underrepresented." *Women and Hollywood*, February 6, 2020. https://womenandhollywood.com/2020-diversity-report-women-and-poc-make-strides-in-film-remain-underrepresented/.

Morrison, Toni. *Sula*. New York: Vintage Books, 1973.

Moynihan, Ruqayyah. "Internet Users Access Porn Websites More Than Twitter, Wikipedia and Netflix." *Business Insider*, September 30, 2018. www.businessinsider.com/internet-users-access-porn-more-than-twitter-wikipedia-and-netflix-2018-9.

Murdock, Jason. "Tinder: How Your Secret Chats and Dating Profiles Could Be Hacked." *Newsweek*, February 22, 2018. www.newsweek.com/tinder-hacking-chats-and-dating-accounts-hijacked-phone-number-815424.

Myers, Justin. "The Age of Sending Nudes Is Upon Us. Here's How to Do It Right." *GQ*, November 18, 2018. www.gq-magazine.co.uk/article/how-normal-is-it-to-send-nudes.

New York City Department of Health and Mental Hygiene. "Safer Sex and COVID-19." June 8, 2020. www1.nyc.gov/assets/doh/downloads/pdf/imm/covid-sex-guidance.pdf.

*NextShark.* "We Went to the Sugar Baby Summit Where Women Learn to Date Rich Guys for Money." August 18, 2016. https://nextshark.com/sugar-baby-summit-2016-seeking -arrangement/.

Nickalls, Sammy. "More Than 50% of People Who Use Tinder Do It Out of Boredom." *Esquire,* September 7, 2017. www.esquire.com/lifestyle/sex/a12149373/tinder-statistics-study/.

O'Brien, Chris. "The Prisoner of Sex.com." *Wired,* August 1, 2003. www.wired.com/2003 /08/sex-com/.

O'Brien, Sara Ashley. "No More Swiping: Hinge Dumps Feature Popularized by Tinder." CNN Business, October 11, 2016. https://money.cnn.com/2016/10/11/technology /hinge-tinder-dating-apocalypse/index.html.

O'Connor, Clare. "Google Sued for Gender Discrimination by Former Female Employees." *Forbes,* September 14, 2017. www.forbes.com/sites/clareoconnor/2017/09/14/google -sued-for-gender-discrimination-by-female-former-employees/#39a4c5e050c9.

Ollstein, Alice Miranda, and Mohana Ravindranath. "How Some—but Not All—Dating Apps Are Taking on the STD Epidemic." *Politico,* December 10, 2019. www.politico.com /news/2019/12/10/dating-apps-stds-080159.

Olson, Loren A. "Do You Need a Hug? I Do: Anxiety in the COVID-19 Pandemic." *Psychology Today,* March 26, 2020. www.psychologytoday.com/us/blog/finally-out/202003/do-you -need-hug-i-do-anxiety-in-the-covid-19-pandemic.

Ortutay, Barbara. "Dating Apps Face US Inquiry over Underage Use, Sex Offenders." Associated Press, January 31, 2020. https://apnews.com/a93a6e2b02b7f979efca92ea7266e9f2.

Padilla, Mariel. "North Carolina Lawmakers Pass Bill to Close Sexual Assault Loopholes." *New York Times,* November 1, 2019. www.nytimes.com/2019/11/01/us/north-carolina -sexual-assault-loophole.html.

Paul, Katie, Inti Landauro, and Ellen Francis, "Love in the Time of Coronavirus? Around the World, Dating Finds a Way." Reuters, March 19, 2020. www.reuters.com/article /us-health-coronavirus-dating-idUSKBN2161U6.

Pauly, Madison, and Julia Lurie. "Domestic Violence 911 Calls Are Increasing. Coronavirus Is Likely to Blame." *Mother Jones,* March 31, 2020. www.motherjones.com/crime-justice /2020/03/domestic-violence-abuse-coronavrius/.

Peat, Jack. "Millennials 'Spend 10 Hours a Week on Dating Apps.'" *Independent,* January 23, 2018. www.independent.co.uk/life-style/dating-apps-millennials-10-hours-per-week -tinder-bumble-romance-love-a8174006.html.

Pelusi, Nando. "Neanderthink: The Appeal of the Bad Boy." *Psychology Today,* January 1, 2009. www.psychologytoday.com/us/articles/200901/neanderthink-the-appeal-the-bad-boy.

Percy, Karen. "'Tinder Rapist' Glenn Hartland Sentenced to Over 14 Years in Prison." ABC News. Last modified May 11, 2019. www.abc.net.au/news/2019-05-10/tinder-rapist -glenn-hartland-sentenced/11101416.

Pew Research Center. "Millennials in Adulthood." March 7, 2014. www.pewsocialtrends.org /2014/03/07/millennials-in-adulthood/.

———. "Modern Parenthood." March 14, 2013. www.pewsocialtrends.org/2013/03 /14/modern-parenthood-roles-of-moms-and-dads-converge-as-they-balance-work-and -family/.

———. "On Pay Gap, Millennial Women Near Parity—For Now." December 11, 2013. www.pewsocialtrends.org/2013/12/11/on-pay-gap-millennial-women-near -parity-for-now/.

Picciani, Elizabeth Naismith. "He Sexually Assaulted Her After They Met on Bumble. Then She Saw Him on Tinder. Then Hinge." ProPublica, March 9, 2020. www.propublica.org/article/he-sexually-assaulted-her-after-they-met-on-bumble -then-she-saw-him-on-tinder-then-hinge.

Pierce, David. "The Oral History of Tinder's Alluring Right Swipe." *Wired*, September 28, 2016. www.wired.com/2016/09/history-of-tinder-right-swipe/.

Popper, Nathaniel. "Young Adults, Burdened with Debt, Are Now Facing an Economic Crisis." *New York Times*, April 6, 2020. www.nytimes.com/2020/04/06/business/millennials -economic-crisis-virus.html.

Porter, Eduardo, and David Yaffe-Bellany. "Facing Adulthood with an Economic Disaster's Lasting Scars." *New York Times*. Last modified May 20, 2020. www.nytimes.com/2020 /05/19/business/economy/coronavirus-young-old.html.

Ramzy, Austin, and Katie Rogers. "Tinder Doesn't Contribute to Hookup Culture (Says Tinder)." *New York Times*, August 12, 2015. www.nytimes.com/2015/08/13/world/asia /tinders-claim-of-many-users-in-north-korea-meets-mockery-online.html.

Rao, Aliya Hamid. "Even Breadwinning Wives Don't Get Equality at Home." *The Atlantic*, May 12, 2019. www.theatlantic.com/family/archive/2019/05/breadwinning -wives-gender-inequality/589237/.

Rector, Kevin. "Online Child Sex Abuse Reports Surge as Kids Spend More Time on Computers Amid Coronavirus." *Los Angeles Times*, May 21, 2020. www.latimes.com/california/story /2020-05-21/child-sex-abuse-and-exploitation-surge-online-amid-pandemic-overwhelming -police.

Rhodan, Maya. "No Satisfaction: Women Are Less Likely to Orgasm During Casual Sex." *Time*, November 11, 2013. https://healthland.time.com/2013/11/11/no -satisfaction-woman-are-less-likely-to-orgasm-during-casual-sex/.

Rodger, Elliot. "My Twisted World: The Story of Elliot Rodger." Unpublished manuscript, January 2014.

Rosman, Katherine. "A 'Sugar Date' Gone Sour." *New York Times*, October 15, 2018. www.nytimes.com/2018/10/15/style/sugar-dating-seeking-arrangement.html.

Rothkopf, Joanna. "Single? Consider a Cross-Dimensional (Human-Hologram) Marriage." *Esquire*, November 13, 2018. www.esquire.com/lifestyle/a25018920/japan-married -hologram-gatebox/.

Rowse, Janine, Caroline Bolt, and Sanjeev Gaya. "Swipe Right: The Emergence of Dating-App Facilitated Sexual Assault. A Descriptive Retrospective Audit of Forensic Examination Caseload in an Australian Metropolitan Service." *Forensic Science, Medicine and Pathology* 16 (February 6, 2020).

Rudder, Christian. "Race and Attraction, 2009–2014." *OkTrends* (blog). OkCupid, September 10, 2014. www.gwern.net/docs/psychology/okcupid/raceandattraction20092014.html.

———. "Why You Should Never Pay for Online Dating." *OkTrends* (blog). OkCupid, April 7, 2010. www.gwern.net/docs/psychology/okcupid/whyyoushouldneverpayforon linedating.html.

Rushkoff, Douglas. *Team Human*. New York: W. W. Norton & Company, 2019.

Sadlier, Allison. "People in Relationships Are Signing Up for Dating Apps During Coronavirus Isolation." *New York Post*, May 1, 2020. https://nypost.com/2020 /05/01/surprising-percentage-of-americans-in-relationships-using-dating-apps-during -coronavirus-isolation/.

Safronova, Valeriya. "Tinder and Bumble Are Seriously at War." *New York Times*, April 4, 2018. www.nytimes.com/2018/04/04/style/tinder-bumble-lawsuit-explainer.html.

Sales, Nancy Jo. *American Girls: Social Media and the Secret Lives of Teenagers*. New York: Knopf, 2016.

———. "Can Hinge Make Online Dating Less Apocalyptic by Losing the Swipe?" *Vanity Fair*, October 11, 2016. www.vanityfair.com/news/2016/10/hinge-relaunch -swipe-dating-apocalypse.

———. "Caution: These Kids Are About to Blow Up." *New York*, August 24, 1998. https://nymag.com/nymetro/nightlife/barsclubs/features/2937/.

———. "Daddies, 'Dates,' and the Girlfriend Experience: Welcome to the New Prostitution Economy." *Vanity Fair*, July 7, 2016. www.vanityfair.com/style/2016/07/welcome-to -the-new-prostitution-economy.

———. "Dispatches from the Gender Gap: Work-from-Home Moms in the Time of Coronavirus." *Vanity Fair*, April 3, 2020. www.vanityfair.com/style/2020/04/dispatches -from-the-gender-gap-motherhood-in-the-time-of-coronavirus.

———. "Friends Without Benefits." *Vanity Fair*, September 26, 2013. www.vanityfair.com /news/2013/09/social-media-internet-porn-teenage-girls.

———. "Hip Hop Debs." *Vanity Fair*, September 2000. https://archive.vanityfair.com /article/2000/9/hip-hop-debs.

———. "It's Not Easy Being a Kentucky Derby Princess." *Vanity Fair*, May 5, 2014. www.vanityfair.com/culture/2014/05/Kentucky-derby-princesses.

———. "The 'Locker Room Talk' of Howard Stern." *Cosmopolitan*, October 20, 2016. https://www.cosmopolitan.com/politics/a6946953/donald-trump-howard-stern -misogyny-sexual-predator/.

———. "The Majority of 11-Year-Olds Own Smartphones. And Experts Are Worried." *The Guardian*, November 1, 2019. www.theguardian.com/commentisfree/2019/nov/01 /smartphones-children-technology-mobile-phones.

———. "Money Boss Player." *Vibe*, May 1999. http://www.nancyjosales.com/wp-content /uploads/2015/05/DonaldTrump2.pdf.

———. "No Thanks, Guys, We Don't Want to Quarantine and Chill." *The Guardian*, April 24, 2020. www.theguardian.com/commentisfree/2020/apr/24/coronavirus-dating-apps -quarantine-and-chill.

———. "A Star Is Bred." *New York*, July 29, 1999. https://www.nancyjosales.com/wp-content /uploads/2015/05/GwynethPaltrow2.pdf.

———. "Teenage Gangland." *New York*, December 16, 1996. http://reprints.longform.org /prep-school-gangsters.

———. "Tinder and the Dawn of the 'Dating Apocalypse.'" *Vanity Fair*, August 6, 2015. www.vanityfair.com/culture/2015/08/tinder-hook-up-culture-end-of-dating.

Sanday, Peggy Reeves. *Fraternity Gang Rape: Sex, Brotherhood, and Privilege on Campus*. New York: NYU Press, 1990.

Savage, Rachel. "Trans People Find Fault with Tinder's Efforts at Inclusion." Reuters,

November 13, 2019. www.reuters.com/article/us-global-rights-tinder-trfn/trans-people
-find-fault-with-tinders-efforts-at-inclusion-idUSKBN1XN2VL.

Schwarz, Hunter. "For the First Time, There Are More Single American Adults Than Married Ones, and Here's Where They Live." *Washington Post*, September 15, 2014. www.washingtonpost.com/blogs/govbeat/wp/2014/09/15/for-the-first-time -there-are-more-single-american-adults-than-married-ones-and-heres-where-they-live/.

Seal, Mark. "The Temptation of Tiger Woods." *Vanity Fair*, May 2010.

Segran, Elizabeth. "Real Dick-Pic Senders Explain Why They Do It." *Refinery29*, February 8, 2015. www.refinery29.com/en-gb/why-men-send-nude-dick-pictures.

Shadel, JD. "A Queer User's Guide to the Wild and Terrifying World of LGBTQ Dating Apps." *Washington Post*, October 8, 2019. www.washingtonpost.com/lifestyle/2019/10 /08/queer-users-guide-wild-terrifying-world-lgbt-dating-apps/.

Shah, Binjal. "#MeToo: How Tinder, Bumble, Hinge Enable Sexual Harassers." *HuffPost*, May 10, 2019. www.huffingtonpost.in/entry/tinder-bumble-hinge-dating-apps-sexual -harassers-me-too_in_5d9318ffe4b0019647ae3683.

Shahvisi, Arianne. "'Men Are Trash': The Surprisingly Philosophical Story Behind an Internet Punchline." *Prospect*, August 19, 2019. www.prospectmagazine.co.uk/philosophy/men -are-trash-philosophy-dating-hate-speech.

Shammas, Brittany. "He Met His Victims on Tinder and Bumble, Prosecutors Say. His Attorneys Say Women Were There to Hook Up." *Washington Post*, September 19, 2019. www.washingtonpost.com/nation/2019/09/19/an-alleged-serial-rapist-met -victims-bumble-tinder-his-attorneys-say-women-were-there-hook-up/.

Siegel, Rachel. "You Swiped Right but It Doesn't Feel Right: Tinder Now Has a Panic Button." *Washington Post*, January 23, 2020. www.washingtonpost.com/technology/2020/01/23 /tinder-panic-button/.

Simpson, Connor. "The Steubenville Victim Tells Her Story." *The Atlantic*, March 16, 2013. www .theatlantic.com/national/archive/2013/03/steubenville-victim-testimony/317302/.

Singer, Natasha. "OkCupid's Unblushing Analyst of Attraction." *New York Times*, September 6, 2014. www.nytimes.com/2014/09/07/technology/okcupids-unblushing-analyst-of -attraction.html.

Singer, Natasha, and Aaron Krolik. "Grindr and OkCupid Spread Personal Details, Study Says." *New York Times*, January 13, 2020. www.nytimes.com/2020/01/13/technology /grindr-apps-dating-data-tracking.html.

Singh, Natasha. "Talk to Your Kids About Porn." *The Atlantic*, August 29, 2018. www.theatlantic.com/ideas/archive/2018/08/talking-to-kids-about-porn/568744/.

Skinner, B. F. *About Behaviorism*. New York: Vintage Books, 1976.

———. "'Superstition' in the Pigeon." *Journal of Experimental Psychology* 38, no. 2 (1948): 168–172.

Smialek, Jeanna. "Millennial Men Leave Perplexing Hole in Hot U.S. Job Market." *Bloomberg*. Last modified November 2, 2018. www.bloomberg.com/news/articles/2018-11-02 /millennial-men-leave-perplexing-hole-in-a-hot-u-s-labor-market.

Solnit, Rebecca. *Men Explain Things to Me*. Chicago: Haymarket Books, 2014.

Soloski, Alexis. "Did Daisy Haggard Create the Next 'Fleabag'? Not Exactly." *New York Times*, November 8, 2019. www.nytimes.com/2019/11/08/arts/television/daisy-haggard-back -to-life.html.

Southall, Ashley. "He Used Tinder to Hunt the Women He Raped and Killed, Police Say." *New York Times*, July 30, 2018. www.nytimes.com/2018/07/30/nyregion/murder-tinder-uber-nurse-queens-nyc.html.

Southern Poverty Law Center. "Daryush 'Roosh' Valizadeh." www.splcenter.org/fighting-hate/extremist-files/individual/daryush-roosh-valizadeh.

Spellings, Sarah. "Transgender Woman Sues Tinder After Her Account Is Deleted." *The Cut*, March 14, 2018. www.thecut.com/2018/03/transgender-woman-sues-tinder-after-her-account-was-deleted.html.

Stampler, Laura. "Inside Tinder: Meet the Guys Who Turned Dating into an Addiction." *Time*, February 6, 2014. https://time.com/4837/tinder-meet-the-guys-who-turned-dating-into-an-addiction/.

Stanton, Elizabeth Cady, et al. "Declarations of Sentiments and Resolutions." July 1848. https://www.womenshistory.org/resources/primary-source/declaration-sentiments-and-resolution.

*The Status of Women in U.S. Media 2019*. New York: Women's Media Center, 2019.

Stern, Scott W. *The Trials of Nina McCall: Sex, Surveillance, and the Decades-Long Government Plan to Imprison "Promiscuous" Women*. Boston: Beacon Press, 2018.

Stevenson, Alison. "This Woman Turned Her Collection of Unsolicited Dick Pics into an Art Show." *Vice*, April 15, 2016. www.vice.com/en_ca/article/ppxjem/this-woman-turned-her-collection-of-unsolicited-dick-pics-into-an-art-show.

Stokel-Walker, Chris. "Tinder May Not Actually Be Very Good for Finding a Partner." *New Scientist*, November 27, 2019. www.newscientist.com/article/2224899-tinder-may-not-actually-be-very-good-for-finding-a-partner/.

———. "Why Is It OK for Online Daters to Block Whole Ethnic Groups?" *The Guardian*, September 29, 2018. www.theguardian.com/technology/2018/sep/29/wltm-colour-blind-dating-app-racial-discrimination-grindr-tinder-algorithm-racism.

Strimpel, Zoe. "The Boy Geniuses of Silicon Valley Are Totally Deluded if They Think They Can Fix Online Dating." *The Telegraph*, October 17, 2016. www.telegraph.co.uk/technology/2016/10/17/the-boy-geniuses-of-silicon-valley-are-totally-deluded-if-they-t/.

Summers, Nick. "The Truth About Tinder and Women Is Even Worse Than You Think." *Bloomberg*, July 3, 2014. www.bloomberg.com/news/articles/2014-07-02/the-truth-about-tinder-and-women-is-even-worse-than-you-think.

Swanson, Ana. "144 Years of Marriage and Divorce in the United States, in One Chart." *Washington Post*, June 23, 2015. www.washingtonpost.com/news/wonk/wp/2015/06/23/144-years-of-marriage-and-divorce-in-the-united-states-in-one-chart/.

Tasca, Cecilia, Mariangela Rapetti, Mauro Giovanni Carta, and Bianca Fadda. "Women and Hysteria in the History of Mental Health." *Clinical Practice and Epidemiology in Mental Health* (October 19, 2012): 110–119.

Taub, Amanda. "A New Covid-19 Crisis: Domestic Abuse Rises Worldwide." *New York Times*, April 6, 2020. www.nytimes.com/2020/04/06/world/coronavirus-domestic-violence.html.

Tavernise, Sabrina. "U.S. Suicide Rate Surges to a 30-Year High." *New York Times*, April 22, 2016. www.nytimes.com/2016/04/22/health/us-suicide-rate-surges-to-a-30-year-high.html.

Thomas, Katie, and Reed Abelson. "Elizabeth Holmes, Theranos C.E.O. and Silicon Valley Star, Accused of Fraud." *New York Times*, March 14, 2018. www.nytimes.com/2018/03/14/health/theranos-elizabeth-holmes-fraud.html.

Thompson, Derek. "The Brutal Math of Gender Inequality in Hollywood." *The Atlantic*, January 11, 2018. www.theatlantic.com/business/archive/2018/01/the-brutal-math-of -gender-inequality-in-hollywood/550232/.

———. "Why Online Dating Can Feel Like Such an Existential Nightmare." *The Atlantic*, July 21, 2019. www.theatlantic.com/ideas/archive/2019/07/online-dating-taking-over -everything/594337/.

Tierney, Allison. "Why Are Trans People Being Banned from Tinder?" *Vice*, December 14, 2017. www.vice.com/en_us/article/xwvaaz/why-are-trans-people-being-banned-from-tinder.

Tiffany, Kaitlyn. "The Tinder Algorithm, Explained." *Vox*. Last modified March 18, 2019. www.vox.com/2019/2/7/18210998/tinder-algorithm-swiping-tips-dating-app-science.

*Times of India*. "Techie Raped by Man She Met on Dating App." February 7, 2016. https://timesofindia.indiatimes.com/city/hyderabad/Techie-raped-by-man-she -met-on-dating-app/articleshow/50885126.cms.

Treacy, Siobhan. "Robot-Human Marriages: The Future of Marriage?" *Electronics360*, November 26, 2018. https://electronics360.globalspec.com/article/13207/robot-human -marriages-the-future-of-marriage.

Turan, Kenneth. "Spike Jonze's 'Her' Shows Love's Perils." *Los Angeles Times*, December 17, 2013. www.latimes.com/entertainment/movies/moviesnow/la-et-mn-her-review 20131218-story.html.

Turkle, Sherry. *Alone Together: Why We Expect More from Technology and Less from Each Other*. New York: Basic Books, 2011.

US Census Bureau. "U.S. Marriage and Divorce Rates by State." January 15, 2020. www .census.gov/library/visualizations/interactive/marriage-divorce-rates-by-state.html.

Valenti, Jessica. "Frat Brothers Rape 300% More. One in 5 Women Is Sexually Assaulted on Campus. Should We Ban Frats?" *The Guardian*, September 24, 2014. www.theguardian .com/commentisfree/2014/sep/24/rape-sexual-assault-ban-frats.

Valizadeh, Roosh. "How to Stop Rape." Rooshv.com, February 16, 2015. www.rooshv.com /how-to-stop-rape.

Van Zuylen-Wood, Simon. "'Men Are Scum': Inside Facebook's War on Hate Speech." *Vanity Fair*, February 26, 2019. www.vanityfair.com/news/2019/02/men-are-scum-inside -facebook-war-on-hate-speech.

Vega, Nicolas. "Stock of Tinder's Parent Company Soars Thanks to Dating Site's 'Secret Sauce.'" *New York Post*, May 8, 2019. https://nypost.com/2019/05/08/tinder-stock -soars-thanks-to-companys-secret-sauce/.

Vincent, James. "Former Facebook Exec Says Social Media Is Ripping Apart Society." *The Verge*, December 11, 2017. www.theverge.com/2017/12/11/16761016/former-facebook-exec -ripping-apart-society.

Vino, Lauren. "Here Is Why Trojan's New Condom Survey Should Have Us All Worried." *MTV News*, September 16, 2014. www.mtv.com/news/1927028/trojan-condom-survey/.

Vinopal, Lauren. "Guys Are Reporting Women on Tinder for the Crime of Not Being Into Them." *Mel*, September 2019.

Vogels, Emily A. "10 Facts About Americans and Online Dating." *Fact Tank* (blog). Pew Research Center, February 6, 2020. www.pewresearch.org/fact-tank/2020/02/06 /10-facts-about-americans-and-online-dating/.